CHINESE FAMILY LAW AND PRACTICE

by Rong Tao Kohtz

ABA AMERICAN BAR ASSOCIATION
International Law Section

Cover design by Sara Wadford/ABA Design

Printed in the United States of America.

27 26 25 24 23   5 4 3 2 1

A catalog record for this book is available from the Library of Congress.

Table of Contents

Supplemental material for *Chinese Family Law and Practice* will be found at ambar.org/ChineseFamilyLaw.

Chapter 5

Chapter 6

Chapter 7

Preface

This book provides the most up-to-date information about statutes, court rules, and reported cases relevant to issues arising from the day-to-day practice of Chinese family law. It aims to serve as a much-needed reference guide of Chinese family law for attorneys and judges around the globe. It offers not only an overview of the rules of Chinese family law but also case analyses to demonstrate how these rules are applied in Chinese courts. In addition, this book aims to offer a critical introduction to Chinese family law for further academic research. It illustrates not only the framework of Chinese family law but also its historical, cultural, and ideological context from a comparative perspective. Last but not the least, this book aims to assist those who are navigating through Chinese family law, whether in China or elsewhere. If the book succeeds in helping any family restore peace and harmony, it will have been worth doing.

This book uses Euro-American legal terminology to describe and analyze Chinese family law to aid a non-Chinese audience's understanding of Chinese legal principals. As a result, misunderstanding, even bias or prejudice, will inevitably stem from this comparative approach. Generally, exercises in comparative law are "likely to miss nuances in the foreign law, to fail to appreciate the way in which one branch of the other country's law interacts with another, or to assume erroneously that the foreign law mirrors U.S. law when it does not."[1] Describing Chinese family law within a Euro-American paradigm may be more prone to generalizations and oversimplifications because every society's family law is a knowledge system constructed with its unique social and cultural norms of family life. As Lawrence Friedman put it, "a computer may be a computer in Iran or Saudi Arabia; but a marriage in these countries is not

1. Bodum USA, Inc. v. La Cafetiere, Inc., 621 F.3d 624, 638–39 (7th Cir. 2010).

at all like a marriage in France or in Finland."[2] "Family law is a mirror of family life."[3] Thus, I should like this book to be used with awareness of its inevitable deficits in describing the complexity and nuances of Chinese family law and practice. Differences aside, this book also attempts to explore our shared human experience, emotions, and values. A marriage in China or Iran or Australia may not be like a marriage in the United States or Finland or Japan; but they are all marriages. If family law is a mirror of family life, then it would show not only our differences but also our similarities. Thus, I should also like this book to be used for understanding our commonalities.

Last, this book is written with critiques of the Anglo-American adversarial legal system as its backdrop. After nearly two decades of practice in the highly charged, adversarial mode of dispute resolution, I appreciate the efficacy of China's conciliatory approach in family law. Thus, I hope to contribute our understanding of the family and family law from the perspective of non-Euro-American traditions.

2. Lawrence M. Friedman, Private Lives: Families, Individuals and the Law 13 (2004).

3. Lawrence M. Friedman, A History of American Law 769 (Oxford University Press, 2019).

Acknowledgments

My thanks first go to my family—my husband, Dr. D. Stave Kohtz; my parents, Dr. Tao Yanxiao (陶远孝) and Chen Tansui (陈潭绥); my daughters, Chani, Hilary, and Finnea; my sister, Dr. Min Tao; and my late parents-in-law, Donald and Nada Kohtz. This book would not have been possible without their support. Chani and Finnea read and edited parts of the manuscript. Hilary helped with the book cover design. I reserve my deepest gratitude for Stave, who offered many astute suggestions and cogent criticisms.

I would like to thank many teachers, colleagues, and friends who have helped me throughout my career, especially Professor Randy Edwards and Professor Michael Dowdle for giving me the opportunity to come to the United States to attend Columbia University Law School and have an unexpectedly rewarding career as an international family lawyer in New York City.

Last but not the least, I thank my colleague and friend, Attorney Zhao Ningning (赵宁宁) for her insightful comments and suggestions.

Chapter 1

Historical and Cultural Context of Chinese Family Law

Chinese family law, with its unique Chinese characteristics (*zhongguo tese*), is a product of China's economic, political, and cultural past and present.[1] The distinctive characteristics of modern Chinese family law reflect China's struggles between fading Marxist ideology and invigorating legal pragmatism, and its toils between enduring Chinese tradition and ambiguous Euro-Anglo modernity.

§ 1.1 Historical Sketch

Family law has been the foundation and core of Chinese law. "In a sense, all traditional Chinese law was 'family law'—or, perhaps more accurately, applied family law."[2] Modern Chinese family law traces its origin to the Republican era (1912–1949). When the Republic of China replaced the last imperial dynasty at the turn of the 20th century, family reform was considered to be the key to building a democratic republic and prosperous nation. The traditional patriarchal family was accused of stifling China's youth on the altar of filial piety. In its place, the Western ideals of free marriage choice; companionate marriage; and the economic and emotional independence of

1. Philip C.C. Huang, *The Modern Chinese Family: In Light of Economic and Legal History*, 37(5) Modern China 459–97 (2011) (pointing out that the conjoining of an urban China and a rural China led to the unique development pattern of modern Chinese family and the laws governing it).

2. Teemu Ruskola, *Conceptualizing Corporations and Kinship: Comparative Law and Development Theory in A Chinese Perspective*, 52 Stan. L. Rev. 1599, 1622 (2000).

the nuclear, conjugal family were promoted as ideals that encouraged productivity, independence, and civic virtue of the new Chinese republic.[3]

In their making of a modern civil code of the Republic of China, based on the European continental model,[4] the republican legal reformers attempted to use these Western family ideals as the blueprint to redefine individual rights in family matters, to reshape gender and family relations, and to construct a new republican social order. The republican reformers explicitly enforced egalitarian, monogamous, heterosexual marriage as the only legitimate form of marriage by upholding gender equality, abolishing concubinage, and allowing divorce.[5] The republican lawmakers did not, however, discard tradition, customs, or the Confucian values entirely. Instead, they made herculean efforts to fit age-old customs and legal concepts into a modern civil code, and to "retain the national character of early laws and customs not repugnant to present conditions of life" or contradictory to "modern doctrines of private law."[6]

For many vexing reasons, the marriage and family law reform in the republican era had little to no bearing on Chinese people's lives at the time.[7] The introduction of modern family law concepts nevertheless made a long-lasting impact on Chinese law. From the 1929 Civil Code of the Republic of China, contemporary Chinese family law inherited a wealth of modern legal concepts, such as "the adoption of individual not the family as the basic unit" of social order; "the right of the parties to marry, without the consent of their parents, on reaching majority; equal rights in men and women for holding separate property"; and "equal right of male and female heirs to share the inheritance."[8]

Maoist Chinese family law took shape after the establishment of the People's Republic of China (the PRC) in 1949, and has undergone several transformations ever since.[9] In the early period of the PRC, the laws of marriage and family were instrumental in the Chinese Communist Party's (the CCP)

---

3. Susan L. Glosser, Chinese Visions of Family and State, 1915–1953, at 3–4 (2013).

4. The Civil Code of the Republic of China (promulgated on May 23, 1929; effective from Oct. 10, 1929).

5. Kathryn Bernhardt, *Women and the Law: Divorce in the Republican Period*, *in* Civil Law in Qing and Republican China 187–214 (Kathryn Bernhardt & Philip C.C. Huang eds., 1994).

6. R.C.W. Sheng, *The Civil Code of China*, 4 China L. Rev. 69, 71 & 76 (1930).

7. *See, e.g.*, Alison W. Conner, *Don't Change Your Husband: Divorce in Early Chinese Movies*, 40 Conn. L. Rev. 1245; and Jiang Dong, *China's Latest Marriage Law Amendment and Family Property: Tradition and Modernity*, 9 Frontiers L. China 604, 609–12 (2014).

8. Sheng, *supra* note 6, at 77.

9. *See, e.g.*, Weifang Liu (刘维芳), Shilun Zhonghua Renmin Gonghe Guo Hunyinfa de Lishi Yanjin (试论《中华人民共和国婚姻法》的历史演进) [*On the People's Republic of China Marriage Law's Historical Development*], Dangdai Zhongguoshi Yanjiu (当代中国史研究) [Contemporary Chinese History Studies] Vol. 1. (2014); and Michael Palmer, *Child and Family Law in China:*

re-engineering of China's social, ethical, and moral order.[10] The Marriage Law (1950) and the Marriage Registration Regulations (1955)[11] abolished arranged marriage and polygamy, and reintroduced monogamous marriage based on free choice and gender equality.[12] At the same time, marriage was politicized. The work unit (*gongzuo danwei*) replaced family (*jiating*) as the building block of Chinese society.[13] Marriage and divorce were not personal choices for one's happiness but apparatuses for the greater goals of the socialist state.[14] While declaring its commitment to gender equality and more protection of women and children, the PRC used the laws of marriage and family mainly as political tools for its own agenda.[15] Some of the Maoist family law concepts and juridical practices remain firmly embedded in Chinese family law and Chinese people's daily lives to this day.[16]

As the reform era began in 1978, China immediately embarked on an ambitious legislative agenda to construct a legal system that could serve a market-oriented economy and society. By the turn of the 21st century, China has made substantial strides in reforming and formalizing its family law framework.[17] Major revisions to the Marriage Law in 2001 were at the center

---

Bringing the Law Back In, *in* The Future of Child and Family Law: International Predictions (Elaine E. Sutherland, ed. 2012).

10. Neil Diamant, Revolutionizing the Family: Politics, Love and Divorce in Urban and Rural China 4–7 (2000).

11. Hunyin Fa (婚姻法) [The Marriage Law] (1950) (hereinafter Marriage Law), arts. 1–3. *See also* Hunyin Dengji Tiaoli (婚姻登记条例), *Preamble* to [The Marriage Registration Regulations] (1955).

12. Marriage Law, *supra* note 11, arts. 7–10. *See, e.g.*, Diamant, *supra* note 10 (studying the impact of PRC Marriage Law of 1950 on marriage and family structures in urban and rural China).

13. Diamant, *supra* note 10, at 3–4.

14. See Philip C.C. Huang, *Divorce Law Practices, the Origins, Myths and Realities of Judicial "Mediation"*, 31(2) Modern China 151–203 (2005).

15. Margaret Y.K. Woo, *Shaping Citizenship: Chinese Family Law and Women*, 15 Yale J.L. & Feminism 99, 101, 106–07 (2003). *See also, e.g.*, Li Peng Qiangdiao Xiugai Hao Hunyinfa Dui Jiaqiang Shehuizhuyi Jingshenwenmin Jianshe Yiyi Zhongda (李鹏强调修改好婚姻法对加强社会主义精神文明建设意义重大) [*Li Peng Emphasizes Amending the Marriage Law Has Significant Impact on Socialist Spiritual Civilization Building*], Renmin Ribao (人民日报) [People's Daily], Oct. 27, 2000. In his speech given on the eve of the new Marriage Law of 2001, Li Peng, the former chairman of the People's Congress of China (PCC), emphasized that the new marriage law was to restore the moral order in Chinese society, to cure the moral ills that had come with the market economy, and most importantly to maintain social stability.

16. William Partlett & Eric C. Ip, *Is Socialist Law Really Dead?*, 48 N.Y.U. J. Int'l L. & Pol. 463 (2016).

17. For detailed reports of China's family law building in the post-Deng era, see Michael Palmer, *Transforming Family Law in Post-Deng China: Marriage, Divorce and Reproduction*, China Q., No. 191, China's Legal System: New Developments, New Challenges 675–95 (Sept. 2007); and Palmer, *supra* note 9.

of China's family law reform.[18] The Marriage Law was revised in response to the demands for legal mechanisms that were capable of handling complex and multifaceted family and marital disputes arising from an increasingly urbanized, diverse society.[19] The 2001 Marriage Law coined the contractual nature of marriage, introduced the concept of nuptial agreement, and instituted an equitable property distribution regime.[20] The marriage law reform received a frenzy of criticism from legal scholars and women's rights advocates for "monetizing" marriage based on imported Western legal concepts, such as contractual marriage, separate property, and nuptial agreement.[21] Despite the intense criticism, to a considerable extent, the 2001 Marriage Law turned away from "close surveillance" of marriage by the socialist state and moved toward privatization of marriage.[22] Overall, the 2001 Marriage Law

---

18. Zhonghua Renmin Gonghe Guo Hunyin Fa (中华人民共和国婚姻法) [THE PEOPLE'S REPUBLIC OF CHINA MARRIAGE LAW] (promulgated Sept. 10, 1980; amended on Apr. 28, 2001) (hereinafter "Marriage Law").

19. *See* Ma Yinan (马忆南), Zhongguo Hunyi Jiatingfa De Chuantong Yu Xiandaihua—Xie Zai Hunyinfa Xiugan Zhiji (中国婚姻家庭法的传统与现代化—写在婚姻法修改之际) [*Chinese Marriage and Family Law's Tradition and Modernization—Written at the Time When the Marriage Law Being Revised*], Beijing Daxue Xuebao (Zhexue Shehuikexue Ban) (北京大学学报 (哲学社会科学版)) 38(1) [J. PEKING UNIV. (Philosophy and Social Sciences)] 60–68 (2001).

20. *See* Huang, *supra* note 1; Valerie L. Chang, *No Gold Diggers: China's Protection of Individual Property Rights in the New Marital Property Regime*, 45 GEO. WASH. INT'L L. REV. 149, 154 (2013).

21. Chinese scholars vehemently opposed the Marriage Law Interpretations (III), which recognizes nonmarital separate property and defines residences acquired prior to the marriage or gifted by one party's parents as nonmarital "individual property." *See, e.g.*, Zhao Xiaoli (赵晓力), Zhongguo Jiating Zibenzhuyihua De Haojiao (中国家庭资本主义化的号角) (*The Bugle Call for the Capitalism-ization of the Chinese Family*) Wenhua Zongheng (文化纵横) [BEIJING CULTURAL REV.] Vol. 1 (2011), (claiming that the new marital property system betrays the Chinese familial value and moral principles); Jiang Shingong (强世功), Sifa Nengdong Xia De Zhongguo Jiating—Cong Zuigaofayuan Guanyu Hunyinfa De Sifa Jieshi Tanqi (司法能动下的中国家庭—从最高法院关于《婚姻法》的司法解释谈起) [*The Chinese Family Under Judicial Initiative—Beginning with the Judicial Interpretations of the Supreme Court*] Wenhua Zongheng (文化纵横) [BEIJING CULTURAL REV.] Vol. 1 (2011), (arguing that the new marital property regime separates the economic partnership and the emotional bond, which are integral components of a marriage, and consequently simplifies the divorce process; the divorce rate would then rise as a result of simpler, cheaper, and easier divorces); ZHANG XIANGLONG (张祥龙), Biaozhunhua Panjue Jiang Daozhi Hunyin He Jiating De Shuailuo (标准化判决将导致婚姻和家庭的衰落) [STANDARDIZATION OF ADJUDICATION WILL CAUSE THE DECLINE OF MARRIAGE AND FAMILY] (arguing that that uniform application of law in property distribution in divorce cases would cause unfair outcomes in divorce cases and consequently discourage people from getting married).

22. Deborah S. Davis, *Privatization of Marriage in Post-Socialist China*, 40(6) MODERN CHINA 551, 551–77 (2014) (an in-depth study of Chinese marriages since 1990 based on census data and interviews with urban residents in Guangzhou and Shanghai).

provided greater protections for individual rights and clearer rules to address the economic reality of China's growing middle class.[23]

Finally, in 2020 family law rules, regulations, and doctrines adopted in the reform era were codified into a coherent framework in the Book of Marriage and Family and the Book of Succession of the Civil Code of the People's Republic of China (the "Civil Code"), which took effect in 2021.[24] The Civil Code is a monumental achievement in modernizing Chinese family law.

§ 1.2 Changing Society

By the turn of the 21st century, the rapid development of a market-oriented economy, high-paced urbanization, swift industrialization, and mass migration had transformed Chinese society. Family structure and marriage, and Chinese people's views of them, changed drastically in this reform era. Domestic migration contributed to the reconfiguration of Chinese women's identities in marriage and family.[25] Global migration brought demographic, cultural, and social diversity into Chinese families.[26] Large extended, multigenerational,

---

23. The SPC and family law practitioners rigorously defended the new marital property regime. *See, e.g.*, Ma Yina (马忆南), Hunyinfa Xin Sifa Jieshi—Lixing Yu Ganqing De Chongtu (婚姻法新司法解释—理性与情感的冲突) [*The New Marriage Law Judicial Interpretations—the Conflict between Rationality and Emotion*], Shehui Guancha (社会观察) 3 [Social Outlook] (2011) (defending the SPC's rules in defining premarital property, separate property, and marital property); Zhang Xianmin (张先明), Pinglun: Yang Lixin Lei Mingguang Jiedu Hunyinfa Jieshi (III) (评论：杨立新、雷明光解读《婚姻法解释（三）》) [Op-Ed: *Yang Lixin and Lei Mingguan Explaining the Judicial Interpretations on the Marriage Law (III)*], Renmin Fayuan Bao (人民法院报) [People's Court Daily] (Sept. 9, 2011) (explaining the necessity of the SPC efforts to unify provisions governing properties in property law, contract law, and marriage law); Song Yuan (宋媛), Lüshi Cheng Xin Hunyinfa Zuixin Jieshi Pianxiang Qiangzhe Xi Wudu (律师称新婚姻法最新解释偏向强者系误读) [*Attorneys Assert the Allegation that Most Recent Judicial Interpretations on the New Marriage Law Favor the Moneyed Party Is a Misreading*], Guoji Xianqu Daobao(国际先驱导报) [International Herald Leader] (Aug. 19, 2011); Long Jun (龙俊), Fuqi Gongtong Caichan De Qianzai Gongyou (夫妻共同财产的潜在共有) [*Inherent Community Ownership in Husband and Wife's Common Property*], Faxue Yanjiu (法学研究) 4 [Chinese J. L.] 20 (2017) (arguing that the new marital property regime does not cause breakdown of marriages and proposing that a spouse's nonmonetary contribution during the marriage must be considered in determining distribution of marital property and debts).

24. Zhonghua Renmin Gongheguo Minfa Dian (中华人民共和国民法典) [the Civil Code of the People's Republic of China] (promulgated on May 28, 2020; effective from Jan. 1, 2021) (hereinafter the "Civil Code").

25. *See* Woo, *supra* note 15, at 102–03.

26. In the case of global migration, marriage migration across the border from surrounding countries into China began two decades ago and is flourishing. Tens of thousands of foreign women are flocking to China for marriage, pushed by poverty at home and sucked in by China's dramatic shortage of women. *See, e.g.*, Simon Denyer et al., *Too Many Men*, Wash.

patriarchal, patrimonial, patrilineal, and patrilocal families are being replaced by a variety of family structures.[27] Individualization and privatization of marriage, family, and personal relations have been palpable.[28] The marriage rate has decreased sharply,[29] while the crude divorce rate has risen dramatically, to a level similar to the crude divorce rates in industrialized countries.[30]

Increases in divorce, bigamy, domestic violence, concubinage, and other social malaises led to public debates over the state of Chinese marriage, family, and society, and the need for legal mechanisms to remedy these social ills infecting Chinese society. The mainstream narrative that emerged from these public debates is that Chinese people are increasingly seen as living in a moral vacuum in which self-interests and predatory instincts are left unchecked.[31] In agreement with this reading of contemporary Chinese society, the Chinese government has put a renewed emphasis on "rule by law"

Post, Apr. 18, 2018, https://www.washingtonpost.com/graphics/2018/world/too-many-men/?utm_term=.a4446e8bb4a9; foreign investors and workers poured into China and many of them married and became long-term residents. *See, e.g.*, Hsiu-Hua Shen, *Becoming "the First Wives": Gender, Intimacy, and Regional Economy between Taiwan and China*, *in* East Asian Sexualities: Modernity, Gender, and New Sexual Cultures (Liu Jieyu et al., eds. 2008).

27. Hu Zhan & Peng Xizhe (胡湛, 彭希哲), Zhongguo Dangdai Jiatinghu Biandong De Qushi Fenxi – Jiyu Renkou Pucha Shuju De Kaocha (中国当代家庭户变动的趋势分析—基于人口普查数据的考察) [*Household Changes in Contemporary China: an Analysis Based on Census Data*], Shehuixue Yanjiu (社会学研究) 3 [Socio. Stud.] 145–244 (2014). *See also* Wang Yuesheng (王跃生), Dangdai Zhongguo Jiating Jiegou Biandong Fenxi (当代中国家庭结构变动分析) [*An Analysis of the Changes in Contemporary Chinese Household Structures*], Zhongguo Shehuikexue (中国社会科学) 1 [Soc. Sci. in China] (2006).

28. Davis, *supra* note 22 (an in-depth study of Chinese marriages since 1990 based on census data and interviews with urban residents in Guangzhou and Shanghai).

29. *See* Zhonghuan Remnin Gonghe Guo Mingzheng Bu 2017 Nian Shehui Fuwu Fazhan Gongbao (中华人民共和国民政部2017 年社会服务发展统计公报) [Ministry of Civil Affairs of the People's Republic of China 2017 Social Services Progress Statistics Report], Figure 14; Jiehun Dengji (wan dui) (结婚登记 (万对) 1985–2016) [Number of Marriage Registrations (Ten Thousand) 1985–2016], Zhonghuan Remnin Gonghe Guo Guojia Tongjiju Guojia Shuju (中华人民共和国国家统计局国家数据)[National Bureau of Statistics of the People's Republic of China National Data], http://www.mca.gov.cn/article/sj/tjgb/2017/201708021607.pdf.

30. The crude divorce rate rose from 0.18 percent in 1978, at the Maoist era level, to 0.44 percent in 1985, to 2 percent in 2010, to 3.02 percent in 2016, and to 3.36 percent in 2019. *See* Cu Lihunlu (粗离婚率 1985–2019) [Crude Divorce Rate 1985–2016], Zhonghuan Remnin Gonghe Guo Guojia Tongjiju Guojia Shuju (中华人民共和国国家统计局国家数据) [National Bureau of Statistics of the People's Republic of China National Data]. The national crude divorce rate in the United States was about 2.9 percent in 2018. Centers for Disease Control and Prevention, National Vital Statistics System, National Marriage and Divorce Rate Trends for 2000–2018. *See also* Yang Juhua & He Shaohua (杨菊华 何炤华), Shehui Zhuanxing Guocheng Zhong Jiating De Bianqian Yu Yanxu (社会转型过程中家庭的变迁与延续) [*Continuity or Change? Chinese Family in Transitional Era*], Renkou Yanjiu (人口研究) 38(2) [Population Rsch.] 36–51 (2014).

31. Andrea E. Pia, *"We Follow Reason, Not the Law": Disavowing the Law in Rural China*, 39 Pol. & Legal Anthropology Rev. 276, 276–79 (2016).

(*fazhi*).[32] The current administration vowed to construct an effective family law system to fill the alleged moral vacuum and to regulate Chinese people's private lives by law.[33]

§ 1.3 Fading Maoist Ideology

In the Maoist era, centuries-old social order had been turned upside down and family law was weaponized to re-engineer marriage, family, and Chinese society.[34] The socialist state, although more successful than its predecessors, was never able to remake Chinese society precisely according to its ideological vision. The state's prescriptions for marriage and family relations were compelling but did not amount to orthodoxy.[35] After 40 years of legal reform, Maoist ideology is fading away both in the books and in practice. Lawmakers, judges, lawyers, legal scholars, and the public are no longer concerned about the nature and function of a socialist marriage in a planned economy or whether a spouse's petite bourgeoisie sentiment is the cause of marital discord.[36] Instead, their attentions have turned to pressing practical issues: How to protect the best interest of the child in acrimonious divorces? What contract law doctrines may be applied to contracts between spouses? Under what circumstances should a paternity test be ordered? How to determine the nature and scope of marital debts at the time of divorce? Can a stay-home wife be compensated for unpaid domestic work in a divorce, and how much? Can

32. Zhonggong Zhongyang Guanyu Quanmian Tuijin Yifazhiguo Ruogan Zhongda Wenti de Jueding (中共中央关于全面推进依法治国若干重大问题的决定) [CCP Central Committee's Decision Concerning Some Important Issues on Promoting Governing the Nation by Law] (Oct. 28, 2014), *see also* Li Peng Qiangdiao Xiugai Hao Hunyinfa Dui Jiaqiang Shehuizhuyi Jingshenwenmin Jianshe Yiyi Zhongda (李鹏强调修改好婚姻法对加强社会主义精神文明建设意义重大) [*Li Peng Emphasizes Amending the Marriage Law Has Significant Impact on Socialist Spiritual Civilization Building*], Renmin Ribao (人民日报) [People's Daily], Oct. 27, 2000 (In his speech given at the eve of the new Marriage Law of 2001, Li Peng, the former chairman of the People's Congress of China (PCC), emphasized that the new marriage law was to restore the moral order in Chinese society, to cure the moral ills that had come with the market economy, and most importantly to maintain social stability.).

33. *See* Liu, *supra* note 9; Palmer, *supra* note 9.

34. *See* Liu, *supra* note 9; Palmer, *supra* note 9.

35. Margaret Kuo, Intolerable Cruelty: Marriage, Law, and Society in Early Twentieth-Century China 5–6 (2012).

36. For a thorough review of Chinese family law scholarship, see Xue Ninglan (薛宁兰), Yu Lifa Xiangban Qianxin: Qishi Nian Lai De Hunyin Jianting Faxue Yanjue (与立法相伴前行: 七十年来的婚姻家庭法学研究) [*Development along with the Legislation: The Study of Marriage and Family Law in the New China*], (暨南学报(哲学社会科学版) 2019年10月总第249期) 10(249) Jinan J. (Philosophy and Social Sciences) 12–28 (2019).

adult children be compelled not only to provide financial support but also emotional support to their elderly parents?[37]

§ 1.4 Enduring Traditions

Many marriage customs derived from China's peasant economy and Confucian tradition have survived imported ideas and laws since the republican era. Centuries-old customs and traditions not only remain relevant to Chinese people's present views of marriage, divorce, and family life but also exert great influence on China's contemporary legislative and judicial processes.[38] Arranged marriages and multigenerational households are common. In the countryside, the beginning of a marriage is marked by a wedding banquet instead of the state-mandated marriage registration. From China's coastal metropolises to its interior countryside, lavish betrothal gifts are exchanged before couples marry, and intense, sometimes fatal, disputes over the return of the gifts erupt when marriages break down. A patriarchal social order is profoundly ingrained not only in private homes but also in the judicial system itself.[39] Child custody cases become family duels for continuation of family bloodlines. Adult children are ordered to visit elderly parents for filial piety.

§ 1.5 Western Influence

Western influence on modern Chinese family law is apparent. Western ideals of free choice of marriage, companionate marriage, and nuclear family have been accepted and widely practiced. The early republican era legislative efforts were led by "jurists, thoroughly trained in the western systems of law, men of learning, of broad vision, and of fine courage."[40] The republican Civil Code drew its key principles primarily from the continental system of jurisprudence. Generalizations about China's membership in the "civil law" family (*dalu faxi*) of nations are, however, somewhat misleading. Anglo-American legal doctrines and theories have influenced modern Chinese law as well. The drafters of the republican Civil Code, in fact, acknowledged adoption

37. Wu Xiaofang (吴晓芳), Dangqian Hunyin Jiating Anjian De Yinan Wentit Tanxi (当前婚姻家庭案件的疑难问题探析) [*Inquiries and Analyses of Current Complex Issues in Marriage and Family Cases*], Renmin Sifa (人民司法) [The People's Judicature] 54–58 (2010).

38. *See* Huang, *supra* note 1.

39. Ke Li, *"What He Did Was Lawful": Divorce Litigation and Gender Inequality in China*, 37(3) Law & Pol'y 153–79 (July 2015) (finding pervasive gender bias of rural legal workers in divorce litigations).

40. E.G.L., *The Private Law of China*, 30(2) Yale L.J. 180–84, 181 (Dec. 1920).

of Anglo-American family law theories and doctrines in the republican Civil Code.[41]

The United States' legal cooperation and assistance was instrumental in China's reconstruction of its legal system in the reform era.[42] American family law principles, methods, and doctrines are easily identifiable in Chinese family law by trained eyes. To name a few: mandatory full financial disclosure in divorce actions; damages for injuries caused by domestic abuse; equitable compensation for a spouse's nonmonetary contribution as a caregiver through property distribution. Thus, the contemporary Chinese family law system may be described as a hybrid legal system[43]—a system of law that incorporates and harmonizes indigenous Chinese legal concepts, customs, and traditions, and transplanted European-Continental and Anglo-American legal doctrines and theories.

41. Sheng, *supra* note 6, at 77.

42. Jerome A. Cohen, *Was Helping China Build Its Post-1978 Legal System a Mistake?*, 61 VA. J. INT'L L. ONLINE 1, 12 (2020). Nicholas Calcina Howson, *"Can the West Learn from the Rest?"—The Chinese Legal Order's Hybrid Modernity*, 32 HASTINGS INT'L & COMP. L. REV. 815, 818–19 (2009).

43. Howson, *supra* note 42.

Chapter 2

Sources of Chinese Family Law

There are three sources of family law in China: legislations, administrative regulations, and judicial interpretations. The People's Republic of China (the PRC) is a unitary nation. Major national legislation comes from the central national organs, namely the National People's Congress (the NPC) and its standing committee.[1] The NPC has the authority to make and revise the Constitution and "basic laws" (*jiben fa*).[2] The NPC Standing Committee may enact laws other than basic laws and may revise basic laws when the NPC is not in session. Any such revisions must be consistent with the basic law's original intent.[3] Local legislations are permitted but are limited in scope. Local People's Congresses and their standing committees of the provinces, autonomous regions, and directly administered municipalities may adopt regional regulations (*defang fa*) to meet regional needs.[4] Local legislations must be consistent with the Constitution and national legislation.[5] The State Council (*guowu yuan*) and other administrative agencies of the central government may adopt administrative regulations (*fagui*)[6] and local governments can adopt regional regulations (*defang fagui*).[7] Last, a unique and important component of Chinese family law is judicial interpretations (*sifa jieshi*) issued by the Supreme People's Court (the SPC). The SPC judicial interpretations are detailed directives on the application of law, which Chinese courts must follow.

---

1. The Constitution of the People's Republic of China (the "Constitution") arts. 62 and 69. *See also* the Legislation Law of the People's Republic of China (the "Legislation Law") art. 7 para. 1.
2. Legislation Law art. 7 para. 2.
3. *Id*. art. 7 para. 3.
4. China has 34 provinces, five ethnic autonomous regions, and four directly administered municipalities (Beijing, Shanghai, Tianjin, and Chongqing).
5. Legislation Law art. 72.
6. *Id*. art. 65.
7. *Id*. art. 82.

§ 2.1 The Constitution

The Constitution of the People's Republic of China is the principal law of the country. It provides ideological principles of Chinese family law, such as parents have the obligation to support their minor children and adult children have the obligation to support their parents.

§ 2.2 The Civil Code

For more than 100 years, legal scholars in China have been laboring for a civil code that is both "modern and Chinese."[8] The first Chinese civil code, the Civil Code of the Republic China came into fruition in 1929. The 1929 Civil Code, albeit with numerous amendments, remains in effect in Taiwan.[9] On the mainland, a new civil code, the Civil Code of the People's Republic of China (the "Civil Code") was promulgated on May 28, 2020 and took effect on January 1, 2021, after decades of legislative efforts.[10] The Civil Code has two major parts on family law: the Book of Marriage and Family and the Book of Succession. In addition, some provisions that are applicable in family law matters, such as guardianship, right to privacy, and forms of property ownership, are scattered throughout the Civil Code.

Although the Civil Code adopted some new family law doctrines, it has largely retained the existing family law provisions with some additions and revisions.[11] The 2001 Marriage Law and some judicial interpretations on the Marriage Law are incorporated into the Book of Marriage and Family, and the 1985 Succession Law are incorporated into the Book of Succession. The

8. Roscoe Pound, *Chinese Civil Code in Action*, 29 Tul. L. Rev. 277, 290 (1954–1955).

9. Legislative History, The Civil Code, available at Laws and Regulation Database of the Republic of China. *See also* R.C.W. Sheng, *The Civil Code of China*, 4 China L. Rev. 69 (1930); and Pound, *supra* note 8.

10. Xue Jun (薛军), Zhongguo Minfa Dian Bianzhuan: Guannian, Yuanjin Yu Silu (中国民法典编纂: 观念、愿景与思路) [Drafting the Civil Code of China: Concepts, Visions and Ideas], Zhongguo Faxue (中国法学)[China Legal Science], Issue 4, 41–64 (2015); Wang Limin (王利明), Minfa Dian De Shidai Tezheng He Bianzhuan Buzou (民法典的时代特征和编纂步骤) [*The Civil Code's Period Characteristics and Drafting Plan*], 8(6) Tsinghua Univ. L.J. 6–16 (2014).

11. Yang Lixin (杨立新), Minfa Dian Hunyin Jiating Bian Wanshan Woguo Qinshu Zhidu De Chengguo Yu Sifa Caozuo (民法典婚姻家庭编完善我国亲属制度的成果与司法操作) [*The Civil Code Marriage and Family Book's Improvement of Our Country's Kinship System and Its Judicial Implementation*] 14(3) Tsinghua Univ. L.J. 191–207 (2020); Ma Yinan (马忆南), Minfa Dian Hunyin Jiating Bian Jiedu (民法典婚姻家庭编解读) [*An Explanatory Reading of the Civil Code Marriage and Family Book*] Zhongguao Minzheng (中国民政) [Chinese Civil Affairs], 2020(23):44–47; and Xia Yinlan (夏吟兰), Minfa Fenze Hunyin Jiating Bian Lifa Yanjiu (民法分则婚姻家庭编立法研究) [*The Civil Code Marriage and Family Book Legislative Studies*] Zhonguo Faxue (中国法学) [China Legal Sci.] Issue 3 (2017) 71–86.

major family law additions and revisions in the Civil Code are (1) the repeal of the prohibition to marry for serious diseases; (2) the addition of compensatory damages for the innocent party when a marriage is annulled for the other party's wrongdoing; (3) the addition of a mandatory waiting period before divorce; (4) the addition of compensation for a spouse's unpaid domestic work; (5) the addition of provisions concerning married couples' debts; (6) the addition of reliefs for the innocent spouse in a divorce; and (7) the addition of compensatory damages for adultery, domestic violence, and other marital fault in a divorce.[12]

§ 2.3 Special Laws

In addition to the Civil Code, there are special laws that apply in family law matters.

As family law matters are civil matters, civil procedural laws govern the adjudication of family law matters. The two major civil procedural statutes relevant to family matters are (1) the PRC Civil Procedure Law (the "Civil Procedure Law");[13] and (2) the PRC Law of the Applicable Laws to Foreign-Related Civil Relations (the "Law on Applicable Laws"),[14] which governs conflict of laws issues in civil matters, including marriage, succession, and other family law matters.

A few special laws are relevant to specific substantive areas of family law. These special laws include:

(1) The Women's Rights and Interests Protection Law;[15]
(2) The Minors Protection Law;[16]

---

12. Wu Xiaofang (吴晓芳), Dui Minfa Dian Hunyin Jiating Bian Xinzeng He Xiugan Tiaowen De Jiedu (对民法典婚姻家庭编新增和修改条文的解读) [*An Explanatory Reading of the Civil Code Marriage and Family Book's New and Amended Provisions*], Renmin Sifa (人民司法) [The People's Judicature], 19.2020, 29–33.

13. Zhonghua Renmin Gonghe Guo Minshi Susong Fa (中华人民共和国民事诉讼法) [The People's Republic of China Civil Procedure Law] (promulgated Apr. 1, 1991, amended on Oct. 28, 2007, Aug. 31, 2012, and June 27, 2017).

14. Zhonghua Renmin Gonghe Guo Shewai Minshi Guanxi Falü Shiyong Fa (中华人民共和国涉外民事关系法律适用法) [The People's Republic of China Law of the Applicable Laws to Foreign-Related Civil Relations] (promulgated on Oct. 28, 2010, effective from Apr. 1, 2011).

15. Zhonghua Renmin Gongheguo Funü Quanyi Baohu Fa (中华人民共和国妇女权益保护法) [The People's Republic of China Women's Rights and Interests Protection Law] (promulgated on Apr. 3, 1992, amended on Aug. 28, 2005).

16. Zhonghua Renmin Gongheguo Weichengnian Ren Baohu Fa (中华人民共和国未成年人保护法) [the People's Republic of China Minors Protection Law] (promulgated on Sept. 4, 1991, amended on Dec. 19, 2006, amended on Oct. 26, 2012, amended on Oct. 17, 2020, effective June 1, 2021).

(3) The Elderly Persons' Rights and Interests Protection Law;[17] and
(4) The Anti-Domestic Violence Law.[18]

These special laws are policy oriented and contain mostly statements of policy goals and general principles for the protections of women, children, and the elderly, but they have few operational provisions. Nevertheless, Chinese courts quite frequently rely on these laws in their decisions.

§ 2.4 Administrative Regulations

The administrative regulations issued at the national and provincial levels are an important component of Chinese law.[19] At the national level, the State Council and its subordinate agencies may enact administrative regulations to implement the Constitution and national laws.[20] The State Council may recommend and propose new legislation to the National Congress.[21] The State Council and the Ministry of Civil Affairs, which are under the State Council, regulate the registration of marriage, divorce, adoption, and guardianship, and manage China's social welfare system. Thus, the State Council and the Ministry of Civil Affairs' administrative regulations in these areas are an important source of Chinese family law, including:

(1) Regulation on Marriage Registration;[22]
(2) Marriage Registration Protocols;[23]
(3) Measures for the Registration of Adoption of Children by Chinese Citizens,[24] and

17. Zhonghua Renmin Gongheguo Laonian Ren Quanyi Baozhang Fa (中华人民共和国老年人权益保障法) [The People's Republic of China Elderly Persons' Rights and Interests Protection Law] (promulgated on Aug. 29, 1996, amended on Aug. 27, 2009, amended on Dec. 28, 2012, amended on Apr. 24, 2015, amended on Dec. 29, 2018) (hereinafter the "Elderly Protection Law").

18. Zhonghua Renmin Gongheguo Fan Jiating Baoli Fa (中华人民共和国反家庭暴力法) [The People's Republic of China Anti-Domestic Violence Law] (promulgated on Dec. 27, 2005, effective on Mar. 1, 2016) (hereinafter the "Anti-Domestic Violence Law").

19. Chang Wang and Nathan Madison, Inside China's Legal System 296–97 (2013).

20. Legislation Law art. 65 para. 1.

21. *Id.* art. 65 para. 2.

22. Zhonghua Renmin Gongheguo Guowuyuan Hunyin Dengji Tiaoli (中华人民共和国国务院婚姻登记条例) [The PRC State Council Regulations on Marriage Registration] (adopted on July 30, 2003, effective from Oct. 1, 2003).

23. Zhonghua Remin Gongheguo Minzheng Bu Hunyin Dengji Gongzuo Guifan (中华人民共和国民政部婚姻登记工作规范) [The PRC Ministry of Civil Affairs Marriage Registration Protocols] (effective from Dec. 8, 2015).

24. Zhongguo Gongmin Shouyang Zinü Dengji Banfa (中华人民共和国民政部中国公民收养子女登记办法) [The People's Republic China Ministry of Civil Affairs Measures for Registration of Adoption of Children by Chinese Citizens] (May 12, 1999).

(4) Measures for the Registration of Adoption of Children by Foreign Citizens.[25]

§ 2.5 Local Laws

The People's Congresses and the People's Governments (*renmin zhengfu*) at local levels, mainly on the provincial level, issue provincial- or local-level legislation and regulations that are suitable to local conditions. Local legislation and regulations are an integral part of the Chinese legal system. To a certain extent, local laws and regulations determine how local courts and law enforcement implement, apply, and enforce national laws. Local laws must not contradict national legislation. National laws and administrative regulations supersede provincial and local laws when local laws conflict with any national law or national administrative regulations.[26]

§ 2.6 Judicial Interpretations

China's highest court, the Supreme People's Court, issues "judicial interpretations" (*sifa jieshi*), which are binding authorities on the interpretation and application of laws. There are two types of SPC judicial interpretations: guidelines on how to apply a specific statute and instructions in response to lower courts' inquires as to how to handle a specific case or a specific type of case. The SPC's judicial interpretations are binding on Chinese courts.

The SPC has issued a series of judicial interpretations that reshaped Chinese family law in the past two decades. The most consequential SPC judicial interpretations in family law are those on the 2001 Marriage Law—Interpretations on Some Issues Concerning the Application of the Marriage Law (I), (II), and (II) (the "Marriage Law Interpretations (I), (II), and (III)").[27] Through the

---

25. Zhonghua Renmin Gongheguo Minzheng Bu Waiguo Gongmin Zai Zhonghua Renmin Gongheguo Shouyang Zinü Dengji Banfa (中华人民共和国民政部外国公民在中华人民共和国收养子女登记办法) [The PRC Ministry of Civil Affairs Measures for Registration of Adoption of Children by Foreign Citizens] (May 25, 1999).

26. Legislation Law art. 88.

27. Zuigao Renmin Fayuan Guanyu Shiyong Zhonghua Renmin Gonghe Guo Hunyin Fa Ruogan Wenti De Jieshi (yi) (最高人民法院关于适用《中华人民共和国婚姻法》若干问题的解释 (一) [The Supreme People's Court Interpretations on Some Issues Concerning the Application of the People's Republic of China Marriage Law (I)] (promulgated by the Sup. People's Ct., Dec. 25, 2001, effective Dec. 27, 2001) 2002 Sup. People's Ct. Gaz. 1 [hereinafter the "Marriage Law Interpretations (I)"]; Zuigao Renmin Fayuan Guanyu Shiyong Zhonghua Renmin Gonghe Guo Hunyin Fa Ruogan Wenti De Jieshi (er) (最高人民法院关于适用《中华人民共和国婚姻法》若干问题的解释 (二) [The Supreme People's Court Interpretations on Some Issues Concerning the Application of the People's Republic of China Marriage Law (II)] (promulgated by the Sup. People's Ct., Dec. 4, 2003, effective Apr. 1, 2004, revised Feb. 20, 2017, effective Mar.

judicial interpretations on the Marriage Law, the SPC implemented detailed rules of a marital property system befitting China's growing market economy and emerging middle class.[28] In addition to the interpretations on the Marriage Law, several SPC interpretations on specific issues related to divorce were major sources of authority in family law matter litigations.[29]

1, 2017) 2017 Sup. People's Ct. Gaz. 6 [hereinafter the "Marriage Law Interpretations (II)"]; and Zuigao Renmin Fayuan Guanyu Shiyong Zhonghua Renmin Gonghe Guo Hunyin Fa Ruogan Wenti De Jieshi (san) (最高人民法院关于适用《中华人民共和国婚姻法》若干问题的解释（三）[The Supreme People's Court Interpretations on Some Issues Concerning the Application of the People's Republic of China Marriage Law (III)] (promulgated by the Sup. People's Ct., July 4, 2011, effective Aug. 13, 2011) 2011 Sup. People's Ct. Gaz. 9 [hereinafter the "Marriage Law Interpretations (III)"].

28. The SPC regularly issues judicial interpretations as directives to the lower courts. When a statute is enacted or amended, the SPC often issues detailed court rules in the form of judicial interpretations or opinions to guide the lower courts' application of the new statute or amendments. For studies on the SPC judicial interpretations, see Li Wei, *Judicial Interpretation in China*, 5 Willamette J. Int'l L. & Disp. Resol. 87 (1997); Eric C. Ip, *The Supreme People's Court and the Political Economy of Judicial Empowerment in Contemporary China*, 24 Colum. J. Asian L. 367 (2011); Keith J. Hand, *Understanding China's System for Addressing Legislative Conflicts: Capacity Challenges and the Search for Legislative Harmony*, 26 Colum. J. Asian L. 139 (2013).

29. Zuigao Renmin Fayuan Guanyu Renmin Fayuan Shenli Lihun Anjian Ruhe Rending Fuqi Ganqing Que Yi Poli D Rugan Juti Yijian (最高人民法院关于人民法院审理离婚案件如何认定夫妻感情确已破裂的若干具体意见) [Several Specific Opinions on How to Determine Whether Spouses' Relationship Has Ruptured] (promulgated by the Sup. People's Ct., Nov. 21, 1989, effective Dec. 13, 1989), 1990 Sup. People's Ct. Gaz. 1; Zuigao Renmin Fayuan Guanyu Renmin Fayuan Shenli Weiban Jiehun Dengji Er Yi Fuqi Minyi Tongju Shenghuo Anjian De Rugan Yijian (最高人民法院关于人民法院审理未办结婚登记而以夫妻名义同居生活案件的若干意见) [Several Opinions on the People's Courts' Adjudication of Cohabiting as Husband and Wife without Obtaining Marriage Registration Cases] (promulgated by the Sup. People's Ct., Nov. 21, 1989, effective Dec. 13, 1989), 1990 Sup. People's Ct. Gaz. 1; Zuigao Renmin Fayuan Guanyu Renmin Fayuan Shenli Lihun Anjian Chuli Caichan Fenge Wenti De Ruogan Jiuti Yijian (最高人民法院关于人民法院审理离婚案件处理财产分割问题的若干具体意见) [Several Specific Opinions on the Handling of Property Division in the People's Courts' Divorce Case Adjudication] (promulgated by the Sup. People's Ct., Nov. 3, 1993, effective Nov. 3, 1993), 1993 Sup. People's Ct. Gaz. 4; Zuigao Renmin Fayuan Guanyu Renmin Fayuan Shenli Lihun Anjian Chuli Zinu Fuyang Wenti De Ruogan Jiuti Yijian (最高人民法院关于人民法院审理离婚案件处理子女抚养问题的若干具体意见) [Several Specific Opinions on the Handling of Child Custody and Support Issues in the People's Courts' Divorce Case Adjudication] (promulgated by the Sup. People's Ct., Nov. 3, 1993, effective Nov. 3, 1993), 1993 Sup. People's Ct. Gaz. 4; Zuigao Renmin Fayuan Guanyu Renmin Fayuan Shenli Lihun Anjian Zhhong Gongfang Shiyong, Chengzu Ruogan Wenti De Jieda (最高人民法院关于人民法院审理离婚案件中公房使用、承租若干问题的解答) [Answers and Explanations to Issues Concerning the Use and Lease of Public Housing in Divorce Case Adjudication] (promulgated by the Sup. People's Ct., Feb. 5, 1996, effective Feb. 5, 1996), 1996 Sup. People's Ct. Gaz. 2; Zuigao Renmin Fayuan Guanyu Shenli Sheji Fuqi Zhaiwu Jiufen Anjian Shiyong Falü Youguan Wenti De Jieshi (最高人民法院关于审理涉及夫妻债务纠纷案件适用法律有关问题的解释) [Interpretations on the Applicable Law in the Adjudication of Cases Concerning Spouses' Debts] (promulgated by the Sup. People's Ct.,

The SPC's past judicial interpretations were repealed upon the enactment of the new Civil Code. However, much of the content of these judicial interpretations have been incorporated into the SPC's judicial interpretations to the Book of Marriage and Family of the Civil Code (I)[30] (the "Marriage and Family Book Interpretations") and judicial interpretations to the Book of Succession of the Civil Code (I) (the "Succession Book Interpretations"), effective on January 1, 2021, the most recent judicial interpretations on family law. The SPC's prior judicial interpretations on family law were repealed simultaneously upon the issuance of the new judicial interpretations. The new sets of judicial interpretations on family law refined, but did not fundamentally change, the three Marriage Law judicial interpretations.

In addition to the SPC judicial interpretations on marriage and succession laws, the SPC's Rules on the Procedural Issues Concerning Chinese Citizens' Application for Recognition of Foreign Country Court Divorce Judgments, a set of court rules on the recognition of foreign divorce judgments, is frequently applied in Chinese courts.[31]

§ 2.7 Reported Cases

Prior court decisions do not have any binding authority in Chinese law. In recent years, the Supreme People's Court and some provincial High People's Courts started to systematically publish representative judgments, decisions, and orders in both civil and criminal matters. Although these reported cases do not create binding precedents, they are useful references for practitioners—judges and lawyers alike. These reported cases undoubtedly are instrumental in improving the consistency of judicial decision-making and

Jan. 16, 2018, effective Jan. 18, 2018), 2018 Sup. People's Ct. Gaz. 5; and Zuigao Renmin Fayuan Guanyu Renmin Fayuan Shouli Shenqing Chengren Waiguo Fayuan Lihun Panjue Youguan Wenti De Guiding (最高人民法院关于人民法院受理申请承认外国法院离婚判决有关问题的规定) [Regulations on the People's Courts' Acceptance of Application for Recognition of Foreign Country Court Divorce Judgment Cases] (promulgated by the Sup. People's Ct., Dec. 1, 1999, effective Mar. 1, 2000), 2000 Sup. People's Ct. Gaz. 2.

30. Zuigao Renmin Fayuan Guanyu Shiyong Zhonghua Renmin Gonghe Guo Minfadian Hunyin Jiating Bian De Jieshi (yi) (最高人民法院关于适用《中华人民共和国民法典》婚姻家庭编的解释 (一)) [the Supreme People's Court Interpretations on the Application of the People's Republic of China Civil Code, Book of Marriage and Family (I)] (promulgated by the Sup. People's Ct., Dec. 25, 2020, effective Jan. 1, 2021) [hereinafter "Marriage and Family Book Interpretations (I)"].

31. Zuigao Renmin Fayuan Guanyu Zhongguo Gongmin Shenqing Chengren Waiguo Fayuan Lihun Panjue Wenti De Guiding (最高人民法院关于中国公民申请承认外国法院离婚判决程序问题的规定) [the Supreme People's Court's Rules on the Procedural Issues Concerning Chinese Citizens' Application for Recognition of Foreign Country Court Divorce Judgments] (promulgated by the Sup. People's Ct., Jan. 16, 2018, effective Jan. 18, 2018), 2018 Sup. People's Ct. Gaz. 5.

predictability of litigation. However, the SPC's reported cases' influence on Chinese courts' judicial decision-making is found to be limited.[32] There are two types of reported cases: Guiding Cases and Typical Cases.

2.7.1 Guiding Cases

Guiding cases are cases reported by the SPC that (1) are of great social concern; (2) involve application of fundamental legal provisions; (3) are typical; (4) are difficult, complex, or novel; or (5) have any other referential value.[33] Cases that are reported and designated by the SPC as "guiding cases" must be referenced by the lower courts and the SPC in similar cases.[34] As of September 1, 2022, the SPC had reported 185 guiding cases. There were several family law guiding cases: (1) Guiding Case No. 50, where the courts held that a child born through artificial insemination with donor sperm was the husband's child;[35] (2) Guiding Case No. 66, where the husband was awarded a larger share of marital property than the wife, who had concealed and transferred the couple's marital retirement savings;[36] (3) and Guiding Case No. 89, where parents' request to give their daughter a nonconforming name was denied, as the name did not conform with Chinese tradition and public order and good morals, and was not in the best interest of the child; and (4) a case that dealt with division of marital property.[37]

---

32. *See, e.g.*, Shucheng Wang, *Guiding Cases and Bureaucratization of Judicial Precedents in China*, 14 U. Pa. Asian L. Rev. 96 (2019).

33. The SPC Provisions Concerning the Work of Guiding Cases art. 2.

34. *Id.* art. 7. For in-depth discussion of the Guiding Cases system, see Mo Zhang, *Pushing the Envelope: Application of Guiding Cases in Chinese Courts and Development of Case Law in China*, 26 Wash. Int'l L.J. 269 (2017).

35. Zhidao Anli 50 Hao: Li Mou, Guo Mou Yang Su Guo Mo He, Tong Mou Mou Jicheng Jiufen An [指导案例50号：李某、郭某阳诉郭某和、童某某继承纠纷案] (Guiding Case No. 50: Li and Guo Sue Guo and Tong Succession Dispute Case) Zuigao Renming Fayuan Guanyü Fabu Di Shi Pi Zhidaoxing Anli De Tongzhi (Fa [2015] 85 Hao) [最高人民法院关于发布第十批指导性案例的通知，(法[2015] 85号)] [the Supreme People's Court's Notification Regarding Publication of the Tenth Set of Guiding Cases (Law [2015] No. 85)].

36. Zhidao Anli 66 Hao: Lei Mou Mou Su Song Mou Mou Lihun Jiufen An [指导案例66号：雷某某诉宋某某离婚纠纷案] (Guiding Case No. 66: Lei Sue Song Divorce Dispute Case), Zuigao Renming Fayuan Guanyü Fabu Di Shisi Pi Zhidaoxing Anli De Tongzhi (Fa [2016] 311 Hao) [最高人民法院关于发布第十四批指导性案例的通知，(法[2016] 311号)] [the Supreme People's Court's Notification Regarding Publication of the Tenth Set of Guiding Cases (Law [2016] No. 311)].

37. Zhidao Anli 89 Hao: "Beiyan Yunyi" Su Jinans Shi Gong'an Ju Lixia Qu Fenju Yanshan Paichusuo Gong'an Xingzheng Dengji An [指导案例89号："北雁云依"诉济南市公安局历下区分局燕山派出所公安行政登记案] (Guiding Case No. 89: "Beiyan Yunyi" Sue Jinan City Police Bureau Lixia District Bureau Yanshan Precinct Police Administrative Registration Case) Zuigao Renming Fayuan Guanyü Fabu Di Shiqi Pi Zhidaoxing Anli De Tongzhi (Fa [2017] 332 Hao) [最高人民法院关于发布第十七批指导性案例的通知，(法[2017] 332号)] [the Supreme People's Court's Notification Regarding Publication of the Tenth Set of Guiding Cases (Law [2017] No. 332)].

2.7.2 Typical Cases

The SPC periodically publishes Typical Cases to address the most pressing legal and policy issues put in front of the Chinese courts.[38] Although the courts are not required to "reference" or follow Typical Cases, Typical Cases "attain unofficial precedent status,"[39] and Chinese courts "generally follow or respect" Typical Cases.[40] As of September 1, 2022, the SPC had published the following family law Typical Cases:

(1) Family and Marriage Typical Cases (the FMTCs),[41]
(2) Domestic Violence Typical Cases (DVTCs),[42]
(3) Crimes Involving Domestic Violence Typical Cases (CDVTCs),[43]
(4) Termination of Guardianship for Violation of Minor's Rights and Interests Typical Cases (TGTCs),[44]

---

38. Liu Zuoxiang (刘作翔), Zhongguo Anli Zhidao Zhidu De Zuixin Jinzhan Ji Qi Wenti (中国案例指导制度的最新进展及其问题) [Chinese Guiding Cases System's Most Recent Developments and Challenge] Dongfang Faxue (东方法学)[Oriental Law], 2015 Vol. 3. Typical cases (*dianxing anli*) should be distinguished from guiding cases (*zhidaoxing anli*) published by the SPC under a formal Guiding Case System (zhidaoxing anli zhidu) established in 2015. Guiding cases, although not precedential, may be referenced in court decisions. For decades, the SPC has published Typical Cases, which have no precedential effect. For in-depth analyses of China's Guiding Case system, see Cao Zhixun (曹志勋), Lun Zhidaoxing Anli De "Canzhao" Xiaoli Ji Qi Caipan Jishu—Jiyu Dui Yigongbu De 42 Ge Mingshi Zhidaoxing Anli De Shizhi Fenxi (论指导性案例的"参照"效力及其裁判技术—基于对已公布的42个民事指导性案例的实质分析)[*Discussing Guiding Cases' "Reference" Authority and Adjudicating Techniques-Based on Didactic Analyses of 42 Published Civil Matter Guiding Cases*]; Bijiaofa Yanjiu (比较法研究)6 J. Comp. L. 111–34 (2016); Zhang, *supra* note 34; Mark Jia, *Chinese Common Law? Guiding Cases and Judicial Reform*, 129 Harv. L. Rev. 2213 (2016); Peter Howard Corne, *Creation and Application of Law in the PRC*, 50 Am. J. Comp. L. 369 (2002).

39. Corne, *supra* note 38, at 410.

40. Judge Luo Xia, *China Judicial Reforms Are Creating Opportunities for Technology Transfer and Licensing*, 52 Les Nouvelles 1, 2 (2017).

41. "Yong Gongkai Cu Gongzheng Jianshe Hexin Jiazhi" Zhuti Jiaoyu Huodong Hunyin Jiating Jiufen Dianxin Anli ("用公开促公正 建设核心价值"主题教育活动 婚姻家庭纠纷典型案例) ["Promote Justice Construct Core Value through Transparency" Focused Education Campaign: Family and Marriage Disputes Typical Cases] (Dec. 4, 2015).

42. Zuigao Renmin Fayuan Gongbu Shiqi Jiating Baoli Dianxing Anjian (最高人民法院公布十起家庭暴力的典型案例) [The Supreme People's Court Published Ten Domestic Violence Typical Cases], 2015 Sup. People's Ct. Gaz. 2.

43. Zuigao Renmin Fayuan Fabu She Jiating Baoli Fanzui Dianxing Anjian (最高法发布涉家庭暴力犯罪典型案例) [The SPC Published Crimes Involving Domestic Violence Typical Cases] (Mar. 4, 2015).

44. Zuigao renmin fayuan guanyu qinhai weichennian ren quanyi bei chexiao jianhuren zige dianxin anli (最高人民法院关于侵害未成年人权益被撤销监护人资格典型案例) [Termination of Guardianship for Violation of Minor's Rights and Interests Typical Cases] (May 31, 2016).

(5) Personal Safety Protection Order Typical Cases (PSPOTCs),[45]
(6) Elderly People's Rights and Interests Protection Typical Cases (EPTCs) (I) and II, and[46]
(7) Minors' Rights and Interests Protection Typical Cases (MPTCs).[47]

The publication of these Typical Cases is a part of the SPC's effort to improve uniformity and predictability of outcomes in family law cases.[48]

A Typical Case report usually contains three parts: "Basic Facts" (*jiben anqing*), which illustrate the fact pattern of the case; "Adjudication Outcome" (*caipan jieguo*), which outlines the trial court and sometimes the appellate court's decisions; and "Exemplary Significance" (*dianxing yiyi*), which is the SPC's commentary on the case. Although the Typical Cases do not report everything that took place in the courtroom in each case, they nonetheless provide a broader understanding of Chinese family law, its application in the courts, and the direction the SPC is steering the Chinese courts to in family law.

2.7.3 Published Decisions

All civil judgments, orders, and decisions are published and searchable in Chinese courts' online database, unless nonpublication is ordered by a court. Recently, an increasing number of family matter decisions are not published for the protection of minor children's privacy. Although Chinese courts' decisions do not have any binding authority over future cases, the published court decisions provide a wealth of information about what facts are critical in a certain type of case, what law applies, or how a particular judge decides on a particular type of case. Because attorneys' information is published in the decisions as well, litigants could get glimpses of attorneys' competency before retaining counsel.

---

45. Zuigo Renmin Fayuan Renshen Anquan Baohu Ling Shi Da Dianxing Anli (最高人民法院人身安全保护令十大典型案例) [The SPC Ten Important Personal Safety Protection Order Typical Cases] (Nov. 25, 2020).

46. Renmin Fayuan Laonian Ren Quanyi Baohu Shi Da Dianxing Anli (人民法院老年人权益保护十大典型案例) [Ten Important the People's Court Elderly People's Rights and Interests Protection Typical Cases] (Feb. 24, 2021); Zuigao Fay Fabu Laonian Ren Quanyi Baohu Dier Pi Dianxin Anli (最高法发布老年人权益保护第二批典型案例) [The SPC Second Set of Elderly People's Rights and Interests Protection Typical Cases] (Apr. 8, 2022).

47. Weichengnian Ren Quanyi Sifa Baohu Dianxing Anli (未成年人权益司法保护典型案例) [Minors' Rights and Interests Judicial Protection Typical Cases] (Mar. 2, 2022).

48. Margaret Y.K. Woo, *Court Reform with Chinese Characteristics*, 27 Wash. Int'l L.J. 241, 260–61 (2017).

Chapter 3

The Chinese Judiciary

The Chinese judiciary has four components: the courts, the procuratorates, lawyers, and notaries. The roles and functions of the Chinese courts and lawyers are self-evident. The procuratorates, whose main task is criminal prosecution, also play an important role in China's civil justice system. Chinese procuratorates may intervene in civil appeals and challenge courts' decisions on behalf of civil litigants. Chinese notaries are licensed legal professionals and they play a significant nonlitigatory role in China's judiciary.

Semi-judiciary state agencies are involved in the regulation of family affairs as well. The Ministry of Civil Affairs and its local Bureaus of Civil Affairs handle registrations of marriage, divorce, and adoption. The Ministry of Public Safety and its local police departments. In addition to governmental agencies, nongovernmental community-based self-governing bodies—that is, Urban Residents' Committees in cities and Villagers' Committees in rural areas—are given considerable power and authority to surveille, manage, and provide essential social services to families.

§ 3.1 The People's Courts

The courts of the People's Republic of China (PRC) are called "the People's Courts." The People's Courts are the "adjudication organs of the State."[1] The People's Courts are divided into two tracks: courts of general jurisdiction and courts of special jurisdiction. Courts of general jurisdiction hear all civil and criminal matters, except for matters related to military, transportation, maritime, and intellectual property, which are adjudicated in special courts with

1. Zhonghua Renmin Gonghe Guo Renmin Fayuan Zuzhi Fa (中华人民共和国人民法院组织法) [The People's Republic of China Organic Law of People's Courts] (promulgated by the National People's Cong. July 1, 1979, effective Jan. 1, 1981, amended Sept. 2, 1983 Dec. 2, 1986, and Oct. 31, 2006) (the "Organic Law of the People's Courts"), art. 2.

exclusive jurisdiction.[2] The People's Courts of general jurisdiction are organized by four levels: (1) the Basic-Level People's Courts (*jiceng remnin fayuan*); (2) the Intermediate People's Courts (*zhongji renmin fayuan*); (3) the High People's Courts (*gaoji renmin fayuan*); and (4) the Supreme People's Court (*zuiguao renmin fayuan*).[3]

Chinese courts function with remarkable efficiency. In family matter cases, years-long acrimonious divorces, ubiquitous in American courts, are rare in China. At the trial court level, most family matters are usually concluded within six months of the commencement of an action, as required by the Civil Procedure Law. The high efficiency and low cost of civil dispute resolution are achieved through a stringent internal "case management" system that closely monitors judges' performance.

3.1.1 Hierarchical Structure of Courts

3.1.1.1 The Supreme People's Court

At the very top of the PRC court system is the Supreme People's Court (the SPC). The SPC reports to the Standing Committee of the National People's Congress (the NPC). The SPC chief justice is elected and appointed by the Standing Committee.[4] The SPC reviews the decisions of all lower courts and has jurisdiction over all regular and special courts.[5] The SPC wields immense judicial power over the lower courts through judicial interpretations and through Guiding Case and Typical Case reports.[6] (For discussions on judicial interpretations Guiding Cases and Typical Cases, see § 2.7.)

3.1.1.2 High People's Court

High People's Courts are established at the provincial level, and they are the highest courts in each province. Each province has only one High People's Court. Every High People's Court hears appeals from the Intermediate People's Courts located in its province. A provincial High People's Court may also exercise jurisdiction as court of first instance over civil cases, with significant impact within the province where it sits.[7]

---

2. Organic Law of the People's Courts art. 15.

3. Organic Law of the People's Courts arts. 12 and 13; *see also* Yulin Fu, *The Chinese Supreme People's Court in Transition*, 59 IUS GENTIUM 13, 13–14 (2017); Margaret Woo, *The Dynamism of China's Civil Litigation System*, 48 IUS GENTIUM 141, 143 (2016).

4. Organic Law of the People's Courts art. 42.

5. *Id*. art. 10.

6. *Id*. art. 18.

7. *Id*. arts. 20 and 21.

3.1.1.3 Intermediate People's Court

Intermediate People's Courts usually sit at the municipal level. An Intermediate People's Court serves as the court of second instance for appeals from the lower courts within its jurisdiction. In addition, it is the court of first instance in major cases that involve foreign parties and cases with significant impact within its geographical jurisdiction.[8]

3.1.1.4 Basic-Level People's Court

Basic-level People's Courts are trial courts of first instance at the county level in rural areas and at the district level in cities. Basic People's Courts have general jurisdiction as courts of first instance.[9]

3.1.2 Courts' Internal Structure

3.1.2.1 Divisions

A Chinese court usually has two parts: the civil part and the criminal part. The civil part is divided into specialized divisions, which usually include civil matter (*minshi*) divisions, commercial matter (*shangshi*) divisions, and family matter (*jiashi*) divisions.[10] A court's civil part maintains several divisions, usually including at least one division specialized in family law matters.

3.1.2.2 Collegiate Bench

Simple civil matters that have few factual disputes, or involve small claims, or are likely to be resolved through mediation are dealt with through a summary procedure (*jianyi chengxu*) presided by a single judge at the Basic People's Court level.[11] A significant fraction of family disputes are resolved through the summary procedure.[12]

---

8. *Id.* arts. 22, 23.

9. *Id.* art. 24.

10. Wang Yaxin & Fu Yulin, Chapter 2 *China: Mainland. Efficiency at the Expense of Quality?*, 31 IUS GENTIUM 11, 12 (2014).

11. Civil Procedure Law arts. 39 para. 2, 133(3), and 157. (To limit the number of cases for full adjudication and trials, all civil cases are assessed and assigned to one of the following litigation tacks: (1) expedited procedure used for cases with little or no factual disputes; (2) mediation used for cases that are more substantial and likely to be settled; (3) simplified procedure used for many civil cases in which the facts are relatively undisputed and the amount in controversy is below RMB5,000 (USD825); and (4) ordinary procedure for cases that will likely require a trial.); Woo, *supra* note 3, at 145–46.

12. The SPC reported that 73.05 percent of cases were heard through the summary procedure. *See* Renminfayuan Xinwen Chuanmei Zongshe (人民法院新闻传媒总社) [The People's Court Media and Press Office], Zuigao Renmin Fayuan Fabu Diyi Jidu Shenpan Zhixing Gongzuo Shuju Xinshou Anjian Shu Jixue Zengzhang Jiean Shu Tongbi Zengjia Zhengti Yunxin

Most cases are heard by a "collegiate bench." The number of members on the collegiate bench must be an odd number that is three or more. Most collegiate benches have three trial judges, or one judge with two People's Jurors, or two trial judges with one People's Juror.[13] The majority view prevails in the adjudication process. Dissenting opinions, if any, can be recorded in the file and kept by the trial court.[14] One member of the collegiate bench acts as the lead trial judge. The role of the lead trial judge is to take primary control of the hearing process; to question the parties or their witnesses at the hearing; to supervise the investigation and collection of evidence (where necessary); and to prepare a draft judgment.[15]

3.1.2.3 Judges

Chinese judges' competence and professionalism have improved greatly in the past 40 years.[16] Trained legal professionals replaced party cadres and retired military officers who were installed as judges in the Maoist era. To qualify as a judge, a candidate must have at least a bachelor's degree in law and three to five years of legal experience, and must have passed the national judicial exam.[17]

The feminization of the legal profession has become a worldwide phenomenon, and Chinese courts are no exception to this global trend.[18] Family matters are often heard by female judges. The general perception is that

---

Shitai Wen Zhong Xiang Hao (最高人民法院发布第一季度审判执行工作数据 新收案件数继续增长 结案数同比增加 整体运行态势稳中向好), [The Supreme Court Releases the First Quarter Adjudication and Enforcement Data—the Number of New Cases Increase Continues, the Number of Concluded Cases Increases at the Same Rate, Overall Function Steady and Improving], Zuigao Renmin Fayuan Xinwen (最高人民法院新闻) [Press Release], https://www.chinacourt.org/article/detail/2018/05/id/3295839.shtml; *see also* Zuigao Renmin Fayuan Sifa Dashuju Zhuanti Baogao Lihun Jiufen (2017) (最高人民法院司法大数据专题报告离婚纠纷 (2017)) [The SPC Judicial Data Subject Report: Divorce Disputes (2017)], http://www.court.gov.cn/upload/file/2017/10/13/16/39/20171013163908_87275.pdf; Zuigao Renmin Fayuan Sifa Dashuju Zhuanti Baogao Lihun Jiufen (2018) (最高人民法院司法大数据专题报告离婚纠纷 (2018)) [The SPC Judicial Data Subject Report: Divorce Disputes (2018)], http://www.court.gov.cn/upload/file/2018/03/23/09/33/20180323093343_53196.pdf.

13. Organic Law of the People's Courts art. 30 para. 1; *see also* Civil Procedure Law, Chapter 3 Trial Organization.

14. Organic Law of the People's Courts art. 30 para. 2.

15. *Id*. art. 30 para 3.

16. Benjamin L. Liebman, *China's Courts: Restricted Reform*, 21 COLUM. J. ASIAN L. 1, 12 (2007).

17. Zhonghua Renmin Gonghe Guo Faguan Fa (中华人民共和国法官法) [The People's Republic of China Judges Law] (promulgated Feb. 28, 1995, effective Feb. 28, 1995, amended June 30, 2001, amended Sept. 1, 2017, and amended Apr. 23, 2019) [hereinafter the "Judges Law"] art. 12 (7).

18. Chunyan Zheng, Jiahui Ai & Sida Liu, *The Elastic Ceiling: Gender and Professional Career in Chinese Courts*, 51 LAW & SOC'Y REV. 168 (2017).

female judges are better suited to handle family law matters because of their feminine virtues: patience, empathy, and motherly disposition.[19] Thus, women judges are often assigned to handle family matters as a measure to diffuse family discord and to protect women, children, and the elderly.

Chinese judges enjoy career security and may not be removed without good cause.[20] Each judge's performance is reviewed annually. Judges' promotion and compensation are usually tied to their annual evaluations.[21] The SPC's and local governments' Judges' Disciplinary Committees (*faguan chenjie weiyuanhui*) oversee allegations of judges' ethical, professional, and criminal misconducts.[22] Disciplinary actions and criminal charges are required for a wide range of judicial misconducts from participation in for-profit activities or dereliction of duty to bribery.[23] Chinese judges are constantly evaluated by hyper-quantified measures for their fairness (*gongzheng*), efficiency (*xiaolü*), and impact (*xiaoguao*).[24] The constant assessment and close surveillance of judges' decision-making is a double-edged sword. On one hand, it helps improve judicial transparency and efficiency. On the other hand, it interferes with judicial independence and autonomy.[25]

3.1.2.4 People's Jurors

People's Jurors (*renmin peishenyuan*) are lay members of collegiate benches in both civil and criminal trials.[26] The People's Juror system, a Soviet Union relic, was adopted by former communist regimes, including the PRC. People's Jurors used to be merely props in the Chinese Communist Party's (CCP's)

---

19. Shuai Wei & Xin Xin, *Does Gender Play a Role in Divorce Mediation? Working Pattern of Women Judges in China*, 19(3) Asian J. Women's Studies 149–71, 151–53 (2013).

20. Judges Law arts. 52–53.

21. *Id.* arts. 41–45.

22. *Id.* art. 48.

23. *Id.* art. 46.

24. Jonathan J. Kinkel & William J. Hurst, *The Judicial Cadre Evaluation System in China: From Quantification to Intra-state Legibility*, 224 China Q., 224, 933–54, 933 (Dec. 2015).

25. For studies on administrative assessment and surveillance of Chinese judges, *see, e.g., id.*; Carl Minzner, *Judicial Disciplinary Systems for Incorrectly Decided Cases: The Imperial Chinese Heritage Lives On, in* Chinese Justice: Civil Dispute Resolution in Contemporary China 58–90 (Margaret Woo & Mary Gallagher eds., 2011); *Randall Peerenboom, Judicial Independence and Judicial Accountability: An Empirical Study of Individual Case Supervision*, 55 China J. 67–92; and Randall Peerenboom, *Judicial Independence in China: Common Myths and Unfounded Assumptions, in* Judicial Independence in China: Lessons for Global Rule of Law Promotion 69–94 (Randall Peerenboom ed., 2010).

26. Zuigao Renmin Fayuan Guanyu Shiyong Zhonghua Renmin Gongheguo Renmin Peishenyuan Fa Ruogan Wenti De Jieshi (最高人民法院关于适用《中华人民共和国人民陪审员法》若干问题的解释) [The SPC Interpretations on the Issues Concerning the Application of the PRC People's Juror Law (promulgated by the Sup. People's Ct., Feb. 18, 2019, effective May 1, 2019) [hereinafter the "Interpretations on the People's Juror Law"] art. 5.

political shows, making symbolic appearances at highly politicized public trials. As judicial transparency has become a serious concern in Chinese society in recent decades, the People's Juror system (*renmin peishenyuan zhidu*) has been renovated and expanded to improve judicial transparency since 2004.[27] In 2018, China enacted the People's Juror Law, which is billed as a great leap to the democratization of the Chinese judicial system.[28]

On paper, Chinese law confers significant power to People's Jurors. As part of a collegiate bench, People's Jurors have the same authority as judges in the adjudication process.[29] People's Jurors may express their independent opinions in open court and communicate with the litigants directly. They may question witnesses and examine evidence.[30] They may even conduct mediation.[31] Contrary to propaganda pieces that lauded People's Jurors who play active roles in resolving contentious family disputes, People's Jurors remain largely symbolic and rarely participate in any courtroom activities.[32]

People's Jurors are given enormous power but are required of little qualification. They are lay people with no legal training who are randomly selected from the local community. Any Chinese citizen over 28, of good moral character, with no criminal record, and not in the legal profession can act as a People's Juror.[33] People's Jurors may be selected from people with expertise or professional knowledge in cases that require special knowledge, expertise, or experience in certain fields.[34] Thus, Chinese courts often appoint respected community members, social workers, or schoolteachers as People's Jurors in family law cases, particularly in cases involving children and/or domestic violence.

---

27. For studies on China's People's Jury system, see, e.g., Xin He, *Double Whammy: Lay Assessors as Lackeys in Chinese Courts*, 50(3) LAW & SOC'Y REV. 733–65 (2016).

28. Zhonghua Renmin Gonghe Guo Renmin Peishenyuan Fa (中华人民共和国人民陪审员法) [The People's Republic of China People's Jurors Law] (promulgated and effective Apr. 27, 2018) [hereinafter the "People's Jurors Law"]. Zhenqi Zhao, Renmin Peishenyuan Fa: Kuoda Sifa Lingyu De Renmin Minzhu (人民陪审员法：扩大司法领域的人民民主) [Expansion of People's Democracy in the Judicial Territory], Li Fa (立法 –中国人大) [Legislations—China People's Congress], Jan. 20, 2019, at 21.

29. Civil Procedure Law art. 39 para. 3; and the People's Juror Law art. 2.

30. The People's Juror Law art. 3.

31. The Interpretations on the People's Juror Law, art. 7.

32. *See, e.g.*, Li Jiancong: Zhewei Peishenyuan You "Sangao" (李建葱：这位陪审员有"三高") [Li Jiancong: This Juror Has "Three Masterful Techniques"], Renmin Fayuan Bao (人民法院报) [the People's Court Daily], July 21, 2018.

33. The People's Juror Law arts. 5–7.

34. The Interpretations on the People's Juror Law art. 3 para. 3.

3.1.2.5 Adjudication Committees

Each Chinese court has an adjudication committee composed of the chief judge, the vice chief judge, and senior judges of the court.[35] The role of the adjudication committee of each court is to review the judges' trial work and discuss major or complicated legal issues arising from the cases pending before the court.[36] When a collegiate bench cannot reach a consensus on certain issues in a case, the lead judge of the collegiate bench must refer these issues to the court's adjudication committee. The adjudication committee then meets to discuss these issues until a majority opinion is formed.[37] The adjudication committee must review the case file and conduct meetings to discuss the case before taking a vote and issuing its opinion. The presiding judge or collegiate bench must be present at the adjudication committee meetings. The adjudication committee may invite legal experts or members of the local People's Congress to participate in its review and discussion of a case.[38] The adjudication committee's opinion must be disclosed in the court's decision.[39]

Adjudication committees used to be the *de facto* internal decision-making body, as prior to the recent judicial reforms generally judgments or court orders had to be approved by adjudication committees. Adjudication committees now serve an advisory role. Only cases that involve sensitive political issues, national security, or complex criminal matters, such as death penalty cases, must be reviewed by the adjudication committee before decisions can be rendered in these cases.[40] Individual judges or collegiate benches may request the adjudication committee's advice in complex civil matters when a collegiate bench cannot reach a majority opinion, or when a judge's decision might be inconsistent with the court's previous decisions, or when a case is remanded, or whenever the adjudication committee's guidance is needed.[41] Only after the request for its advice is approved by the court's chief judge, can a court's adjudication committee intervene and provide its opinion.[42] Because most family law cases are routine, nonpolitical, and straightforward, adjudication committees rarely intervene in family law matters.

---

35. Organic Law of the People's Courts art. 36.

36. *Id.* art. 37.

37. *Id.* art. 38.

38. Zuigao Renmin Fayuan Guanyu Jianquan Wanshan Renmin Fayuan Shenpan Weiyuanhui Gongzuo Jizhi De Yijian (最高人民法院关于健全完善人民法院审判委员会工作机制的意见) [the SPC's Opinions on Perfecting and Improving the People's Court Adjudication Committees' Institutional Mechanism] (promulgated by the Sup. People's Ct., Aug. 2, 2019, effective Aug. 2, 2019) [hereinafter the "Adjudication Committee Opinions"], art. 18.

39. Organic Law of the People's Courts art. 39.

40. The Adjudication Committee Opinions art. 8.

41. *Id.* art. 9.

42. *Id.* art. 10.

3.1.2.6 Language

Mandarin Chinese is the official language written and spoken in Chinese courts. However, the courts located in an ethnic minority autonomous region must use the regional ethnic language as the official working language and must provide interpreters to litigants who are not familiar with the ethnic language.[43] Foreign litigants may request Chinese courts to provide interpreters at the litigants' own expense.[44] There are no rules concerning the qualifications and appointment of court interpreters. In practice, litigants usually bring their own interpreters.

Documents submitted to Chinese courts in any language other than Chinese must be accompanied with Chinese translations. When there is any dispute over the accuracy of the Chinese translations, the parties may choose a neutral translator or request a court-appointed translator.[45]

3.1.2.7 Court Fees

Court fees are charged according to the SPC's rules of court fees. There are three types of court fees: (1) case fees (*anjian shouli fei*), that is, filing fees; (2) application fees (*shengqing fei*), similar to motion fees paid in the U.S. courts, for specific applications for interim or permanent reliefs; and (3) disbursement of costs.[46]

In property disputes, case fees are levied based on percentages of the value of the disputed transactions or property.[47] Case fees for divorce actions are from RMB50 to RMB300 for cases in which the value of disputed property is no more than RMB200,000. In divorce actions where the value of disputed property is more than RMB200,000, an additional case fee is levied at the level

43. The Constitution art. 134; Zhonghua Renmin Gongheguo Minzu Quyu Zizhi Fa (中华人民共和国民族区域自治法) [the People's Republic of China Reginal Ethnic Autonomy Law] (promulgated by the National People's Cong. on May 31, 1984; effective October 1, 1984); amended on February 28, 2001) [hereinafter "Ethnic Autonomy Law"] art. 47.

44. Civil Procedure Law art. 240.

45. Zuigao Renmin Fayuan Guanyu Shiyong Zhonghua Renmin Gonghe Guo Minshi Susong Fa De Jieshi (最高人民法院关于使用中华人民共和国民事诉讼法的解释) [the Supreme People's Court's Interpretations on the Civil Procedure Law of the People's Republic of China] (promulgated by the Sup. People's Ct., Dec. 18, 2014, effective Feb. 4, 2015, amended Dec. 23, 2020, and amended Mar. 22, 2022; effective Apr. 19, 2022) 2022 Sup. People's Ct. Gaz. 7 [hereinafter the "Civil Procedure Law Interpretations"] art. 525.

46. Zuigao Renmin Fayuan Susong Feiyon Jiaona Banfa (最高人民法院诉讼费用交纳办法) [The Supreme People's Court Rules on Litigation Fee Payments] (Oct. 24, 2010) [hereinafter "Litigation Fee Payments Rules"] art. 6.

47. Litigation Fee Payments Rules art. 13(1).

of 0.5 percent of the property value.[48] In other nonproperty disputes, such as child custody or guardianship, the case fees range from RMB50 to RMB100.[49]

Generally, the losing party pays the court fees and costs.[50] In family matters, usually there are no winners or losers. Thus, parties in family disputes, such as divorces, are encouraged to settle court fees.[51] When the parties fail to reach a settlement, court fees and litigation costs are then allocated between the parties by the courts.[52]

§ 3.2 The People's Procuratorates

The People's Procuratorates are China's state prosecutorial organ. In addition to criminal prosecution, the procuratorates have the power of legal supervision in civil matters.[53] The procuratorates can intervene in civil procedures by filing an appeal or request for reconsideration to an appropriate court when the procuratorates find that a judgment or order should be reviewed for legal, factual, or procedural errors, or that a judgment or order may be detrimental to national interests or public interests.[54] The procuratorates may appeal a civil judgment or order on their own motion or upon a party's application.[55]

The procuratorates' power to intervene in civil matters gives the state a unique opportunity to provide legal assistance to vulnerable parties or to participate in high-impact civil cases. For example, in *Zhang v. Di*, a protracted divorce action, the Supreme People's Procuratorate appealed on the wife's behalf in the SPC on the grounds, *inter alia*, that the lower courts failed to protect the wife and the parties' child's interest by awarding the husband the family home, and made the wife and child homeless.[56] The procuratorates' intervention in civil matters is infrequent. For example, Chinese procuratorates filed appeals or requests for reconsideration in only 5,814 civil cases in the entire country in 2017.[57]

---

48. *Id*. art. 13(2)1.
49. *Id*. art. 13(2)3.
50. *Id*. art. 29 para. 1.
51. *Id*. art. 33.
52. *Id*. art. 33 and art. 29 para. 2.
53. Civil Procedure Law art. 14.
54. *Id*. art. 208.
55. *Id*. arts. 208, 209.
56. (2015) Min Kang Zi Di 9 Hao ((2015) 民抗字第9号).
57. Wu Xiaomei (伍晓梅) ed. Zhongguo falü nianjian (中国法律年鉴) [Chinese Law Yearbook], 2018, 1189.

§ 3.3 Lawyers

China's legal profession has grown exponentially since the 1990s. Many Chinese attorneys and judges are educated and trained both in China and in Anglo-American and Western European jurisdictions. Some well-trained and highly skilled Chinese attorneys have been attracted to family law practice and become family law specialists in recent years. Nevertheless, when working with Chinese attorneys, one should be sensitive to the differences in the legal systems, cultures, and languages.

Chinese attorneys are licensed and regulated by the Ministry of Justice.[58] Generally, the Chinese government has supported the development of the legal profession. A key feature of the regulation of the Chinese legal profession is that attorneys' fees are regulated by local Bureau of Justice and consumer protection agencies.[59] Municipalities often publish an advisory schedule for attorneys' fees and disbursements. Although the advisory fee schedule is not mandatory, it usually sets the fee standards in the community.

§ 3.4 Notary Offices

China's notary offices (*gongzheng chu*) is a vital component of Chinese legal system. Modeled after the Latin Notary, Chinese notary offices conduct a wide range of legal functions that are normally performed by lawyers, courts, and state agencies in Anglo-American jurisdictions. Chinese notary offices are entrusted by the state with the authority to certify the authenticity and legality of civil juridical acts, and facts or documents of legal significance.[60] Chinese notaries (*gongzheng yuan*) are not menial officeholders that witness execution of legal instruments, but rather private legal professionals licensed by the state,[61] and subject to professional, civil, and criminal liability for miscarriage of their office.[62]

58. Zhonghua Renmin Gongheguo Lüshi Fa (中华人民共和国律师法) [The Lawyers Law of the People's Republic of China] (promulgated by the National People's Cong. on May 15, 1996, amended on Dec. 19, Oct. 28, 2007, Oct. 26, 2012, and Sept. 1, 2017) [hereinafter the "Lawyers Law"] arts. 2 and 4.

59. Lawyers Law art. 59.

60. Zhonghua Renmin Gongheguo Gongzheng Fa (中华人民共和国公证法) [The Notary Law of the People's Republic of China] (promulgated by the National People's Cong. Aug. 28, 2005; amended Apr. 24, 2015 and Sept. 1, 2017) [hereinafter the "Notary Law"], art. 2.

61. *Id.* art. 16.

62. *Id.* arts. 41–43.

3.4.1 Authentication

Chinese notaries play a pivotal role in Chinese family law system. A major function of Chinese notaries is authenticating "fact" by verifying and memorializing the "fact," which may be the occurrence of a legal action or event, or the existence of a legal relationship or status, in a notary deed (*gongzheng shu*). A notary deed is a public document taken as probative basis for establishing a fact,[63] and can only be invalidated by a notary office (*gongzheng chu*) or a court.[64] For example, upon an interested party's request, a notary can issue a notary deed of the marriage of a person after verifying the documentation of the marriage. (See Appendix XIV, Notary Deed of Marriage, available online.) The notary deed of marriage is deemed as probative evidence of the marriage. If a party needs to prove the marriage in a civil action, such as an intestate inheritance dispute or a divorce action, the notary deed of marriage alone is sufficient to prove the marriage.[65]

3.4.2 Legal Counseling

Chinese notaries provide essential nonadversarial, nonlitigation legal services in family law matters. Like the Latin notary, Chinese notary offices are "charged with the public function of receiving, interpreting, and giving legal form to the intent of the parties, preparing the documents pertinent to the desired end and issuing copies that attest to their content."[66] In other words, Chinese notaries draft, attest, and record nonlitigation legal instruments, particularly instruments concerning succession, guardianship, adoption, divorce, and family property, such as wills, gift agreements, prenuptial agreements, post-nuptial agreements, and estate distribution agreements. Chinese notaries are basically neutral counselors for all parties that request their services in nonadversarial family matters.[67] To illustrate: Zhang and Wang are divorced. Their divorce agreement provides that (1) Zhang, the father,

---

63. *Id*. art. 36.

64. *Id*. arts. 39, 40.

65. Zuigao Renmin Fayuan Guanyu Minshi Susong Zhengju De Ruogan Guiding (最高人民法院关于民事诉讼证据的若干规定) [the Supreme People's Court's Several Provisions on Evidence in Civil Procedures] (promulgated by the Sup. People's Ct., on Dec. 6, 2001; amended on Oct. 14, 2019, effective from May 1, 2020), art. 10(7), providing that a party does not need to provide any evidence as to a fact that has been established by a notarial certificated.

66. Pedro A. Malavet, *Counsel for the Situation: The Latin Notary, a Historical and Comparative Model*, 19 Hastings Int'l & Comp. L. Rev. 389, 434 (1996), citing Ediciones Repertorio Notarial De Comerio De Escribanos De La Provincia De Buenos Autas, Congresos Y Jornadas 37 (1969).

67. Wu Rong (吴蓉), Cong ADR Dao ODR Kan Gongzheng Zai Shehui Zhili Chuangxin Zhong De Zuoyong Fahui Ji Ziwo Wanshan (从ADR 到ODP看公证在社会治理创新中的作用发挥及自我完善) (From ADR To ODR Notary's Functions and Self-Improvement in Social Governance Innovation), Zhongguo Gongzheng (中国公证) [Chinese Notary], 2020(09):38–47, 43–44.

should have residential custody of their child, and Wang would pay Zhang RMB500 per month for child support; (2) Wang should have the ownership of the marital home and in exchange Wang should pay Zhang RMB60,000; and (3) Zhang should retain the right of occupancy of the marital home and may live there with the parties' child after the divorce. A couple of years after the divorce, Zhang plans to relocate to another city. Wang and Zhang want to modify the divorce agreement due to Zhang's relocation. Instead of going to court, they can go to a notary office (*gongzheng chu*) and have their divorce agreement modified and notarized. They bring to the notary an amended divorce agreement stating that (1) the residential custody of their son would be changed from Zhang to Wang, and Zhang should pay Wang RMB500 per month for child support; (2) Wang should have the ownership of the marital home and in exchange Wang would pay Zhang RMB90,000; and (3) Zhang would relinquish the right to occupancy of the marital home and turn the home over to Wang. The notary first verifies Zhang and Wang's identifies, marital status, child, and property. Then, the notary reviews Zhang and Wang's divorce agreement and their proposed amendments. He discusses with the couple various relevant issues, such as whether the modification is reasonable, whether the modification is consensual, whether the marital home has been transferred to Wang according to the divorce agreement, and whether the amendment is lawful as it concerns child custody and support.[68] Having reviewed the circumstances of the case and the draft amendment, the notary edits, corrects, and finalizes the amendment, and then presents it to Zhang and Wang for their approval and signatures. Finally, the notary issues a notary deed of the amended divorce agreement after Wang and Zhang execute the amended divorce agreement.[69]

The Chinese notary system is an invaluable source of information for family law practitioners. Chinese notaries maintain a permanent record of life events, family affairs, and private and commercial transactions that have been through the notary system.[70] For example, wills prepared and attested by notaries are recorded in local notary systems' databases. Although there is not

---

68. Lu Zhenjun (吕振军), Zhe Fen Lihun Xieyishu Keyi Gongzheng Ma? (这份离婚协议书可以公证吗?) [Can This Divorce Agreement Be Notarized?] Zhongguo Gongzheng (中国公证) [Chinese Notary], 2008(02):51–52.

69. Yang Changcheng (杨长城), Lihun Xieyi Biangeng De Xiaoli Tanjiu Ji Qi Gongzheng Shencha (离婚协议变更的效力探究及其公证审查) [The Effect of Divorce Agreement Modification and Its Notary Inspection], Zhongguo Gongzheng (中国公证) [Chinese Notary], 2017(05):59–64, 64.

70. Zhongguo Gongzhen Xiehui (中国公证协会) [China Notary Association], Woguo Gongzheng Falü Fuwu Tixi De Jianshe Yu Wanshan (我国公证法律服务体系的建设与完善) [Our Country's Notary Legal Service System's Construction and Improvement], Zhongguo Sifa (中国司法) [Justice of China], 2016(01):57–61, 61.

a national database of notarized wills, many jurisdictions, such as Shanghai, have searchable databases of wills.[71]

3.4.3 Conservator

A distinct function of a Chinese notary is the power to serve as conservator of the property of a ward, heir, testamentary beneficiary, or minor under the doctrine of "lodgment" (*ticun*).[72] When there is an unmet condition of an obligor's performance, or when it is impossible to know exactly who a debtor's creditor(s) might be, a debtor or an obligor tendering the performance may lodge the prestation (property or money payment) for the creditor(s) in lieu of performance. Lodgment may be made in a notary office for preservation and tendering the payments when the condition of the obligor's performance is met.[73] In other words, Chinese notary offices may act as conservators to manage and preserve protected persons' property and make disbursements when the conditions of disbursements are met. For example, a notary office may manage a ward's property and make disbursements to the ward's guardian according to the ward's guardianship appointment order. To ensure both parties' compliance, a divorcing couple may agree to lodge certain property in a notary's office, who will tender the property to a party after the party has complied with the divorce agreement. In Shanghai, some courts encourage payor parents to lodge child support payments in notary offices at the time of the divorce so that the notary offices can make periodic disbursements to the custodial parents.[74]

§ 3.5 Government Agencies

The Ministry of Civil Affairs and its local bureaus handle civil registrations of marriage, divorce, and adoption, and provide essential social welfare services. Local Bureaus of Civil Affairs often implement local rules and policies

---

71. Li Yong Etc. (李勇), Yizhu Gongzheng Chengxu He Gongzheng Yizhu Jicheng Zhong De Youguan Zhidu (遗嘱公证程序和公证遗嘱继承中的有关制度) [Wills Notarization Procedure and Relevant Mechanisms in Notarized Will Succession] Zhongguo Gongzheng (中国公证) [Chinese Notary], 2018(04): 11–12, 12.

72. Notary Law art. 12(2).

73. Ticun Gongzheng Guize (提存公证规则) [The Lodgment Notarization Rules] (promulgated by the Ministry of Justice on June 2, 1995) art. 2.

74. Shangahi Shi Xuhui Qu Renmin Jianchayuan Hui Tong Qu Fayuan, Qu Sifa Ju, Qu Jiaoyu Ju Guanyu Sheli Fuyang Fei Ticun Jianguan Zhidu De Shishi Fangan (上海市徐汇区人民检察院会同区法院、区司法局、区教育局关于设立抚养费提存监管制度的实施方案) [The City of Shanghai Xuhui District Procuratorate Jointly with District Court, District Bureau of Justice, District Bureau of Education Operational Plan on Establishing Child Support Lodgment and Supervision System].

of marriage, divorce, and adoption registrations. These local rules and policies are an important part of local law concerning marriage, divorce, and adoption.

China's police departments are called the "Public Safety Bureaus" (*gong'an ju*). Their main tasks are crime prevention and problem solving at the neighborhood level. A local Public Safety Bureau precinct's (*paichu suo*) primary duty is to conduct community policing, including foot patrols, home visits, and community engagement. The relationship between the local police and residents is described as "the police are fishes, and the people are water," suggesting that broad public support is pivotal for the police's survival. Although the relationship between the police and the community may be highly strained from time to time, most Chinese people trust their local police and are satisfied with their performance, and are willing to cooperate with the police.[75] The Public Safety Bureaus also maintain China's household registration system, where vital records of every household are kept. For a discussion of China's household registration, see subsection 5.2.2.

§ 3.6 Community Governance

Urban Residents' Committees and Villagers' Committees are community-based semi-self-governance organizations. These organizations are given extraordinary power and responsibility in dispute resolution, social service delivery, and community governance. China ended rural and urban collectives in the early 1980s and established a community governance structure that consists of Urban Residents' Committees and Villagers' Committees. These community committees are led by members elected by the community and are supervised and funded by local governments. They provide essential services in rural villages and city neighborhoods.[76]

In the countryside, each village's Villagers' Committee is responsible for administrating the village land; operating village-owned enterprises; mediating civil disputes; managing the village's revenues and expenditures; and overseeing the village's public safety, sanitation, and social welfare services.[77] Members of the Villagers' Committee are elected by the members of the village and confirmed by the local government.[78]

---

75. Liu, Siyu, Yuning Wu, Ivan Sun & Feng Li, *Neighborhood Context, Police Legitimacy and Willingness to Help the Police in Shanghai, China*, 43(6) POLICING 947–62 (2020).

76. The Constitution art. 121.

77. Zhonghua Renmin Gongheguo Cunmin Weiyuan Hui Zuizhi Fa (中华人民共和国村民委员会组织法) [The People's Republic of China Villagers' Committee Organic Law] (promulgated by the National People's Cong. Nov. 4, 1998, amended Oct. 28, 2010) [hereinafter "Villagers' Committee Organic Law"] arts. 8, 9.

78. Villagers' Committee Organic Law arts. 2, 3, and 5.

Urban Residents' Committees are the counterparts of Villagers' Committees in urban neighborhoods. Urban Residents' Committees are established, funded, and supervised by local governments.[79] An Urban Residents' Committee has five to nine members, including salaried staff and unpaid elected committee members from the community.[80] Urban Residents' Committees' principal duties include educating the public on laws and regulations; mediating civil disputes; and most importantly assisting local governments in community policing, public sanitation, and social welfare services.[81]

Urban Residents' Committees and Villagers' Committees have multifaceted roles in family matters: They mediate in family disputes. They cooperate with the police and assist the court to enforce personal safety protection orders for domestic violence victims.[82] They intervene and report abuse or neglect of minor children or elderly people.[83] They appoint guardians for minor children and incapacitated people or sometimes assume guardianship.[84] They notify a decedent's heirs of the decedent's death. [85]

§ 3.7 Civil Justice with Chinese Characteristics

The modern Chinese civil justice system is usually studied and critiqued from two perspectives: its affinity with China's legal tradition and its affiliation with China's political present. Commentary on China's civil justice system has been tainted by a misconception that conforming with the anti-litigation Chinese culture and tradition, Chinese judges avert adjudication in civil matters, act more as mediators than adjudicators, and work to produce compromise.[86] Implied in this myth is an indictment that Chinese people's cultural

79. Zhonghua Renmin Gongheguo Jumin Weiyuan Hui Zuizhi Fa (中华人民共和国居民委员会组织法) [the People's Republic of China Urban Residents Committee Organic Law] (promulgated by the National People's Cong. Nov. 4, 1998, amended Oct. 28, 2010) (hereinafter "Urban Residents' Committee Organic Law") art. 17 and art. 20.

80. Urban Residents' Committee Organic Law art. 3.

81. *Id.* arts. 7, 8.

82. Anti-Domestic Violence Law art. 17.

83. *Id.* arts.13, 14.

84. The Civil Code arts. 27, 31.

85. *Id.* art. 1150.

86. Philip C.C. Huang's studies on the civil justice system in the Qing Dynasty and the Maoist period in the PRC dispel this misconception. Huang found that although a substantial portion of civil disputes were settled informally through community mediators or the Qing magistrates or the PRC judges, the formal system exercised substantial influence on those settlements and compromises. *See, e.g.*, Philip C.C. Huang, *Codified Law and Magisterial Adjudication in the Qing*, *in* CIVIL LAW IN QING AND REPUBLICAN CHINA 142–86 (Kathryn Bernhardt & Philip C.C. Huang ed.) (2008); Philip C.C. Huang, *Divorce Law Practices, the Origins, Myths and Realities of Judicial "Mediation"* 31(2) MODERN CHINA 151–203 (2005); PHILIP C.C. HUANG, COMMUNITY

preference for informal settlement and compromise has led to Chinese courts' inherent lack of judicial transparency, consistency, and predictability. Such oversimplification is incorrect.

China's judiciary has been characterized by the West as nothing but the socialist state's tool to pursue political goals. There is no doubt that in the Maoist era, China's judicial system was intended to be and, in fact, was a political bureaucracy whose primary function was to serve the CCP's political agenda. To the present time, the state continues to use the judicial system as a political tool.[87] However, after four decades of institution building, in part in cooperation with the global legal community, the Chinese civil justice system has become a "respectable legal system" founded on the principal tenets of due process and fairness, staffed with trained professionals, and competent to meet the needs of the world's largest population and second largest economy.[88] Its primary function is to administrate justice; resolve disputes; and provide essential services to individuals, families, and businesses. In family law matters, the Chinese judiciary has transformed from a Maoist political bureaucracy to a specialized, problem-solving service provider.

3.7.1 Administrate Justice

The Chinese civil justice system's principal function is to administrate justice and to restore social order and harmony. Hence, Chinese judges are more concerned with substantive justice than with procedural justice, and are more inclined to render results that serve perceived fairness than to strictly apply the letter of the law.[89] Most of them have a strong sense that their deci-

---

MEDIATION, PAST AND PRESENT, IN CHINESE CIVIL JUSTICE CHINESE CIVIL JUSTICE, PAST AND PRESENT 135–72 (2012).

87. *See, e.g.*, Ben Liebman, *A Return to Populist Legality: Historical Legacies and Legal Reform, in* MAO'S INVISIBLE HAND (Sebastian Heilman & Elizabeth J. Perry eds., 2010); and Carl F. Minzner, *China's Turn Against Law*, 59 AM. J. COMP. L. 935, 984 (2011).

88. Jerome A. Cohen, *Was Helping China Build Its Post-1978 Legal System A Mistake?*, 61 VA. J. INT'L L. ONLINE 1, 12 (2020).

89. Jiahong He, *Promoting the Procedural Justice in China*, 7 FRONTIERS L. CHINA 171, 171–72 (2012); *see also* Gao Qicai et al. (高其才 王晨光 冯泽周), Chengxu, Faguan Yu Shenpan Gongzheng—Shanghai Dengdi Faguan Fangtan Zongsu (程序、法官与审判公正 -上海等地法官访谈综述) [*Procedure, Judge and Fair Adjudication—Review of Interviews with Judges from Shanghai and Its Surrounding Areas*], Faxue (法学) [L. & SCI.] Vol. 8 (2000) 6, 6–8, (finding that Chinese judges are more concerned with substantive justice based on extensive interviews with judges in Shanghai); Jiang Guohua & Han Yuting, (江国华 韩玉亭), Lun Faguan de Juese Kunjing (论法官的角色困境) [*On the Dilemma of Judges' Role*], (法制与社会发展) [L. & SOC. DEV.] Vol. 2 (2015), 15–28, (finding that Chinese judges are more concerned of substantive justice based on a series of surveys conducted among nearly 3,000 Chinese judges on four issues: (1) whether maintaining social stability overweigh neutral adjudication in their judicial decision making process; (2) whether the facts and applicable law overweigh public opinion or political influence in their

sions should go beyond legal technicality and balance legalism against other essential factors—social norms, common sense, and *qingli* (accepted code of conduct).[90]

In the United States, family law judges, with their *parens patriae* authority, have more discretion than in any other fields of private law.[91] Similarly, Chinese judges are expected to exercise judicial discretion in family law matters and act as *fumu guan* (father and mother official), a Chinese term equivalent to *parens patriae*, not only for children but also for the elderly, for family units, and for their communities.[92] The societal expectation that family law judges must advocate substantive justice, fairness, and preservation of personal relations further reinforce Chinese judges' emphasis on substantive justice.[93]

---

decision-making in a case; (3) whether political policy consideration outweighs the existing law in their judicial decision-making process; (4) whether substantive justice outweighs procedural justice in their judicial decision making process).

90. *See, e.g.*, Wang Qun (王群), Lun Faguan De Zhize Ji Qi Juese Diwei (论法官的职责及其角色定位) [*On Defining Judges' Duties and Role*], Faxue （法学) [Jurisprudence], July 22, 2013 (asserting that to apply law correctly based on objective facts is the minimum duty of a judge and every judge has a higher duty, which is to protect social justice and fairness).

91. Marsha Garrison, *How Do Judges Decide Divorce Cases? An Empirical Analysis of Discretionary Decision Making*, 74 N.C. L. Rev. 401 (1996); *see also* Solangel Maldonado, *Bias in the Family: Race, Ethnicity, and Culture in Custody Disputes*, 55 Fam. Ct. Rev. 213 (2017) (describing judges' use of discretionary power in custody disputes in U.S. courts).

92. Jiang & Han, *supra* note 89 (finding the belief that an ideal judge should not be an indifferent neutral arbitrator based on a survey among litigants, attorneys, and judges on whether an ideal judge would be neutral or proactive in adjudicating a case); *see also* Feng Yuqing et al., *Popularized Judiciary in Rural China: Paternalistic Approaches and Enchanted Legal Consciousness*, 44 Hong Kong L.J. 651 (2014) (an empirical study on divorce litigants' expectations and perception of judges in rural Chinese courts, and the judges' paternalistic approach in adjudication to meet the litigants' expectations); Cai Hong (蔡 红), Yongxin Jiangtou Fali Qing Naxin Tiejin Qunzhong Xin (用心讲透法理情 拿心贴近群众心) [Take Pains to Explain the Sense of Law, Through Your Heart to Approach the People's Hearts] (a local judge's essay on the local people's expectations of local judges as "fumu guan" and how local judges could meet these expectations by handling family disputes with compassion, diligence, patience, and fairness).

93. In recent years, Chinese public opinion has increasingly demanded judicial discretion. *See, e.g.*, Ji Weidong, *The Judicial Reform in China: The Status Quo and Future Directions*, 20 Ind. J. Global Legal Stud. 185, 211 (2013) (discussing the impact of a widely accepted belief that judicial performance should be evaluated by the degree of people's satisfaction and that judges can adjust the application of law in accordance with mainstream attitudes); Benjamin L. Liebman, *Malpractice Mobs: Medical Dispute Resolution in China*, 113 Colum. L. Rev. 181 (2013) (finding state over-responsiveness to individual grievances manifested in medical malpractice cases, where Chinese courts have adopted flexible interpretations of existing law and regulations to appease litigants and have resisted legal standards that the public view as unfair.); Jiang & Han, *supra* note 89, at 24–25 (finding that Chinese litigants and attorneys want judges to act proactively and judges attempt to remain neutral based on a survey among litigants, attorneys and judges on whether an ideal judge would be neutral or proactive in adjudicating a case); *see also* Zhang Hai Long et al. (张海龙 宝峰), Jiji Tansuo Jiashi Shenpan Xin Moshi (积极探索家事审判新

3.7.2 Seek Order and Harmony

Chinese culture, custom, and Confucian philosophy emphasize stability and harmony in human relations.[94] China's civil dispute resolution places social order and harmony over individual litigants' interests and emphasizes social duty over individual rights.[95] As a result, China's family matter proceedings are conciliation oriented and mediation centered. Mediation is preferred over litigation in family matters. In divorce actions, Chinese courts must conduct mediation in divorce actions and can only proceed with the adjudication process after mediation efforts have failed. Approximately 40 percent of family and marriage cases are settled through mediation each year in the last decade.[96]

Mediations are administrated by the presiding judge, ergo labeled "judicial mediation."[97] "Judicial mediation" in Chinese courts is similar to the formal or informal settlement conferences hosted by the presiding judge or the judge's staff throughout the course of family matter proceedings in the United States.[98] Around the globe, judges are more and more involved in facilitating resolution and settlement of family conflicts.[99] "Judicially hosted" settlement conferences or mediations are hailed by some attorneys and judges as

---

模式) [*Actively Explore New Family Matter Adjudication Models*] Renmin Fayuan Bao (人民法院报) [People's Court Daily] (Sept. 18, 2018), 2 (suggesting that the goal of family law matter adjudication is to restore harmony and the courts should explore innovative conciliatory dispute resolution methods to achieve this goal).

94. Cao Pei, *The Origins of Mediation in Traditional China*, Disp. Resol. J. 32–35 (May 1999); Xiaobing Xu, *Different Mediation Traditions: A Comparison between China and the U.S.*, 16 Am. Rev. Int'l Arb. 515, 515 (2005); *see also* Huang, *supra* note 86, Ch. 7 Court Mediation, Past and Present (2012).

95. Woo, *supra* note 3, at 148–49.

96. *See* Reminfayuan Shenli Hunyin Jiating, Jicheng Yishen Anjian Anjian Tiaojie Jianshu (人民法院审理婚姻家庭，继承一审案件案件调解件数) [Number of Marriage Family and Succession Cases of the First Instance Mediated], Zhonghuarmgongheguo Guojia Tongjiju Guojia Shuju (中华人民共和国国家统计局国家数据) [National Bureau of Statistics of the People's Republic of China National Data].

97. Civil Procedure Law art. 94. For observations and discussions on China's judicial mediation, see Minzner, *supra* note 87; Kwai Hang Ng & Xin He, *Internal Contradictions of Judicial Mediation in China*, 39 Law & Soc. Inquiry 285 (2014). *See also* Margaret Y.K. Woo, *Court Reform with Chinese Characteristics*, 27 Wash. Int'l L.J. 241, 252–56 (2017).

98. For in-depth comparison of Chinese judicial mediation and Western ADR approaches, including mediation, see Huang (2012), *supra* note 86, at 195–99.

99. Jean-François Roberge & Dorcas Quek Anderson, *Judicial Mediation: From Debates to Renewal*, 19 Cardozo J. Conflict Resol. 613, 614 (2018); *see also* Ellen E. Deason, *Beyond "Managerial Judges": Appropriate Roles in Settlement*, 78 Ohio St. L.J. 73 (2017) (discussing judges' increasing involvement in settling disputes in U.S. courts).

the "cheaper, better, faster" family dispute resolution approach.[100] Although effective, as opponents to judge-facilitated mediation correctly point out, a presiding judge's impartiality may be undermined by acting as a mediator.[101] Nonetheless, the inherent flaws of judicially hosted mediation or judicial mediation administrated by the presiding judge are hardly institutional, systemic problems unique to Chinese courts.

Chinese courts are criticized by legal scholars for their preference for mediation in family dispute resolution.[102] The criticism is out of touch with the needs of families, who are usually eager to resolve their conflicts. Mediation has been widely accepted as a more conciliatory, cost-efficient, and effective alternative to adversarial litigation in family law proceedings.[103] Recognizing the detrimental impacts of the adversary process on family litigants,[104] numerous jurisdictions, including 32 states in the United States, require mediation in family matter proceedings.[105] Chinese judges, as many of their counterparts around the world, are under the pressure to settle and end disputes quickly, for many reasons, such as burgeoning dockets or litigants' complaints of delay and mounting legal cost caused by the delay. The primary reason for Chinese courts' extensive use of mediation may well be that mediation is a better dispute resolution approach than protracted litigation in family disputes. Scholarly studies on judicial mediation in Chinese family law proceedings based on court archives, interviews, and courtroom observations have not yet provided

---

100. Gregory D. Brown, *The Judicially Hosted Settlement Conference-My Case in the Balance: Musings of a Trial Attorney*, Disp. Resol. Mag., Spring 2011, at 8; *see also* Hon. Kristena A. LaMar, *I Think I Blew It*, Disp. Resol. Mag., Spring 2011, 12–14 (suggesting that in family disputes, settlement conferences conducted by presiding judges and attended by the litigants are more effective than with mediations conducted by a neutral); Hon. Stephen G. Crane, *Judge Settlements versus Mediated Settlements*, Disp. Resol. Mag., Spring 2011, 20–22 (insightful review of pros and cons of judicially hosted settlement conferences and private mediations); Wayne D. Brazil, *Judicial Mediation of Cases Assigned to the Judge for Trial–Magistrate Judges Celeste F. Bremer and Karen K. Klein*, Disp. Resol. Mag., Spring 2011, 24–27 (two judges' insights in judge-conducted settlement conferences).

101. Brazil, *supra* note 100, at 26; *see also* Ng et al., *supra* note 97.

102. Woo, *supra* note 97, at 252–56; *see also* Carl F. Minzner, *supra* note 87.

103. Holly Joyce, *Comment, Mediation and Domestic Violence: Legislative Responses*, 14 J. Am. Acad. Matrim. L. 447, 447 (1997).

104. Rebecca Aviel, *Family Law and the New Access to Justice*, 86 Fordham L. Rev. 2279, 2280 (2018).

105. Jacqueline Nolan-Haley, *Mediation: The Best and Worst of Times*, 16 Cardozo J. Conflict Resol. 731, 738 (2015); *see also* Overview of Judicial Mediation in the World: Mediation, the Universal Language of Conflict Resolution, First International Conference on Judicial Mediation, Paris, October 16–17, 2009 (Béatrice Brenneur eds 2010); European Network of National Observatories on Childhood, Family Mediation in the European Union Survey Report (June 2005) and National Council of Juvenile and Family Court Judges, Custody Mediation Where Domestic Violence Is Present.

sufficient evidence to demonstrate whether Chinese judges' strong penchant for mediation is motivated primarily by self-interests or whether it is more of a logical response to family litigants' needs and preferences.[106]

3.7.3 Judicial Efficiency

The Chinese civil justice system is incredibly efficient. Every case processed through Chinese courts is streamlined, monitored, and tightly controlled through a case management system from the commencement of the action to the pronouncement of the judgment. Supervising judges, such as the president of the court and the chief judge of each division, closely monitor and manage each case throughout its life cycle in the court to ensure that each deadline is strictly followed. Judges' performances are managed by each court's Judicial Management Office (*sifa guanli bangongshi*). The Judicial Management Office conducts bi-annual and annual reviews of the judges and inspections of the cases processed by the court where it sits and the lower courts within its jurisdiction. A judge's promotion and, sometimes, compensation are directly tied to the results of these reviews and inspections. Whether cases are timely concluded within the statutory time limits set by the Civil Procedure Law is one of the most important evaluation criteria in Judicial Management Office reviews.[107]

---

106. *See, e.g.*, Huang (2005), *supra* note 86 (studying China's divorce law practices based on archival records of 216 court cases spanning from 1953 to 1995); Martha J. Bailey, *Mediation of Divorce in China*, 8 CAN. J.L. & SOC. 45 (1993) (a study on divorce mediation based on group interviews in 1990); Feng Yuqing & Cao Qing, *Popularized Judiciary in Rural China: Paternalistic Approaches and Enchanted Legal Consciousness*, 44 HONG KONG L.J. 651 (2014) (a study on divorce adjudication at a trial court in rural China based on court archives, courtroom observations and interviews); Xin He, Routinization of Divorce Law Practice in China: Institutional Constraints' Influence on Judicial Behavior, 23 INT'L J.L. POL'Y & FAM. 83 (2009) (a study on court-mediated reconciliation based on interviews and courtroom observations); Jian Wang, *To Divorce or Not to Divorce: a Critical Discourse Analysis of Court-Ordered Divorce Mediation in China*, 27 INT'L J.L. POL. & FAM. 74–96 (2013) (a study on mandatory mediation in 48 divorce cases based on recordings of the mediation sessions); Margaret Y.K. Woo, *Shaping Citizenship: Chinese Family Law and Women*, 15 YALE J.L. & FEMINISM 99, 101, 106–07 (2003) (a study on divorce litigations based on in-depth interviews with 29 female divorce litigants); Xin He & Kwai Ng, *Pragmatic Discourse and Gender Inequality in China*, 47 LAW & SOC'Y REV. 279 (2013) (a study on Chinese courts' practice in divorce cases based on observations of more than 20 divorce trials); Xin He & Kwai Hang Ng, *In the Name of Harmony: The Erasure of Domestic Violence in China's Judicial Mediation*, 27 INT'L J.L. POL. & FAM. 97 (2013) (examined judicial medication in Chinese courts based on observations of court hearings, trials, and interviews with judges); Kwai Hang Ng & Xin He, *Internal Contradictions of Judicial Mediation in China*, 39 LAW & SOC. INQUIRY 285 (2014).

107. Wang & Fu, *supra* note 10, at 26–28. *See also* Yulin Fu, *Court Management in ransformation China*, 6(1) PEKING UNIV. L.J. 81–103 (2018); and Fuhua Wang, *The History and Future of Civil Judicial Case Management in China*, 6(1) PEKING UNIV. L.J. 237–71 (2018).

Chinese courts have been criticized for pushing a "quick resolution over adjudication and the delivery of justice" in family law disputes.[108] The criticism overlooks litigants' interests and priority in family dispute resolution. Generally, a quick, low-cost resolution of a family dispute is a welcomed outcome in family matters. More than litigants in other types of cases, "family litigants repeatedly and overwhelmingly invoke speed and cost as one of their highest priorities," and willingly, "knowingly and voluntarily forgo the opportunity to deploy doctrinal principles that might increase their take in return for a faster, smoother, more certain resolution."[109] This is not to say that Chinese courts' efficiency does not come at a cost. The tight control over the courts' adjudication process invites questions of due process, neglect of vulnerable interest groups, and interference with judicial independence.[110] Nevertheless, the rapid growth of a matrimonial bar and explosion of family law cases in courts suggest robust public trust in China's family law system, despite its flaws.

3.7.4 Judicial Independence and Transparency

China's judicial independence and transparency have been under scrutiny for decades. At the institutional level, Chinese courts' independence was questioned for the CCP's political influence and control. At the individual level, Chinese judges were viewed as being caught in inescapable social and personal influences ingrained in Chinese culture. Through institutional reform, Chinese judiciary has achieved greater autonomy and transparency in the last two decades.

3.7.4.1 Political Influence

Most Western commentators judge Chinese judiciary not by its competency as adjudicators but by its ability as an institutional check on the CCP's power.[111] Similar to U.S. judges, Chinese judges are political appointees by national, provincial, or local level legislatures.[112] Thus, for many decades, scholars have sharply criticized the Chinese judiciary for its lack of independence,

---

108. Xin He & Kwai Hang Ng, *In the Name of Harmony: The Erasure of Domestic Violence in China's Judicial Mediation*, 27 INT'L J.L. POL. & FAM. 97, 99 (2013).

109. Aviel, *supra* note 104, at 2296; *see also* Hon. Lynda B. Munro (Ret.) et al., *Administrative Divorce Trends and Implications*, 50 FAM. L.Q. 427, 440–41 (2016) (describing simplified marriage dissolution evolved as litigants and courts' need for "a more efficient, less public, and more cost-effective" process to replace the costly and protracted traditional adversarial divorce).

110. For critiques of Chinese civil justice system, *see, e.g.*, CHINESE JUSTICE: CIVIL DISPUTE RESOLUTION IN CONTEMPORARY CHINA (Margaret Y.K. Woo & Mary E. Gallagher, ed.) (2011).

111. Larry Catá Backer, Between the Judge and the Law: Judicial Independence and Authority with Chinese Characteristics, 33 CONN. J. INT'L L. 1, 14 (2017).

112. Judges Law art. 18.

impartiality, and integrity.[113] Chinese courts have been tasked with implementing CCP policies that varied from the 1980s' "strike hard" anti-crime campaigns to, most recently, promoting "harmony."[114] Indeed, the recent rise of nationalistic authoritarian control over Chinese society poses a threat to what the liberal legal reform has achieved at the turn of the 21st century.[115]

As Chinese judges become more professional and independent in recent years, the CCP maintains its political control over Chinese judiciary through so-called court presidents (*yuanzhang*). Court presidents are head administrators of Chinese courts. Because court presidents are political appointees, they must embrace local needs and address local political concerns not necessarily for their own interests but certainly for their courts' funding and status, which depend on the local government. Thus, local political demands can be internalized in courts via court presidents, who might pressure judges to bend the rules to fit local needs.[116]

It is naïve to presume a sterile, apolitical judiciary, and to judge the Chinese judiciary against such an impossible standard. Chinese judges are undoubtedly political. So are all judges, because courts are sites where societal narratives are forged, popular expression is constructed, and politics are played.[117] For instance, in the United States, federal judges are partisan appointees, and state judges are selected through political elections. During the Trump era, some states' family courts opened their courtrooms to immigration enforcement agents to arrest undocumented domestic violence victims, whereas other courts provided the victims sanctuary. If judges were 100 percent apolitical, there would have not been partisan battles for U.S. Supreme Court justice appointments. In recent years, China's judicial reform has significantly curtailed the CCP's direct supervision and interference with Chinese courts' day-to-day operation and given Chinese judges considerable autonomy as a specialized profession.[118] The CCP's eventual, albeit reluctant, detachment form Chinese courts is inevitable. From a practical point of view,

---

113. *See, e.g.*, Xin He, *The Politics of Courts in China*, 2(2) CHINA LAW & SOC'Y REV. 129–53 (2017); KENNETH DAM, THE LAW-GROWTH NEXUS (2006); KWAI HANG NG & XIN HE, EMBEDDED COURTS: JUDICIAL DECISION-MAKING IN CHINA (2017).

114. Woo, *supra* note 3, at 144.

115. Minzner, *supra* note 87; and CARL MINZNER, END OF AN ERA: HOW CHINA'S AUTHORITARIAN REVIVAL IS UNDERMINING ITS RISE (2018).

116. Yun-Chien Chang & Ke Xu, *Decentralized and Anomalous Interpretation of Chinese Private Law: Understanding A Bureaucratic and Political Judicial System*, 102 MINN. L. REV. 1527, 1532 (2018).

117. Larry Catá *Backer, Between the Judge and the Law: Judicial Independence and Authority with Chinese Characteristics*, 33 CONN. J. INT'L L. 1, 19 (2017).

118. JUDICIAL INDEPENDENCE IN CHINA: LESSONS FOR GLOBAL RULE OF LAW PROMOTION (Randle Perenboom ed., 2010); Yuedan Wang, *"Detaching" Courts from Local Politics? Assessing the Judicial Centralization Reforms in China*, CHINA Q. 2020-07-03, at 1–20; Minzner, *supra* note 87;

it will be an impossible task for any political party to hold a tight grip on a judicial system that must serve 1.4 billion people and the world's second largest economy.

3.7.4.2 Personal Influence

The perceived judicial corruption of Chinese courts is disconcerting, particularly to foreign litigants. Legal scholars long attributed China's allegedly rampant judicial corruption to personal connections (*guanxi*)—a set of cultural practices through which powers are transmitted by "favor giving" (*guanxi*) via personal connections.[119] In simpler terms, these scholars allege that the culprit of China's judicial corruption is Chinese people's inherent cultural tendency to exert and accept personal influences, and then act unethically. This Orientalist depiction of Chinese judiciary insinuates that Chinese judges can never be truly independent, impartial, and fair because they are Chinese. This innuendo is biased and wrong.

It might be true that Chinese people had to use personal connections and informal channels to address their grievance or resolve their disputes when there were no reliable institutional dispute resolution mechanisms.[120] However, when a functional judicial system is available to them, there is no evidence that Chinese people would prefer "*guanxi*" (favor giving), in other words "corruption," over legitimate means. For example, in the first decade of the 1882 Chinese Exclusion Act, Chinese immigrants brought over 7,000 lawsuits in U.S. federal courts to challenge the act, and they won many of these cases,[121] presumably not by giving favors to the U.S. federal court judges. In contemporary China, the growing number of family matter disputes brought in Chinese courts dispels the myth that Chinese people prefer "*guanxi*" over law. It also supports the observation that the Chinese judiciary has become an independent, specialized profession and has gained considerable public trust and confidence as a result.[122] This is not to say that personal influences and

and *Overcoming Embeddedness: How China's Judicial Accountability Reforms Make Its Judges More Autonomous*, 43 Fordham Int'l L.J. 737 (2020).

119. *See, e.g.*, Wang Xiaoqiang (王小强), Touguo Mianzi De Guanxian Kongzhi—Yi Duofang Shengcunxing Zhihui Boyi Wei Jichu (透过面子的关系案控制—以多方生存性智慧博弈为基础) [*Controlling "Guanxi" Cases through Faces—Based on Game-of-Survival Wisdom of Multiple Parties*], 12 Xiangjiang Falü Pinglun (湘江法律评论) [Xiangjiang L. Rev.] 249, 265 (2015). Xin He, Kwai Hang Ng, *"It Must Be Rock Strong!" Guanxi's Impact on Judicial Decision Making in China*, 65 Am. J. Comp. L. 841 (2017).

120. Mayfair Mei-Hui Yang, Gifts, Favors, and Banquets: The Art of Social Relationships in China (1994).

121. Lucy E. Salyer, Laws Harsh as Tigers: Chinese Immigrants and the Shaping of Modern Immigration Law, xiii (1995).

122. Yueduan Wang, *Overcoming Embeddedness: How China's Judicial Accountability Reforms Make Its Judges More Autonomous*, 43 Fordham Int'l L.J. 737 (2020).

corruptions are in any way negligible, but there is little doubt that the Chinese judiciary has become an independent, professional legal institution and has earned tremendous public trust and confidence in the recent decades.

3.7.5 Uneven Justice

China is a vast country with diverse social norms, cultural environments, and economic development levels. Local needs likely demand decentralized interpretations of national laws. The unique institutional environment in China has led to the decentralized development of private law in a unified system. Specifically, statutes are often interpreted differently across provinces.[123] For instance, a rural court that serves a low-income agrarian population might be more inclined to order filial support than an urban court that does not feel much pressure to meet the needs of the aging poor. Chinese provincial courts have considerable autonomy and power to devise differing solutions to similar legal issues to meet local needs.

Access to justice is geographically uneven along the rural and urban divide. Urban areas, particularly global cities like Beijing, Shanghai, and Guangzhou, have staffed all levels of courts with highly educated judges, many of whom are trained both in China and Euro-American jurisdictions. In affluent cities, access to licensed attorneys is readily available, not only through the private legal market but also through legal aid services. In stark contrast, licensed attorneys are scarce in China's vast countryside, and the rising demand for legal services among rural residents is not being met. Confronted with the high demand for legal services and shortage of licensed lawyers, China established a basic-level legal workers system (*jiceng falil gongzuozhe*), which allows paraprofessional law practitioners to provide limited legal services. The basic-level legal workers provide essential legal services to underserved populations in rural areas.[124] However, the quality of their services is somewhat questionable.[125]

---

123. Chang & Xu, *supra* note 116, at 1530–31.

124. Ke Li, *Relational Embeddedness and Socially Motivated Case Screening in the Practice of Law in Rural China*, 50(4) Law & Soc'y Rev. 920–52; 927–29 (Dec. 2016).

125. Ke Li, *"What He Did Was Lawful": Divorce Litigation and Gender Inequality in China*, 37(3) Law & Pol'y 153–79 (2015).

Chapter 4

Civil Procedure Law and Rules in Family Matters

Family matter disputes are general civil matters heard in the courts of general jurisdiction. Most family matters are dealt with in the civil division or family matter division in Basic-level People's Courts or Intermediate People's Courts. Family law proceedings are governed by the Civil Procedure Law, the Supreme People's Court's Interpretations on the Civil Procedure Law of the People's Republic of China,[1] and the Supreme People's Court Several Provisions on Evidence in Civil Procedures.[2] Special family matter procedures and rules are being implemented as part of China's family matter adjudication reform.

Chinese civil proceedings are guided by five principles. First, the courts must safeguard parties' equal rights in due process.[3] Second, the courts should make efforts to mediate in civil suits and encourage conciliation and settlement. However, mediation must be voluntary and lawful.[4] Third, parties have the right to present their legal position and evidence, and the right to

1. Zuigao Renmin Fayuan Guanyu Shiyong Zhonghua Renmin Gonghe Guo Minshi Susong Fa De Jieshi (最高人民法院关于使用中华人民共和国民事诉讼法的解释) [the Supreme People's Court's Interpretations on the Civil Procedure Law of the People's Republic of China] (promulgated by the Sup. People's Ct., Dec. 18, 2014, effective Feb. 4, 2015, amended Dec. 23, 2020, and amended Mar. 22, 2022; effective Apr. 19, 2022) 2022 Sup. People's Ct. Gaz. 7 [hereinafter the "Civil Procedure Law Interpretations"].

2. Zuigao Renmin Fayun Guanyu Minshi Susong Zhengju De Ruogan Guiding (最高人民法院关于民事诉讼证据的若干规定) [the Supreme People's Court's Several Provisions on Evidence in Civil Procedures] (promulgated by the Sup. People's Ct. on Dec. 6, 2001, amended on Oct. 14, 2019, effective from May 1, 2020) 2020 Sup. People's Ct. Gaz. 3 [hereinafter "SPC Rules of Evidence in Civil Procedure"].

3. Civil Procedure Law art. 8.

4. *Id*. art. 9.

respond to the opposing party's legal position and evidence.[5] Fourth, parties have the duty to act in good faith.[6] Thus, the courts may sanction frivolous claims, false testimony, and other unfair practices in civil litigation. Fifth, parties have the right to dispose their own procedural and substantive rights in civil litigation.[7] In other words, parties have the right to decide whether to or not to pursue any lawful civil claims and whether to initiate, or continue, or discontinue civil proceedings.

§ 4.1 Jurisdiction

The People's Courts are divided into two tracks: courts of general jurisdiction and courts of special jurisdiction. Courts of general jurisdiction hear all civil and criminal matters, except for matters related to military, transportation, maritime, and intellectual property, which are adjudicated in special courts with exclusive jurisdiction.[8] Family law matters are heard in courts of general jurisdiction. The jurisdiction of a court of general jurisdiction is determined by two parameters. One is hierarchical jurisdiction based on the complexity of a dispute, and the other is territorial jurisdiction based on the geographic location of the parties and their dispute.

Jurisdictional objections must be raised within 15 days after the defendant is served.[9] If a defendant has answered without raising any jurisdictional objections, the court is presumed to have proper jurisdiction, unless another court has proper hierarchical jurisdiction or exclusive jurisdiction as provided by law.[10] If a defendant has made both jurisdictional objections and substantive replies to the complaint, the court must examine the defendant's objections and render its decision within 15 days after the defendant makes the objections.[11] In the event that the court sustains the defendant's objection, the court must transfer the case to a court with proper jurisdiction.[12] Trial courts' jurisdictional rulings are appealable.

5. *Id.* art. 12.
6. *Id.* art. 13 para. 1.
7. *Id.* art. 13 para. 2.
8. Organic Law of the People's Courts art. 15.
9. Civil Procedure Law art. 127 para. 1.
10. *Id.* art. 127 para. 2.
11. Civil Procedure Law Interpretations art. 223 para. 2.
12. Civil Procedure Law art. 127 para. 1.

4.1.1 Hierarchical Jurisdiction

The People's Courts of general jurisdiction are organized through a hierarchical system called "the four levels of courts and two trials to conclude a case" (*siji liangshen zhongshen*).[13] "Four levels" mean that there are four tiers of the People's Courts: the Basic-level People's Courts (*jiceng remnin fayuan*), Intermediate People's Courts (*zhongji renmin fayuan*), provincial High People's Courts (*gaoji renmin fayuan*), and the Supreme People's Court (SPC) (*zuiguao renmin fayuan*).[14] "Two trials to conclude" means that each action may have two trials before its conclusion, first at the court of first instance and then at the court of the second instance where an appeal is taken. The People's Courts of general jurisdiction at each level may exercise initial jurisdiction as the court of first instance based on the importance and complexity of a case,[15] and its higher court at the next level has the appellate jurisdiction as the court of second instance.[16] Actions that are concluded after the second trial by a court of second instance are final and not appealable.[17] However, under specified circumstances a re-adjudication (*zaishen*) through the trial supervision procedure (*shenpan jiandu chengxu*) may be allowed after an appeal.[18]

Hierarchical jurisdictions of courts at different levels are primarily determined by the value of claims, according to the SPC's rules on hierarchical jurisdiction.[19] The Basic-level People's Courts have jurisdiction over most marriage and family law matters as the original court of first instance. However, high-net-worth family matters may be under the jurisdiction of the Intermediate People's Courts or even the High People's Courts. For instance, the SPC ruled that a post-nuptial agreement dispute that involved over RMB350 million (approximately USD 55 million) should be heard by the Intermediate People's Court of the City of Haikou because the disputed amount exceeded the Basic-level People's Courts' jurisdiction.[20]

---

13. Margaret Woo, *The Dynamism of China's Civil Litigation System*, 48 IUS GENTIUM 141, 143 (2016).

14. Organic Law of the People's Courts arts. 12–13; see also Yulin Fu, *The Chinese Supreme People's Court in Transition*, 59 IUS GENTIUM 13, 13–14 (2017); Woo, *supra* note 13.

15. Civil Procedure Law arts. 17–20.

16. *Id*. ch. 14 Procedure of Second Instance.

17. *Id*. art. 175.

18. *Id*. ch. 16 Procedure for Trial Supervision.

19. Zuigao Renmin Fayuan Guanyu Tiaozheng Gaoji Renmin Fayuan He Zhongji Renmin Fayuan Guanxia Diyi Shen Minshang Shi Anjian Biaozhuen De Tongzhi (最高人民法院关于调整高级人民法院和中级人民法院管辖第一审民商事案件标准的通知) [The Supreme People's Court's Notice on Adjustment of Jurisdictional Standards of Civil and Commercial Matters in the High People's Courts and Intermediate People's Courts] (promulgated by Sup. People's Ct. on July 17, 2018, effective from Aug. 1, 2018) 2018 Sup. People's Ct. Gaz. 11.

20. (2019) Zuigao Min Xia Zhong 231 Hao ((2019) 最高法民辖终231(号)).

4.1.2 Territorial Jurisdiction

A court's territorial jurisdiction is generally based on either party's residence or habitual residence at a place. A person's residence is where their household registration (*huji*) is located.[21] A person's habitual residence is where he/she has lived continuously for at least a year at the time of the commencement of the action.[22] For a place to qualify as a person's habitual residence, the place must meet three criteria: (1) the person has lived in the place for more than a year; (2) the person's presence at the place has been continuous without interruption; and (3) the person must be present at the place at the time of the action.[23] If a person's household registration has been revoked and the person does not have a habitual residence, then the court at the place where their last household registration was located has jurisdiction.[24]

4.1.2.1 Defendant's Residence

Generally, civil matters fall under the territorial jurisdiction of the Basic-level People's Court at the place where the defendant's residence or habitual residence is located.[25] After a case has been accepted, any change of either party's household registration or habitual residence does not affect the court's jurisdiction.[26] If a defendant's household registration and habitual residence are at different locations, then the court at the place where the defendant's habitual residence is located has personal jurisdiction over him/her.[27] If a defendant's household registration has been revoked and the defendant does not have any habitual residence, then the court at the place where the defendant's last household registration was located has jurisdiction.[28]

4.1.2.2 Plaintiff's Residence

As exceptions to the general principle that a suit must be brought in the jurisdiction where the defendant's residence or habitual residence is located, the court where the plaintiff's residence or habitual residence is located may exercise jurisdiction: (1) in actions concerning personal relationships, such as divorce, or child custody where the defendant does not reside within the territory of the PRC or has disappeared;[29] (2) in suits for filial support, dependent

21. Civil Procedure Law Interpretations art. 3.
22. *Id.* art. 4.
23. (2020) Zui Gao Fa Min Xia 91 Hao ((2020) 最高法民辖91号).
24. Civil Procedure Law Interpretation arts. 6, 7.
25. Civil Procedure Law arts. 17, 21.
26. Civil Procedure Law Interpretations art. 37.
27. Civil Procedure Law art. 21.
28. Civil Procedure Law Interpretation arts. 6, 7.
29. Civil Procedure Law art. 22.

support, or child support that have multiple defendants who reside in different jurisdictions;[30] (3) in any divorce action where the defendant has left the marital domicile for more than a year;[31] or (4) in any divorce action where both parties are living abroad temporarily.[32]

In divorce actions involving Chinese nationals living abroad permanently, Chinese courts have jurisdiction (1) if the parties were married in China and habitually reside outside of China, and if the court of the foreign country where both parties habitually reside has declined jurisdiction for the reason that the court where the marriage was entered has proper jurisdiction, then the Chinese court where the marriage was entered or either party's last domicile is located has jurisdiction over the parties' divorce;[33] (2) if the parties were married outside of China and habitually reside outside of China, and if the court of the foreign country where both parties habitually reside has declined jurisdiction because of the parties' nationality, then the Chinese court where either party's last domicile is located has jurisdiction over the parties' divorce;[34] (3) if one party resides abroad and one party resides in China, the Chinese court has jurisdiction over the parties' divorce, regardless of which party initiates the divorce action;[35] (4) if one party brings a divorce action in the foreign country where he/she resides and the other party brings an action in China, the Chinese court may exercise jurisdiction over the parties' divorce;[36] or (5) in post-divorce property division actions where both parties are Chinese nationals residing abroad, the court where the parties' major asset is located has jurisdiction.[37] For further discussions on Chinese courts' jurisdiction over Chinese nationals living abroad, see subsection 12.2.1.2.

4.1.2.3 Guardianship

The court of the protected individual's domicile has the jurisdiction over suits for contest or modification of guardianship.[38] For further discussions on Chinese courts' jurisdiction over guardianship of minor children living abroad see subsection 12.2.1.3.

---

30. Civil Procedure Law Interpretations art. 9.
31. *Id.* art. 12.
32. *Id.* art. 16.
33. *Id.* art. 13.
34. *Id.* art. 14.
35. *Id.* art. 15 para. 1.
36. *Id.* art. 15 para. 2.
37. *Id.* art. 17.
38. *Id.* art. 10.

4.1.3 Exclusive Jurisdiction

As exceptions of general territorial jurisdiction, the Civil Procedure Law designates exclusive jurisdiction over certain disputes.

4.1.3.1 Real Property

Courts at the place where a real property is located have exclusive jurisdiction over any real property disputes,[39] including disputes over ownership, partition, and easement of real property. However, disputes over spouses' respective rights and interests in real property are not real property disputes but rather disputes over marital status and personal relations. Therefore, such disputes are not under the exclusive jurisdiction of the courts where the real property is located, and the general jurisdiction rules that govern marital and domestic disputes should be applied to determine jurisdiction.[40] For example, in *Chen v. Jian*, Chen and Jian were divorced in Guangzhou. The parties' divorce agreement provided that Jian must transfer the parties' home in Guangzhou to Chen, and either party could bring an action at "the current location" (*dangdi*), if any dispute arose from the agreed property transfer. After the divorce, Jian failed to transfer the title of the parties' marital home to Chen as required by the divorce agreement. Chen sued Jian in a Basic-level court in Chongqing, where Jian lived. The Chongqing court ruled that it did not have jurisdiction over the dispute, as the disputed home was located in Guangzhou, and transferred the case to a Guangzhou court. The Guangzhou court rejected the transfer on the ground that post-divorce property disputes were not real property disputes but rather disputes concerning the parties' marital relationship under the jurisdiction of the court of the defendant's habitual residence. The lower courts sought decisions from the province's High People's Court. The Chongqing High People's Court issued a decision, with the Guangdong Province concurrence, that the Chongqing Court had jurisdiction, as disputes arising from marital property are not real property disputes under the exclusive jurisdiction of the court where the real property is situated. Furthermore, the Chongqing Court held that the choice of forum clause in the parties' divorce agreement was too vague to enforce, and consequently was unenforceable.[41]

In *Ren v. Wang*, the SPC clarified the distinction between exclusive jurisdiction over disputes concerning real property and general territorial jurisdiction over disputes arising from real property distribution between spouses. The SPC affirmed that the jurisdiction over real estate distribution incidental to a divorce is determined by the jurisdictional rules governing marriage

39. Civil Procedure Law art. 33 (1).
40. (2020) Zui Gao Fa Min Xia 14 Hao ((2020) 最高法民辖14号).
41. (2018) Yu Min Xiao 64 Hao ((2018)渝民辖64号).

and family matters, not real property. In *Ren v. Wang*, the parties agreed in a divorce settlement agreement that Wang should transfer to Ren the parties' home in Anhui after the divorce. After the divorce, Wang refused to complete the agreed property transfer, and moved back to Guizhou where her household registration was. Ren sued Wang in Guizhou to enforce the divorce settlement agreement. The Guizhou courts declined to take jurisdiction on the ground that the disputed home was located in Anhui and therefore Anhui had exclusive jurisdiction over the home. The SPC reversed the Guizhou courts' decision and held that disputes arising from real property division in connection with a divorce are not disputes under the exclusive jurisdiction of the courts where the real property is located because these disputes are not real estate disputes subject to exclusive jurisdiction but rather family matter disputes subject to the rules on general territorial jurisdiction. Thus, the SPC ruled that Guizhou, where Wang was living after the divorce, had jurisdiction over the parties' dispute over their former marital home.[42]

4.1.4 Choice of Forum

Generally, the parties to a dispute concerning a contract or property may, by written mutual agreement, designate a specific court to adjudicate the dispute.[43] In property disputes arising from cohabitation, dissolution of marriage, or termination of adoption, the parties may, by written agreement, choose a jurisdiction where either party resides; or where the disputed property is located; or where any agreement concerning the cohabitation, marriage, or adoption was entered or performed, provided that the parties' choice of forum does not violate any law on hierarchical jurisdiction and exclusive jurisdiction.[44] For detailed discussions on choice of forum, see subsection 12.2.3.

4.1.5 *Forum Non Conveniens*

Chinese courts may reject a suit for *forum non conveniens* if the suit has no connections with China or a Chinese national. For further discussion of *forum non conveniens*, see subsection 12.2.5.

4.1.6 Parallel Proceedings

When a Chinese court and the courts of a foreign country both have proper jurisdiction, the Chinese court may accept a suit even if a parallel suit

42. (2020) Zui Gao Fa Min Xia 14 Hao ((2020) 最高法民辖14号).
43. Civil Procedure Law art. 34.
44. Civil Procedure Law Interpretations art. 34.

between the same parties has been filed or is pending in a foreign court; and the Chinese court must reject the request of the foreign court or either party to enforce the foreign court's judgment or order from the parallel suit unless a bilateral or international treaty between China and the foreign country provides otherwise. However, a Chinese court must reject any suit in which a foreign country has adjudicated the same disputes and entered a judgment or order that has been recognized by Chinese courts.[45] For further discussions of parallel proceedings in Chinese courts and foreign country courts, see subsection 12.2.4.

4.1.7 Enforcement Jurisdiction

Enforcement of a judgment or order that is final and effective may be brought at the court that entered the judgment or order, or at a court in the jurisdiction where the person subject to the enforcement resides or property subject to the enforcement is located.[46] Enforcement of provisional orders of security lien, garnishment or attachment, or confirmation of mediated settlement agreement may be brought in the court that issued the order or in the court of the jurisdiction where the subject property is located.[47]

§ 4.2 Parties

To participate in a legal action, a person must have full legal competency. A minor or an incompetent person must be represented by their legal representative (*fading dailiren*). The court must appoint a legal representative for the minor or incompetent person who is unrepresented in an action.[48] A party may be represented by one or two litigation representatives (*susong dailiren*).[49] Litigants can retain trained legal professionals, including licensed attorneys and community legal service workers (*jiceng falu fuwu gongzuozhe*) as their "litigation representatives" (*susong daili ren*).[50] A party may also appoint a close relative or an employee,[51] or someone from their workplace, community, or any affiliated entity to act as their "litigation representative."[52] Parties may participate in an action through their litigation representatives, usually their attorneys, without appearing in person. However, parties in a divorce

45. *Id.* art. 533.
46. Civil Procedure Law art. 224.
47. Civil Procedure Law Interpretations art. 462.
48. Civil Procedure Law art. 57; *see also* Civil Procedure Law Interpretations art. 83.
49. Civil Procedure Law art. 58 para. 1.
50. *Id.* art. 58 (1).
51. *Id.* art. 58 (2).
52. *Id.* art. 58 (3).

action must appear in person unless they are not competent to express themselves or they have submitted a written statement about their stance in the action.[53]

§ 4.3 Case Acceptance

A trial court procedure has four stages: (1) case acceptance, (2) service of process, (3) trial, and (4) pronouncement of the judgment. The initial stage of a lawsuit is "case acceptance" (*li'an*). In the case acceptance stage, the "Docketing Division" (*lian bu*) of each court acts as the gatekeeper of the case manage system.[54] After receiving a complaint and its accompanying filings, the Docketing Division will not only conduct a clerical and procedural review of the filings but, more importantly, it will examine and decide on jurisdictional issues and, at least to certain extent, the merit of the plaintiff's substantive claims. Cases that do not meet jurisdictional and other statutory criteria or are deemed baseless by the Docketing Division will be rejected.[55] The Docketing Division often conducts mediation and persuades the plaintiff to withdraw the action upon the parties' settlement.[56]

A plaintiff must submit a written complaint to commence an action. (See Appendix IV, Complaint, available online.) If a plaintiff is illiterate, the court will take the plaintiff's oral statements and make a record as the plaintiff's complaint.[57] A complaint may not contain any personal insults or offensive language.[58] A complaint must clearly state the parties' identities, the plaintiff's claims, and the factual and legal basis of the plaintiff's claims.[59] A complaint must identify the plaintiff's evidence, the source of the evidence, and witnesses.[60] (See Appendix VI, Evidence List, available online.) In practice, complaints or answers often include a packet of documentary evidence or a list of evidence to be introduced.

If the complaint meets the statutory criteria, the court will accept it, place the case on the court's docket within seven days, issue a notice of acceptance

---

53. *Id.* art. 62.

54. Nanping Liu & Michelle Liu, *Justice without Judges: The Case Filing Division in the People's Republic of China*, 17 U.C. Davis J. Int'l L. & Pol'y 283, 289 (2011).

55. Zuigao Renmin Fayuan Guanyu Renmin Fayuan Dengji Lian Ruogan Wenti De Guiding (最高人民法院关于人民法院登记立案若干问题的规定) [The SPC's Provisions on Issues Concerning People's Courts' Case Acceptance] (promulgated by the Sup. People's Ct. on April 13, 2015, effective on May 1, 2015) 2015 Sup. People's Ct. Gaz. 8, art. 10.

56. *Id.* art. 15.

57. Civil Procedure Law art. 120.

58. Civil Procedure Law Interpretations art. 210.

59. Civil Procedure Law art. 121.

60. *Id.*

and levy a case acceptance fee.[61] For an action to be accepted, it must meet all the following criteria: (1) the plaintiff must have the standing to bring the action; (2) the defendant has been identified; (3) the pleadings are sufficiently specific; and (4) the action must fall in the court's jurisdiction.[62] In addition, the court must reject a divorce complaint if the plaintiff had brought a previous divorce action that was dismissed or withdrawn within the past six months, unless the court finds any new reason or circumstances that might justify a divorce.[63]

After receiving the payment of case acceptance fee, the court will assign a judge or collegiate bench to the case and notify the plaintiff of the assignment. The court will also serve the complaint and the notice to respond on the defendant and notify the defendant of the assignment of a judge or tribunal. The parties may request the recusal of the assigned judge or any member of the collegiate bench for conflict of interest or any other good cause.[64] Defendants may submit written answers within 15 days of the service of the complaint[65] (See Appendix V, Answer, available online.) The content and format of an answer are similar to a complaint. A defendant's failure to submit a written answer has no procedural or substantive effects.[66]

§ 4.4 Service of Process

The parties do not have the obligation to effect service of any judicial documents through the course of a legal action. Chinese courts are responsible for service of process in civil actions.[67] Within five days of the acceptance of a case, the court must serve the defendant.[68] In practice, courts usually contact the parties to arrange for service of process of judicial documents, such as summons and complaints. In actions where the defendants are not in China, service may be undertaken through diplomatic channels or in accordance with the Hague Convention on the Service Abroad of Judicial and Extrajudicial Documents in Civil and Commercial Matters. For discussions of service of process outside of China, see subsection 12.5.2.

61. *Id.* art. 123.
62. *Id.* art. 119.
63. *Id.* art. 124 (7).
64. *Id.* art. 44.
65. *Id.* art. 125 para. 1.
66. *Id.* art. 125 para. 2.
67. *Id.* art. 84.
68. *Id.* art. 85.

§ 4.5 Pre-Trial Procedures

4.5.1 Pre-Trial Provisional Remedies

4.5.1.1 Preservation

Protective orders for preservation (*baoquan*) to prevent irreparable damage may be issued before an action is commenced,[69] during a pending action,[70] or in connection with enforcement after an action is concluded.[71] Preservation remedies include seizure, sequestration, and freezing of assets.[72] Injunctions and restraining orders may be entered against certain acts as well.[73]

Applications for preservation must be heard and decided promptly, and must be decided within 48 hours in case of emergency.[74] Courts may issue preservation orders *ex parte* or on notice.[75] However, courts may require security before issuing pre-action preservation orders.[76] During a pending action, the court may determine whether the party seeking a preservation order must provide security based on the circumstances of the case.[77] The amount of security is determined by the possible damage that might be caused by the preservation measures when a spouse seeks preservation of the other spouse's separate property or marital community property.[78] Preservation orders must be enforced immediately upon issuance.[79]

4.5.1.2 Advance Enforcement

"Advance enforcement" (*xianyu zhixing*) is a *pendente lite* relief for a needy party during the pendency of an action. Pending final determinations of child support, filial support, or spousal support, courts may grant advance enforcement, including advance payments of support.[80] Advance enforcement is available only when the parties' rights and duties are clearly defined, the party seeking the relief will suffer severe hardship if advance enforcement is not granted, and the advance enforcement order will not cause the

69. *Id.* art. 101.
70. *Id.* art. 100 para. 1.
71. Civil Procedure Law Interpretations art. 163.
72. Civil Procedure Law art. 103 and Civil Procedure Law Interpretations art. 154.
73. Civil Procedure Law art. 100 para. 1.
74. *Id.* art. 100 para. 3.
75. *Id.* art. 100 para. 1.
76. Civil Procedure Law Interpretations art. 152 para. 1.
77. *Id.* art. 152 para. 2.
78. Marriage and Family Book Interpretations (I) art. 85.
79. Civil Procedure Law art. 100 para. 3.
80. *Id.* art. 106.

respondent undue hardship.[81] Advance enforcement allows a needy party to attach and garnish an obligor's income and assets for support.

4.5.2 Disclosure and Collection of Evidence

The party contending an allegation bears the burden of proof.[82] Thus, the burden to collect and produce evidence is on the party that asserts a claim.[83] Chinese law does not provide extensive discovery devices.[84] Consequently, parties have to rely upon discovery orders,[85] and courts' sanction power in collecting evidence.[86] Nevertheless, parties' ability in pre-trial collection and exchange of evidence has been improved under the recently amended civil procedure law and rules.

Chinese courts are designed to seek "objective facts" (*keguan shishi*), to apply the law "correctly" based on the "objective facts," and to deliver justice and order.[87] Therefore, Chinese judges are given expansive "fact-seeking" power. As "fact-seekers" instead of "facts-finders," Chinese judges, not the parties, lead the discovery process.[88] At a trial, the presiding judge or collegiate bench, not the parties, examines the evidence, questions the witness, and makes active inquiries into the merits of each case.[89] The presiding judge, not the law, allocates the parties' burden of proof in each case.[90] Chinese judges may investigate and collect evidence *sua sponte* in specific types of cases, including cases concerning divorce, custody, and other personal relations.[91] To ensure accuracy and impartiality, a court's *sua sponte* investigation and collection of evidence must be conducted by at least two judges and a court clerk.[92] Any error of facts or law may constitute grounds for reversal because

81. *Id.* art. 107.

82. *Id.* art. 64 para. 1.

83. *Id.* art. 64.

84. John J. Capowski, *China's Evidentiary and Procedural Reforms, the Federal Rules of Evidence, and the Harmonization of Civil and Common Law*, 47 Tex. Int'l L.J. 455, 470–71 (2012), at 468–69; *see also* Judge Elizabeth Fahey & Judge Zhirong Tao, *The Pretrial Discovery Process in Civil Cases: A Comparison of Evidence Discovery between China and the United States*, 37 B.C. Int'l & Comp. L. Rev. 281 (2014) (comparing judges' roles in evidence-gathering process).

85. Civil Procedure Law Interpretations arts. 94–96.

86. Civil Procedure Law arts. 65, 67.

87. *Id.* art. 2; *see also* Philip C.C. Huang, Chinese Civil Justice, Past and Present 135–72 (2012).

88. Fahey & Tao, *supra* note 84.

89. Capowski, *supra* note 84, 470–71.

90. Civil Procedure Law Interpretations arts. 90–93.

91. Civil Procedure Law arts. 64, 67; Civil Procedure Law Interpretations arts. 94, 96; Zhong Jianhua et al., *Establishing the Truth on Facts: Has the Chinese Civil Process Achieved This Goal?*, 13 J. Transnat'l L. & Pol'y 393, 400 (2004); Capowski, *supra* note 84, at 468–69.

92. Civil Procedure Law Interpretations art. 97.

Chinese judges must ascertain all relevant facts in each case, including undisputed or unalleged facts.[93] Therefore, Chinese courts' appellate review is not limited to questions of law.[94] Instead, the appellate court must review the trial court's application of law as well as its findings of fact, and may even question the parties and conduct additional investigation *sua sponte*.[95]

There are three major avenues for pre-trial evidence production in civil litigations: (1) mandatory initial disclosure, (2) evidence production through investigative orders, and (3) supervised evidence exchange.

4.5.2.1 Initial Disclosure

Generally, parties must provide evidence that supports their initial pleadings in their complaint or answer.[96] Parties usually submit an evidence packet together with their complaint or answer. An initial disclosure packet typically includes (1) the name, address, and telephone number of each party; (2) documents that the disclosing party may use to support claims or defenses; and (3) a description, by category and location, of all documents, electronically stored information, and tangible things that the disclosing party possesses or controls and may use to support its claims or defenses.

4.5.2.2 Financial Disclosure in Divorce Actions

Mandatory financial disclosure in divorce actions involving property disputes has been implemented in Chinese courts since 2018.[97] Courts must serve both parties a "family matter party's property disclosure form" (*jiashi anjian dangshiren caichan shengbao biao*) simultaneously with case acceptance notices and summons. Sanctions for failure to truthfully disclose martial property or separate property range from reprimand, reduction of property distribution share, negative reporting to the social credit reporting system and employment credit system, fines, to imprisonment for obstruction of civil litigation.[98] (See Appendix VIII, Divorce Litigants Financial Disclosure Form, available online.)

---

93. Zhong et al., *supra* note 91, at 419–21.

94. Civil Procedure Law art. 169.

95. *Id.* art. 168.

96. *Id.* arts. 121, 125.

97. Zuigao Renmin Fayuan Guanyu Jinyibu Shenhua Jiashi Shenpan Fangshi He Gongzuo Jizhi Gaige De Yijian (Shixing) (最高人民法院关于进一步深化家事审判方式和工作机制改革的意见(试行)) [The Supreme People's Court Opinions on Further Reforms of Family Matter Adjudication Procedures and Mechanisms (Trial Implementation)] (promulgated by the Sup. People's Ct. on July 18, 2018) 2018 Sup. People's Ct. Gaz. 11, [hereinafter the "Family Matter Adjudication Procedures"] art. 44.

98. Family Matter Adjudication Procedures art. 44.

4.5.2.3 Investigation Orders

A party may request that the court investigate and collect evidence when the party is unable to obtain the evidence for reasons not under the party's control,[99] or when the evidence sought is not accessible by the party because access to the records is restricted by government agency or because the records involve national security, commercial secretes, or personal privacy.[100] Parties must obtain investigative orders in order to compel production of evidence from an adverse party or third-party witnesses. In other words, parties may not demand production of evidence from an adverse party or third parties directly. Requests for investigation orders must be specific and must be made before the evidence submission deadline in an action.[101]

The court must reject an investigative request for evidence that is irrelevant, is used to support frivolous claims, or has little evidentiary value.[102] In divorce actions, upon a party's application, the court may issue investigative orders to financial institutions and employers to compel production of material evidence.[103] Investigative requests must be reasonable. For instance, a Hebei court rejected a wife's request to investigate the husband's business records from 1996 to 2020, finding that the wife's request was overly broad, and akin to a fishing expedition for irrelevant evidence.[104]

4.5.2.4 Family Matter Investigators

A court may investigate and collect evidence *sua sponte* in civil actions whenever the court deems it necessary to conduct its own investigation.[105] Chinese courts' *sua sponte* investigative authority is, however, restricted to collection of evidence relevant to national interest, public interest, potential crime, procedural matters, or "personal status and relation."[106] Since family matters are matters concerning personal status and relation, Chinese courts may conduct their own investigations to collect evidence in family matters, including appointing experts or family matter investigators to conduct investigations on the court's behalf.[107]

---

99. Civil Procedure Law art. 64 para. 2. *See also* the SPC Rules of Evidence in Civil Procedure art. 2 para. 2.
100. Civil Procedure Law Interpretations art. 94.
101. The SPC Rules of Evidence in Civil Procedure art. 20.
102. Civil Procedure Law Interpretations art. 95.
103. Family Matter Adjudication Procedures art. 43.
104. (2021) Ji 06 Min Zhong 296 Hao ((2021) 冀06民终296号).
105. Civil Procedure Law art. 64 para. 2.
106. Civil Procedure Law Interpretations art. 96.
107. Family Matter Adjudication Procedures art. 15.

Upon parties' applications or the courts' own initiation, Chinese courts may conduct investigations and collect evidence in guardianship, visitation, and custody proceedings that involve minors.[108] Chinese courts may appoint "family matter investigators" (*jiashi diaochayuan*), a Japanese legal transplant, for a broad range of investigations in divorce, child custody and support, filial support, and any other matters that the court deems necessary.[109] Family matter investigators may interview the parties, their parents, and children over the age of eight, and visit the parties' neighborhood, workplace, and the children's school.[110] Courts may select family matter investigators from professionals trained in mental health, law, education, and related fields, or from lay persons recommended by governmental agencies, women's federations, communist youth associations, and community organizations.[111]

4.5.2.5 Forensic Examination

Parties may request a court to order forensic examinations and appoint forensic examiners, such as forensic accountants, real estate appraisers, or medical examiners in domestic matters. Parties may also select neutral forensic experts by agreement. A court may appoint forensic examiners when the parties fail to select any by agreement.[112] Requests for a forensic examiner must be relevant and material to the allegations or claim asserted by either party, and must be made before the evidence submission period is closed.[113]

Forensic examiners are entitled to obtain case materials and interrogate parties and witnesses.[114] A forensic examiner must complete the examination and make a written report to the court within the time period ordered by the court.[115] A forensic report must specify the examiner's opinions, the theoretical basis and methodology used in the examination, and the process of the examination.[116] Parties may object to forensic reports in writing,[117] and seek leave to submit written rebuttal forensic reports or call their own expert to testify at trial.[118]

---

108. *Id.* art. 42.
109. *Id.* art. 21.
110. *Id.* art. 22.
111. *Id.* art. 17.
112. Civil Procedure Law art. 76.
113. Civil Procedure Law Interpretations art. 121.
114. Civil Procedure Law art. 77.
115. *Id.*; and the SPC Rules of Evidence in Civil Procedure art. 35.
116. The SPC Rules of Evidence in Civil Procedure art. 36.
117. *Id.* art. 32.
118. Civil Procedure Law Interpretations art. 122.

4.5.2.6 Inspection

Upon a party's request or on its own initiation, the court may conduct on-site inspections.[119] When the court examines physical evidence on-site or the site in question, it must make a written record of the time, place, participants, method, and outcome of the on-site inspection.[120] In family matters, Chinese courts may conduct home visits and inspections.

4.5.2.7 Evidence Submission

Pre-trial collection of evidence is closely supervised by the court. Parties must submit, to the court, evidence (*juzheng*) that will be offered at the trial by the deadlines set by the court. At the beginning of the pre-trial phase, the court must serve both parties with a notice of evidence production (*juzheng tongzhi*) that specifies each party's burden of proof, the deadlines for evidence submission, the circumstances under which orders for investigation and collection of evidence may be issued, and the legal consequences for noncompliance.[121]

4.5.2.7.1 Time Limit

Collection, exchange, and submission of evidence must be completed within the "evidence submission period" (*juzheng qixian*) set by the court. Applications for investigative orders must be made within the evidence submission period as well. An "evidence submission period" must be for at least 15 days, and may be extended by agreement with leave.[122] A court may allow additional time for the parties to submit additional evidence to refute, supplement, or correct the evidence that has been submitted.[123] In the event that a party is unable to collect certain evidence for good cause, the court may also extend the time for submission.[124] A party that has failed to timely produce evidence and caused undue delay in a legal action may be fined.[125]

4.5.2.7.2 Evidence Exchange

At the closing of an evidence submission period, the court may hold an evidence exchange session to narrow down the issues of facts and resolve evidentiary disputes.[126] The date for evidence exchange may be stipulated by the parties or designated by the court.[127] The evidence submission closes

---

119. *Id.* art. 124.
120. The SPC Rules of Evidence in Civil Procedure art. 43.
121. *Id.* art. 50.
122. Civil Procedure Law Interpretations art. 99 paras. 1 and 2.
123. *Id.* art. 99 para. 3. *See also* the SPC Rules of Evidence in Civil Procedure art. 51.
124. The SPC Rules of Evidence in Civil Procedure art. 52.
125. *Id.* art. 59.
126. Civil Procedure Law art. 133 (4).
127. The SPC Rules of Evidence in Civil Procedure art. 56 para. 2.

on the date when evidence exchange is conducted.[128] During an evidence exchange session, the court must make a record of the facts and evidence that are not disputed by the parties, and the allegations and evidence that are disputed.[129] The parties may raise objections to the authenticity and relevancy of the evidence that has been submitted.[130] If either party wishes to submit rebuttal evidence after the evidence exchange, the court must arrange for a further exchange of evidence.[131]

4.5.2.8 Preservation of Evidence

Parties may seek preservation of evidence before their evidence submission period has ended.[132] Evidence may be preserved by seizure, sequestration, audio recording, video recording, duplication, forensic examination, and court inspection.[133] The court may order a party seeking preservation of evidence to provide security if the preservation measures might cause damages to the person who possesses the evidence.[134] If a preservation order has caused damages in property, the applicant of the preservation order is liable for such damages.[135]

§ 4.6 Trial

After the closing of disclosure, collection, exchange, and submission of evidence, the trial process begins. The court may hold a pre-trial conference. A pre-trial conference is a proactive case management mechanism to improve the quality of the trial and to provide the parties with an opportunity to settle. At the pre-trial conference, the court may (1) ascertain the plaintiff's pleadings and the defendant's responses; (2) review any amendment or supplement to the parties' pleadings; (3) examine evidence submitted and address any remaining issues of investigative orders, forensic examination, disclosure, inspection, or evidence preservation; (4) coordinate evidence exchange; (5) summarize the focal points of the upcoming trial; and (6) mediate a settlement.[136] After the pre-trial conference, the court may provide a "summary of disputes" (*guina zhengyi jiaodian*). The summary of disputes identifies the key issues in facts and law to be tried. It serves as a roadmap for the trial.

128. *Id*. art. 56 para. 1.
129. *Id*. art. 57.
130. *Id*. art. 60.
131. *Id*. art. 58.
132. Civil Procedure Law art. 81; and the Civil Procedure Law Interpretations art. 98.
133. The SPC Rules of Evidence in Civil Procedure art. 27.
134. *Id*. art. 26.
135. *Id*. art. 28.
136. Civil Procedure Law Interpretations art. 225.

Trials (*tingshen*) in Chinese courts are highly formulaic. Judges take an active inquisitory role at the trial. They are free to question the parties or their witnesses directly. The exchange between the parties is controlled by the presiding judge. Trials in family matters are usually more informal and relaxed. Some courts are experimenting with hearing family law matters in a living room-like setting. Nonetheless, family matter judges rarely stray away from the scripted trial process that is conducted in six stages: (1) introduction, (2) in-court investigation, (3) oral argument, (4) closing statements, (5) mediation, and (6) pronouncement of judgment.

4.6.1 Introduction

As a trial session starts, a court clerk reads the transcript or plays the audio recording of courtroom etiquette. Then the presiding judge or collegiate bench enters the courtroom. The presiding judge or the lead judge of the collegiate bench will then introduce him/herself, the members of the collegiate bench, and the clerk. The parties will be asked if they request any court staff's recusal. Parties in divorce actions or other family matters may request the court to close the courtroom to protect the parties' privacy.[137]

If no recusal is requested, the presiding judge will make a brief opening remark on the nature and status of the case and ascertain each party and their litigation representatives' identity. Attorneys will also submit to the court copies of attorney certificates (*lushi zheng*) and the client's authorization of legal representation (*shouquan weituo shu*).

4.6.2 In-Court Investigations

In-court investigations (*fating diaocha*) are conducted in the following order: (1) each party presents an opening statement; (2) after the court reads the witnesses their rights and obligations, the parties and their witnesses testify and the statements of absent witnesses are read; (3) documentary evidence, physical evidence, audio-visual recordings, and electronic data are introduced; (4) expert opinions are read; and (5) transcripts of survey are read.[138]

4.6.2.1 Parties' Statements

First, the plaintiff states the relief sought and the factual and legal basis for the complaint. The presiding judge, then, will inquire whether the plaintiff wishes to amend, withdraw, or add any pleadings. After the plaintiff's opening statement, the defendant presents an opening statement in response. The judge, then, asks the defendant to clarify whether he/she wishes to amend,

137. Civil Procedure Law art. 134.

138. *Id.* art. 138.

withdraw, or add any responsive pleadings, including counterclaims. At the trial, either party may add, abandon, or modify their claims or request joinder of a third party.[139]

4.6.2.2 Presentation of Evidence

The plaintiff presents evidence first. New evidence that has not been previously disclosed or exchanged in the pre-trial evidence submission period may be introduced at the trial.[140] As permitted by the court, the defendant may examine and inspect the plaintiff's evidence, and question the plaintiff and the plaintiff's witnesses, including experts.[141] After the plaintiff's presentation of evidence, the defendant will do the same. Based on the in-court presentation of evidence, either party may request additional investigation, forensic examination, or inspection.[142]

The court must examine the evidence presented by the parties and question them and their witnesses. The court must ascertain whether each piece of evidence (1) is consistent with the original, if a duplicate or copy is submitted; (2) is relevant; (3) is properly notarized or certified; (4) is acquired through lawful means, for example, a witness's testimony is not given under coercion; (4) is authenticate; and (5) is provided by a witness with interest or ties to either party.[143] Some evidence, such as the parties' testimony, must be corroborated.[144] Furthermore, the court must examine the evidence's relevancy to the case.[145]

4.6.3 Oral Argument and Closing Statements

After examination of evidence and testimonies, a court debate (*fating bianlun*) is conducted in the following order: (1) the plaintiff's arguments, (2) the defendant's arguments, (3) the arguments of the third party joined in the action, (4) debate among the parties, and (5) the final statements by all parties.[146] The presiding judge or collegiate bench can question the parties during the debate. In practice, the court may allow or request that each party submit additional written statements of representation (*daili ci*) as summary and/or supplement of their oral arguments after the debate.

---

139. *Id.* art. 140.
140. *Id.* art. 139 para. 1.
141. *Id.* art. 139 para. 2.
142. *Id.* art. 139 para. 3.
143. The SPC Rules of Evidence in Civil Procedure art. 87.
144. *Id.* art. 90.
145. *Id.* art. 88.
146. Civil Procedure Law art. 141.

4.6.4 Mediation

Mediation has become a widely accepted alternative to the adversarial legal process in emotionally charged family law proceedings around the world.[147] Chinese judges are encouraged to make best efforts to assess each case's unique circumstances, diffuse conflicts, and resolve disputes through mediation.[148] Throughout the trial process, the court may encourage the parties to attend mediation. In divorce actions, mediation is required before a trial unless both parties decline to participate.[149] Mediation is conducted in closed sessions. In practice, parties often submit to the court and exchange mediation plans (*tiaojie jihua*) as settlement proposals to facilitate a settlement.

Chinese courts generally follow well-crafted SPC guidelines in cases where domestic violence is alleged. The SPC does not prohibit mediation when domestic violence is alleged. Instead, the SPC provides some cautionary instructions: First, judges must not blame the victim, or try to justify a perpetrator's action. Second, judges must protect the victim and balance the power structure between the victim and the abuser. Third, judges should hold private meetings (caucuses) with each party separately in high-conflict situations to protect the victim. Fourth, a court may engage community mediators, professional mediators, or family members to facilitate the mediation. Last, judges must take control of the mediation process by (1) setting the order in which the parties may speak; (2) controlling the content of the parties' statements, and sanctioning any statements or conduct intended to intimidate or harass the other party; (3) controlling the length of time that each party may speak based on the principle of "empower the vulnerable and control the domineering" (*furuo yiqiang*); (4) supporting and encouraging the victims to advocate for their own rights; and (5) reviewing the parties' agreement reached through the mediation and advising the victim if an agreement is clearly unfair; and if the victim insists on accepting an unfair agreement, the court must ensure that the victim entered the agreement willingly without coercion and duress.[150]

---

147. Holly Joyce, Comment, *Mediation and Domestic Violence: Legislative Responses*, 14 J. AM. ACAD. MATRIM. L. 447, 447 (1997).

148. FMTC 5.

149. Civil Procedure Law Interpretations art. 145 para. 2.

150. Zuiggao Renmin Fayuan Sheji Jiating Baoli Hunyin Anjian Shenli Zhinan (最高人民法院涉及家庭暴力婚姻案件审理指南) [The Supreme People's Court Guidelines for Hearing Marriage Cases Involving Domestic Violence], arts. 53–62 (March 2008) [the "DV Guidelines"], arts. 70–71.

4.6.5 Court Record

A court clerk is responsible for managing the file, taking minutes of the hearing, and sometimes drafting legal documents in the trial process. Each courtroom has a simultaneous monitoring system through which the parties and the judge can read the clerk's transcription and make corrections in real time. At the conclusion of each hearing or trial, the parties must review, correct, and sign the trial transcript (*tingsheng jilu*).[151] The minutes and transcripts are included in the court case file. The case files are accessible only to the parties and their counsel.

4.6.6 Judgment/Decree/Order

Usually, a written judgment must be entered within six months after the court's acceptance of the case.[152] If a judgment or order is placed on record in open court orally, the parties may request a written judgment.[153] Civil judgments are published by the courts unless leave is granted for nonpublication for good reasons, such as privacy.[154] An increasing fraction of family matter judgments and orders are not published for privacy reasons.

§ 4.7 Appeals

Civil judgments, orders, or rulings are appealable as of right at the courts of second instance. After the appeal, either party may request a retrial through an "adjudication supervision procedure" (*shenpan jiandu chengxu*).

4.7.1 Appeals in the Court of Second Instance

An appeal from a judgment must be taken within 15 days from the date of service of the judgment,[155] and an appeal from an order or ruling must be taken within ten days from the date of service of the order or ruling.[156] An appellant must submit a written appeal (*shangsu shu*) through the original court of first instance.[157] The appellee is not required to submit a written response.[158]

---

151. Civil Procedure Law art. 147.
152. *Id.* art. 149.
153. Civil Procedure Law Interpretations art. 253.
154. *Id.* art. 254.
155. Civil Procedure Law art. 164 para. 1.
156. *Id.* art. 164 para. 2.
157. *Id.* art. 165.
158. *Id.* art. 167.

An appellate court must review the lower court's findings of fact and application of law.[159] If an appellate court that serves as the court of second instance decides to conduct a new trial, it must follow the same procedural and evidentiary rules as those in the courts of the first instance.[160] An appellate court may choose not to conduct a trial if the parties did not present any new factual, evidentiary, or legal issues.[161] In addition, it may decide without a trial when the decision on appeal is concerning procedural issues, such as case acceptance, jurisdiction objection or decisions, and there are no issues of facts but issues of law on the appeal.[162]

After an appellate review or a new trial, an appellate court may (1) dismiss the appeal and sustain the original judgment or ruling if the lower court's decision is "clear in fact finding" (*shishi qingchu*) and "correct in application of law" (*shiyong falü zhengque*); (2) reverse, vacate, or modify the original judgment or ruling if the lower court has erred in its fact finding or application of law; (3) vacate the lower court's decision and remand the case to the original court of first instance for retrial, or conduct a new trial by the appellate court if the lower court has erred in its fact finding; (4) vacate the lower court's decision and remand the case if there are some serious procedural violations by the lower court.[163] Furthermore, in an appeal of a denial of divorce by the original court of first instance, if the divorce is granted on appeal, the appellate court may mediate the ancillary issues, such as child custody and support, and property division upon the parties' consent to mediation, or remand the ancillary issues to the original court of first instance.[164]

4.7.2 Adjudication Supervision Procedure

"Adjudication supervision procedure" (*shenpan jiandu chengxu*) is "a procedure for additional, but discretionary, reviews" of final judgments and orders that may contain errors.[165] After all channels of appeal have been exhausted, the adjudication supervision procedure may be invoked by courts *sua sponte*,[166] or by parties,[167] or by procuratorates[168] to seek a retrial. A retrial

159. *Id.* art. 168.
160. *Id.* art. 174.
161. *Id.* art. 169 para. 1.
162. Civil Procedure Law Interpretations art. 331.
163. Civil Procedure Law art. 170.
164. Civil Procedure Law Interpretations art. 327.
165. Margaret Y.K. Woo, *Adjudication Supervision and Judicial Independence in the P.R.C.*, 39(1) Am. J. Compar. L. 95–119, 97 (Winter 1991).
166. Civil Procedure Law art. 198.
167. *Id.* art. 199.
168. *Id.* arts. 208, 209.

is warranted if any errors of fact, errors of law, procedural errors, or judicial misconducts that could have changed the outcome of a case have been found through the adjudication supervision procedure.[169]

A party may file a petition for retrial through adjudication supervision procedure in the original court of first instance or the court directly above the original court of first instance within six months after the judgment, order, or mediated decree has taken effect.[170] Repeated petitions for retrial are not allowed. A petition must be denied if the same petition has been previously denied by a court or rejected by a procuratorate, or a retrial has been granted for the same cause alleged in the petition.[171]

A procuratorate may appeal civil judgments or orders on its own motion or upon a party's application.[172] In addition, upon a party's petition, the procuratorates may move for reconsideration or appeal a court's decision made in an adjudication supervision procedure if (1) the court has rejected a party's retrial petition; (2) the court has failed to issue a ruling within the statutory time frame; or (3) the court's decision is clearly erroneous.[173]

A case may be retried by an adjudication supervision court or remanded to a lower court if there is any consequential error in application of law in the original judgment.[174] Consequential errors of law occur when (1) the law that a court's decision relied on is not applicable to the case; (2) a court's allocation of liability is inconsistent with the parties' contract or the law; (3) a court's decision relied on laws that have been repealed or laws that have not yet taken effect; (4) a court's application of law violates the rules concerning retroactivity of law; (5) a court's application of law violates the rules concerning applicability of law; and (6) the application of law clearly conflicts with the legislative intention.[175]

An adjudication supervision court may order a retrial or remand if the lower courts have made consequential evidentiary errors,[176] or there is sufficient new evidence that may change the outcome of the case.[177] New evidence may be admitted in an adjudication supervision proceeding if such evidence is material to prove consequential errors in the factual findings or the conclusion of law of the original decision, and was not previously introduced due

169. *Id.* art. 200.
170. Civil Procedure Law art. 205.
171. Civil Procedure Law Interpretations art. 381.
172. Civil Procedure Law arts. 208, 209.
173. *Id.* art. 209.
174. *Id.* art. 200 (2) and (6).
175. Civil Procedure Law Interpretations art. 388.
176. Civil Procedure Law art. 200 (1), (3), (4) and (5).
177. *Id.* art. 200 (2).

to reasonable causes.[178] Reasonable causes for failure to introduce a piece of evidence include (1) the evidence existed before the conclusion of the trial but was discovered after the trial for objective reasons; (2) the evidence was discovered before the conclusion of the trial but could not be obtained or offered within the statutory time frame for objective reasons; or (3) the evidence did not exist before the original trial was concluded and therefore could not be offered.[179] For example, the Beijing High People's Court ordered a retrial in an adjudication supervision procedure after finding that a husband had concealed evidence of marital funds and a home that he purchased without the wife's knowledge, and submitted falsified documentary evidence during the trial.[180]

Evidence that could have been introduced during a trial or appeal may not be introduced in an adjudication supervision proceeding. For example, new property appraisals are routinely rejected in adjudication supervision proceedings. In *Sheng v. Chu*, Sheng sought the ownership and occupancy of the parties' marital home. However, Sheng refused to obtain an appraisal of the home during the trial in the basic-level court and during the appeal in the intermediate court. The High People's Court of Shangdong Province found that Sheng's request for an appraisal of the marital home was time barred, as she failed to comply with the lower court's orders to appraise the home and failed to request the court to appoint an appraiser both at the original court of first instance and the court of second instance.[181] In *Zhou v. Wu*, the Shanxi Province High People's Court refused to admit the appraisal of the parties' marital home as new evidence in the adjudication supervision proceeding. The court held that the appraisal did not qualify as new evidence admissible in an adjudication supervision proceeding because it could have been offered in the proceedings in the original court of first instance and in the court of second instance.[182]

4.7.3 Stay

An appeal automatically stays the execution of a judgment or order from the original court of first instance in that a civil judgment, order, or ruling becomes final only after the conclusion of the appeal at the court of second instance. An adjudication supervision proceeding brought by a party does not stay the final judgment or order.[183] If a retrial is granted after an adjudication

178. Civil Procedure Law Interpretations art. 385.
179. *Id.* art. 388 (1), (2) and (3).
180. (2019) Jing Min Shen 3097 Hao ((2019) 京民申3097号).
181. (2019) Wan Min Shen 2773 Hao ((2019) 皖民申2773号).
182. (2019) Jin Min Shen 2033 Hao ((2019) 晋民申2033号).
183. Civil Procedure Law art. 199.

supervision review, the original judgment or order may be stayed by the court during the retrial.[184] However, support judgments, orders, or rulings for elderly parents, adult dependents, and minor children may not be stayed.[185]

§ 4.8 Enforcement Procedure

When an obligor or debtor has failed to comply with a judgment or court order that has taken effect, the obligee or creditor may bring an enforcement proceeding at the court of first instance at the place where the obligor or debtor resides, or at the place where the subject property is located.[186]

The respondent or an interested third-party subject to enforcement may file objections and is entitled to a hearing on the objections.[187] The decision on a party's objection to enforcement is appealable.[188] However, the appeal does not necessarily stay the enforcement measures.

A notice of enforcement must be entered and served on the defaulting party when the court finds the party against whom enforcement is sought has failed to perform his or her legal obligations.[189] When the defaulting party has failed to comply with the notice of enforcement, the court can garnish the defaulting party's income, and seize, freeze, transfer, or auction the defaulting party's property to satisfy his or her obligations.[190] The court must reserve necessary living expenses for the defaulting party and his or her dependent family members.[191]

184. *Id.* art. 206.
185. *Id.*
186. *Id.* art. 224.
187. *Id.* art. 225.
188. *Id.* art. 227.
189. *Id.* art. 240.
190. *Id.* arts. 242, 243.
191. *Id.* art. 243.

Chapter 5

Fundamental Concepts and Principles of Chinese Family Law

Chinese family law regulates relationships between a heterosexual couple and their children in a nuclear family as well as relations among kin related by blood or marriage, particularly relatives sharing the same household. Inasmuch, Chinese family law primarily governs the personal relationships between family members of a household.

§ 5.1 Principles of Chinese Family Law

Chinese family law is guided by the deep commitment to monogamous, heterosexual, egalitarian marriage. The unique characteristics of Chinese family law are manifested in its stated principles. As stated in the Civil Code, the principles of Chinese marriage and family law are (1) the state regulates and protects the family and marriage; (2) marriages must be entered by choice and free of coercion; (3) marriages are heterosexual and monogamous; (4) men and women enjoy equal status in marriage; and (5) the state protects the lawful interests of women, minors, the elderly, and the disabled.[1]

Marriage is monogamous. A married person is prohibited from having a sexual relationship with any other person that is not their spouse. Bigamous marriages are null and void. Bigamy is a crime that can be committed not only by a person that is already married but also by a person who has knowingly married another person that is already married.[2] Marriage is limited to opposite-sex couples. Although there have been discussions of legalizing same-sex marriage in China, same-sex marriages are not legal. Men and

1. The Civil Code art. 1041.

2. Zhonghua Renming Gongheguo Xingfa (中华人民共和国刑法) [The Criminal Law of the People's Republic of China] (the "Criminal Law") art. 258.

women enjoy equal rights and share equal responsibilities in marriage and family life. Pre-communist China was an agrarian, patriarchal society, where marriage was a means to consolidate and perpetuate family wealth. Liberating young people from patriarchal control of marriage was one of the CCP's political commitments.[3] Marriage by parental imposition (*baoban hunyin*), marriage by purchase (*maimai hunyin*), and any interference in the freedom of marriage have been banned since the CCP takeover.[4] Interference with freedom of marriage by violence (*baoli ganshe hunyin ziyou*) is a crime punishable by fine and imprisonment.[5] To curb skyrocketing bridal prices and lavish weddings in both urban and rural China, any exaction of money or property by means of marriage is prohibited.[6]

The PRC Constitution proclaims that "marriage, family, mothers and minor children are entitled to the state's protection.[7] A natural person's personal rights arising from marriage, family and other domestic relations are entitled to legal protection,"[8] and "marriage and family are entitled to the state's protection."[9] These provisions give the state the authority to protect freedom of marriage, gender equality, and the rights of the vulnerable in the private domestic sphere. At the same time, they grant the state the license to interfere with family privacy, sexuality, and reproductive rights.

Chinese family law purposefully emphasizes protection and support of women, minor children, elderly parents, and disabled family members. The emphasis is necessitated by China's reliance of families as a social safety net. At the same time, it mirrors Chinese culture, which views family harmony and financial support of one's children, parents, and disabled family members as matters of the greatest importance.

§ 5.2 Natural Person

A "natural person" is defined as a living human being. "Natural person" is a legal construct of personhood for individuals as opposed to "legal person," which is a legal construct of personhood for corporations and other

3. Margery Wolf, *Marriage, Family, and the State in Contemporary China*, 57(2) PAC. AFFAIRS 213–36, 215–18, (Summer 1984).
4. Philip C.C. Huang, *Morality and Law in China, Past and Present*, 41(1) MODERN CHINA 3–39, 22 (2015).
5. Criminal Law art. 257.
6. The Civil Code art. 1042.
7. The Constitution art. 49.
8. The Civil Code art. 112.
9. *Id*. art. 1041.

organizations.[10] Natural persons have equal civil rights.[11] "Natural person" is the most fundamental concept in Chinese family law, as a person's rights and duties within a family are determined according to his/her capacity as a natural person. Chinese family law is structured around a conceptual framework that starts with "natural person" (*ziran ren*) and expands to a network of reciprocal rights and duties stemming from a natural person's relationships within a family, including his/her relationship with his/her spouse, children, parents, siblings, and other members of his/her household.

5.2.1 Time of Birth and Time of Death

A natural person's legal capacity for civil rights and obligations starts from the moment of his/her birth and ends at the moment of his/her death.[12] The Civil Code does not define "live birth" or "death." The time of birth and the time of death of a natural person are determined by the times recorded on the birth certificate or death certificate; or, in the absence of a birth certificate or death certificate, the times recorded in the household registration (*hukou*) or any other valid identity registration. If there is any other evidence sufficient to refute the recorded time of birth or death, the time proved by such evidence shall prevail.[13] Although an unborn child is not recognized as a natural person, the fetus is entitled to protection from harm, including protection from loss of testamentary legacy or succession. A fetus is presumed to have legal capacity in succession. A posthumous child is entitled to succession rights if the child is born alive. If a child is stillborn, the fetus's legal personality in succession is treated as if it has never existed.[14]

5.2.2 Age and Civil Legal Capacity

A person's age determines their civil legal capacity. Under the Civil Code, there is no single age at which a person moves from childhood to adulthood. A person reaches full legal capacity in three stages.

A minor under the age of eight is "a person without civil legal capacity" (*wu minshi xingwei nengli ren*), who can only carry out judicial acts through their guardian, who is their "legal representative" (*fading daibiao ren*).[15]

Eight is the age at which a natural person acquires limited legal capacity. A minor over the age of eight is "a person with limited civil legal capacity"

---

10. *Id.* arts. 57, 58.
11. *Id.* art.14.
12. *Id.* art.13.
13. *Id.* art. 15.
14. *Id.* art. 16.
15. *Id.* arts. 20, 23.

(*xianzhi minshi xingwei nengli ren*). A person with limited legal capacity may independently perform juridical acts that could benefit him/herself and cause him/herself no harm or liability, or judicial acts that are appropriate for his/her age and intelligence,[16] and may perform any other juridical acts through his/her legal representative, or with his/her legal representative's consent or ratification.[17]

Eighteen is the age of majority. A natural person under the age of 18 is a minor.[18] When a natural person reaches the age of 18, he/she becomes an adult, acquires full legal capacity, and can perform juridical acts (*falü xingwei*) independently.[19] However, a person over 16 years of age may be deemed as "a person with full legal capacity" (*wanquan minshi xingwei nengli ren*) if he/she primarily relies on his/her own earned income to support him/herself.[20]

5.2.3 Loss of Legal Capacity

An adult who is unable to understand the nature of his or her conduct is a "person without civil legal capacity" (*wu mingshi xingwei nengli ren*). A person without legal capacity can only carry out juridical conduct through his/her legal representatives.[21]

An adult who is unable to fully understand his/her conduct is a "person with limited civil legal capacity" (*xianzhi mingshi xingwei nengli ren*). A person with limited civil legal capacity may independently perform juridical acts that benefit him/herself and cause him/her no harm or liability, or judicial acts that are appropriate for his/her age and intelligence. However, he/she may perform other juridical acts only through his/her legal representative, or with his/her legal representative's consent or ratification.[22]

The guardian of a person without legal capacity or a person with limited legal capacity is the legal representative of said person.[23] Any interested person or entity may apply to a court for a determination of an adult's legal capacity.[24] An adult who has been determined by a court as a person without legal capacity or a person with limited legal capacity may apply to a court, by him/herself or through an interested party, for a determination of his/her legal capacity based on the recovery of his/her intelligence or mental health.[25]

---

16. *Id.* art. 19.
17. *Id.*
18. *Id* .art. 17.
19. *Id.* art. 18.
20. *Id.* art. 18.
21. *Id.* art. 21.
22. *Id.* art. 22.
23. *Id.* art. 23.
24. *Id.* art. 24 para. 1.
25. *Id.* art. 24 para. 2.

Entities that have standings to seek the determination of a person's legal incapacity include but are not limited to any Urban Residents' Committee (*jumin weiyuan hui*), Villagers' Committee (*cunmin weiyuan hui*), school, medical care institution, Women's Federation (*funu lianhehui*), Disabled Persons' Federation (*canjiren lianhehui*), organization legally formed for seniors, and Civil Affairs agency.[26]

5.2.4 Declared Absence or Death

A natural person may be declared as absent when he/she has disappeared for more than two years.[27] When an absentee reappears, the declaration of his/her absence must be revoked by a court.[28] The absentee's property should be managed by a custodian.[29] If the absentee reappears, the property may be reclaimed.[30]

When a person has been disappeared for more than four years or more than two years after an accident, he/she may be declared as deceased.[31] The date of the declaration of death of a person is the date of the person's death; however, if a person is declared dead because of his/her absence after an accident, the day of the accident is his/her date of death.[32]

If a person who was declared dead reappears, the declaration of his/her death should be revoked by a court.[33] He/she may reclaim his/her property.[34] His/her marriage may be resumed from the date of revocation of the declaration of death, unless the other spouse has remarried or has submitted to the Civil Affairs Bureau a written statement of refusal to resume marriage.[35] However, if his/her child has been legally adopted by another person, the adoption may not be terminated on the ground that the adoption is without his/her consent.[36]

5.2.5 Residency and Domicile

A natural person's domicile is the residence recorded in their household registration (*hukou*) or any other valid identity registration; but if their habitual

26. *Id.* art. 24 para. 3.
27. *Id.* art. 40.
28. *Id.* art. 45.
29. *Id.* arts. 42–44.
30. *Id.* art. 45 para. 2.
31. *Id.* art. 46.
32. *Id.* art. 48.
33. *Id.* art. 50.
34. *Id.* art. 53.
35. *Id.* art. 51.
36. *Id.* art. 52.

residence is different from the residence in their household registration, their habitual residence shall be deemed as their domicile.[37] For discussion of household registration, see 5.3.2.

§ 5.3 Family and Household

5.3.1 Family

In Chinese society, "family" is understood in three forms. The simplest form is a conjugal nuclear family that consists of a married couple and their unmarried offspring. In a more extended form, a family is a multigenerational household in one enclosed compound (*yuan*) that typically includes a set of parents and their adult children's families. This extended family structure is common, especially in rural China. In a further extended form and in a broader sense, a family (*jia*) is synonymous with a clan (*zu*), consisting of a group of households bonded together by kinship.[38]

Recognizing the multiple forms and meanings of "family," the Civil Code defines the relationships between members of a family by different degrees of kinship, blood, marriage, and/or co-residence. Members of a person's family include relatives (*qingshu*), close relatives (*jin qingshu*), and family members (*jiating chengyuan*). A person's relatives (*qingshu*) are relatives related by blood or by marriage.[39] A person's close relatives (*jin qingshu*) are their spouses, parents, children, siblings, paternal grandparents, maternal grandparents, paternal grandchildren, maternal grandchildren.[40] A person's family members (*jiating chengyuan*) are their spouses, parents, children, and close relatives who reside with them in the same household (*gongtong shenghuo*).[41] Family members have a duty to provide care and financial support to each other. Parents, as well as stepparents, grandparents, and adult siblings, have the duty to support, protect, discipline, and educate the minor children in the family.[42]

Heterosexual marriages are the nexus of Chinese family units. Marriage as a status creates rights and obligations not only between the parties *inter se* but also between the parties and the members of their respective natal family. Customarily, the bride joins the groom's natal household after the wedding. With the rise of nuclear families and rapid urbanization, this custom has become obsolete in Chinese cities. The custom of the bride joining the groom's

---

37. *Id.* art. 25.

38. Wen Yen Tsao, *The Chinese Family from Customary Law to Positive Law*, 17 HASTINGS L.J. 727, 736 (1966).

39. The Civil Code art. 1045 para. 1.

40. *Id.* art. 1045 para. 2.

41. *Id.* art. 1045 para. 3.

42. *Id.* arts. 1067, 1072, 1074, 1075.

extended family, however, remains quite prevalent in rural China. To ensure that the wife's natal family enjoys a status equal to the husband's, the Marriage Law of 1980 expressly provided that a husband may join his wife's natal household, a wife may join her husband's natal household, or the husband and wife may establish their own household, whichever both parties may agree to. The provision is kept in the Civil Code.[43]

5.3.2 Household

Every Chinese national is assigned to a household. To a certain extent, a Chinese person lacks the true individualistic status as an individual, especially in rural China, because every person's status is always defined by his/her membership in a household and his/her relationship with the members of the household.

Members of agricultural villager-groups are not treated as individual farmers, instead collectively as farming households (*nongcun chengbao jinying hu*). Agricultural lands are collectively owned by villages composed of households living within the village boundary. Each household in a village receives allotted agricultural land (*chengbao di*) on a per capita basis under a 30-year contract with the village.[44] Agricultural land allotment contracts are contracts between villages and their member farming households, not individual members of the households. Therefore, the birth of a child or the death of a family member or the addition of a new daughter-in-law usually does not affect the household's land allotment or any entitlements derived from it. Land reallocation takes place only when member households of a village collectively decide that a redistribution is necessary.[45]

A household registration (*hukou*) is assigned to every Chinese person. Upon birth, a person becomes a member of the household to which their parents belong and is registered to the household under the so-called household registration system (*hukou zhidu*). After a person reaches majority, he/she becomes a member of a household of the collective (*jiti hu*), usually a college, workplace, or the military, if they leave their birth household for education or employment or military service. Alternatively, they may remain in their birth household. When a person marries, he/she may remain in his/her birth household, or join his/her spouse's household, or start a new household. When a person moves, his/her household registration is changed to the place where he/she moves to.

---

43. *Id.* art. 1050.
44. *Id.* art. 55.
45. Sherry Tao Kong & Jonathan Unger, *Egalitarian Redistributions of Agricultural Land in China through Community Consensus: Findings from Two Surveys*, 69 China J., 1–19 (Jan. 2013).

China's household registration system is a regulatory scheme for population and migration control. An ancient system native to China, the household registration system has been a useful tool for policing, taxation, and economic planning for many centuries. A major function of the contemporary household registration system is to differentiate Chinese population into two categories: rural (*nongcun*) and urban (*chengshi*). A rural household registration (*nongcun hukou*) guarantees land rights and entitlements to resources collectively owned by the village that a person's household belongs to. An urban household registration (*chengshi hukou*) guarantees a person's eligibility to social benefits provided by the city where a person's household registration is at, such as access to the city's public schools and health care systems, and generously subsidized housing.[46]

China's household registration system is relevant to family law practice in at least three aspects. First, a person's household registration serves as prima facie evidence of a person's age, gender, marital status, and family relationships. Second, a person's household registration location (*hukou suozaidi*) is his/her legal residence and thus determines the territorial jurisdiction of marriage, divorce, adoption, guardianship, and succession. Third, a person's household registration is closely correlated to their social benefits entitlements, including urban housing entitlements and rural land entitlements, which may have considerable market value in China's rapidly growing economy.

---

46. Jesper W. Zeuthen & Michael B. Griffiths, *The End of Urban-Rural Differentiation in China? Hukou and Resettlement in Chengdu's Urban-Rural Integration*, *in* POLITICS AND MARKETS IN RURAL CHINA 220 (Bjö Alpermann ed., 2011).

Chapter 6

Marriage: Husband and Wife

Marriage is central to Chinese family life and Chinese family law. Marriage of a heterosexual couple—a husband and wife—forms the nexus of a Chinese family. It defines the rights and obligations within a Chinese family, and the family's social and economic status.

§ 6.1 Defining Marriage

Chinese law does not define "marriage" in any definitive terms. There is not a definition for "marriage" in the newly minted Civil Code. Most Chinese legal scholars accept "marriage" as "a legal union of a man and a woman entered for the purpose of a permanent joint life and defined by spousal rights and duties."[1] Nevertheless, the Civil Code sets the unequivocal tenets of marriage: "*hunyin ziyou*," a marriage must be a free choice; "*yifu yiqi*," a marriage is between one husband and one wife, in other words monogamous and heterosexual; and "*nannü pingdeng*," the male and female are equal in a marriage.[2] Thus, marriage could be defined as a consensual, monogamous union of two equal partners of opposite-sex under Chinese law.

Marriage is a state-sanctioned institution under Chinese law. A marriage begins upon the completion of marriage registration,[3] and ends when a divorce registration, divorce judgment, or mediated divorce decree that

---

1. *See, e.g.*, Cao Shiquan (曹诗权, Etc.), Hunyin Jiating De Gainian (婚姻家庭的概念) [The Definitions of Marriage and Family]; Hunyin Jiating Jicheng Fa (婚姻家庭继承法) [Marital-Family and Succession Law] (2006); Xia Yinlan & Xue Ninglan (夏吟兰; 薛宁兰), Hefaxing Wei Hunyin Benzhi Zhi Bian (合法性为婚姻本质之辩) [An Argument for Legality as Marriage's Intrinsic Nature]; Minfa Dian Zhi Hunyin Jiating Bian Lifa Yanjiu (民法典之婚姻家庭编立法研究) [The Civil Code's Marriage and Family Book Legislative Studies] (2016).
2. The Civil Code art. 1041 para. 2.
3. *Id.* art. 1049.

dissolves the marriage takes effect.[4] State approval through marriage registration (*hunyin dengji*) is required to establish a marriage. Marital life is under state regulation. Sex outside of marriage, although widespread, is considered disreputable by society and is punished as unlawful when it involves married persons.[5] As equal partners, spouses' reciprocal rights and duties are defined, protected, and enforced by the state, albeit a limited role is played by custom, tradition, and informal institutions. A marriage ends when the state grants its dissolution.

§ 6.2 Entering a Marriage

Under Chinese law, there are three requirements for entering a marriage: (1) the marriage is entered voluntarily with both parties' consent,[6] (2) both parties to the marriage are eligible to marry;[7] and (3) the marriage must be registered with a marriage registration authority, namely, a local Civil Affairs Bureau, according to the law.[8]

6.2.1 Consent

Marriage must be consensual. The husband and wife must enter the marriage at their freewill. Neither party can be forced to marry under duress or coercion.[9] Marriage entered under coercion or duress is voidable. A person who has concluded a marriage under duress or coercion may apply to the court for its annulment. For discussions of voidable marriage, see subsection 7.3.2.

6.2.2 Eligibility to Marriage

There are four criteria for marriageability. The bride and groom must be unmarried, from opposite sexes,[10] of marriageable age,[11] and not lineally or collaterally related by blood within the third degree of kinship.[12] A marriage is void if either party is not eligible to marry because of bigamy, consanguinity, incurable illness, or nonage.[13] For discussions of void marriage, see subsection 7.3.1.

4. *Id.* art. 1080.
5. *Id.* art. 1042 para. 2.
6. *Id.* art. 1046.
7. *Id.* arts. 1046–1048.
8. *Id.* art. 1049.
9. *Id.* art. 1046.
10. *Id.*
11. *Id.* art. 1047.
12. *Id.* art. 1048.
13. *Id.* art. 1051.

6.2.2.1 No Prior Spouse Living

China limits marriage to heterosexual couples, *"yifu yiqi"* (one husband, one wife).[14] Bigamy is a crime, which is actually prosecuted and punished. Prospective spouses must be unmarried at the time of entering a new marriage. If a party has a prior spouse that is living, that prior marriage needs to be dissolved before a new marriage can be entered.

The marriage of a person who is declared dead terminates upon the date of the declaration of death. If a person remarries after their prior spouse has been declared dead, their marriage to the prior spouse who has been declared dead may not be resumed in the event that the prior spouse reappears.[15] However, termination of a marriage upon a declaration of death does not give a person who is declared dead the license to remarry another person. In other words, if an absent person who is declared dead remarries another person without dissolving their prior marriage, his/her subsequent marriage would be bigamous and void.[16]

6.2.2.2 Gender

Under Chinese law, marriage is between a man and woman.[17] Therefore, parties to a marriage must be of opposite sex. Same-sex couples cannot legally get married in China. However, foreign same-sex marriages entered in jurisdictions that have legalized same-sex marriages could potentially be recognized under Chinese law, depending on the spouses' country of habitual residence and nationality. Pursuant to the Law on Applicable Laws, the validity of a marriage is determined by the law of the country of the spouses' common habitual residence or common nationality, or by the law in the country where the marriage is celebrated if the spouses do not have a common habitual residence or a common nationality.[18] Thus, when either spouse is a foreign national or has habitual residence outside of China, a same-sex marriage might be recognized in China if the place of marriage has legalized same-sex marriage, provided that recognition of such foreign same-sex marriage is not contrary to China's public policy.[19] On the other hand, if both spouses in a same-sex marriage are Chinese nationals or habitually reside in China, their marriage will not be recognized as legally valid under Chinese law

14. *Id.* art. 1046.
15. *Id.* art. 51.
16. Di Yuanjian (翟远见), Lun Xuangao Siwang Ji Qi Chexiao Zi Hunyin Shang De Xiaoli (论宣告死亡及其撤销在婚姻上的效力) [*On the Effects of Declaration of Death and Its Revocation on the Validity of Marriage*] Zhongguo Faxue (中国法学) [China Legal Sci.] Issue 2, 42–60, 49–50 (2021).
17. The Civil Code arts. 1041, 1046, and the Regulation on Marriage Registration art. 1.
18. Law on Applicable Laws art. 21.
19. *Id.* art. 5.

because the validity of their marriage is dictated by Chinese law. China has yet to develop a coherent body of law on the recognition of foreign same-sex marriages.[20]

Transgender people may legally marry a person of opposite sex under Chinese law.[21] Chinese citizens have the right to choose their gender identity. A person may change his or her gender recorded in the household registration after having medical gender reassignment procedures in medical facilities authorized and regulated by local governments.[22] In 2004, Zhang Lin and her husband registered the first legal marriage between a transgender woman and a man in Chengdu. After Zhang underwent gender reassignment procedures, her gender classification was changed from "male" to "female" in her household registration, and she was issued a new national identification card (*shenfen zheng*) that identified her as a "female." With the new identification documents, Zhang and her husband registered their marriage.[23] In 2002, the SPC had suggested that a spouse's gender reassignment should not affect the validity of an existing, valid marriage if the marriage was initially entered by two persons of opposite sex and was entered in compliance with the laws and

20. Zhang Bijiang (张碧江), Shilun Shewai Tongxin Hunyin De Falü Shiyong (试论涉外同性婚姻的法律适用) [*Preliminary Discussions on Applicable Law of Foreign Same-Sex Marriages*] Lanzhou Jiaoyu Xueyuan Yuanbao (兰州教育学院学报) [J. LANZHOU INST. OF EDUC.] ,Vol. 32, No. 3, 105–52 (Mar. 2016); and Yang Fan (杨帆), Lun Shewai Tongxin Hunyin De Falü Shiyong Wenti (论涉外同性婚姻的法律适用问题) [*On the Issues Concerning Applicable Law of Foreign Same-Sex Marriages*] Fazhi Yu Shehui (法制与社会) [LEGAL SYS. & SOC'Y] 2016 Issue 8 Vol. 2, 173–74.

21. Wong Li & Wan Xiao (翁里, 万晓), Bianxing Ren De Xinbie Biangengquan Ji Qi Hunyin Jiating Falü Wenti Yanjiu (变性人的性别变更权及其婚姻家庭法律问题研究) [*A Study on Transgender People's Right to Sex Change and Related Marriage and Family Law Issues*], Ningxia Daxue Xuebao Sheke Ban (宁夏大学学报社科版) [J. NINGXIA UNIV. (Humanities & Social Sciences Ed.)], Vol. 38, No. 1 (Jan. 2016), 105. For a review of China's policy on transgender people's rights to gender identity and marriage, *see* Wu Guopin (吴国平), Bianxing Ren Hunhou Bianxinquan Ji Qi Hunyin Jiating Guanxi Wenti Tanxi (变性人婚后变性权及其婚姻家庭关系问题探析) [*On Transgender's Right of Gender Transition after Marriage and the Relationship in Marriage and Family*], Xinan Zhengfa Daxue Xuebao (西南政法大学学报) [J. SW. UNIV. OF POL. SCI. & L.] Vol. 13, No. 3, 59–68 (June 2011).

22. Gong'an Bu Guanyu Gongmin Shishi Bianxing Shoushu Hou Biangeng Hukou Dengji Xingbie Xiangmu Youguan Wenti De Pifu (公安部关于公民实施变性手术后变更户口登记性别项目有关问题的批复) [THE MINISTRY OF PUBLIC SAFETY RESPONSE TO ISSUES CONCERNING CHANGE OF GENDER CLASSIFICATION AFTER CITIZENS UNDERGOING SEX-CHANGE OPERATIONS] (Gongzhi (公治) (2002) No. 131); *see also* Weisheng Bu Baigong Ting Bianxing Shoushu Jishu Guanli Guifan (Shixin) 2009 Nian 11 Yue 13 Ri (卫生部办公厅变性手术技术管理规范(试行) 2009年11月13日) [The Ministry of Health Executive Office Sex-Change Surgical Technique Management Regulation (Interim) Nov. 13, 2009].

23. Quanguo Shouli Bianxing Ren Hunli Wuyi Juxin (全国首例变性人婚礼五一举行) [The Nation's First Transgender Person's Wedding Took Place on May 1], China Courts, https://www.chinacourt.org/article/detail/2004/03/id/108659.shtml.

regulations of marriage.[24] However, the SPC has not provided any further guidance on whether a spouse's gender reassignment during the marriage affects the validity of an existing marriage.[25]

6.2.2.3 Age

A man must be at least 22 years old, and a woman must be at least 20 years old to be eligible to marry.[26] Marriages entered by any persons under the marriageable age are void. See discussions of void marriage due to nonage in subsection 7.3.1.2.

6.2.2.4 Consanguinity

Marriage is prohibited between a man and a woman who are lineal relatives by blood or collateral relatives by blood up to the third degree of kinship.[27] Marriages prohibited between blood relatives are void as well. See discussions of void marriage due to consanguinity in subsection 7.3.1.3.

6.2.3 Marriage Registration

The Civil Code requires that every marriage must be registered with a marriage registration authority (*hunying dengji jiguan*), namely, a local Civil Affairs Bureau (*minzheng jü*). Completion of marriage registration marks the establishment of a marital relationship. Marriage registration is a simple and straightforward process.

6.2.3.1 Marriage Registration Procedure

Prospective spouses must appear in person at the marriage registration authority to apply for marriage registration.[28] Marriage by proxy is not permitted.

Chinese nationals and their foreign spouses may register their marriages at the marriage registration authority with proper jurisdiction, which is usually where the Chinese spouse's household registration is located.[29] Foreign

---

24. Zuigao Renmin Fayuan Guanyu Hunyin Dangshiren Yifang Bianxing Hou Ruhe Jiechu Hunyin Guanxi Wenti De Dafu (Minban Han [2002] 127 Hao) (最高人民法院关于婚姻当事人一方变性后如何解除婚姻关系问题的答复(民办函[2002]127号)) [The Supreme People's Court's Response Regarding Issues Concerning How to Dissolve a Marriage after the Sex-Change of One Party to the Marriage], *see also* Guopin, *supra* note 3, at 63–64; *see also* Wong Li & Wan Xiao, *supra* note 21, at 106.

25. Wong Li & Wan Xiao, *supra* note 21, at 106.

26. The Civil Code art. 1047.

27. *Id*. art. 1048.

28. *Id*. art. 1049.

29. The Regulations on Marriage Registration art. 4 para. 2.

nationals must provide copies of passports, an affidavit of marriageability, and proof of termination of previous marriage.[30] Chinese authorities no longer register marriages between foreign nationals.[31]

The marriage registration authority must ascertain the parties' identities, consent to marry, and marriageability. The parties must provide required information to prove their eligibilities to marry, such as personal identification, proof of termination of previous marriages, and proof of no consanguinity.[32] If the couple meets the eligibility to marry, the marriage registration authority will register the marriage and issue a marriage certificate to each spouse. Issuance of the marriage certificates marks the beginning of a legally recognized marital relationship.[33]

6.2.3.2 Defective Marriage Registrations

A spouse may seek revocation of marriage registration for procedural defects in the marriage registration through administrative review or administrative litigation.[34] Marriage registration defects (*hunyin dengji xiaci*) refer to errors incurred during the process of marriage registration. Some marriage registration defects, such as typographical errors in marriage certificates, are minor. Some defects, such as registering the marriage under false identity or using falsified documents, are material. Some marriage registration defects are substantive. Some marriage registration defects are procedural, such as registration at a wrong location. Chinese law does not have any clear rules as to what defects would warrant revocation of a marriage registration.

A marriage can only be declared void or be voided on statutory grounds.[35] When a marriage registration authority revokes a marriage registration, a marriage is effectively "canceled" or "voided." The policy allowing revocation of marriage registrations was intended to push marriage registration authorities to scrutinize parties' marriageability. However, the policy has essentially

---

30. *Id.* art. 5, and the Marriage Registration Protocols art. 35.

31. Minzheng Bumen Guifanxin Wenjian Sheding De Zhenming Shixiang Quxiao Mulu Fujian 2 (Minzheng Bu Gongao Di 456 Hao) (民政部部门规范性文件设定的证明事项取消目录 附件2 (民政部公告第456号)) [Catalog of Cancellation of Certification Matters Set Forth in Ministry of Civil Affairs Departmental Regulatory Documents (Ministry of Civil Affairs Publication No. 456)], Appendix II, Item 2. http://www.mca.gov.cn/article/xw/tzgg/201903/20190300016006.shtml.

32. The Regulations on Marriage Registration art. 5 and the Marriage Registration Protocols art. 28.

33. The Civil Code art. 1049.

34. The Marriage and Family Book Interpretations (I) art. 17 para. 2.

35. The Civil Code arts. 1051, 1052, 1053, and the Marriage and Family Book Interpretations (I) art. 17 para. 1.

expanded grounds for marriage annulment without statutory basis.[36] In an advisory to the Ministry of Civil Affairs, the SPC suggested that marriage registration defects, even if the defect is material, should not affect the validity of marriage.[37]

Without clear statutory rules on defective marriage registrations, Chinese courts' decisions, including the SPC's, in revocation of defective marriage registration cases are hardly consistent. For example, some Chinese courts ordered revocation of marriage registrations due to a spouse's concealment of their foreign country citizenship and some courts declined to do so, citing statute of limitation or immateriality of the defect. In the matter of Ji Lili and James Jing Zhang, the Anhui courts ordered revocation of the parties' marriage registration, in that James, a naturalized Dutch citizen of Chinese origin, did not provide any documentation that he was unmarried, and used his old Chinese passport to register the marriage with Lili in a local Civil Affairs Bureau, which did not have the authority to register marriages involving foreign nationals. In 2015, James and Lili registered their marriage in Anhui Province after James obtained Dutch citizenship. James used his Chinese passport to register the marriage. In 2018, James sued Lili for divorce in a Hangzhou court. In the divorce action, the Hangzhou court found that the parties' marriage registration was defective because James concealed his foreign nationality from the marriage registration authority. The Hangzhou court dismissed the divorce action and ordered the parties to seek determination of validity of their marriage registration in a court in Anhui, where the marriage was registered. Soon after the Hangzhou court's order, James brought an action in Anhui in 2019. The Anhui courts then ordered revocation of the marriage registration, finding that the local Civil Affairs Bureau registered the parties' marriage without authority and failed to ascertain James's status as an unmarried person. The SPC affirmed the Anhui courts' decision that the parties' marriage registration should be revoked because it was issued without authority by a local Civil Affairs Bureau that did not have the authority to register marriages involving foreign nationals, and the Civil Affairs Bureau

---

36. Sun Ruojun (孙若军), Xiaci Jiehun Dengji Chuli Fangshi De Tixihua Sikao (瑕疵结婚登记处理方式的体系化思考) [*The Systematic Thinking of Handling Mode to the Defective Marriage Registration*] Zhonghua Nuzi Xueyuan Yuanbao (中华女子学院学报) [J. China Women's Univ.] Dec. 2014, 5–12, 5–6; *see also* Ran Keping & Zeng Jia (冉克平, 曾佳), Minfadian Shiye Xia Hunyin Dengji Xiaci De Kunjing Ji Qi Lujin Xuanze (民法典视野下婚姻登记瑕疵的困境及其路径选择) [*On the Dilemma of Marriage Registration Defects and Its Path Selection*], Hebei Faxue (河北法学) [Hebei Law Sci.] Vol. 38, No. 10 (Oct. 2020), 47–58, 53.

37. Wang Liren (王礼仁), "Hunyin Dengji Xiaci" Zhong De Hunyin Chengli Yu Bu Chengli ("婚姻登记瑕疵"中的婚姻成立与不成立) [Is a Marriage with "Marriage Registration Defects" Valid or Invalid], Renmin Sifa (人民司法) [the People's Judicature] Issue 11, 2010, 30–36, 32, and 33, citing the SPC's advisory letter to the Civil Affairs Ministry (Fayan (法研) [2002] 81).

failed to check James's marriageability.[38] The SPC's affirmation in the Matter of Ji Lili and James Zhang obviously contradicts its previous stance that procedural defects in marriage registration do not warrant revocation of a marriage registration.

Unlike the Anhui courts in the Matter of Ji Lili and James Zhang, not many Chinese courts are willing to hold the marriage registration authority responsible beyond the examination of the formality of the documentation presented by marriage registration applicants, as a marriage registration authority's inspection of the parties' identity and marriageability is not an examination of substance (*shizhi jiancha*) but a limited examination of formality (*xingshi jiancha*). Thus, the Shanghai court in the Matter of Chen opined that the Civil Affairs Bureau is not responsible for the defects in the marriage registration as there was no way for the Bureau to know that the wife had become a Canadian citizen by examining the documentation provided by the parties without any substantive inquiries; and the Bureau should not be required to go beyond examination of formality as it is not authorized to make any substantive inquiries. In addition, the judges indicated that the wife's nationality alone was immaterial to the validity of the parties' marriage registration or the marriage itself.[39]

The statute of limitation in actions against administrative agencies is six months from the date of the notice of an administrative act,[40] or one year from the discovery of the cause of action to contest an administrative act.[41] Consequently, many litigants, who discovered defects in their marriage registrations

---

38. (2019) Wan Xing Zhong 789 Hao ((2019) 皖行终789号); and (2020) Zui Gao Xing Shen 11360 Hao ((2020) 最高法行申11360号).

39. Xu Fangfang & Zhou Shen (徐芳芳, 周圣), Jiaru Waiji Wei Zhuxiao Guonei Huji Neidi Jumin Hunyin Dengji Xingwei De Xiaoli (加入外籍未注销国内户籍内地居民婚姻登记行为的效力) [*The Effects of Marriage Registrations of Mainland Residents Who Have Acquired Foreign Nationality and Not Yet Cancelled Their Mainland Household Registration*] Renmin Sifa (人民司法) [THE PEOPLE'S JUDICATURE] 16.2015, 81–85.

40. Zhonghua Renmin Gonghe Guo Xinzheng Susong Fa (中华人民共和国行政诉讼法) [The People's Republic of China Administrative Procedure Law] (promulgated Apr. 4, 1989, amended Nov. 1, 2014, and amended June 27, 2017) [hereinafter the "Administrative Procedure Law"] art. 46.

41. Zuigao Renmin Fayuan Guanyu Shiyong Zhonghua Renmin Gonghe Guo Mingzheng Susong Fa De Jieshi (最高人民法院关于使用中华人民共和国行政诉讼法的解释) [the Supreme People's Court's Interpretations on the Civil Procedure Law of the People's Republic of China] (promulgated by the Sup. People's Ct., Nov. 13, 2017, effective Feb. 8, 2018) 2018 Sup. People's Ct. Gaz. 4 [hereinafter the "Administrative Procedure Law Interpretations"] art. 64. The SPC's previous Judicial Interpretations on the Administrative Procedure Law, issued in 2000, provided a two-year statute of limitation from the discovery of a cause of action, and a five-year statute of limitation from the discovery or notice of an administrative act. The SPC Judicial Interpretations on the Administrative Procedure Law ([2000] No. 8, eff. Mar. 10, 2000) arts. 41, 42.

years after the registration, are barred from seeking revocation of a marriage registration.[42] Chinese courts differ in whether the statute of limitation starts to run. For example, the Beijing High People's Court also held that the one-year statute of limitation applies in cases where defects in a marriage registration have been discovered after the marriage registration has been issued. Thus, the court dismissed a daughter's action to revoke her late father's marriage registration brought 14 months after the daughter discovered the alleged defects.[43] Some Chinese courts, however, held the statute of limitation to revoke a defective marriage registration should start from the date of registration. For example, in *Mahoney v. Song*, the Guangdong courts held that the statute of limitation for actions concerning defective marriage registrations started to run from May 12, 2000, which was the date of the marriage registration, and not from September 2017, when the husband discovered the defect in the marriage registration. In the *Mahoney* case, the husband discovered that the marriage registration was defective in September 2017 and brought the action to revoke the marriage registration in October 2017.[44] Similarly, the Qinghai High People's Court held that the statute of limitation to revoke a marriage registration starts to run from the date of the registration and not from the discovery of any defects in the registration.[45]

6.2.4 *De Facto* Marriage

Under Chinese law, marriage is a state-sanctioned status, independent of religion or custom. A traditional, or customary, or religious wedding ceremony does not confer a legal marital status. Nor does long-term cohabitation. A legally binding marriage requires the state's approval obtained through the marriage registration process. However, the marriage registration requirement is often ignored, particularly in rural China where tradition and custom, instead of formal laws, define marriage and family relations. Some peasants are unaware that a marriage is not official until it is formally registered in the civil registry. More often, the registration requirement is simply ignored, as young couples are customarily married at the age of 18 or 19, before they have

---

42. Ran Keping & Zeng Jia (冉克平, 曾佳), Minfadian Shiye Xiao Hunyin Dengji Xiabi De Kunjing Ji Qi Lujin Xuanze (民法典视野下婚姻登记瑕疵的困境及其路径选择) [*On the Dilemma of Marriage Registration Defects and Its Path Selection*], Hebei Faxue (河北法学) [Hebei Law Sci.] Vol. 38, No. 10 (Oct. 2020), 47–58, 54.

43. (2020) Jin Xing Shen 867 Hao ((2020) 京行申867号); *see also* (2019) Jin 03 Xing Zhong 1223 Hao ((2019) 京03行终1223号).

44. (2018) Yue Xing Zhong 1504 Hao ((2018) 粤行终1504号) and (2017) Yue 09 Xing Chu 150 Hao ((2017) 粤09行初150号).

45. (2020) Qing Xing Shen 22 Hao ((2020) 青行申22号).

reached the legal age required for marriage.[46] As a result, *de facto* marriages (*shishi hunyin*) that are not formally registered with the marriage registration authority remain common in rural China.[47]

6.2.4.1 *De Facto* Marriages before and after February 1, 1994

De facto marriages entered prior to February 1, 1994, are recognized as legal marriages.[48] *De facto* marriages entered after February 1, 1994, may be registered retroactively, and if the parties fail to register their *de facto* marriage retroactively, then their relationship must be treated as nonmarital cohabitation.[49] A *de facto* marriage is defined as a marriage in which the spouses have openly cohabitated as husband and wife and have been accepted as husband and wife by the members of their community. The essential elements of a *de facto* marriage are (1) the parties were both single and eligible to marry at the time of the marriage; (2) the parties have cohabitated as husband and wife; (3) the parties have established a reputation as husband and wife in their community.[50] For example, in *Chen v. Chen*, the court found that the date of the couple's marriage was retroactive to 1991 for three reasons: (1) the parties were eligible to marry in 1991 when they started living together; (2) they lived together as husband and wife since 1991, including having two children and moving the wife's household registration to the husband's household; and (3) they registered the marriage retroactively.[51]

6.2.4.2 Retroactive Registration

Couples in *de facto* marriages may register their marriages retroactively.[52] The effect of the registration starts retroactively from the date when the parties' marriage would have met substantive requirements for a legal marriage.[53] For example, if a couple has entered a *de facto* marriage before reaching the

46. Wang Lixiang (王理想), Dangqian Nongcun Hunyin Wenti Yanjiu (当前农村婚姻问题研究) [*A Study on Contemporary Rural Marriage Issues*], Fazhi Bolan (法制博览) [Legality Vision] 2021(02), 67–69, 67.

47. "Yong Gongkai Cu Gongzheng Jianshe Hexin Jiazhi" Zhuti Jiaoyu Huodong Hunyin Jiating Jiufen Dianxin Anli ("用公开促公正 建设核心价值" 主题教育活动 婚姻家庭纠纷典型案例) ["Promote Justice Construct Core Value through Transparenc"" Focused Education Campaign: Family and Marriage Disputes Typical Cases] (Dec. 4, 2015) [hereinafter "FMTC"], 44. Jin Mei (金眉), Lun Woguo Shishi Hunyin Zhidu Zhi Wanshan (论我国事实婚姻制度之完善) [*Discussions on Refining Our Country's De Facto Marriage Regulations*] Nanjing Shehui Kexue (南京社会科学) [Nanjing J. Soc. Sci.] 2017 Issue 10, 81–83.

48. The Marriage and Family Book Interpretations (I) art. 7(1).

49. Id. art. 7(2).

50. Jin, *supra* note 47, at 81–83.

51. (2020) Zhe 07 Min Zhong 4361 Hao ((2020) 浙07民终4361号).

52. The Civil Code art. 1049.

53. The Marriage and Family Book Interpretations (I) art. 6.

marriageable age, the date of their valid marriage would be the date when both parties reached the minimum marriage age. Date of marriage is crucial in determining spouses' rights and duties. Allowing couples to register their marriage retroactively would undoubtedly benefit them as a family unit and benefit the partner who had made substantial nonmonetary contribution to the relationship.

In disputes over the date of a marriage, Chinese courts often use the marriage registration records as *prima facie* evidence of the parties' intention and relationship.[54] For example, in a collection action brought by Cai against a married couple Hong and Wu, Hong and Wu claimed that they were married in 2006, and thus a home in Wu's name acquired in 2004 was Wu's separate property not subject to Cai's collection of Hong's debt. Cai provided the court with the retroactive marriage registration forms that Wu and Hong submitted to register their *de facto* marriage retroactively from 1996. Based on the marriage registration records, the court found Hong and Wu were married in a de facto marriage since 1996 and thus Hong had 50 percent share in the home acquired in 2004.[55]

After a period of cohabitation, couples may register their marriage as a new marriage or register the marriage retroactively from the date of their *de facto* marriage. If the marriage is registered as a new marriage, the date of the marriage is the date of registration; and if the marriage is registered as a *de facto* marriage, retroactively, the date of the marriage is usually an earlier date when they started living together as declared in their declarations submitted in connection with the retroactive marriage registration. The registration form for a new marriage is a Marriage Registration Application Declaration (*shenqing jiehun dengji shengming shu*) (Appendix I, available online), and the form for retractive registration of a *de facto* marriage is Retroactive Marriage Registration Application Declaration (*buban jiehun dengji shengming shu*) (Appendix II, available online). Most laypersons are not aware that there are two different forms with different legal implications. Choosing the right form has significant legal consequences, as illustrated in the case of Li Jianguang and Zhang Lu. Li and Zhang started living together in 1998 and had a son in 1999 while Zhang was married to another man and Li was married to another woman. In 2000, Zhang divorced her ex-husband. In 2002, Li divorced his ex-wife. In 2005, Zhang and Li registered their marriage and submitted the Marriage Registration Application Declaration forms used for registering new marriages. In 2013, Li and Zhang separated. In 2015, Zhang filed for divorce. During their relationship from 1998 to 2015, the couple amassed a significant

54. Pu Yi (蒲毅), Buban Jiehun Dengji De Shiwu Rending (补办结婚登记的实务认定) [*Retroactive Marriage Registration Practice and Verification*] Fazhi Bolan (法制博览) [Legality Vision] 2021 Issue 2, Vol. 1, 70–71.

55. (2019) Lu 01 Min Zhong 4102 Hao ((2019) 鲁01民终4102号).

amount of wealth. In the divorce action, Zhang and Li disputed the date of their marriage. Zhang argued that their 2005 marriage registration was intended to and should be retroactive from the 2002; and that the date of their marriage was the date when Li's divorce in 2002, as that was the date when both parties became eligible to marry and therefore was the date of their *de facto* marriage. Li argued that the parties' date of marriage was in 2005, when the marriage was registered, as the parties neither intended to nor applied for a retroactive marriage registration. The Inner Mongolian High People's Court agreed with Li and affirmed the lower court's decision that the date of Li and Zhang's marriage was in 2005 and the seven luxury homes purchased in Li's name in Beijing and Inner Mongolia before the date of the parties' marriage registration were Li's premarital assets.[56]

The requirement of retroactive registration of a *de facto* marriage is intended to give couples in *de facto* marriages the opportunity to cure the formality defect of their marriage and legitimize the marriage. However, the requirement has also created some legal quandaries. For example, retroactive registration is not possible if one spouse is deceased. A surviving spouse in a *de facto* marriage entered after February 1, 1994, has no inheritance rights if their partner dies intestate before the marriage is registered.[57] This is an extremely unfair situation in decades-long *de facto* marriages.

6.2.4.3 *De Facto* Marriage and Bigamy

The PRC Criminal Code defines bigamy as an offense when a married person knowingly marries a person or cohabits with a person openly as husband and wife.[58] Thus, a person could be guilty of bigamy even though one of their marriages is not a legal marriage but a de facto marriage that has not been legally registered.[59]

The most common case of bigamy is when a person has entered a subsequent *de facto* marriage or bigamous cohabitation before the person's prior legal marriage is dissolved. The *Zhou Jiangchun* case is a typical bigamy case based on a legal marriage and a subsequent de facto marriage. Zhou Jiangchun married Hong Baoying in 1989. While married to Hong Baoying, Zhou started living with Huang Shumei openly as husband and wife in 2007. In 2014, Hong Baoying filed a criminal complaint against Zhou Jiangchun for bigamy. Zhou Jiangchun was found guilty and sentenced to one year and six months imprisonment. Zhou Jiangchun appealed. The SPC denied his appeal

56. (2015) Nei Min Kang Yi Zi Di 00025 Hao ((2015) 内民抗一字第00025号).
57. The Marriage and Family Book Interpretations (I) art. 8.
58. The Criminal Law art. 258.
59. Zhang Yawei (张雅维), Xing Min Falü Chongtu Shijiao Xiao De Chonghun Zui Rending (刑民法律冲突视角下的重婚罪认定) [*Determining the Crime of Bigamy from the Perspective of Criminal and Civil Law Conflicts*], 山东社会科学 2020, (06), 188–92.

and found that Zhou was guilty of bigamy as he cohabitated with another woman openly as husband and wife for years while he was still married to his first wife, and that the length of Zhou's sentence was appropriate because Zhou's action is a severe violation of the monogamous marriage system.[60]

Chinese courts have jurisdiction over foreign nationals who are married to another person and cohabitate with their Chinese partners in China for more than a year, as the bigamous act occurred within China's territory.[61] For instance, a Japanese man and his Chinese partner were both found guilty of bigamy by the Shanghai court. The Japanese man lived with his Chinese partner openly as husband and wife and had a child together before the man could divorce his wife in Japan. Unable to get his wife to consent to a divorce, the Japanese man forged his wife's signature and obtained a divorce. He then married his Chinese partner in China. The man's Japanese wife found out about the divorce obtained by fraud. She had the divorce invalidated in Japan and then brought criminal charges against her husband and his Chinese partner in Shanghai. The Shanghai court found that the Japanese man and his Chinese partner knowingly and openly lived together as husband and wife while the man was married to another woman and were therefore found guilty of bigamy.[62]

A person who entered a *de facto* marriage and subsequently entered a registered marriage could also be guilty of bigamy if the first *de facto* marriage was not terminated when the subsequent marriage was registered.[63] In 2017, the SPC upheld Dou Weijun's 1987 bigamy conviction after Dou's 30-year-long appeals. Dou was a schoolteacher. He had a relationship with Song from 1977 to 1986. In 1977, Dou and Song tried to register their marriage on their "honeymoon" but failed due to a lack of certain documents. Dou and Song made marriage announcements and lived as husband and wife during Dou's visits to Song. Dou and Song had a son. During their relationship, Dou and Song lived apart in two different provinces. Dou visited Song and their son on Chinese New Year holidays and school summer vacations from 1977 to 1986. Nevertheless, Dou and Song never obtained a marriage registration. On May 24, 1984, Dou married his colleague, Li, who was also a schoolteacher. Song filed a criminal complaint for bigamy against Dou in 1986. Dou was found guilty and was incarcerated. Dou fought his conviction for 30 years. In 2017, the SPC upheld Dou's bigamy conviction, finding that Dou married Li in 1984

60. (2018) Zui Gao Fa Xing Shen 109 Hao ((2018) 最高法刑申109号).

61. Zhang Huasong (张华松) Shewai Chonghun Fanzui De Guanxia Ji Yuwai Zhengju De Shenhe Yu Caixin (涉外重婚犯罪的管辖及域外证据的审核与采信) [*Determination of Jurisdiction and Examination and Admission of Foreign Evidence of Foreign-Related Bigamy*] Renmin Sifa (人民司法) [The People's Judicature] 06/2011, 56–57.

62. *See id.*; (2010) Hu Yi Zhong Xin Chu Zi Di 135 Hao ((2010) 沪一中刑初字第135 号).

63. (2020) Chuan Xin Zai 2 Hao ((2020) 川刑再2号).

when Dou was still married to Song in a *de facto* marriage that was recognized by law as a valid marriage in 1984, and therefore his bigamy conviction was correct.[64] Dou and his wife, Li were both fired soon after Dou's conviction and could not obtain any employment thereafter. As a result, Dou, Li, and their son have suffered extreme poverty.[65]

§ 6.3 Marital Rights and Duties

The Civil Code provides two types of marital rights and duties: personal rights and duties and property rights and duties. In general, couples are free to define their property rights and duties by written agreements, whereas personal obligations between spouses, such as obligations of mutual respect, fidelity, and support, may not be altered by contracts.

6.3.1 Duty of Fidelity and Mutual Respect

The Civil Code provides that spouses must be faithful, and must respect and love each other.[66] The provision is not merely a proclamation of moral values. It imposes the duty of fidelity and mutual respect on spouses and provides the legal basis for legal remedies to infidelity, domestic abuse, and misappropriation of marital property. For discussions on divorce relief for infidelity, domestic abuse, and misappropriation of marital property, see § 8.7.

6.3.2 Equal Status

Chinese law emphasizes gender equality between a husband and wife, and all family members.[67] Spouses are equal life partners in carrying out the most fundamental functions of a family—raising children, caring for each other, and tending to the elderly. The husband and wife are also equal economic partners in generating income, creating family wealth, and making family financial decisions. Equal status of a husband and wife is the very foundation of community matrimonial property regime, which most Chinese couples choose as the mode of their family economy.

---

64. (2017) Zui Gao Fa Xin Shen 458 Hao ((2017) 最高法刑申458号).

65. Zoufang Weiwen Kunnan Jiating Guanai Minsheng Chuandi Wennuan (走访慰问困难家庭 关爱民生传递温暖) [Home Visit an Indigent Family, Care the People's Welfare Deliver Compassion], Henan Xinxi Gang (河南信息港) [Henan Information Online] (Aug. 1, 2018) (on file with the author).

66. The Civil Code art. 1043.

67. *Id.* art. 1055.

6.3.3 Right to One's Own Name

Both husband and wife are entitled to have their own names.[68] The "right to a name" is a natural person's right to decide, use, and change their own name and to permit or prohibit use of their name by another person or entity in a manner that is consistent with public order and good morals.[69] The right to a name is inherent to an individual's identity and legal status. Before the communist takeover, many Chinese women never had their own legal names. They were referred to by their fathers' family names before they were married and assumed their husbands' family names after they married into the husbands' families. The namelessness of Chinese women highlights in a dramatic way the gender inequality and cruelty in pre-PRC China.[70]

Chinese women's right to a name was first codified in the Marriage Law of 1950. The legal recognition of women's right to their own names was a milestone in Chinese women's fight for gender equality. Contemporary Chinese women are no longer nameless.

6.3.4 Right to Liberty of the Person

Married persons' right to liberty of the person is intended to liberate married women from a subservient status and protect their rights to participate in activities outside of home. It is widely accepted in Chinese society that women cannot attain and maintain equal status as men at home or in society if they are confined in the domestic sphere at home, and that gender equality can only be achieved by guaranteeing women's ability to work outside of the home to earn their own income and to participate in political and social activities. Consistent with this gender ideology, the Civil Code provides that both the husband and wife have the liberty of person to participate in production, work, study, and social activities outside of their home; and neither the husband nor the wife can restrict or interfere with the other party's lawful activities in the public sphere.[71]

6.3.5 Equal Parental Rights and Responsibilities

Parents have the equal rights and duties to care for, educate, and protect their minor children.[72] Parental rights and duties are shared equally between the

---

68. *Id.* art. 1056.
69. Id. art. 1021.
70. Rubie S. Watson, *The Named and the Nameless: Gender and Person in Chinese Society*, 13(4) Am. Ethnologist 619–31, 619 (Nov. 1986).
71. The Civil Code art. 1057.
72. *Id.* art. 26.

husband and wife.[73] The pointed proclamation of husband and wife's equal parental rights is to counter a common belief in rural China that children belong to their father's family and must remain in their father's natal household in the event of the parents' separation or divorce. For discussions of parental rights and obligations, see Chapters 9 and 10.

6.3.6 Spousal Support

A husband and a wife have the obligation to support each other financially. If a party fails to provide sufficient support for his/her spouse, the needy spouse may seek spousal support (*fuyang*) during the marriage.[74] Commenting on Typical Case *Huang v. Zhang*, the SPC stressed that spousal maintenance during the marriage was both a moral duty and a legal obligation. Huang and Zhang had been married since 1989 but lived separately for many years. Huang was in poor health and suffered depression. She had been on medical leave from work since 2009. Huang and her 90-year-old mother were living off Huang's meager rental income and disability payments from her employer. Zhang was not much better off than Huang, although his income was higher than Huang's. Zhang filed for divorce several times over the years. However, his divorce complaint was denied every time because Huang objected to the divorce vehemently. Instead of divorcing Zhang, Huang brought an action against Zhang for spousal support in 2014. Considering that Huang needed financial support, the court ordered Zhang to pay Huang a modest amount of monthly spousal maintenance based on the couple's respective financial resources and the couple's adult son's ability to support Huang.[75] Huang opposed the divorce probably because the marital spousal maintenance obligation generally terminates upon dissolution of the marriage. Under Chinese law, post-divorce spousal maintenance (*jinji bangzhu*) is very limited in terms of amount and duration and is only available to an indigent spouse.[76] Considering the financial consequence of the divorce, a non-moneyed spouse, usually the wife, often objects to a divorce not because she wants to stay in a bad marriage but because her standard of living could deteriorate greatly after a divorce, especially if the parties have few assets.[77] For discussions on post-divorce spousal support, see § 7.8.

---

73. *Id.* art. 1058.
74. *Id.* art. 1059.
75. FMTC 37.
76. The Civil Code art. 1090.
77. Jiang Yue & Zhuang Limei (蒋月，庄丽梅), Wo Guo Ying Jianli Lihun Hou Fuyangfei Geifu Zhidu (我国应建立离婚后扶养费给付制度) [*Our Country Should Establish Post-Divorce Maintenance Payment System*], Zhongguo Faxue (中国法学) [China Law Sci.], 1998, vol. 3, 50–56, 50.

6.3.7 Spousal Agency

Under Chinese law, marriage is an equal economic partnership. Such partnership implies not only the husband and wife's equal and individual financial standings but also their joint ownership and liability. Therefore, marital status creates an agency relationship between spouses. Both spouses may be held liable for transactions, especially debts, that are contracted by one spouse who has acted as the other spouse's agent under the implied spousal agency/principal doctrine.[78] A non-acting spouse's liability for his or her spouse's acts is, however, limited by the "necessaries doctrine," under which a person can only be bound by transactions contracted by his or her spouse to meet the ordinary necessary needs of the family's daily life.[79] In other words, spouses' joint liability for debts incurred by one spouse is limited to the scope of family necessities, and a nondebtor spouse is not liable for the debtor spouse's debts that are not for ordinary family and personal expenses.[80]

6.3.8 Right to Community Property

Spouses have equal rights to use, enjoy, and dispose of marital community property.[81] Not all property acquired by either or both spouses during the marriage is the spouses' "community property." The Civil Law provides that property derived from earnings or efforts of spouses during the marriage is marital property, specifically (1) wages, bonuses, and any compensations for services; (2) income from production, business management, or investment; (3) income from intellectual property; (4) inheritance, bequest, or gifts; and (5) any other properties acquired with marital community property.[82]

Spouses' equal rights to community property means that marital assets are divided equally between the spouses upon dissolution of the marriage. Equal rights also means that a married person is entitled to use, enjoy, and dispose of marital property freely without the other spouse's unreasonable interference, and at the same time, he/she may not dispose marital property without his/her spouse's knowledge or consent. For instance, in *Zhao Weijuan v. Yang Shen and Yang Weishan*, the court ordered the husband's father to return half of the funds that the husband gifted to him because the wife did not consent to the gift. Zhao Weijuan and Yang Shen are married. Without Zhao's knowledge or consent, Yang Shen transferred RMB2,800,000 to his father, Yang Weishan. Zhao sued for dissolution of marital property regime.

78. The Civil Code art. 1060.
79. *Id.* art. 1060.
80. *Id.* art. 1064.
81. *Id.* art. 1602 para. 2.
82. *Id.* art. 1602 para. 1.

The court denied Zhao's request but ordered the father-in-law to return half of the funds to Zhao. The court held that the funds transferred to Yang Weishan were Yang Shen and Zhao Wijuan's marital community property, and because the amount of funds was relatively substantial and was not for daily household needs, the parties must consult with each other as equals, and Yang's gift to his father was void because it was made without his wife's consent.[83]

When a spouse gifts marital property to a "*disan zhe*" (a third party) with whom he/she has an extramarital affair, the spouse is in violation of his/her spouse's interests in the marital community property. Thus, grieved spouses routinely sue their spouses' lovers for recovery of marital property, and succeed in Chinese courts. In *Sun v. Xu*, Sun and Guo were a married couple, and Xu was Guo's mistress. Guo and Xu broke up, and Guo reconciled with his wife, Sun. Sun sued Xu for recovery of marital funds in the sum of RMB1.03 million. Xu admitted that Guo gave her RMB600,000 in anticipation of his divorce. Xu alleged that she had returned a total of RMB580,000 to Guo and Sun. Sun admitted that Xu returned RMB170,000. The court ordered Xu to return RMB430,000 to Guo and Sun, finding that Guo gave Xu RMB600,000, and Xu returned RMB170,000 to Guo and Sun. The court ruled that Guo had no right to give marital funds to Xu without Sun's permission and that Xu was unjustly enriched as she accepted Guo's gift with the full knowledge that Guo had no right to gift her marital funds without Sun's permission.[84] Furthermore, Guo's betrayal of his wife was a violation of ethics as well as his legal duty of fidelity.[85]

6.3.9 Right to Separate Property

A married woman's right to own and control property was limited prior to the socialist rule in mainland China. Women's inability to own property continued until very recently in rural Chinese communities outside of the mainland.[86] The Civil Code provides that both spouses have the right to own separate properties, including (1) property acquired before marriage; (2) compensation for personal injuries; (3) property acquired by bequest, gift, or contract that is expressly given to one party; (4) personal items exclusively used

---

83. (2020) Ji 0408 Min Chu 3320 Hao ((2020) 冀0408民初3320号).

84. (2017) Lu 03 Min Zhong 3662 Hao ((2017) 鲁03民终3662号).

85. For The Court's Commentary on Sun V. Xu, see Yang Fu Yuan & Rong Mingxiao (杨富元, 荣明潇), Dui Fuqi Yifang Shanzi Chufen Gongtong Gongyou Caichan Zhong Budang Deli Qingqiu Quan De Bawo (对夫妻一方擅自处分共同共有财产中不当得利请求权的把握) [*Balance the Claim of Unjust Enrichment from One Spouse's Unilateral Disposition of Joint Property*], Renmin Sifa (人民司法) [The People's Judicature] 11.2019, 14–17.

86. Rubie S. Watson, Inequality Among Brothers: Class and Kinship in South China 61–72 (1985); and Women's Property in Republican China: Rights and Practice. Republican China.

by one party; and (5) any other property that should be a spouse's separate property.[87] In addition, property defined as separate property by spouses' written agreement is separate property.[88] For discussions of separate property, see § 8.2.

6.3.10 Right to Regulate Spousal Property Relationship by Contract

Spouses have the right to define their property relationship by agreement before or during the marriage. They may select the specific form in which title is held and determine their respective share in any or all of their property acquired before and/or during the marriage by written agreements.[89] As a basic principle, spousal agreements concerning property are binding. In other words, married couples can opt-out all or part of their assets from the community property regime by written agreements. For discussions of spousal agreements concerning property, see § 8.3.

6.3.11 Right to Inherit from Each Other

Spouses are entitled to inherit from each other.[90] If a surviving spouse is unable to provide for him/herself, a portion of the deceased spouse's estate must be appropriated for their support before the remainder of the estate is distributed according to the deceased spouse's will.[91]

---

87. The Civil Code art. 1063.
88. *Id.* art. 1065.
89. *Id.* art. 1605.
90. *Id.* art. 1061.
91. *Id.* art. 1141 and the Succession Book Interpretations art. 25.

Chapter 7

Dissolution of Marriage

Although certain aspects of a marriage may be contractual under Chinese law, a valid marriage is a permanent status and can only be dissolved by a marriage registration authority (*hunying dengji jiguan*) or a court when the marriage has irrevocably broken down. Chinese courts usually discourage divorce and encourage reconciliation to "better maintain social stability and improve the social happiness index" by "exercising caution in granting divorces."[1] Couples are routinely denied divorce and ordered to go home to fix their marriages. In 2017, 63 percent of divorce applications were denied for failure to establish that the marital relationship has irretrievably broken down (*ganqing poli*).[2]

Divorces may be obtained based on the parties' mutual consent by completing the divorce registration with a marriage registration authority, namely, a Civil Affairs Bureau.[3] Divorces obtained through divorce registration are commonly known as "divorce by agreement" (*xieyi lihun*). If a couple cannot agree to a divorce, either party may bring an action for divorce in court and seek a judgment of divorce.[4] Divorces obtained through the judicial system are commonly known as "divorce by litigation" (*susong lihun*). A marriage is dissolved upon completion of divorce registration or entry of a judgment of divorce (*lihun panjue shu*) or mediation decree of divorce (*lihun tiaojie shu*).[5] If

1. "Yong Gongkai Cu Gongzheng Jianshe Hexin Jiazhi" Zhuti Jiaoyu Huodong Hunyin Jiating Jiufen Dianxin Anli ("用公开促公正 建设核心价值"主题教育活动 婚姻家庭纠纷典型案例) ["Promote Justice Construct Core Value through Transparency" Focused Education Campaign: Family and Marriage Disputes Typical Cases] (Dec. 4, 2015) [hereinafter "FMTC"], 15.

2. The SPC Sifa Dashujü Zhuanti Baogao Lihun Jiufen (司法大数据专题报告 离婚纠纷) [Judicial Key Data Subject Report: Divorce Disputes], http://www.court.gov.cn/upload/file/2017/10/13/16/39/20171013163908_87275.pdf.

3. The Civil Code art. 1076.

4. *Id*. art. 1079.

5. *Id*. art. 1080.

a divorced couple wants to resume their marital relationship after the divorce, they must re-register the marriage.[6]

In addition to divorce, marriage-like relationships can be ended by judicial actions under Chinese law. A void marriage may be ended by a declaratory judgment that declares a marriage void.[7] A marriage may be dissolved by an annulment if the marriage was entered under duress or a spouse had concealed some serious illness.[8]

§ 7.1 Divorce Registration

7.1.1 Divorce Registration Procedure

Most divorces in China are consensual and are handled by the marriage registration authorities. A divorce may be obtained based on the parties' mutual consent by registering the divorce with a marriage registration authority.[9] Foreign nationals and their Chinese national spouses are eligible to divorce through registration if the marriage was registered in China.[10] Divorcing couples must appear in person at a Civil Affairs Bureau with proper jurisdiction where either party's household registration is located, or where the Chinese national spouse's household registration is located if the other spouse is not a Chinese national.[11]

A divorce registration application must include divorce application declaration forms, divorce agreement, marriage certificate, identification documents, and other documents required by the local Civil Affairs Bureau.[12] A written divorce agreement on the parties' consent to the divorce and

6. *Id.* art. 1083.

7. Zuigao Renmin Fayuan Guanyu Shiyong Zhonghua Renmin Gonghe Guo Minfadian Hunyin Jiating Bian De Jieshi (Yi) (最高人民法院关于适用《中华人民共和国民法典》婚姻家庭编的解释 (一)) [the Supreme People's Court Interpretations on the Application of the People's Republic of China Civil Code, Book of Marriage and Family (I)] (promulgated by the Sup. People's Ct., Dec. 25, 2020, effective Jan. 1, 2021) [hereinafter "Marriage and Family Book Interpretations (I)"] art. 14.

8. The Civil Code arts. 1052, 1053.

9. *Id.* art.1076.

10. Zhonghua Renmin Gongheguo Guowuyuan Hunyin Dengji Tiaoli (中华人民共和国国务院婚姻登记条例) [The State Council of the PRC Regulations on Marriage Registration] (adopted on July 30, 2003, effective from Oct. 1, 2003) [hereinafter the "Marriage Registration Regulations"] art. 10.

11. *Id.* art. 10.

12. Zhonghua Remin Gongheguo Minzheng Bu Hunyin Dengji Gongzuo Guifan (中华人民共和国民政部婚姻登记工作规范) [The Ministry of Civil Affairs of the PRC Marriage Registration Protocols] (effective from Dec. 8, 2015) [hereinafter the "Marriage Registration Protocols"] art. 55.

settlements of all issues related to child custody, child support, property, and debts must be submitted as part of a divorce registration application.[13]

The divorce registration process has made a divorce simple, fast, and economical. Critics of the divorce registration blame it for the rising divorce rate in the recent decades. Thus, a 30-day "divorce cooling period" has been added in the Civil Code. After the Civil Affairs Bureau's receipt of the divorce registration application, the parties must wait for a 30-day "divorce cooling period" (*lihun lengjing qi*) before they are able to obtain a certificate of divorce. The divorce cooling period starts to run from the date of the return receipt issued by a Civil Affairs Bureau to a divorcing couple when their divorce registration application is accepted by the Bureau. Either party may withdraw the divorce application within 30 days after the receipt of such application by the Civil Affairs Bureau.[14] Within 30-days after the divorce cooling period has elapsed, both parties must apply in person for a certificate of divorce at the Civil Affairs Bureau, and the parties' divorce application will be deemed withdrawn in the event the parties fail to appear in person to apply for a certificate of divorce.[15]

Divorce registration applications will be denied if (1) the parties have not reached a divorce settlement agreement; (2) either party is a person without legal capacity (*wu minshi xingwei nengli ren*) or a person with limited legal capacity (*xianzhi mingshi xingwei nengli ren*); and (3) the parties' marriage was not registered in mainland China.[16] Divorce registrations cannot be issued to persons with limited legal capacity or persons without legal capacity.[17]

7.1.2 Defects or Errors in Divorce Registrations

Generally, defects in the Civil Affairs Bureaus' handling of divorce registration do not affect the validity and finality of a divorce, and a defective divorce registration may not be revoked. For instance, Liang and Huang were married in China in 1985, and divorced in 2015 by obtaining a divorce registration from a local Civil Affairs Bureau in Jiangsu Province. During the marriage, Huang immigrated to Singapore and became a citizen of Singapore. In 2018, the Civil Affairs Bureau found that Huang was not a Chinese citizen at the time of the divorce registration and therefore the Bureau did not have the authority to issue the divorce registration. The Bureau notified Liang of the error and revoked the divorce registration. Liang objected to the revocation of the divorce registration. The Jiangsu Province High People's Court ordered the Bureau to reinstate the

13. The Marriage Registration Regulations art. 11.
14. The Civil Code art. 1077 para. 1.
15. *Id*. art. 1077 para 2.
16. The Marriage Registration Regulations art. 12.
17. *Id*. art. 12(2).

divorce registration in that the Bureau had no authority to revoke the divorce registration for its own error. The court held that the parties and/or innocent third parties would be unfairly prejudiced if divorce registrations could be revoked for errors in the registration process because the parties and interested third parties had relied on the validity and finality of the divorce and the revocation of a divorce registration would likely cause harm to the parties' subsequent spouses or children.[18] Similarly, the Henan Province High People's Court vacated a local Civil Affairs Bureau's revocation of a divorce registration in *Wang v. Minyang County*. In this case, Wang and her ex-husband registered their divorce in Minyang County, which was not the place of their household registration and therefore did not have the jurisdiction to register the divorce. The court held that the divorce registration should not be revoked for the Bureau's lack of jurisdiction to issue it in that the revocation of a divorce registration for procedural errors would unfairly "alter the parties' marital status and would have significant impact on their personal rights."[19]

§ 7.2 Judicial Divorce

When the spouses cannot agree to a divorce, either party may bring an action for divorce.[20] If the spouse of a person without civil legal capacity has abused, neglected, or engaged in any other conduct that violated the incapacitated person's lawful rights and interests, the incapacitated person's parents, children, close relatives, and any person or organization that is willing to act as a guardian may apply to the court to disqualify the spouse as the incapacitated person's guardian and to appoint a new guardian. After a new guardian is appointed, the new guardian may bring an action for divorce on behalf of the incapacitated person.[21]

7.2.1 Mandatory Mediation

Mediation is mandatory in all divorce actions.[22] A divorce is predicated upon a couple's failure to reconcile after mediation. In a divorce action, the court must first try to mediate a reconciliation. If the parties reconcile, they will

18. (2018) Su Xing Zhong 1715 Hao ((2018) 苏行终1715号); *see also* Huang He and Lü Changcheng (黄河, 吕长城), Yuequan Wuxiao Yuanze Bu Shiyong Yu Lihun Dengji (越权无效原则不适用于离婚登记) [Actions Beyond Authorization Void Principle Inapplicable in Divorce Registration], Renmin Sifa (人民司法) [The People's Judicature] 17.2020, 104–05 (the presiding judges' commentary on the case).

19. (2016) Yu Xing Zhong 1452 Hao ((2016) 豫行终1452号).

20. The Civil Code art. 1079 para. 1.

21. The Marriage and Family Book Interpretations (I) art. 62.

22. The Civil Code art. 1079 para. 2.

stipulate a so-ordered mediated reconciliation agreement in open court and discontinue the action. If the parties do not reconcile, the court must try to mediate a divorce settlement agreement to dissolve the parties' marriage and settle all relevant ancillary issues, such as child custody, visitation, child support, and property division. A Chinese mediated divorce settlement agreement is similar to a U.S. so-ordered stipulation of settlement that is executed by both parties and signed by the presiding judge. Only after all mediation efforts have failed, may the court proceed to adjudicate the divorce and ancillary issues.

Mediation is often a formality in simple divorce cases. For example, in *Tao v. Ba*, the parties' marriage was arranged by their families through matchmakers. They were married for a few months and had no children or marital property. Apparently, the wife had some mental health issues. After a brief mediation by the court, she consented to the divorce. A mediated decree of divorce was entered based on their agreement to divorce.[23]

7.2.2 Divorce Ground: Breakdown of Mutual Affection

The sole ground for divorce is "breakdown of mutual affection" (*ganqing polie*). The Civil Code provides that a divorce is warranted when a couple's mutual affection has broken down (*ganqing polie*).[24] Confronted with the explosion of divorces among young people born after 1980, some called to restrict no-fault divorce based on the breakdown of marital relationship by requiring a waiting period.[25] The Civil Code has implemented a 30-day waiting period in divorce registration. However, no waiting period is required in divorce actions. In practice, Chinese courts have implemented a six-month waiting period in first-time divorce actions for decades. Chinese courts generally do not find "breakdown of mutual affection" in a first-time divorce action when one spouse seeks a divorce and the other spouse objects. As a new divorce action cannot be brought within six months after the first divorce is dismissed or withdrawn, the parties are compelled to wait for at least six months before filing for divorce again.[26]

Breakdown of mutual affection cannot be readily established in Chinese courts. Parties' admission or testimony alone is not sufficient to prove

23. (2020) Yu 1625 Min Chu 4904 Hao ((2020) 豫1625民初4904号).

24. The Civil Code art. 1079 para. 2.

25. *See, e.g.*, Quan Jing (权静), Guanyu Jiali Wu Guocuo Lihun Xianzhi Zhidu De Falü Sikao (关于建立无过错离婚限制制度的法律思考—以包头市昆都仑区人民法院近5年1033件80后离婚案件为样本) [Some Thoughts on Establishing Restrictions to No-Fault Divorce Law—Samples from Baotou City Dulun District People's Court Most Recent 5 Years' 1033 Cases of Born-After-80's Divorces], Renmin Sifa (人民司法) [The People's Judicature] 21.2014, 72–74.

26. Civil Procedure Law art. 124(7) and Civil Procedure Law Interpretations art. 214.

breakdown of mutual affection. Whether there is an irretrievable breakdown of mutual affection (*ganqing polie*) is determined by the totality of the circumstances of a case. The case of Jin and Quan is a Typical Case where the court denied the wife's complaint for a divorce. Jin and Quan were married for ten years and have a daughter and a son. The husband admitted that the couple argued often during their ten-year-marriage but vehemently opposed the divorce. After hearing both parties' testimonies, the court found that the parties' marriage had a good foundation (*hunying jichu hao*) and their mutual affection had not ruptured despite that they have frequent arguments about trivial affairs in their family life.[27]

Squabbles over housework or other family affairs do not justify a divorce, particularly when young children are involved. Thus, the court refused to grant a divorce in Tang and Jiang's case although both parties wanted to end the marriage. Tang and Jiang were married in 2009. Each of them had a failed first marriage. Tang had a daughter from her previous marriage. Tang and Jiang had a daughter born of their marriage in 2013. Less than a year after the child's birth, Tang filed for divorce. Both parties wanted a divorce and alleged that they had argued a lot because of differences in personality and lifestyle. The trial court found that the parties' mutual affection (*ganqing*) had not irretrievably broken down and denied Tang's divorce petition. The court determined that the parties' reconciliation was possible because they were compatible as well-educated professionals of good moral character and had a good relationship in the first five years of their marriage before their daughter's birth. The trial court denied Tang's divorce petition and asked the parties to consider the welfare of their children and be more supportive and considerate to each other.[28]

Similarly, in *Zhao v. Yang*, the court declined to grant a divorce after finding that the parties might be able to reconcile. Zhao and Yang got married within six months after they had met. After four years of marriage, Zhao and Yang had two daughters. Zhao left home and stayed with her parents after an argument with Yang. Yang begged her to return home several times. Zhao refused to return and filed for divorce. The court found that Zhao and Yang's relationship was fractured but not yet broken and a divorce would be detrimental to the children's welfare. Thus, the court denied Zhao's divorce petition and directed the parties to make good efforts to maintain family harmony and provide their children a nurturing environment.[29]

In recent years, there has been an increase of "gray divorces" of elderly couples after decades-long marriages. The bar to prove "breakdown of mutual affection" is higher in long marriages. For example, in *Li v. Zhang*, the court

27. (2014) Sun Tong Min Yi Chu Zi Di 06537 Hao ((2014) 宿埇民一初字第06537号).
28. FMTC 28.
29. FMTC 47.

declined to grant the wife a divorce, although the parties had been separated for more than ten years during a 20-some-year marriage. The court found that the wife visited the husband and their adult children regularly, although she had been a migrant worker for more than ten years and the couple recently built a new home together. Thus, the court found that their "mutual affection" had not broken down and denied the wife's request for a divorce.[30]

The SPC suggested that "gray divorces" should not be readily granted, as older couples' marriages are more about family responsibilities and their divorces would affect not only themselves but also their children and even grandchildren; and that older couples are more likely than not to resolve their marital discords and repair their relationships after having been able to do so for decades. Thus, there is little reason for the courts to dissolve a long marriage because of the couple's temporary marital discontent. In *Liu v. Li*, Liu and Li married in 1980. They had a son, who also married and had his own children. After 32 years of marriage, Liu filed for divorce in 2012. The court denied his petition. Liu brought his second divorce action in 2014. The court again denied his petition for divorce. The court reasoned that Li and Liu had been married for nearly 40 years and had gone through many hardships together; and that although the couple quarreled over the years, their marital relation had not irretrievably broken down. The court scolded Li for her short temper and directed her to be more considerate to Liu's feelings. The court also asked Liu to forgive Li for her bad temper and repair the marriage for the sake of their son and grandchildren.[31]

On the other hand, divorces are sometimes quickly granted when the court finds that a marriage between two older persons was a marriage for convenience and lacked a foundation of mutual affection (*quefa ganqing jichu*). In *Peng v. Li*, Peng was 70 years old, and Li was 52 when they got married. The couple fought often because their adult children could not get along. Six years after their marriage, the couple separated, and Peng filed for divorce. The court found that Peng and Li's marriage was both parties' second marriage and lacked a solid foundation of mutual affection (*quefa ganqing jichu*). The court quickly granted the divorce.[32]

7.2.3 Circumstances under Which a Divorce Should Be Granted

It is often difficult for a court to determine whether a couple's mutual affection is all but lost and their marriage is not salvageable. Thus, the Civil Code prescribes five statutory circumstances under which a divorce should be

30. (2014) Ding Min Chu Zi Di 1019 Hao ((2014) 定民初字第1019号).
31. FMTC 15.
32. FMTC 24.

granted as under these circumstances the parties' mutual affection can be presumed broken down.[33] These circumstances are:

(1) Bigamy or cohabitation with a third-party,
(2) Domestic violence, or maltreatment or abandonment of any family member,
(3) Gambling, drug abuse, or any other addictions,
(4) Living separately for more than two years due to "lack of mutual affection" (*ganqing buhe*); and
(5) Any other circumstances that have caused a breakdown of spouses' mutual affection.[34]

Divorce may be granted when the court finds the couple's "mutual affection" has broken down due to any circumstances that may render a divorce inevitable. For instance, divorce is warranted when a couple's relationship has been wrecked by disagreements over whether or when to have children.[35] A spouse's long sentence for serious crimes also justifies a divorce because a spouse's criminal activities would inevitably disrupt a family's normal life and damage the spouses' relationship.[36]

Substance abuse warrants a divorce, as in Tan and Kong's case. Tan and Kong started living together in 1985 when Kong was 17 years old. They were married in 1992 and had two children. Tan had been incarcerated for 13 years, since 1996, for drug trafficking. Kong started abusing illegal drugs in 1998 and had been struggling with drug addiction ever since. Tan filed for divorce in 2013. Considering Kong's long history of drug abuse, the court granted the divorce over Kong's objection.[37]

A divorce is usually granted after the spouses have lived separately for more than two years due to marital disagreements, as the separation is clear evidence of irretrievable breakdown of the couple's mutual affection. In *Sun Fengjie v. Wang Yuping*, Sun and Wang were married in 1993 and had a daughter in 1994. The parties argued often and had physical altercations during the marriage. They separated in 2007. In 2011, the parties entered a divorce settlement agreement but did not obtain a divorce registration, purportedly because their daughter was preparing for her college entrance exam. Sun filed for divorce in 2012 and then again in 2013. He withdrew his complaint at

33. Xue Ninglan (薛宁兰), Lihun Fa De Susong Shijian Ji Pingxi (离婚法的诉讼实践及其评析) [Divorce Law Litigation Practice and Commentary], Faxue Luntan (法学论坛) [Legal Forum] No. 4, Vol. 29, Ser. No. 154) (July 2014), 15–23.

34. The Civil Code art. 1079 para. 3.

35. The Marriage and Family Book Interpretations (I) art. 34.

36. (2017) Jing Min Zhong 694 Hao ((2017) 京民终694号).

37. (2014) Jiang En Fa Cheng Min Chu Zi Di 29 Hao ((2014) 江恩法城民初字第29号).

both times due to lack of evidence for breakdown of mutual affection (*ganqing polie*). Sun filed for divorce a third time in 2014. The trial court granted the divorce despite Wang's vehement objection. Wang appealed. The appellate court affirmed the divorce in that there was sufficient evidence of irretrievable breakdown of the parties' marital relation in that the parties had been living separately since 2007 and had only communicated with each other with written notes and text messages. The court found that it was clear Sun and Wang's mutual affection had irretrievably broken down (*ganqing polie*) after living separately for more than two years.[38]

The occurrence of any of the statutory circumstances does not necessarily necessitate a divorce if the parties still have mutual affection for each other and the marriage remains viable. However, there are cases in which domestic violence is trivialized by the court for the sake of keeping a marriage together. For example, in *Zhang v. Liu*, a Shanghai court denied the wife's divorce complaint despite the wife's allegations of the husband's violent behavior, as the court found that the parties' marriage was still viable.[39] Similarly, the court denied the wife's request for a divorce in *Chen v. Chen*, where the wife alleged that the husband was verbally abusive and addicted to gambling, and he neglected her and their three children. After the trial, the court found that the husband "used bad language out of frustration and anger" and that the husband did not gamble but liked to play cards with the wife's father. The court also found that the parties were likely to reconcile and that the divorce would be harmful to the parties' three young children. Therefore, the court refused to grant the wife a divorce.[40]

Domestic violence victims often have difficulty in collecting evidence of the abuse. Far too many times, stringent evidentiary requirements have essentially forced domestic victims to stay in an abusive marriage as well. In *Min v. Sun*, the wife alleged that the husband had physically abused her during the marriage, he had been arrested for assaulting her, and the parties had been separated for three years. However, the Hubei Province High People's Court declined to admit evidence of domestic violence because the wife's delay in offering the evidence was not excusable. The High People's Court affirmed the lower court's denial of the wife's complaint for a divorce for lack of evidence and held that the husband should be given another chance to save the marriage.[41]

---

38. FMTC 28.
39. (2020) Hu 0113 Min Chu 28226 Hao ((2020) 沪0113民初28226号).
40. (2020) E 02 Min Zhong 2045 Hao ((2020) 鄂02民终2045号).
41. (2018) E Min Shen 481 Hao ((2018) 鄂民申481号).

7.2.4 Disappearance

The spouse of a person who is declared by court as absent is entitled to a divorce.[42] A person may be declared as absent after two years of disappearance.[43] Mere disappearance is not sufficient to warrant a divorce. The left-behind spouse must obtain a declaratory decree of absence of the other spouse. In *Lü v. Hou*, the court declined to grant a divorce, although the husband abandoned the wife and child and disappeared after an argument. The court found that the wife and her witnesses failed to offer sufficient evidence of the circumstances surrounding the husband's disappearance and therefore a divorce cannot be granted based on the husband's alleged disappearance.[44]

7.2.5 Separation after Prior Divorce Action

Divorce should be granted for irretrievable breakdown of mutual affection (*ganqing poli*) if the parties have been separated for more than a year after dismissal of a previous application for divorce.[45] In *Liu v. Tai*, the appellate court reversed the trial court's denial of divorce, finding that the parties' mutual affection had broken down, as the parties had been separated for more than two years after a prior divorce action brought by the wife, Liu.[46]

7.2.6 Grounds to Deny a Divorce

7.2.6.1 Active Duty

A divorce between an active military servicemember and their civilian spouse must obtain the servicemember's consent unless the servicemember has engaged in gross misconduct.[47] This restriction covers both enlisted and career servicemembers in active military service. It does not apply when both spouses are in active duty of military service. "Gross misconduct" includes (1) bigamy, cohabitation with a third-party; (2) gambling, drug abuse, and other addictions; (3) domestic violence, and maltreatment or neglect of family members; and (4) any other gross misconduct that may cause breakdown of spouses' mutual affection.[48]

---

42. The Civil Code art. 1079 para. 4.
43. *Id*. art. 40.
44. (2014) Bo Min Chu Zi Di 33 Hao ((2014) 博民许初字第33号).
45. The Civil Code art. 1079 para. 5.
46. (2019) Liao 05 Min Zhong 1499 Hao ((2019) 辽05民终1499号).
47. The Civil Code art. 1081.
48. The Marriage and Family Book Interpretations art. 64.

7.2.6.2 Pregnancy

Chinese custom reveres expecting mothers and requires an extended period of maternity care and rest for mothers after giving birth. Thus, the Civil Code provides that during pregnancy or within a year after the wife has given birth, a husband may not seek a divorce unless a court deems it appropriate to allow the husband to sue for a divorce, or the wife seeks a divorce.[49] Thus, in *Liu v. Chen*, the trial court, which sits in a rural town, denied a husband's complaint for divorce that was made about three months after his wife gave birth to the couple's second daughter.[50] Following the custom and the long-established policy, the Civil Code provides that a husband is not permitted to bring a divorce action during a wife's pregnancy, or within one year after the birth of a child, or within six months after termination of a pregnancy.[51] However, divorce actions that are brought by wives or any divorce actions brought by the husband that the court deems necessary may be allowed.[52]

§ 7.3 Annulment

Marriages could be found invalid for two reasons under Chinese law: (1) the marriage is a void marriage (*wuxiao hunyin*) that a party was, or both parties were, not eligible to marry at the time of the marriage;[53] or (2) the marriage is a voidable marriage (*ke chexiao hunyin*) that may be voided by a court on statutory grounds.[54]

A void marriage is *void ab initio*. No legal action is required to end a void marriage as it is deemed never to have taken place. For practical reasons, an action to declare a marriage void (*xuanbu hunyin wuxiao*) is nevertheless necessary to end a void marriage, particularly when the parties need to resolve issues related to property or children. In contrast, if a marriage is voidable, it is valid until a court annuls it in an action to void a marriage (*hunyin chexiao*).

In the past two decades, the SPC has developed a set of rules concerning property division and children in nonmarital cohabitation relationships.[55] In actions concerning invalid marriages, the courts must divide the property between the parties as if they were in a cohabitation relationship. In the event, a marriage is voided or annulled, the innocent party is entitled to

49. The Civil Code art. 1082.
50. (2015) Yong Leng Min Chu Zi Di 135 Hao ((2015) 永冷民初字第135号).
51. The Civil Code art. 1082.
52. *Id*. art. 1082.
53. *Id*. art. 1051.
54. *Id*. art. 1052.
55. *See, e.g.*, Cohabitation Opinion; Marriage Law Interpretations (I) arts. 2, 4, 5; Marriage Law Interpretations (II) arts. 1, 2.

compensation from the party that is at fault.[56] However, such compensation must not infringe on the property rights of the at-fault party's new spouse.[57] The invalidity of the parents' marriage does not affect the rights of their children. The Civil Code provisions concerning parents and children are applicable to children born of void or voidable marriages. [58]

7.3.1 Action to Declare a Marriage Void

Either spouse or any interested party may seek a declaratory judgment to declare that a marriage is null and void on statutory grounds. A court may not declare a marriage void on any other grounds.[59] During the lifetime of the parties to the marriage, or after the death of one or both parties,[60] an action for a declaration of a void marriage may be brought on the statutory grounds of (1) bigamy, (2) nonage, or (3) consanguinity.[61]

In an action to declare a marriage void brought by an interested party, both parties to the marriage must be joined as defendants; and if one of the parties is deceased, the surviving party is the defendant.[62] Interested parties who may bring an action to declare a void marriage include (1) either party's close relatives or relevant community organizations, if the ground is bigamy; (2) close relatives of the nonaged party, if the ground is nonage; and (3) either party's close relatives, if the ground is consanguinity.[63] If an action is brought on the ground of bigamy, the lawful spouse from a bigamous party's first marriage may be joined as a third party.[64]

A court may not allow a plaintiff to withdraw the complaint for a declaratory judgment of a void marriage after the court has accepted the case. In an action for declaration of a void marriage, the court may not mediate the dispute over the validity of the marriage and must enter a judgment after conducting a fact-finding trial on the validity of the marriage.[65] However, the court may conduct mediation sessions for issues concerning property division and child custody and support.[66] If one party brought a divorce action and the other party brought an action for declaration of a void marriage, the

56. The Civil Code art. 1054 para. 2.
57. *Id.* art. 1054 para. 1.
58. *Id.*
59. The Marriage and Family Book Interpretations (I) art. 17.
60. *Id.* art. 14.
61. The Civil Code art. 1051.
62. The Marriage and Family Book Interpretations (I) art. 15.
63. *Id.* art. 9.
64. *Id.* art. 16.
65. *Id.* art. 11 para. 2 and art. 12.
66. *Id.* art. 11 para. 3.

court must stay the divorce action until the court has entered a judgment in the declaratory action.[67]

7.3.1.1 Bigamous Marriage

A bigamous marriage is void if it is entered when one spouse is already married to another person. In *Chen v. Huang*, Huang concealed her prior marriages from Chen and married Chen. Chen later found out Huang was still married to two other men in Hong Kong when she married Chen in Fujian Province. Chen sued for an annulment on the ground of bigamy in a Fujian court. The court granted him the annulment. The Fujian court also convicted Huang of bigamy and sentenced her to six months of imprisonment but suspended the sentence for one year.[68]

7.3.1.2 Nonage

Under the Civil Code, a woman must be at least 20 and a man must be at least 22 to be legally eligible to marry.[69] In *Luo v. Wu*, Luo brought the action to declare her marriage to Wu void after she reached majority. Luo was born on December 13, 1998. Luo's adoptive father falsified her date of birth and married her to Wu when she was 15 years old in 2013. Two years later, Luo fled from Wu's home. In 2018, she managed to obtain documentation of her birth and brought an action to declare her marriage to Wu void on the ground that she had not reached the marriageable age when she married Wu. On December 10, 2018, a few days before Lou turned 20, the court entered a judgment to declare the marriage void. [70]

7.3.1.3 Consanguinity

Marriages between parties related by blood within third degrees are prohibited. A marriage between first cousins is void, as first cousins are blood relatives within third degrees. Thus, a Shanxi court declared the marriage between Pu and Ma void pursuant to Article 1048 and Article 1051(2) of the Civil Code, in that Pu and Ma were first cousins.[71]

7.3.1.4 Ratification

It is well-established that a declaratory judgment to declare a marriage void may not be granted when a couple voluntarily cohabitates as a married

67. *Id*. art. 13.
68. (2017) Min 05 Min Zhong 1767 Hao ((2017) 闽05民终1767号).
69. The Civil Code art. 1047.
70. (2018) Nei 0802 Mn Chu 6738 Hao ((2018) 内0802民初6738号).
71. (2021) Shan 0728 Min Chu 311 Hao ((2021) 陕0728民初311号).

couple when the condition that rendered the marriage void no longer exists.[72] Thus, in *Chang v. Li*, the court declined to declare Chang and Li's marriage void because Li's divorce from another man came two days after Chang and Li's remarriage. Chang and Li had been previously married to each other. They were divorced on March 19, 2013. Li married Zhang on March 20, 2013. Chang and Li remarried and completed their remarriage registration on September 8, 2015. However, Li's divorce registration with Zhang was not finalized until September 10, 2015. In June 2020, the Civil Affairs Bureau confiscated Chang and Li's marriage certificates when the Bureau noticed that the marriage certificates were issued before Li's divorce registration was finalized. Chang was furious and sought a declaration of void marriage on the ground of Li's two-day bigamy. The court denied his claim and held that Li's previous marriage had been already dissolved, and therefore Chang and Li's marriage was ratified because the condition that might render their marriage void no longer existed.[73]

Early marriages are common in rural China. Thus, it is not unusual for a spouse to bring an action to declare a marriage void for nonage after a long marriage. Chinese courts routinely reject attempts to invalidate a marriage after a long period of cohabitation after the parties reached the marriage age. For example, Zhen and E married in 1993 when Zhen was 17. Because she was too young to marry, Zhen used her older sister's birth record to register the marriage with E. Zhen and E had two sons. Twenty-three years later, in 2016, Zhen sought to declare her marriage to E void on the ground that she was not eligible to marry due to nonage at the time of the marriage registration. The court declined to declare the marriage void but granted a divorce. The court held that Zhen and E's marriage was valid because the parties had voluntarily cohabitated for more than two decades after they reached the marriage age, and the condition that rendered the parties' marriage no longer existed when Zhen brought the action to declare the marriage void.[74]

7.3.2 Action to Void a Marriage

Chinese courts do not grant annulments easily. As a Beijing court put it, "marriage is sacred and solemn, and marriage should be entered with caution and seriousness. Marriages cannot be casually annulled and can only be annulled when the statutory requirements are met."[75] A marriage may be voided or annulled (*che xiao*) only when it was entered into under duress,[76] or when

72. The Marriage Law Interpretations (I) art. 8.
73. (2020) Jin 0106 Min Chu 22623 Hao ((2020) 京0106民初22623号).
74. (2016) Gan 1124 Min Chu 1459 Hao ((2016) 赣1124民初1459).
75. (2019) Jing 0106 Min Chu 4190 Hao ((2019) 京0106民初4190号).
76. The Civil Code art. 1052.

a party concealed serious illness.[77] Furthermore, only the party who was coerced to enter the marriage has the standing to bring an annulment action.[78] In other words, a party who forced the other party to marry him/her does not have the standing to bring an annulment action.

An action for an annulment of marriage must be made within a year from the time when the duress or coercion has ceased,[79] or within a year from the time when the plaintiff has regained personal freedom if he/she had been unlawfully confined.[80] For example, in *Song v. Hou*, the Beijing High People's Court found that a wife's annulment action was untimely because she brought the annulment action in more than one year after the marriage and more than one year after she regained personal freedom from the alleged unlawful confinement by the husband.[81]

7.3.2.1 Coercion

Mutual consent freely given is the prerequisite of a valid marriage. If a person would not have entered a marriage but for coercion or duress, the marriage must be voided.[82] Threats to harm a party's or their close relatives' lives, body, health, reputations, or property constitute duress and coercion to induce a marriage.[83] Allegations of coercion are frequently rejected, except in cases of unlawful imprisonment or where the defendants admitted to the alleged coercion.[84]

Chinese courts generally place a stringent burden of proof on the plaintiffs. A plaintiff must first prove that the defendant's action constitutes "coercion": (1) the coercive act was intentional; (2) the coercive act was carried out; (3) the coercive act caused the victim fear; (4) the victim expressed their fear; and (5) the coercive act was unlawful.[85] Furthermore, the plaintiff must establish the causality between the defendant's coercion and the parties' marriage by proving that (1) he/she was coerced; (2) the defendant was the person who coerced the plaintiff; and (3) the marriage was induced by the coercion but

77. *Id.* art. 1053.

78. The Marriage and Family Book Interpretations (I) art. 18 para. 2.

79. The Civil Code art. 1052 para. 2.

80. *Id.* art.1052 para. 3.

81. (2019) Jing Min Shen 5420 Hao ((2019) 京民申5420号).

82. The Civil Code art. 1052 para. 1.

83. The Marriage and Family Book Interpretations (I) art. 18 para. 1.

84. Yang Jinling (杨晋玲), Songyi Huo Feisong: Wuxiao Hunyin Yu Ke Chexiao Hunyin Anjian De Shenli Chengxu Wenti Tanxi—Jiyu Shizheng De Fenxi (讼抑或非讼: 无效婚姻与可撤销婚姻案件的审理程序问题探析—基于实证的分析) [Litigation or Not: The Procedural Issues in the Adjudication of the Invalid Marriage and Revocable Marriage Cases—An Empirical Analysis], Zhonghua Nüzi Xueyuan Xuebao (中华女子学院学报) Journal of China Women's University, Mar. 2021, No. 2, 46.

85. *Id.*

not any other reasons. For example, in *Yang v. Wang*, a Beijing court refused to annul the parties' remarriage for lack of evidence of coercion. Yang and Wang had been married for 16 years and had two children before they were divorced. A month after they were divorced, Yang and Wang remarried. Yang sought to annul her second marriage to Wang on the ground that she was forced to remarry him after he physically assaulted her, threatened her friend, and vandalized her home. Yang provided the police reports and medical records of her injuries and evidence of the damages in her home. However, the court found that although there was evidence that Yang was assaulted and injured by Wang, Yang did not provide sufficient evidence to prove that she would have not married Wang if he had not assaulted and harassed her. Therefore, the court rejected Yang's request for annulment for lack of evidence that the marriage was induced by Wang's coercion.[86]

In *Yan v. Long*, the wife was denied an annulment because she married the husband under the coercion of her mother but not her husband. After the husband and wife registered the marriage, the wife confided to the husband that her mother forced her to marry him. The husband was sympathetic to the wife and the parties did not consummate the marriage. The wife then sought an annulment of the marriage and the husband testified that he consented to the annulment because his wife was forced by her mother to marry him. However, the court declined to annul the marriage, holding that a marriage may be annulled only when one spouse coerced the other spouse into the marriage but not when a spouse was coerced by a third party to marry. The court found that although the wife was forced into the marriage by her mother, the husband entered the marriage voluntarily and he did not coerce the wife.[87]

7.3.2.2 Concealment of Serious Illness

A person must disclose his/her serious illness before entering a marriage. If a spouse failed to disclose any serious illness truthfully, the other spouse may seek an annulment within a year after he/she has discovered or should have discovered the illness.[88] The Civil Code does not define what illnesses are serious enough that a marriage may be annulled. There are no clear rules about what type of illness and how serious the illness must be to justify an annulment. As a result, Chinese courts' decisions in annulment cases are highly discretionary. For example, the Beijing High People's Court found that a wife's concealment of sexually transmitted diseases did not warrant an annulment

86. (2020) Jin 02 Min Zhong 8623 Hao ((2020) 京02民终8623号).
87. (2019) Jing 0106 Min Chu 4190 ((2019) 京0106民初4190号).
88. The Civil Code art. 1053.

of marriage.[89] A court granted an annulment when a wife concealed an inherited defect that made it impossible for her to have children.[90] A Sichuan court granted the husband an annulment where the wife concealed a long history of chronic schizophrenia from the husband, and she had been hospitalized since the fourth month after the wedding.[91] In contrast, a Tianjin court denied the wife's request for an annulment where the husband was impotent and was diagnosed with acute schizophrenia and other mental disorders two months after the parties married. The court found that the husband did not have a history of any mental illness prior to the marriage, and, therefore, he did not conceal his illness from the wife. Furthermore, the court held that acute schizophrenia is not a serious disease that could render a person ineligible to marry, as it was not subject to the mandatory medical examination for marriage registration.[92]

7.3.3 Effects of Invalid Marriages

A void or voidable marriage is invalid *ab initio*. Thus, parties to an invalid marriage do not have the rights and obligations of a married couple, such as the right to inherit from each other.

Parents' marital status has no bearing on a child's rights or entitlements. The invalidity of the parents' marriage does not affect the rights of their children. Children born of a marriage that is void or is voided enjoy the same rights as children born of a valid marriage. The Civil Code provisions concerning parents and children are applicable to children born of void or voidable marriages.[93] The courts have statutory authority to determine custody and support of the parties' children in an action for declaration of a void marriage or an action to void a marriage.

In actions concerning invalid marriages, properties acquired during parties' cohabitation are treated as joint community property unless there is sufficient evidence of one party's sole ownership.[94] In the event a marriage is voided or annulled due to one party's fault or wrongdoing, the court may favor the innocent party in property distribution and award the innocent party compensation from the party that is at fault.[95] For example, in *Yang v. Liu*, Yang married Liu in 1998 in Beijing. Liu was from Taiwan. During the marriage, Liu and Yang lived in Shanghai and had a daughter. In 2007, Liu

89. (2020) Jing Min Shen 2076 Hao ((2020) 京民申2076号).
90. (2021) Zhe 0109 Min Chu 452 ((2021) 浙0109民初452号).
91. (2021) Chuan 3434 Min Chu 426 Hao ((2021) 川3434民初426号).
92. (2021) Jin 0106 Min Chu 770 Hao ((2021) 津0106民初770号).
93. The Civil Code art. 1054 para. 1.
94. The Marriage and Family Book Interpretations (I) art. 22.
95. The Civil Code art. 1054 para. 2.

suddenly disappeared amid some debt disputes and left Yang to deal with his creditors. One of the creditors sued Yang and Liu jointly in 2007 in a Shanghai court. In the collection action, Yang discovered that Liu married Shen in 1994 in Shanghai, and Shen divorced Liu in 2009 after having no contact with Liu since 2006. The Shanghai court placed a restraining order on an apartment in Yang's name in connection with the collection action against Yang and Liu. Yang brought an action in Beijing for a declaration that her marriage to Liu was void and the apartment in her name was her sole property, and for compensation from Liu for causing the marriage void. The Beijing court declared the marriage void as Liu was married to Shen when he married Yang, and awarded Yang RMB50,000 as compensation for damage caused by Liu's deceit.[96]

96. (2014) Chao Min Chu Zi Di 37161 Hao ((2014) 朝民初字第37161号).

Chapter 8

Dissolution of Marital Property Regime

Chinese law views a marriage as an egalitarian companionship as well as an equal economic partnership based on a community property regime under which both spouses enjoy equal power to use, alienate, or encumber the community of the marital estate earned or acquired during the marriage. Chinese law favors marital property presumption. When there is no sufficient evidence to ascertain the nature of a certain asset acquired by either spouse, such asset is generally imputed as marital property.[1] The presumption favoring marital property is overwhelmingly supported by the public, who also views a married couples' property as "community property" or "family property" regardless of when or how the property was acquired.

Chinese society's strong support for marital community property regime can be traced to China's traditional household economy, which remains somewhat prevalent both in urban and rural China. It can also be attributed to the legacy of "socialist marriage," a CCP creation built on the elimination of private ownership and individualistic property rights.[2] Rural communes and urban state-owned enterprises as well as families were conceptualized as collective units of the socialist planned economy. Diminished within these units was a person's social, political, and economic identity as an individual. Ideology aside, more importantly the socialist economic institutions left long-lasting effects on family financial structure. In China's socialist economy, families did not have any private possessions for production, but economic entitlements that were tied to spouses' assigned roles in the socialist economy and

1. Gongtong Caichan De Jieding (共同财产的界定) [Defining Marital Property] in Zhongguo Hunyinfa Shiyi (中华人民共和国婚姻法释义) [The National People's Congress Explanatory Report on the People's Republic of China Marriage Law] [hereinafter "Marriage Law Explanatory Report"], art. 39, http://www.npc.gov.cn/npc/flsyywd/minshang/2002-07/11/content_297448.htm.

2. Deborah S. Davis, *Privatization of Marriage in Post-Socialist China*, 40(6) Modern China 553 (Nov. 2014).

their marital status. For example, urban housing was assigned based on a person's, usually the husband, seniority and rank at the workplace, marital status, and household size.[3] A "socialist marriage" was essentially a communal unit to share meager entitlements.[4] The reintroduction of private ownership and legitimization of individualistic rights attacked but failed to destroy the core logic of the socialist economy.[5] The fragmented socialist ideal of marriage was supplemented not only by individualistic views of marriage and family but also the returned pre-socialist Confucian kinship norms.[6] New laws that recognized and enforced a married person's separate identity, particularly as a separate property owner, have been met with strong resistance. As a result, Chinese courts struggle to balance the ideal that marriage forms a permanent communal conjugal household, and spouses' individual interests in a privatized family economy.

Consistent with the egalitarian marriage ideal, marital property is distributed equally between the spouses at the time of divorce. However, division of the marital estate is not always equal. Judicial deviations from equal division are encouraged in the interests of minor children, women, and an innocent spouse,[7] and compensation for a spouse's nonmonetary contribution in the care of minor children and elderly parents.[8] With more women leaving the workforce to become homemakers and greater gender inequality in income,

3. Sun Minyang (孙鸣阳), Lun Chengshi Zhigong Zhufang Fenpei He Fangzu Zhidu De Gaige (论城市职工住房分配和房租制度的改革) [On Urban Employees' Housing Distribution and Rent System Reform], Jinji Yanjiu (经济研究) [Econ. Rsch. J.] Issue 7 (1983), 58–59.

4. Wang Shuyun (王叔云), Juyou Zhongguo Tese De Shehuizhuyi Jinji Zhidu—Xuexi Xin Xianfa De Tihui (具有中国特色的社会主义经济制度一学习新宪法的体会) [Socialist Economic System with Chinese Characteristics—Reflections from Learning the New Constitution] Caijin Kexue (财经科学) [Fin. & Econ.] Issue 3 (1983) 1–10; and Ruan Hui & Wu Song (阮辉, 吴淞), Guanyu Zhengque Chuli Jiti Jinji He Jiating Jinji Guanxi (关于正确处理集体经济和家庭经济关系) [On Properly Handling the Relation between Collective Economy and Family Economy] Inzhi Yanjiu (印支研究) [Indo-China Studies] Issue 1 (1984), 65; Sun Xiulu (孙秀禄), Guanyu Jianli Zhigong Jiating Nongchang De Jige Lilun Wenti (关于建立职工家庭农场的几个理论问题) [Several Theoretical Issues on Establishing Employee Family Farms] Zhonguo Nongcun Guancha (中国农村观察) [China Rural Survey] Issue 2 (1985), 63–65; And Chen Xin (陈星); Woguo Xinxing Jiating Jinying He Shehuizhuyi Nongye Xiandaihua (我国新型家庭经营和社会主义农业现代化) [Our Country's New Family Management and Socialist Agriculture Modernization], Qiushi (求实) [Truth Seeking] Issue 1 (1984), 1–7.

5. On the persistence of socialist political, legal, and economic ideologies in the post-Mao reform era, see Michael William Dowdle, *Of Parliaments, Pragmatism, and the Dynamics of Constitutional Development: The Curious Case of China*, 35 N.Y.U. J. Int'l L. & Pol. 1, 124 (2002); and Tao Rong, *Employees' Property Rights in China's State-Owned Enterprise Reorganization*, 13 Colum. J. Asian L. 153 (1999).

6. Teemu Ruskola, *People, Inc.? Law, Economic Enterprise, and the Development of Inequality in China*, 67 Am. J. Comp. L. 383, 406 (2019).

7. The Civil Code art. 1087.

8. *Id.* art. 1088.

every facet of economic significance in a marriage—the wife's unpaid housework, the husband's gainful employment, and their respective acquisition or loss of job skills, professional licenses, career prospects, and future entitlements—will require Chinese courts in the coming years to refine the concept of an egalitarian marital economic partnership. In facing these challenges, Chinese courts must balance the financial interests and needs of each spouse, their children, and their elderly parents.

§ 8.1 Marital Community Property

Marital community property is mainly property acquired through the couple's labor or efforts during the marriage. Not all property acquired during the marriage is the spouses' "community property." The Civil Code provides that marital community property includes the following property acquired by the spouses during the marriage: (1) wages, bonuses, and any compensations for services; (2) income from production, business management, or investment; (3) income from Intellectual Property; (4) inheritance, bequests, or gifts; and (5) any other properties should be included as marital community property.[9] In summary, whether an asset is marital community property is determined by the time of acquisition and the source of acquisition. If an asset is acquired during the marriage and with marital funds or efforts, then it is the spouses' marital community property regardless which spouse holds the title. For example, in *Liu v. Cao*, the Beijing No. 2 Intermediate People's Court reviewed the source of funds used to acquire a home during the marriage to determine whether the home titled solely in the husband's name was martial community property.[10]

8.1.1 Employment Earnings

Earnings from employment, including wages, bonuses, and any compensations for services (*laowu baochou*) earned during the marriage are community property of the husband and wife.[11] Compensations for services include employee benefits, such as employee subsidies and allowances.

9. *Id.* art. 1602 para. 1.

10. Zhu Jiang (朱江) Ed., Liu Mou Sui Cao Moumou Lihun Hou Caichan Jiufen An (刘某诉曹某某离婚后财产纠纷案) [Liu Mou Sue Cao Moumou Post-Divorce Property Dispute Case], Beijing Shi Di Er Zhongji Renmin Fayuan Jindian Anli Fenlei Jingjie Hunyin Jiating Juan (北京市第二中级人民法院经典案例分类精解婚姻家庭卷) [Classification and Detailed Explanation of Classic Cases from the Second Intermediate People's Court of Beijing: Volume Marriage and Family Law] (2013).

11. The Civil Code art. 1602(1).

Compensations for services are simply substitutes for cash earnings and thus are marital community property.

Delayed or deferred employment compensation can be a significant part of a marital estate. Since 2010, Chinese banking regulatory authority has required that 40 percent to 50 percent of the annual variable compensation of senior commercial bank managers must be deferred over three years or longer.[12] However, there is not any clear statutory provision or SPC guidance on the issues concerning deferred or delayed cash compensation for a spouse's efforts made during the marriage but not yet received at the time of the divorce.

8.1.2 Income

Income from production, business management, or investment received during the marriage is the community property of a married couple.[13] Income from businesses or properties acquired with marital funds is naturally the marital community property of spouses.

Income from separate property may also be marital property if the income is generated by a spouse or both spouses' labor or efforts.[14] In *Wang v. Zhang*, Zhang had some rental properties purchased prior to the marriage, and some purchased during the marriage with proceeds from the sale of his premarital real estate property; and Wang had rental properties that she acquired before marriage. In addition, Zhang invested premarital funds in several structured personal financial products that required the investor's direct management. In the parties' divorce action, the court found that (1) the rental income accumulated from each party's separate real estate properties during the marriage was marital because of their active management of the rental properties; (2) most of the appreciation of each party's real estate properties remained each party's separate property as the increase of value was due to market forces and inflation, except that a small fraction of the appreciation of Zhang's real estate properties was marital, as Zhang used some marital funds in some transactions related to these properties; and (3) the appreciation and income

---

12. Zhongguo Yinghangye Jiandu Guanli Weiyuan Hui Guanyu Yingfa Shangye Yinghang Wenjian Xinchou Jianguan Zhiying De Tongzhi (Ying Jian Fa [2010] 14 Hao (中国银行业监督管理委员会关于印发《商业银行稳健薪酬监管指引》的通知 (银监发[2010]14号)) [Notice of China Banking Regulatory Commission on Issuing the Supervisory Guidelines on Sound Compensation in Commercial Banks (No. 14 [2010] China Banking Regulatory Commission)] art. 16. *See also* Wei Jiang, Yunguo Liu, Gerald J. Lobo, Yue Xu, Deferred Cash Compensation and Risk-Taking: Evidence from the Chinese Banking Industry, 53 Pacific-Basin Fin. J. 432–48, (2019).

13. The Civil Code art. 1602(2).

14. The Marriage and Family Book Interpretations (I) art. 26.

from Zhang's investments were marital property because Zhang put in time and efforts to manage the investment during the marriage.[15]

8.1.3 Intellectual Property Income and Proceeds

"Intellectual property income and proceeds" (*zhishi chanquan shouyi*) earned during the marriage is marital community property.[16] Only intellectual property income and proceeds that have been earned during the marriage or, as established by clear evidence, will be earned in the future is marital property.[17] In other words, speculative future income is not marital property.

Copyright, patent, or other intellectual property acquired during the marriage is the creator-spouse's separate property. A creator is the sole owner of intellectual property, as intellectual property is a property right as well as a status under Chinese law. A nontitled spouse is only entitled to the income and profit, such as royalties, generated by an intellectual property during the marriage, but not control of the intellectual property. For example, in *Zhu v. Xing*, Xing was a singer and songwriter. Xing co-wrote several songs with Song, and later bought Song's share in the copyrights and became sole owner of the copyrights of these songs. In Xing and Zhu's divorce action, Zhu sought a share in the copyrights and future income from the songs. The Beijing No. 2 Intermediate People's Court found that half of the copyrights of the songs that Xing co-authored was Xing's personal property and that half of the copyrights was clearly marital property as it was purchased with marital funds. The court found that as Xing is the creator of these songs, he could have better use of the copyrights. Furthermore, since Zhu provided no evidence that these songs were performed and generated any income during the marriage, the court could not speculate the future income or profit from the copyrights. Thus, the court awarded Xing the entire interest in the songs' copyrights and ordered Xing to reimburse Zhu half of the marital funds that he used to acquire the co-author's share of the copyrights.[18]

8.1.4 Inheritance and Gifts

In Chinese tradition, married couples are treated as conjugal households, and family wealth is passed on through generations of households instead of individuals. In other words, inheritance, bequests, or gifts are passed to a

---

15. Zhu, *supra* note 10, Zhang Moumou Su Wang Moumou Lihun Jiufen An (张某某诉王某某离婚纠纷案) [Zhang Moumou Sue Wang Moumou Divorce Dispute Case].

16. The Civil Code art. 1602(3).

17. The Marriage and Family Book Interpretations (I) art. 24.

18. (2014) Er Zhong Min Zhong Zi Di 02678 Hao ((2014) 二中民终字第02678号).

married couple's household, not individual spouses. This custom is adopted in the Civil Code. The Civil Code provides that inheritance, bequests, or gifts received by either spouse during the marriage are community property unless the donor of a bequest of gift expressly specifies that the bequest or gift is given to a spouse individually.[19]

Spouses' joint right to third-party gifts and inheritance is most relevant to marital homes. Marital homes are the main asset of most Chinese families. Customarily, the husband's parents, sometimes together with the wife's parents, finance the purchase of the newlyweds' new home. The disposition of a marital home at the time of divorce, thus, not only involves the spouses but also their parents, who often have contributed their life savings to the couple's home. Thus, it can be extremely unfair to the contributing parents to treat a marital home that they purchased with their life savings for their child's benefits as the young couple's marital property. On the other hand, if the marital home remains separate property of the spouse (usually the husband) whose parents have provided the funds to acquire the home, the other spouse (usually the wife) will be left with no meaningful assets when the marriage fails.[20] To balance the various interests involved in marital homes, the SPC has stipulated that if a marital home is purchased before the marriage by a spouse's parents, the home should be deemed as a premarital gift to the spouse whose parents provided the funds for the purchase, whereas if a marital home is purchased after the marriage by a spouse's parents, the home should be deemed as a gift to both spouses, unless the parties have expressly agreed otherwise in writing.[21] For instance, in the case of *Yu v. Li*, the court found that the marital home purchased with funds from Li's parents during the marriage was Yu and Li's marital property, as Li's mother did not expressly designate the gift to Li in writing. However, considering that Li's parents paid over RMB500,000 for the down payment, the court awarded RMB500,000 more to Li when dividing the equity of the home between Yu and Li.[22] For further discussions of disposition of a marital home purchased with funds from a spouse's parents, see subsection 8.6.3.

---

19. The Civil Code art. 1602.

20. Yang Jinling (杨晋玲), Fuqi Caichan Zhuanhua De Helixing Sikao—Yi Fangchan "Jiamin" Re Wei Beijing (夫妻财产转化的合理性思考—以房产"加名"热为背景) [Fairness Consideration in Marital Property Transmutation—In the Context of "Adding Name" on Real Property Mania] Yunnan Daxue Xuebao Faxue Ban (云南大学学报法学版) [J. Yunnan Univ. L. Ed.], Sept. 2013, Vol. 26 No. 5, 126–33.

21. The Marriage and Family Book Interpretations (I) art. 29.

22. (2020) Zhe Min Zai 153 Hao ((2020）浙民再153号).

8.1.5 Other Marital Property

Properties acquired through spouses' active efforts during the marriage and income from either spouse's active investment of separate property during the marriage are all marital community properties.[23] Appreciation of either party's separate property, except for passive income and growth, is marital community property as well.[24] Marital community property also includes entitlements acquired during the marriage, including social security entitlements that either party has earned or has acquired vested interest in,[25] and entitlements received by state-owned enterprises employees, such as housing subsidies (*zhufang butie*) and bankruptcy resettlement compensation (*pochan anzhi buchang fei*).[26]

§ 8.2 Separate Property

Separate property, as an exception to marital community property, is construed narrowly in the Civil Code. Separate property includes (1) property acquired before marriage; (2) compensation for personal injuries; (3) property acquired by bequest, gift, or contract that is expressly given to one spouse; (4) personal items exclusively used by one spouse; and (5) any other property that should be a spouse's separate property.[27] In addition, property defined as separate property by the spouses' written agreement is separate property.[28]

8.2.1 Premarital Property

Premarital property is separate property and remains separate property during the marriage.[29] Under the doctrine of transmutation, a separate property asset can be converted into marital property either by conveyance, by agreement, by comingling separate and marital property, or by joint use of the separate property. Chinese law rejects the doctrine of "transmutation" by commingling or joint use.[30] Property that is originally a spouse's separate property does not change its nature into marital community property during

23. The Marriage and Family Book Interpretations (I) art. 25 (1).
24. *Id*. art. 26.
25. *Id*. art. 25 (2) and (3).
26. *Id*.
27. The Civil Code art. 1063.
28. *Id*. art. 1065.
29. The Marriage and Family Book Interpretations (I) art. 31.
30. He Jian (贺剑), Lun Funqi Geren Caichan De Zhuanhua Guize (论夫妻个人财产的转化规则) [On the Doctrine of Transmutation of a Spouse's Separate Property] Faxue (法学) [Law Science] Issue 2 (2015), 50–54.

the marriage unless the parties have agreed otherwise in writing.[31] Therefore, joint use or commingling of separate property and marital property does not convert separate property into marital property.

Nevertheless, the appreciation in value attributed to the titled spouse or both spouses' efforts and labor is marital and subject to distribution at the time of divorce.[32] In addition, if the titled spouse transfers their separate property to the parties' joint name, the separate property becomes marital joint property. For instance, a Ningxia court awarded the wife about 20 percent of the marital home that was gifted to the husband by his parents before the marriage because the husband added the wife's name on the deed during the marriage. However, considering that the wife made no contribution to the acquisition of the home and her abuse of the parties' child, the court did not divide the family home equally between the husband and wife.[33]

8.2.2 Gifts and Inheritance to One Spouse

Property acquired by bequest, gift, or contract that is expressly given to one spouse is the recipient's separate property.[34]

If the marital home is purchased before the marriage by a spouse's parents, the home is deemed as a premarital gift to the spouse whose parents provided the funds for the purchase, whereas if the marital home is purchased after the marriage by a spouse's parents, the home is deemed as a gift to both spouses, unless the parties have agreed otherwise in writing.[35] In other words, if the marital home is purchased before the marriage with funds from a spouse's parents, the marital home is the spouse's separate property and will remain their separate property.

8.2.3 Betrothal Gifts and Dowry

Exchanging betrothal gift and dowry has been a Chinese tradition for centuries. The Chinese government waged numerous campaigns against it and had attempted to outlaw betrothal gifts. The government labeled marriages contracted through exchanging betrothal gifts as "money marriages" (*jingqian hunyi*)—marriages based on money instead of love. However, betrothal gifts have not only survived but thrived in recent years. With greater gender imbalance and growing family wealth, the cost of betrothal gifts, often referred to

31. The Marriage and Family Book Interpretations (I) art. 31.
32. *Id*. art. 26.
33. (2020) Ning 02 Min Zhong 540 Hao ((2020) 宁02民终540号).
34. The Civil Code art. 1063(3).
35. The Marriage and Family Book Interpretations (I) art. 29.

as the "bride price," has skyrocketed.[36] In some rural areas, the customary amount of betrothal gift is at the level of five to six times a villager's average annual income.[37]

The "money marriage" problem has become a serious legal issue. Both the number of disputes and the disputed amounts continue to rise. Many disputes over betrothal gifts have led to severe violence in rural areas.[38] Chinese courts' proper handling of betrothal gift disputes is of great importance in "maintaining a harmonious and stable social order."[39]

The nature of gifts exchanged in anticipation of a marriage is not clearly defined in Chinese law. It is not at all clear whether betrothal gifts are conditional gifts that must be returned when an engagement breaks, or when a marriage ends. Nor is it clear whether betrothal gifts remain a recipient-spouse's separate property after the marriage or become a couple's marital property. Despite the ambiguity about the nature of betrothal gifts, the SPC has adopted three general rules on adjudicating betrothal gift disputes: (1) betrothal gifts or dowry must be returned if the parties do not marry; (2) betrothal gifts or dowry must be returned at the time of divorce if the parties have registered the marriage but have not lived together; and (3) betrothal gifts or dowry must be returned at the time of divorce if the premarital gifts have caused the donor hardship in supporting him/herself.[40]

In *Guo v. Lu*, the wife was ordered to return the betrothal gifts from the husband's family when the parties divorced. Guo and Lu's marriage was arranged by their parents through a matchmaker. The Guo family paid the Lu family a significant amount of cash as betrothal gifts over approximately one and a half years. As soon as the agreed amount was paid in full, the couple registered their marriage and held a wedding ceremony. However, Lu refused to live with Guo after the wedding. The marriage was never consummated. Guo filed for divorce and demanded Lu's family to return the betrothal gifts. Lu opposed the divorce and refused to return the gifts, claiming that according to Confucius's teaching, a husband cannot divorce a rightful wife, such

36. The skyrocketing cost of betrothal gifts has been widely reported; *see, e.g.*, Josh Ye, *How Much Does It Cost a Man to Get Married in China? Clue: It Involves a Flat and Wads of Cash*, S. China Morning Post (Feb. 20, 2017), https://www.scmp.com/news/china/society/article/2072313/cost-bridegroom-gifts-secure-permission-marry-soars-china.

37. Guao Linyu, Shang Linghui, Xue Na, Wu Xiling, Wang Zemin (郭林玉, 尚凌晖, 薛娜, 武喜玲, 王泽民), Guanyu Nongcun Hunyin Falü Wenti De Yanjiu – Yi Gansu Sheng Pingliang Shi Lingtai Xian Du Dian Zhen Wei Li (关于农村婚姻法律问题的研究—以甘肃省平凉市灵台县独店镇为例) [A Study on Rural Marriage Law Issues—The Two of Dudian in Lingtai County, Pingliang City, Gansu Province], Fazhi Bolan (法制博览) [Legal Envision] Issue 1. Vol. 2 (2020), 44–46, 44.

38. FMTC 13.

39. FMTC 37.

40. The Marriage and Family Book Interpretations (I) art. 5.

as her, who is acquired through a formal marriage arranged by the parents and matchmakers and celebrated by a proper wedding (*mingmei zhengqu*). The court found that the parties had never lived together, and the marriage was arranged by their parents. Therefore, the court granted Guo a divorce, and ordered Lu to return Guo the betrothal gifts but allowed Lu to keep the furnishings and household appliances that her family gave to the couple as Lu's dowry.[41]

The case of Wang Peng and Xu Lili was much more complicated. Before Wang and Xu were married, the Wang family borrowed RMB110,000 to pay for Wang Peng's betrothal gifts given to Xu Lili. The Wang family gave the Xu family a total of RMB100,000 in cash and a motorcycle. In addition, Wang's parents purchased new furniture and appliances for the young couple prior to the marriage. In the second year of the marriage, Xu purchased a commercial van for Wang with the cash given to her as a betrothal gift. Wang drove the van for hire to support the family. In the third year of the marriage, Xu left the marital residence after an argument with Wang and the parties separated. Wang then filed for a divorce. The court found that Wang and Xu's mutual affection was irretrievably broken down and granted the divorce. The court also found that without the van, Wang would not be able to support himself or repay the debts that his family borrowed to pay for the betrothal gifts, and that the Wang family would suffer extreme financial hardship if the Xu family were to retain the betrothal gifts. Therefore, the court ruled that Wang could keep the van and Xu's parents must return the motorcycle to Wang's parents.[42]

Disputes over betrothal gifts and engagement gifts occur in urban areas as well. Chinese courts rely on the same SPC rules to determine whether engagement gifts should be returned, particularly when the parties do not marry. *Sun v. E* is one of the earlier cases concerning engagement gifts in urban areas. Sun and E both live in Beijing. They participated in a popular dating show, "If You Are the One," and got engaged on the show. In anticipation of the marriage, E introduced Sun to his parents and gifted a BMW to Sun. Sun broke the engagement before the wedding. She refused to return the car to Sun and claimed that E's gifts to her were unconditional, as the custom of betrothal gifts was not practiced in Beijing. The Beijing court rejected Sun's argument and ordered Sun to return the car. The court found that the car was a betrothal gift conditioned on the parties' marriage and Sun would be unjustly enriched if she were to keep the car.[43] Later, in *Liu v. Zhou, et al.*, the Beijing court ordered Liu's ex-girlfriend Zhou and her mother to return the funds that Liu

41. FMTC 13.
42. FMTC 27.
43. Zhu, *supra* note 10, Sun Moumou Su E Moumou Hunyue Caichan Jiufen An (孙某某诉鄂某某婚约财产纠纷案) [Sun Moumou Sue E Moumou Engagement Property Dispute Case].

transferred to them as engagement gifts because the parties did not marry.[44] Whether a gift is an engagement gift or an unconditional gift is determined by the totality of the circumstances in more complex cases. For instance, after examining the funds transfers throughout the parties' courting period, the Beijing High People's Court found that the last large transfer of RMB1 million from Yu, the boyfriend, to Yan, the girlfriend, was an engagement gift conditioned on the parties' anticipated marriage and was not an unconditional birthday present as Yan alleged. The court found that Yu showered Yan with small cash gifts throughout their relationship, but he transferred the RMB1 million when the parties were making plans for marriage and the purchase of a marital home. Thus, the Beijing court ordered Yan to return the one million yuan to Yu, as the sum is a betrothal gift that must be returned when the parties did not marry.[45]

Engagement gift cases show that Chinese courts exercise great discretion in determining under what circumstances these gifts must be returned and how much. Liu and Zhai's case was heard in the courts in Zibo City, a small city in Eastern China. Liu was 20 and Zhai was 16 when they were "married" at a traditional wedding ceremony. Since neither party had reached the legal marriage age, they could not register the marriage. Liu and Zhai soon had a daughter. A couple years later, Zhai left Liu and their daughter for another man. Liu then sued Zhai for the return of betrothal gifts on the ground that Zhai failed to marry him. The Zibo City court held that although the SPC judicial interpretations allow return of betrothal gifts if the parties did not marry, the judicial interpretations did not require return of the entirety of the gifts, and that the court must determine the amount to be returned based on each party's fault and circumstances of the case. Having reviewed the amounts transferred from Liu's parents and Liu to Zhai and her parents, the court found that Zhai and Liu had lived together for a couple of years and had a child, and some of the transfers were spent on the parties' household expenses. The court also found that Liu attempted to marry Zhai, who was a minor at the time of their *de facto* marriage, and it was not Zhai's fault that the parties could not legally marry and instead it was Liu's fault to attempt to circumvent the legal requirements for marriage. However, considering that Liu's family in fact paid Zhai and her family a significant amount of betrothal gifts and that Liu was raising the parties' child without Zhai's help, the court ordered Zhai to repay Liu a portion of the gifts that she received from the Liu family.[46]

44. (2020) Jing 02 Min Zhong 11598 Hao ((2020) 京02民终11598号).
45. (2020) Jing Min Shen 601 Hao ((2020) 京民申601号).
46. (2020) Lu 03 Min Zhong 2475 Hao ((2020) 鲁03民终2475号).

§ 8.3 Agreements Concerning Property

Prenuptial agreements contemplating property division upon divorce had been held void as against public policy in encouraging divorce in the United States until 1990s. Today, prenuptial agreements and postnuptial agreements in contemplation of divorce are no longer *per se* unenforceable.[47] The views on contracts between spouses followed a similar path of development in China. Prenuptial agreement was a novel concept in Chinese society. The public heatedly debated issues such as whether prenuptial agreements induce divorces and whether fidelity could be enforced by contracts between the husband and wife.[48] As individual and family wealth has accumulated rapidly in China since the 1990s, the support for traditional communal, conjugal property regime has quickly given way to a contractual view of marriage. Prenuptial agreement and post-nuptial agreement are now common and widely accepted among the younger generation.

The Civil Code provides that spouses may define their property rights by contract.[49] This provision has two aspects. On one hand, couples are free to structure their own property relationship by agreement in writing and tailor their respective interests in properties acquired prior to the marriage and during the marriage. They may keep all or some of their property as separate property. They may also make all their property community property. They may hold their properties in sole ownership of one spouse, or joint ownership of both spouses, or mixed ownership.[50] On the other hand, personal rights and duties arising from marriage, such as mutual respect and marital fidelity, are not property rights and therefore may not be altered by private agreements.

Prenuptial or postnuptial property agreements may be modified, terminated, or rescinded by the parties' later agreement. Absent fraud, duress, or unconscionability, Chinese courts generally uphold a valid prenuptial agreement.

---

47. Adrienne Hunter Jules & Fernanda G. Nicola, *The Contractualization of Family Law in the United States*, 62 AM. J. COMP. L. 151, 161 (2014).

48. *See, e.g.*, Min Weiguo (闵卫国) Lun Fuqi Zhongcheng Xieyi Yu Lihun Sunhai Peichang (论夫妻忠诚协议与离婚损害赔偿) [On Marital Fidelity Clause and Divorce Damage Compensation], Falu Shiyong (法律适用) [J. L. APPLICATION] 2013, Issue 5, 54–57, arguing that spouses' agreement on compensation for emotional damage caused by infidelity that caused divorce should be enforceable.

49. The Civil Code art. 1065.

50. *Id.* art. 1065 para. 1.

8.3.1 Timing

Property agreements between spouses may be entered before the marriage, during the marriage, or at the time of a divorce. Spouses may designate, by agreement, separate or joint ownership of properties acquired before the marriage as well as properties acquired during the marriage.[51] Thus, the Civil Code provisions concerning property agreements between spouses are applicable to prenuptial agreements, post-nuptial agreements, and divorce property settlement agreements.

8.3.2 Formality

Inter-spouse property agreements must be in writing and must not be ambiguous. When a property agreement is too vague or ambiguous to be enforced, the statutory classification of marital property and separate property shall apply.[52] A property agreement between the spouses must be in writing and be signed by the parties.[53] Verbal prenuptial agreements or post-nuptial agreements are not enforceable. Although prenuptial agreements or post-nuptial agreements do not have to be notarized, they must be signed by both parties.

A duly executed prenuptial agreement is given the same presumption of legality as any other contract and, in the absence of fraud, duress, or any other misconduct, is presumed to be valid. Thus, in *Wei v. Zhang*, the Beijing court upheld a prenuptial agreement after finding that the agreement was properly executed and there was no evidence of any cause that might render it unenforceable.[54]

8.3.3 Consent

Spouses' agreement concerning property must be entered into voluntarily, without fraud or duress, and with full knowledge of the consequences of the agreement. Both parties must have full legal capacity to give the consent. If either party has no legal capacity or has limited legal capacity when the property agreement is entered, such agreement is not binding. The party seeking to invalidate the agreement bears the burden of proof to prove incapacitation, fraud, duress, or any other misconduct.

An inter-spouse property agreement must be consensual and free from duress, fraud, or mistake. The court may set aside any agreement that was entered against a party's true intention, or under duress, or through fraud, or by mistake. Therefore, the Jiangsu Province High People's Court set aside a

---

51. *Id.* art. 1065 para. 2.
52. *Id.* art. 1065 para. 1.
53. *Id.* art. 1065 para. 1.
54. (2020) Jing Min Shen 1738 Hao ((2020) 京民申1738号).

post-nuptial agreement in which the husband agreed to transfer a real estate property to the wife. The court found that the husband was held, beaten, and severely injured by the wife and her relatives and was forced to sign the agreement during the beating.[55] Duress defense requires a showing of actions that have caused serious injuries to a person's body, reputation, or property, or have caused a person's reasonable fear of such injuries. For example, in *Qiao v. Zhao*, a Jiangsu court found that the husband's threat not to marry the wife during her difficult pregnancy did not amount to duress or coercion that could render the parties' prenuptial agreement invalid.[56]

8.3.4 Limits of Contractual Freedom

Spouses' freedom to contract their property is not unlimited. Agreements concerning property must not violate any laws, regulations, or public order and good morals (*gongxü liaosu*); and may not be premised on a scheme to infringe others' legal rights.

8.3.4.1 Loyalty Agreement

The Marriage Law first introduced the concept of contract between spouses in 2001.[57] The introduction of marital contracts was viewed as a new emphasis on personal choice, and a shift from family-centered marriage to individual-centered marriage. The public opinion first reacted quite negatively to this Western legal transplant but quickly turned its attention to the Chinese adaptation: loyalty agreements, which often impose hefty penalties on unfaithful spouses. Chinese courts are divided on the enforceability of "loyalty agreements" but agree that although infidelity must be condemned, only bigamy, adultery, and other serious breaches of marital fidelity may be penalized by a moderate monetary compensation to the innocent spouse.[58] Two local courts' decisions illustrate the Chinese courts' divisions and consensus on the issues related to loyalty agreements.

In *Chen v. Gao*, the Intermediate People's Court of Cangzhou, a small city in northern China, declined to award the husband's premarital residence to the wife pursuant to the parties' "Husband and Wife Loyalty Agreement," which provided that if one party betrayed the other party, the party that was

55. (2018) Su Min Shen 4062 Hao ((2018) 苏民申4062号).
56. (2020) Su 10 Min Zhong 1012 Hao ((2020) 苏10民终1012号).
57. Marriage Law art. 19.
58. Song Yang (宋洋) Funqi Zhongcheng Xieyi Shenpan Yanjiu—Yi 30 Caipan Wenshu Wei Yang Ben (夫妻忠诚协议审判研究一以30 份裁判文书为样本) [A Study on Spousal Loyalty Agreement Adjudication—30 Judgments As Samples] Sichuan Wenli Xueyuan Bao (四川文理学院学报) [Sichuan Univ. of Arts & Sci. J.] Vol. 29 No. 6 (Nov. 2019), 35, and 38–39. *See also* Davis, *supra* note 2, at 565.

at fault must forfeit all of his/her properties to the other party. The Cangzhou court held that the parties' loyalty agreement was enforceable. The court explained:

> The legal effect of "Spouses Loyalty Agreement," such as the one signed by both parties, is currently controversial among scholars. Nor is there a uniform standard for determining the enforceability of such agreements in judicial practice. If a loyalty agreement is entered with the parties' consent, the law must recognize its validity. Article 2 of the Contract Law of the People's Republic of China provides that "[c]ontract referred in this Law is an agreement between natural persons, legal persons or other entities as equal parties for the establishment, modification of a relationship involving the civil rights and obligations of the parties." Obviously, the entry of a loyalty agreement is a manifestation of the parties' contractual terms on their private life. In other words, a loyalty agreement should be protected by law if it is an expression of true intentions of both parties, if it is based on the premise of equality, voluntariness, and no coercion, if it does not violate any provisions of the law, or harm the others, or the public interests of the society, and if it has all essential elements of a valid contract under the contract law. Furthermore, the moral content of spouses' duty of fidelity falls within the scope of law and recognition of loyalty agreements' enforceability is consistent with the legislative intent of the Marriage Law and is beneficial to the protection of equal, harmonious, and civil marital and family relationships.[59]

However, the Cangzhou court found that the husband's conduct did not amount to a "betrayal" punishable under the parties' loyalty agreement because the husband chatted with women online and met some of them at his home, but he did not have sex with any of these women. The court found that the husband's conduct might have hurt the wife's feelings, but it did not amount to a violation of the duty of fidelity between a husband and wife in that the duty of fidelity only requires married couples not to engage in extramarital sex. Therefore, the Cangzhou court refused to award the husband's properties to the wife.[60]

The Ju County People's Court disagreed with the Cangzhou court in its opinion in the case of Zhong and Liu. Ju County is a small rural county of Shangdong Province in eastern China. Before the marriage, Liu signed a note stating that he promised not to see his ex-wife alone or take her calls, and that if he failed to keep his promise, he would pay Zhong RMB300,000 and give all his properties to Zhong. During the marriage, Liu re-signed the same note four times to reaffirm his commitment. Finally, the parties entered a written agreement that Liu would pay Zhong RMB300,000 and all his cash savings if he broke his promise not to have any contact with his ex-wife. Liu simultaneously executed a promissory note for RMB300,000 to Zhong as guarantee. Zhong and Liu eventually broke up because Liu had numerous contacts with his ex-wife. Liu filed for divorce and tried to enforce the parties' agreement in the Ju County court. However, the court refused to enforce the agreement. The court opined that:

---

59. (2015) Cang Min Zhong Zi Di 268 Hao ((2015) 沧民终字第268号).
60. *Id.*

> The parties' written agreement and Liu's notes are essentially "loyalty agreements." The "RMB300,000 loan" provided in the parties' agreement and the promised compensation of RMB300,000 or RMB600,000 are not a loan or compensation that actually incurred but rather the wife's demand for "emotional injury compensation" intended to prevent the husband's interaction with his ex-wife. The duty of fidelity provided in Article 4 of the Marriage Law is a moral obligation. A contract in which a spouse uses this moral obligation as consideration to trade with the other spouse cannot be considered as a contract defining civil right and obligation. A marriage in its nature is a consensual union of two people of opposite sexes for a life together. The bond that holds a marriage together is both spouses' cherished feeling for each other. Using monetary penalty as predetermined punishment for breaking such bond does not sustain the stability of a marriage but causes alienations between spouses. Restriction of a spouse's freedom to divorce in fact is contrary to the basic principle of law and inconsistent with the common people's good morals. Article 2 of the Contract Law provides that "Contract referred in this Law is an agreement between natural persons, legal persons or other entities as equal parties for the establishment, modification of a relationship involving the civil rights and obligations of the parties. Agreements concerning marriage, adoption, guardianship, and any other personal status shall be governed by the provisions of other laws." Therefore, "loyalty agreements" concerning personal status are not governed by the Contract Law. Article 46 of the Marriage Law already clearly defines the four circumstances under which an innocent spouse may seek compensation for damages from the other spouse as: (1) bigamy; (2) a married person's cohabitation with a third-party; (3) domestic violence; (4) maltreatment or abandonment of a family member. The Marriage Law does not provide that a party's breach of ordinary loyalty can give rise to any liability for compensatory damages. The existing legal grounds for compensation for serious breach of fidelity are bigamy and a married person's cohabitation with a third party. In this case, Zhong did not offer any evidence that Liu had committed either offense. Therefore, Zhong's request for Liu to compensate her in the amount of 300,000 has no legal basis."[61]

The Ju County court's decision was affirmed on appeal.[62]

In recent years, Chinese courts seem to follow the Cangzhou court's line of reasoning more often than not and have upheld loyalty agreements and imposed agreed penalties in cases involving serious marital infidelity and misconduct. For example, the Chengdu Intermediate People's Court found the husband violated the loyalty agreement by engaging in extramarital affairs and solicitating prostitution and awarded the parties' marital property and the husband's separate property to the wife pursuant to the parties' loyalty agreement.[63] A Shanghai trial court also found that the parties' loyalty agreement was binding and enforceable and fined the husband, who lived openly with his paramour and had a child with her. However, the court reduced the penalty from RMB200,000 to RMB50,000 and made the award as compensation for the emotional harm that the wife had suffered from the husband's infidelity.[64]

61. (2014) Ri Min Yi Zhong Di 835 Hao ((2014) 日民一终字第835号).
62. *Id.*
63. (2019) Chuan 01 Min Zhong 1078 Hao ((2019) 川01民终1078号).
64. (2020) Hu 0115 Min Chu 46816 Hao ((2020) 沪0115民初46816号).

8.3.4.2 Creditors

Spouses' prerogative to hold family property either as individuals or jointly makes it possible for spouses to shield assets from creditors. In response to spouses' collusive schemes to defeat creditors, Chinese law prohibits inter-spouse agreements designed to shield assets from any *bona fide* creditors and innocent third parties. *Chen v. Huang and Wang* illustrates a common scheme that couples use to invade debts in China. Huang and Wang were married. Wang borrowed a total of RMB 250,000 from his business associate, Chen. The loan was secured by Wang and Huang's marital home. Immediately before the loan became due, Wang and Huang signed a property settlement agreement under which Huang was to receive the parties' assets, including the home, and Wang was to assume the parties' debts. Wang and Huang obtained a divorce by registration and transferred the home to Huang. Chen found out about the transfer in his collection action against Wang and Huang. The court found that Huang and Wang faked the divorce, and their property agreement was entered in bad faith to shield their assets from a *bona fide* creditor, Chen. The court voided the property transfer from Wang to Huang and attached the home for the unpaid debt owed to Chen.[65]

The Civil Code tries to balance the protection of creditors and spouses' freedom to contact. Thus, the Civil Code provides that if a creditor has the knowledge of the spouses' agreement to keep their property separate, any debt owed to the creditor by the debtor spouse can only be satisfied solely with the debtor spouse's separate property. [66] However, a spousal property agreement does not shield the spouses from a third party if the creditor did not know or could have not known of such agreement. A creditor can hold both spouses jointly liable for the debt incurred in one spouse's sole name unless the property agreement has been disclosed to the creditor.[67] Thus, the Beijing No. 3 Intermediate People's Court rejected a wife's claim that the purchases made by her husband were the husband's separate debt pursuant to the couple's prenuptial agreement, and she was not liable for the nonpayment of these purchases. The court found that the merchant had no notice or knowledge of the couple's prenuptial agreement and thus the prenuptial agreement had no effect on the merchant, who is a *bona fide* third party.[68] Furthermore, an agreement between the spouses that limits either spouse's ability to contract transactions may not be used against any *bona fide* third parties.[69]

65. (2020) Su 08 Min Zhong 1412 Hao ((2020)苏08民终1412号).
66. The Civil Code art. 1065 para. 3.
67. The Marriage and Family Book Interpretations (I) art. 37.
68. (2015) San Zhong Min Shen Zi Di 00569 Hao ((2015) 三中民申字第00569号).
69. The Civil Code art. 1061.

8.3.5 Enforcement

Absent fraud, duress, or unconscionability, Chinese courts generally uphold valid prenuptial or post-nuptial agreements and dispose parties' separate and marital properties according to their agreements at the time of divorce.

The validity and enforceability of a prenuptial agreement are often disputed at the time of divorce when a spouse regrets having transferred or promised to transfer a premarital home to the other party pursuant to a prenuptial agreement. The spouses who owned these premarital homes often argue the transfer as a "unilateral gift" that lacks consideration and may be rescinded freely. Chinese courts have repeatedly rejected such characterization. Generally, transfer of one spouse's premarital home to another spouse's sole name or to the parties' joint names may be rescinded only before the title transfer is registered.[70] Thus, in *Li v. Yang* the court refused to rescind the transfer of title on the husband's premarital home from him to the parties, finding that the husband transferred his premarital home to the parties jointly pursuant to the parties' prenuptial agreement and the title transfer had been completed.[71] In *Tang Ping v. Xie Yuhua,* the Anhui Province High People's Court held that the husband was entitled to rescind the gift of a premarital home from him as a sole owner to the parties as joint owners because he did not complete the transfer.[72]

When determining whether a premarital home has transformed into marital property pursuant to the parties' prenuptial or post-nuptial agreement, Chinese courts' decisions are usually based on the totality of the circumstances. As the Guangzhou Intermediate People's Court put it in *Zhao v. Yang,* "determination of marital community property and separate property involves spouses' personal status, property relationship, and ethical and moral issues concerning marriage and family," "to which commercial laws and doctrines, such as the Contract Law, designed to maintain fairness in transactions do not apply."[73] In *Zhao v. Yang,* the parties entered a post-nuptial agreement in which the husband agreed to transfer a home that he purchased shortly before the marriage to the parties, and the parties agreed to pay the mortgage and all carrying expenses of the home with marital funds. The parties and their children lived in the home. The parties paid for the home's mortgage and carrying expenses with marital funds in accordance with their agreement. However, the husband did not make the transfer. The Guangzhou court held that the parties' family home was marital community property because the wife contributed to the home by paying the mortgage payments

70. The Marriage and Family Book Interpretations (I) art. 32.
71. (2020) Ji Min Shen 61 Hao ((2020) 冀民申61号).
72. (2019) Wan Min Shen 36 Hao ((2019) 皖民申36号).
73. (2020) Yue 01 Min Zhong 15350 ((2020) 粤01民终15350号).

and other expenses and making the home into the parties' and their children's family home. The court found that the issue whether the husband could rescind his "gift" was irrelevant because the parties had a duly executed post-nuptial agreement in which the husband agreed to the transfer in exchange for the wife's contribution to mortgage payments. The Guangzhou court commented that the home might not have been a separate property to begin with as it was purchased immediately prior to the marriage and the home was largely paid for with marital funds, although the husband paid a small down payment with his separate money.[74]

Considering the totality of the case, Chinese courts have voided agreements that gifted one spouse's premarital home to the other spouse or to both spouses. In *Jiang v. Rao*, Jiang sought to set aside a prenuptial agreement and to void the transfer registration that transferred half of the interest in Jiang's premarital home to his wife, Rao. In the parties' prenuptial agreement, Jiang agreed to transfer half of the interest in his premarital home to Rao, and Rao agreed to share the mortgage payments with Jiang equally. Five years after the marriage, Jiang fell ill and was hospitalized several times for severe depression for over a year. Jiang could no longer work and had no income. Rao abandoned Jiang after he became ill. She then filed for divorce and sought her share in the home. Jiang was declared incompetent and was represented by his mother. The court found that Jiang was incapacitated and unable to support himself, and he needed ongoing medical treatment and care. The court held that Jiang was entitled to rescind the gift not only because the title transfer was not completed but more importantly because he has no income and is no longer able to work and support himself due to his illness and incapacity. The court set aside the prenuptial agreement and awarded Jiang the home.[75]

Similarly, in *Zhang v. Bai*, considering overall fairness and equity, the Chongqing court terminated a post-nuptial agreement in which the husband was given one-half of the wife's interest in a home that was her separate property. The wife, Zhang, and her sister co-owned a home. Zhang had a 90 percent interest in the home. Zhang and Bai entered a post-nuptial agreement providing that the couple would share the mortgage payments equally, and Bai would receive half of the wife's interest in the home. Bai did not make any mortgage payments during the marriage. In fact, he was abusive to the wife and essentially abandoned the wife. The Chongqing court found that the prenuptial agreement must be terminated due to Bai's noncompliance with his payment obligation.[76]

If the spouses enter a loan agreement for marital funds that are lent to one spouse for his or her own separate business or personal matters, such loan

74. *Id.*
75. (2020) Wan 07 Min Zhong 1167 Hao ((2020) 皖07民终1167号).
76. (2020) Yu Min Shen 1175 Hao ((2020) 渝民申1175号).

agreement is an inter-spouse agreement concerning marital property and may be enforced at the time of the divorce.[77] In *Zhang v. Lu*, the parties executed a promissory note during the marriage for a loan of RMB30 million that Lu lent to Zhang. Lu brought a civil lawsuit against Zhang for repayment of the loan after the parties' divorce as a creditor. Zhang argued that the transaction was an inter-spouse loan between the couple's companies and not for his personal use, and the disputed funds were marital property that had been accounted for in their divorce action. The SPC affirmed the lower courts' finding that the promissory note was a loan agreement enforceable under the contract law. The SPC further held that even if the disputed amount were marital property, Zhang must repay it as it was for his personal use and he could bring a post-judgment action as the promissory note was not addressed in the divorce action.[78]

§ 8.4 Marital Debts

As consumption becomes a driving force of the Chinese economy, Chinese families increasingly rely on credit. Purchases of major goods—homes, cars, home renovations, or education—and spending on luxuries like vacations or jewelry, are largely financed by consumer loans. The expansion of credit has led to a significant increase of consumer indebtedness and, for some, over-indebtedness.[79] As a result, the conflict between creditors' need to collect and an innocent spouse's need for protection from debts incurred unilaterally by his or her spouse has been vigorously litigated in court and in public opinion since the early 2000s.

In 2003, the SPC issued judicial interpretations that allowed creditors to hold spouses jointly liable for debts incurred in a spouse's sole name during the marriage.[80] Creditors could reach a couple's community property, even after the divorce or the debtor spouse's death, for satisfaction of debts incurred during the marriage unless the non-debtor spouse could prove that the debts were not marital.[81] This pro-creditor approach is widely adopted in many Western jurisdictions, and is consistent with the doctrine of marital agency that a couple is jointly liable for any transaction engaged by either spouse during the marriage, and the couple bears the burden of showing that

77. The Marriage and Family Book Interpretations (I) art. 82.

78. (2020) Zui Gao Fa Min Shen 1585 Hao ((2020) 最高法民申1585号); and (2019) Zhe Min Zhong 725 Hao ((2019) 浙民终725号).

79. Huifen Yin, *Consumer Credit and Over-indebtedness in China*, 27 Int'l Insolvency Rev. 58, 60–62 (2018).

80. The Marriage Law Interpretations (II), art. 24.

81. Zhu, *supra* note 10, Yao Mou Su Su Mou Zhaiquan Jiufen An (姚某诉苏某债权纠纷案) [Yao Mou Sue Su Mou Creditor's Right Dispute Case].

the transaction did not benefit the marital community. The strategic implications of these rules are apparent. If marital property law limits a creditor's recourse to a debtor spouse's separate property, a married person can use marriage as a wealth shield by transforming property that would have been available to their creditors into community property safe from his creditors, while continuing to enjoy actual control of the property.[82] For example, in *Liang Siyun v. Li Lianping, et al.*, the wife, Liang, attempted to stop a foreclosure on the marital home by her husband's 37 creditors. The creditors sought to foreclose on the couple's marital home, which was valued at RMB4,222,500. Liang argued that the marital home, which was purchased by the husband prior to the marriage in cash, was marital property and therefore should not be foreclosed to satisfy the husband's separate debt. The Guangdong Province High People's Court found that the husband purchased the marital home prior to the marriage and the home was his separate property subject to the foreclosure.[83] If Liang's husband had put the home in the parties' joint names and made it marital, his 37 creditors would not have been able to foreclose on the home.

In the Chinese public's view, however, a spouse's interest in the marital community property is morally superior to a creditor's interest. Women's rights advocates were particularly vocal and called for protection of divorced and widowed wives' financial security against their husbands' creditors.[84] The populist backlash against the law favoring creditors reflected a glaring flaw in the theory of marital community. Despite the utopian metaphor of the marital community under modern marriage laws, spouses do not merge into one, inseverable union, but rather remain as two separate individuals who can independently incur liability, for the betterment of the community or to its detriment. Indeed, if one spouse's creditor has an unfettered right to foreclose on marital community property regardless of the circumstances in which the obligation was incurred, a non-debtor spouse's interest in the marital estate may be exposed to creditors' recourse without his/her knowledge or consent. This result is clearly at odds with the premise of marriage as a union of two consenting equals.[85] The backlash against the SPC's creditor-friendly approach gradually pushed Chinese law toward favoring the protection of

82. Marie T. Reilly, *In Good Times and in Debt: The Evolution of Marital Agency and the Meaning of Marriage*, 87 Neb. L. Rev. 373, 391–92 (2008).

83. (2020) Yue Min Zhong 1110 Hao ((2020) 粤民终1110号).

84. Dan Shuhua (但淑华), Dui Hunyin Fa Jiesh Er Di Ershsi Tiao Tuiding Fuqi Gongton Zhaiwu Guize Zhi Fansi (对《婚姻法解释（二）》第二十四条推定夫妻共同债务规则之反思) [Rethinking the Presumption Rule of Married Couple's Joint Debts in China] Funü Yanjiu Luncong (妇女研究论丛) [Collection of Women's Studies] No. 6 Ser. No. 138 Nov. 2016, 66–72.

85. Reilly, *supra* note 82, at 393.

non-debtor spouses.[86] The new Civil Code requires a creditor to first establish that a spouse's debt has benefited the marital community before invading the spouses' community property.

8.4.1 Joint Debts

The rule governing marital joint debt is simple: debts jointly signed (*gong qian*) and jointly spent (*gong yong*) by a married couple are their joint debts. Spouses are liable for debts that he/she expressly contracts to be liable. Debts incurred during the marriage in both spouses' names or in one spouse's name but with the other spouse's consent or acquiescence are all marital joint debts.[87] The application of the seemingly simple rule is, however, complicated.

Generally, a spouse is not liable for debts in the other spouse's sole name. In some situations, a spouse could become jointly liable for debts incurred in the other spouse's sole name by imputation. Imputation of marital debts is guided by the doctrine of necessaries. The Civil Code provides that debts incurred in one spouse's sole name may be imputed as joint marital debts when they are incurred for ordinary necessaries of family life (*jiating richang shenghuo xueyao*).[88] The Civil Code further provides that any debt that is incurred in one spouse's sole name and exceeds the ordinary necessaries of family life may not be imputed as marital debt unless the creditor can prove that such debt was used for the spouses' joint living expenditure and/or joint business or was incurred with both spouses' express consent.[89] In addition, although premarital debts normally are not marital joint debts, a spouse's premarital debt that was used on ordinary necessities of family life may be imputed as marital debt as well.[90]

Imputation of marital debts is important when the debtor-spouse is insolvent. The debtor-spouse's insolvency inescapably requires either the non-debtor spouse or the creditor to bear the loss from the debtor's failure to pay. The Civil Code provisions related to marital debts are designed to protect non-debtor spouses and to shield marital assets from creditors of a spouse's separate debts.[91] Thus, it is extremely difficult for creditors to hold non-debtor

86. Huang Haitao (黄海涛), Fuqi Gongtong Zhaiwu De Sifa Rending (夫妻共同债务的司法认定) [Judicial Determination of Spouses' Joint Debts], Renmin Sifa (人民司法) [The People's Judicature] 19.2015, 70.

87. The Civil Code art. 1064 para. 1.

88. *Id.* art. 1064 para. 1.

89. *Id.* art. 1064 para. 2.

90. The Marriage and Family Book Interpretations (I) art. 33.

91. Pei Hua (裴桦), Minfa Dian Fuqi Zhaiwu Tiaokuan De Buzu Yu Yingdui (《民法典》夫妻债务条款的不足与应对) [The Inadequacy of the Marital Debt Provisions in the Civil Code and Its Remedy], Jiaoda Faxue (交大法学) SJTU L. Rev. No. 1 (2021), 5–6, and 15; and Huang Haitao, *supra* note 86, at 71–72.

spouses jointly liable for debts incurred by their spouses without their express consent. Before a creditor could hold a non-debtor spouse jointly liable for a debt not in the spouse's name, the creditor must first prove that the debts incurred by the debtor spouse are for marital use and therefore are marital. Creditors' burden to prove marital debts is exceedingly burdensome, as demonstrated in Shen Shuhua and Wang Xuejun's case. Eight creditors brought separate actions against Shen and Wang to vacate Shen and Wang's divorce judgment as an attempt to foreclose on the marital property that Wang received from the divorce to satisfy over RMB32 million in loans borrowed in Shen's sole name. Shen Shuhua, the wife, and Wang Xuejun, the husband, married in 2006. In 2010, Shen started a company in the city of Baoding with an initial investment of approximately RMB24 million. Shen's business was successful and provided the couple with a lavish lifestyle, including various luxurious homes and cars. Wang filed for a divorce in 2015 and the parties have battled over property distribution in court ever since.[92] During the divorce action, Shen Shuhua sold 42 percent of her stake in the company to several investors and then borrowed RMB32 million from them. The loans were secured by the parties' apartment in Beijing. Wang alleged that Shen and her investors colluded in concocting these loans as a scheme to conceal marital assets. The Beijing court eventually awarded Wang RMB14 million and the parties' apartment in Beijing and allocated the eight loans to Shen. Since Shen's assets were insufficient to satisfy the loans, the investors sought to vacate the divorce judgment and foreclose on the parties' Beijing apartment that was awarded to Wang in the parties' divorce action. The Beijing courts and the SPC rejected the investors' bid to vacate the divorce judgment in that the creditors lacked standing to challenge the divorce judgment and that they could simply bring a collection action against both Shen and Wang jointly by proving that the loans were the parties' joint marital debts.[93] Soon after the SPC's decisions, Li, another creditor of Shen's, sued Shen and Wang in the city of Baoding, and alleged that the RMB3.5-million loan Shen borrowed from him was the parties' joint marital debt. The Baoding courts found the loan was not Wang and Shen's marital debt for four reasons: (1) Wang did not sign the loan agreement or acquiesce to the loan; (2) the loan was not identified as marital debt in the parties' divorce action; (3) the amount of the loan exceeded the ordinary needs of a family; and (4) Li did not provide sufficient evidence that the loan was spent on the parties' joint living or business expenditures. Thus, the Baoding courts ruled that

92. (2017) Jing 0105 Min Chu 83294 Hao ((2017）京0105民初83294号).

93. (2020) Zui Gao Fa Min Shen 691 Hao ((2020）最高法民申691号), (2020) Zui Gao Fa Min Shen 702 Hao ((2020) 最高法民申702号, (2020) Zui Gao Fa Min Shen 703 Hao ((2020) 最高法民申703号), (2020) Zui Gao Fa Min Shen 704 Hao ((2020) 最高法民申704号), (2020) Zui Gao Fa Min Shen 754 Hao ((2020) 最高法民申754号), (2020) Zui Gao Fa Min Shen 787 Hao ((2020) 最高法民申787号), and (2020) Zui Gao Fa Min Shen 795 Hao ((2020) 最高法民申795号).

Li's loan to Shen was not Shen and Wang's marital debt and Wang was not liable for the loan.[94] The Baoding courts' decision was deeply troubling as to whether a particular debt was for "necessaries" should be determined based on the economic circumstances and expectations of a particular family, rather than a minimum standard of living.[95] In Shen and Wang's case, it would not have been hard for Li, the creditor, to believe that a RMB3.5-million loan was in line with Shen and Wang's lavish lifestyle. The couple's marital assets were worth 10 to 15 times the amount that Shen borrowed from Li. However, it was impossible for Li to offer any evidence that the proceeds of the loan were spent on the parties' joint expenditures. As a result, the court found that Li failed to prove the loan was used for marital purchases, and shielded Wang's share of marital property from Li. After division of the martial property, Shen's share of community property was insufficient to satisfy all the loans in her name. Li was left with no recourse, despite that there are substantial marital assets now controlled by Wang.

The stringent burden of proof of marital debts significantly limits creditors' recourse against a debtor's spouse. First, the purpose of a loan is rarely stated in commercial loan agreements or promissory notes between individuals. Even if a loan agreement or promissory note states that the debt is borrowed for marital purposes, such a loan instrument itself is not sufficient evidence of the spouses' joint intent to borrow. Second, creditors have little access to evidence of the parties' family life to prove that a loan is borrowed for marital purposes, is used for marital purposes, and is not more than the family's ordinary household needs. Last, creditors have no control over how the debtor-spouse spends loan proceeds, even if the loan is originally borrowed for joint marital expenditures.[96]

Marital debts must be repaid with marital community property before creditors can invade either spouse's separate property. In other words, if a spouse borrows to pay for family necessities, they cannot be held solely responsible for the debt, and the spouses' marital community property must be used to satisfy the debt before a creditor could collect from either spouse's separate property. For example, in *Zhou v. Zhao*, Zhou Xinglin lent Zhao Xin RMB87,000 to pay for the mortgage on his marital home. Zhao defaulted on the loan. Zhou attempted to foreclose on Zhao's marital home. Zhao's wife objected to the foreclosure as the marital home was purchased by her before the marriage and was therefore her separate property. The court declined to foreclose on the marital home in that the debt owed to Zhou was marital debt and the wife's separate property could not be foreclosed for joint marital debt. The court opined that the creditor, Zhou should have first sued the couple

94. (2020) Ji 06 Min Zhong 3821 Hao ((2020) 冀06民终3821号).
95. Reilly, *supra* note 82, at 377.
96. Pei, *supra* note 91, at 7.

jointly; and if there was no sufficient marital property to satisfy the loan, Zhou then could sue Zhao's wife and foreclose on her separate property.[97]

In the event of a divorce, marital debts must be repaid with community property; and if there is insufficient community property to satisfy the marital debts, the remainder of the debts must be allocated between the spouses.[98] Creditors of marital debts may collect from either spouse. If one spouse ends up paying any debt for which the other spouse is responsible under the divorce judgment, the paying spouse may seek indemnification from the defaulting spouse according to the allocation of debts provided in the parties' divorce agreement or divorce judgment.[99] This right to indemnification is often meaningless because typically the defaulting spouse is insolvent when the indemnification issue arises.

8.4.2 Nonmarital Debts

Obviously, premarital debts are the sole obligation of the person incurring them.[100] Some debts are treated as personal debts for which the debtor-spouse is solely responsible, although the debts are incurred during the marriage. For example, debts incurred for illegal activities such as gambling and illegal drug abuse are nonmarital debts. Loans borrowed to buy gifts to a paramour are also nonmarital debts.[101] Furthermore, a spouse is not responsible for any "fake debts" concocted by one spouse in collusion with a third party.[102]

8.4.3 Allocation of Marital Debts and Liabilities

At the time of divorce, marital debts jointly created by both spouses must be discharged with marital property; and if the amount of marital property is insufficient to satisfy marital debts, the remaining debts are allocated between the spouses.[103] However, the allocation of debts between the spouses does not affect the creditors' ability to collect from either spouse.[104] For example, Wang Zhaoping and Tian Song were married. They borrowed RMB30,000 from Tian Song's sister Tian Na. Since the couple had no marital property, the court divided their marital debts evenly, including the debt owed to Tian Na. Wang Zhaoping and Tian Song were each ordered to pay RMB15,000 to Tian Na.[105]

---

97. (2021) Zhe 0782 Zhi Yi 37 Hao ((2021) 浙0782执异37号).
98. The Civil Code art. 1089.
99. The Marriage and Family Book Interpretations (I) art. 35.
100. *Id.* art. 33.
101. *Id.* art. 34 para. 2.
102. *Id.* art. 34 para. 1.
103. The Civil Code art. 1089.
104. The Marriage and Family Book Interpretations (I) art. 35.
105. (2017) Liao Min Chu 9737 Hao ((2017) 辽0211民初9737号).

However, neither of them paid Tian Na. Tian Na sued both Wang Zhaoping and Tian Song for the unpaid debt. The court held that Tian Song and Wang Zhaoping were jointly and inseverably liable for the debt, and Tian Na may bring an enforcement proceeding against either Tian Song or Wang Zhaoping if they fail to repay the loan by the date set by the court.[106]

To evade collection of debts, some couples have concocted "fake divorces" (*jia lihun*)—fraudulent divorce settlements designed to shield marital assets from creditors. "Fake divorces" have been widely reported by Chinese media. In *Du Feng v. Zhang Yuliang and Huang Shuqing*, Zhang Yuliang and Huang Shuqing were a married couple. Zhang borrowed RMB25 million from Du Feng on March 22, 2012, and promised to pay Du back within ten days. Zhang only repaid RMB1.25 million to Du. On December 10, 2012, Huang and Zhang entered a divorce agreement and obtained a divorce. Within a month after the divorce, Zhang transferred the couple's savings and real properties to Huang, transferred a construction company in his name to Huang's sole name, and transferred 50 percent of his other business holdings to Huang. In addition, Zhang agreed to pay and had paid Huang RMB30,000 per month and 50 percent of his income. When Du sued, the couple first claimed that their marriage was void because Zhang was not at the legal marriage age when they married. The Beijing No.1 Intermediate People's Court rejected Zhang and Huang's claim and held that their marriage was valid. The couple then argued that the loan from Du was not marital debt and was Du's separate debt incurred for his businesses. The court found that Zhang's businesses were the couple's only source of income and their family expenses, including Huang's and the parties' children's personal expenses, were paid directly by Zhang's construction companies. The court held that Huang had shared the profits and income from Zhang's businesses, and she must share the liabilities and loss of the businesses as well. Thus, the court found that the loan that Zhang borrowed from Du was a marital debt that benefited the marital community, and Zhang and Huang were jointly liable for it.[107] Clearly, Zhang and Huang transferred their properties to Huang through a "divorce settlement" to shield assets from Du's collection.

§ 8.5 Dissolution of Community Property Regime during the Marriage

A marital property regime may be dissolved without a divorce on two grounds:

(1) A spouse has caused significant damages to the spouses' community property by concealing, transferring, selling, destroying, or

106. (2020) Liao 02 Min Zhong 5440 Hao ((2020) 辽02民终5440号).
107. (2014) Yi Zhong Min Zhong Zi Di 1189 Hao ((2014)一中民终字第1189号).

squandering the spouses' community property, or by incurring marital debts by fraud.[108]

(2) A spouse does not agree to pay for medical treatment of serious illness of a person to whom their spouse owes statutory support obligation.[109]

A spouse is obligated to support him/herself, his/her minor children,[110] and his/her close relative who is not self-supporting, including parents,[111] stepparents,[112] grandparents,[113] adult children,[114] and siblings.[115]

Although the Civil Code permits division of marital property during the marriage, Chinese courts take the position that dissolution of marital property regime should not be granted as a rule and can only be granted as exceptions under extraordinary circumstances.[116] A marital community property regime cannot be dissolved on any other grounds but the statutory grounds provided in the Civil Code.[117] For example, a Zhejiang court granted a wife's request to divide marital property after she found out her husband transferred more than RMB1 million to a third party without her consent. The court found the husband's action severely damaged the parties' joint property interest, and the severity of his action warranted dissolution of the parties' marital property regime.[118] Following the same logic, a Guangdong court rejected a wife's request to dissolve the parties' marital property regime because the court found that considering the parties' wealth of more than USD100 million, a husband's sporadic large expenditures, ranging from USD30,000 to 50,000, did not amount to any financial wrongdoing that would have harmed the parties' joint interest; and in fact the parties' family wealth increased by many folds in the years of the husband's alleged misconduct.[119]

Requests for dissolution of marital property regime based on one spouse's unwillingness to pay for medical treatment are rarely made. The case of Yan and Guo is one of these rare cases. In the case of Yan, the court granted Yan's request for division of marital property on the ground that Yan's husband withheld marital funds that Yan needed for her medical treatment and care. Yan had a stroke and had been bed-bound for more than two years.

108. The Civil Code art. 1066 para. 1.
109. *Id.* art. 1066 para 2.
110. *Id.* art. 1071.
111. *Id.* art. 1067.
112. *Id.* art. 1072.
113. *Id.* art. 1074.
114. *Id.* art. 1071.
115. *Id.* art. 1075.
116. (2020) Zhe 01 Min Zhong 407 Hao ((2020) 浙01民终407号).
117. The Marriage and Family Book Interpretations (I) art. 38.
118. *See supra* note 116.
119. (2019) Yue 1973 Min Chu 3362 Hao ((2019) 粤1973民初3362号).

The court found that Guo refused to care for Yan or to pay for her medical care, and Yan needed funds to pay for continuing care and treatment. Thus, the court divided the parties' marital assets and awarded Yan a significantly larger share based on her needs for medical care.[120] In contrast, in *Pei v. Liu*, the court rejected a wife's request for division of martial property for medical treatment because the wife's kidney disease was not a "serious illness." Pei and Liu were entitled to a significant amount of compensation from the state for land acquisition. The funds from the compensation were held in trust by their Villagers' Committee. The husband refused to allow Villagers' Committee to release any funds because of his dispute with the village. The wife sought dissolution of marital property regime so that she could receive the compensation funds for medical treatment. The court rejected her request as the statute only permits division of marital property for treatment of serious disease. The court did not find that the wife's kidney disease qualified as a "serious illness."[121]

The Civil Code does not explicitly address creditors' recourse when dissolution of marital property regime undermines creditors' ability to collect. Chinese courts are keenly aware of couples' possible collusion to evade debts. Thus, dissolution of marital property claims are rejected when the interests of *bona fide* creditors are at stake. For instance, in *Tan Xiumei v. Cui Chengjian*, Tan sought dissolution of marital property regime as an attempt to block Cui's foreclosure on the four properties she and her husband jointly owned. Tan's husband, Ren, was personally liable for a RMB23,237,500 loan that he borrowed from Cui. When Ren defaulted on the loan, Cui brought an enforcement proceeding to attach four real estate properties jointly owned by Tan and Ren. Under Chinese law, if the property subject to foreclosure is jointly owned by the debtor and third parties, the court must first partition the jointly owned property before the creditors could foreclose on the debtor's share of the property. Thus, Tan sought to stay Cui's collection and partition of the properties that she and Ren owned. The Xinjiang High People's Court denied Tan's request to divide the properties because Tan did not have either of the statutory grounds for dissolution of marital property regime.[122]

Chinese courts' strong stance against dissolution of marital property regime favors creditors, and fails to afford adequate protection for non-debtor spouses. In *Chen v. Wu*, the Fujian Province High People's Court rejected the wife Chen's request for dissolution of marital property regime. Chen asked the court to dissolve the parties' marital property regime so that she could buy her husband out of the family home. Instead, the court allowed her husband's

---

120. (2012) E Hanyang Min Yi Chu Zi Di 00615 Hao ((2012) 鄂汉阳民一初字第00615号).
121. (2020) Jin 0106 Min Chu 2474 Hao ((2020) 晋0106民初2474号).
122. (2021) Xin 40 Min Zhong 298 Hao ((2021) 新40民终298号).

creditor to foreclose on Chen's family home to satisfy the debts that her husband owed. There was no question that the debts were Chen's husband's separate debt. Neither was there any question that Chen had at least a 50 percent ownership interest in the family home, or that Chen and her children would lose their only home if the home were foreclosed. Since Chen did not have any statutory grounds for dissolution of marital property regime, the court ordered the family home be auctioned and 50 percent of the sale proceeds be paid to Chen.[123]

§ 8.6 Division of Marital Property upon Divorce

Divorcing couples are encouraged to settle property division by agreements. If the parties fail to reach an agreement on marital property and marital debts, a court will make distributions based on the actual circumstances of the property and follow the principle of prioritizing the interests of the children and the wife.[124] In practice, marital property is divided evenly, 50–50, between the spouses. Chinese courts may consider the needs of the children and women, and specific circumstances of the family, and deviate from equal division. Moreover, a court may make an additional distributive award to an innocent spouse as compensation for damages caused by the other spouse's martial fault.[125]

8.6.1 Divorce Agreements

Parties must settle all issues of property and children and memorialize their settlement terms by a written divorce agreement (*lihun xieyi*) before they can apply for divorce registration. A divorce agreement must be filed for divorce registration. Divorce obtained based on a divorce agreement by divorce registration is referred to as "divorce by agreement" (*xieyi lihun*). A divorce agreement (*lihun xieyi*) is a free-standing contract entered by the parties voluntarily outside the judicial system. It is different from a settlement agreement reached through mediation within a divorce action. A settlement agreement entered after judicial mediation is not a free-standing contract but an integral part of the parties' mediated divorce decree (*lihun tiaojie shu*).

There is no statute of limitation to enforce a divorce agreement because a divorce agreement is a legal instrument that affects the parties' personal

123. (2020) Min Min Zhong 1899 Hao ((2020) 闽民终1899号).

124. The Civil Code arts. 1087, 1089.

125. Xue Ninglan (薛宁兰), Lihun Fa De Susong Shijian Ji Qi Pingxi (离婚法的诉讼实践及其评析) [divorce law litigation practice and its commentary], Faxue Luntan (法学论坛) [Legal Forum] No. 4, Vol. 29, Ser. No. 154 (July 2014), 20–21.

status. Thus, in *Shan v. Ma*, a Xinjiang court compelled an ex-husband to complete the title transfer of the parties' marital home to the ex-wife pursuant to their divorce agreement entered about 20 years ago.[126]

8.6.1.1 Condition: Divorce

A divorce settlement agreement does not take effect if the parties do not divorce.[127] In *Tang v. Liao*, the parties entered a divorce agreement on February 13, 2017, and then another divorce agreement on March 20, 2017. The parties registered their divorce based on their March 20, 2017, agreement. Tang sought property distribution in accordance with the parties' February 13, 2017, agreement, instead of the March 20, 2017, agreement. The Sichuan Province High People's Court held that the earlier agreement entered on February 13, 2017, was not legally binding as the parties did not divorce after entering the agreement.[128] In *Zhang Hongjie v. Wu Xiaoxi*, the parties entered a divorce agreement on February 7, 2012. In the parties' divorce action, Wu disputed the terms of the divorce agreement, whereas Zhang sought to enforce the agreement. The court found that the parties' divorce agreement was not binding because the parties were not yet divorced, and as a result their divorce agreement had not yet taken effect. The court further held that if a party reneges a divorce agreement in a divorce action, the court must redistribute the parties' marital community property.[129]

Even a partially performed divorce agreement is not enforceable if the parties did not divorce after the agreement was signed. For instance, in *Lin v. Li*, the couple was married in 1999 and executed a divorce agreement in 2005. They divided between themselves some of the 15 companies and 12 real estate properties according to the 2005 divorce agreement. However, the parties did not divide all of their marital properties and did not divorce. In 2012 Lin filed for divorce in court. In the divorce action, Li sought to enforce the divorce agreement but Lin asked the court to ignore the parties' divorce agreement and redistribute the couple's marital property. The Shanghai court held that Li and Liu's divorce agreement was unenforceable because the agreement's enforceability was conditioned upon the parties' obtaining a divorce registration. Thus, the court distributed the disputed properties between the parties.[130]

---

126. (2021) Xin 0103 Min Chu 1375 ((2021) 新0103民初1375).

127. The Marriage and Family Book Interpretations, art. 69 para. 1.

128. (2020) Chuan Min Shen 1283 Hao ((2020) 川民申1283号).

129. (2015) Chuan Min Shen Zi Di 621 Hao ((2015) 川民申字第621号).

130. Xu Wenwen (徐文文), Yi Bufen Lüxin De Fu Xieyi Lihun Tiaojian Canchan Fenge Xieyi De Xiaoli (已部分履行的附协议离婚条件财产分割协议的效力) [The Effect of Partially Performed Property Division Agreement with the Condition of Consented Divorce] Renmin Sifa (人民司法) [The People's Judicature] 08.2016, 44–46.

When a divorce settlement agreement is found invalid or unenforceable, Chinese courts try to balance parties' interests and supply appropriate remedies to ensure a fair marital property division. In *Liu v. Kong*, Liu, the wife, returned to her parents' home within weeks after the wedding and the parties remained separated ever since. Soon after Liu returned to her parents, the parties' families started negotiating the return of betrothal gifts given by the Kong family to Liu. During the negotiations, Liu acknowledged that she received a total of RMB43,200 from the Kongs. Kong prepared a list of betrothal gifts that were given to Liu. Liu signed and acknowledged the list. Liu's brother also endorsed the list and made a notation on the list, stating that the parties would obtain a divorce registration. The wife's family promised to repay the husband's family RMB43,200. However, Liu and Kong did not finalize the divorce registration. Instead, Liu filed for divorce in court and Kong counterclaimed for return of betrothal gifts on the list. The court found that the list endorsed by Liu, Kong, and Liu's brother was not enforceable, as a property settlement agreement entered in connection with a divorce registration is void in the event that the parties fail to complete the divorce registration. The trial court, nonetheless, admitted the betrothal gift list endorsed by Liu and her brother into evidence, accounted for Kong's betrothal gifts and Liu's dowry, and determined that after offsetting the dowry that Liu brought to the Kong family, Liu must return Kong RMB14,840.[131]

8.6.1.2 Duress or Coercion

It is well settled that absent any fraud or duress, a divorce agreement is enforceable and binding. An action to set aside a divorce agreement must be dismissed if the agreement was not induced by fraud or coercion.[132] Thus, having found no evidence of fraud, coercion, or any misconduct that might render the parties' divorce agreement unenforceable, the court ordered the ex-husband to transfer the parties' former marital residence to the wife pursuant to the parties' divorce agreement in *Zhang v. Li*.[133]

Generally, to prove duress or coercion, a party must introduce evidence that coercive conduct forced an involuntary consent to the divorce agreement. There can be no claim of duress if a party has the alternative of refusing to settle. In *Zhang v. Li*, the husband sought to set aside the parties' divorce agreement, alleging that he entered into the divorce agreement under duress and coercion. The husband alleged that he was beaten and detained for more than ten hours, was forced to sign the divorce agreement under threat from his ex-wife, daughter, son-in-law, and more than ten hitmen hired by his ex-wife,

131. FMTC 32.
132. The Marriage and Family Book Interpretations (I) art. 70 para. 2.
133. (2021) Wan 03 Min Zhong 494 Hao ((2021) 皖03民终494号).

and then was taken to the Civil Affairs Bureau to register the divorce. He also alleged that the ex-wife distributed defamatory pamphlets in his paramour's neighborhood and threatened to distribute the pamphlets again if he had not complied with her demands. The Beijing court found the husband's allegations not creditable; if Zhang had truly feared for his personal safety, he could have reported the alleged incidents to the police or the officials at the time of the divorce registration and could have not had to register the divorce.[134]

8.6.1.3 Binding Effect

Divorced couples may seek to set aside their divorce agreements after the divorce. Parties frequently attempt to set aside the entirety or part of divorce agreements after the fact.[135] Generally, Chinese courts must uphold a divorce agreement if there are no findings of fraud, duress, or any other gross misconduct.[136]

There is no statute of limitation to enforce a divorce agreement as it is entered in connection with dissolution of marriage and affects the parties' personal status. Thus, in *Shan v. Ma*, a Xinjiang court compelled an ex-husband to complete the title transfer of the parties' marital home to the ex-wife pursuant to their divorce agreement entered about 20 years ago.[137]

A divorce agreement is legally binding between the parties and against third parties. To illustrate: Liu Chunhua and Gao Liming were divorced. Their divorce agreement provided that Liu should have the ownership and right to exclusive occupancy of the parties' marital home, and the title of the apartment should be transferred to her after the divorce. Before the title of the apartment was transferred to Liu, Gao's creditors tried to foreclose on the apartment. Liu sought to stop the foreclosure on her apartment. The court found that Gao incurred the debts after the divorce and Liu acquired full ownership of the apartment pursuant to the parties' divorce agreement. The court held that the title of a property alone was not sufficient evidence to prove ownership. Thus, the court held that Liu's apartment could not be used to satisfy Gao's post-divorce debt, for which Liu was not liable.[138]

As the Beijing No. 2 Intermediate People's court stated in *Wang v. Li*, specific provisions of a divorce agreement must not be readily voided or modified

---

134. (2016) Jin 0105 Min Chu 12732 Hao ((2016) 京0105民初12732号).

135. Zhu, *supra* note 10, Li Mou Yu Wang Moumou Lihun Huo Caichan Jiufen An (李某与王某某离婚后财产纠纷案) [Li Mou and Wang Moumou Post-Divorce Property Dispute Case].

136. Marriage and Family Book Interpretations art. 70.

137. (2021) Xin 0103 Min Chu 1375 ((2021) 新0103民初1375).

138. Cheng Yuanyuan (程媛媛), Lihun Xieyi Dui Wei Guohu Fangchan De Yueding Ke Zuque Qiangzhi Zhixing (离婚协议对未过户房产的约定可阻却强制执行) [Divorce Agreement Provisions Concerning Real Property Not Yet Transferred Can Bar Compulsive Enforcement] Renmin Sifa (人民司法) [The People's Judicature] 11.2019, 107–11.

because a divorce agreement is usually a multifaceted agreement that encompasses a variety of matters, such as child support, property, and debt; and spouses' consent to divorce is contingent on each party's satisfaction with the parties' divorce agreement as a whole. More importantly, a divorce agreement is not a contract in the general sense and is different from an ordinary civil contract, as it is not purely profit driven and always involves considerations of the parties' emotions, their personal life, and their children's well-being. In the case of Wang and Li, Wang and Li agreed that Wang would receive a store front in Li's name and would assume the loans borrowed to buy the store front. After the parties obtained a divorce through registration, Li refused to transfer the title to Wang and Wang sued. Li alleged that the store was his separate property, and he did not enter the divorce agreement voluntarily. Li also attacked the fairness of the agreed transfer. The Beijing No. 2 Intermediate Court found that there was no evidence that Li entered the divorce agreement against his will and thus the court compelled him to transfer the title to Wang although the store was Li's separate property.[139]

Divorcing parents frequently agree to gift the family home to their children when the children reach majority. Some parents who have occupied the family home for years after the divorce try to rescind the "gift" when it is time to turn over the home to their children. Chinese courts are inclined to uphold the divorce agreements in these cases based on two theories. Some courts apply contract law rules and treat the "gift" to parties' children as an irrevocable contract between the parents, with the child(ren) as beneficiary, and as part of the parents' support obligation to their children. Other courts, such as the Beijing No. 2 Intermediate People's Court, find contract law inapplicable to divorce agreement and decline to tear a divorce agreement apart to set aside the "gift" provisions. In the case of *Cao v. Cao*, the Beijing No. 2 Intermediate People's Court reversed the lower court's decision to set aside a "gift agreement," which was part of the parents' divorce agreement. In *Cao v. Cao*, the daughter sued her father for the title and possession of an apartment that her father had occupied since the parents' divorce. The parents agreed that the father could live in the marital residence with the daughter until she turned 18 and must turn over the residence to the daughter. The mother did not move out of the marital residence until a couple of years after the divorce and the daughter moved in with her. When the daughter turned 18, she requested the father turn over the apartment to her. The daughter also alleged that the father failed to comply with his support obligation provided in the divorce agreement and refused to pay for her college tuition. The apartment was rented out and the daughter wanted the rental income to pay for college.

139. Zhu, *supra* note 10, Li Mou Yu Wang Moumou Lihun Hou Caichan Jiufen An (李某与王某某离婚后财产纠纷案) [Li Mou and Wang Moumou Post-Divorce Property Dispute Case].

The father argued that he was entitled to rescind the gift contract as he had not yet transferred the apartment to the daughter. The trial court agreed with the father and found that the father was entitled to rescind the gift contract pursuant to the Contract Law. On appeal, the Beijing No. 2 Intermediate People's Court reversed the lower court's decision and reiterated its stance articulated in *Wang v. Li* that the Contract Law is not applicable to divorce agreements, and a divorce agreement may not be set aside haphazardly.[140]

The SPC reaffirmed the Beijing No. 2 Intermediate People's Court's approach in *Yu v. Gao*. In the case of Yu and Gao, Yu and Gao were married in 2001 and had a son in 2003. The parties were divorced through mediation in 2009. The parties' divorce settlement agreement provided that Yu must transfer the marital residence to the parties' son after Yu paid off the mortgage. In 2013, Yu brought a post-judgment proceeding to set aside the parties' divorce settlement agreement and for distribution of the marital residence between Gao and him. Gao argued that gifting the marital residence to the parties' son was an integral part of the parties' settlement agreement in exchange for her assuming all marital debts, and she would have not agreed to the divorce or to assume the entire marital debts. Both the trial court and the Beijing No. 2 Intermediate People's Court, which heard Yu's appeal, agreed with Gao and declined to set aside the parties' agreement to gift the former marital home to their son. The SPC explained that although the Contract Law permits a grantor to unilaterally rescind any contract to give a gift before such contract is performed, the Contract Law provision is not applicable to any divorce settlement agreement, such as the one in the case of Yu and Gao. The SPC a party to a divorce settlement agreement may not unilaterally rescind the parties' agreement to gift any marital property to a third party as part of the divorce settlement, particularly if marital property is gifted to the parties' minor child(ren).[141]

Following *Yu v. Gao*, a Liaoning court upheld a divorce agreement entered nearly 18 years earlier, and compelled the husband to turn over the parties' former marital home to the parties' adult son. The court echoed the SPC's opinion in *Yu v. Gao*, stating that

> the gift in this case is different from ordinary gift because the gift is contracted through a divorce agreement, is not a free-standing gift contract, and is interconnected with the issues of dissolution of marital status, division of marital community property, and child custody and support; therefore, the gift provision may not be severed from the divorce agreement or be set aside arbitrarily. The husband's refusal to comply with the gift agreement has no legal basis and is dishonest. Thus, this court cannot condone his action.[142]

140. Zhu, *supra* note 10, Cao Mou Su Cao Moumou, Yang Mou Zengyu Hetong Jiufen An (曹某诉曹某某、杨某赠与合同纠纷案) [Cao Mou Sue Cao Moumou, Yang Mou Gift Contract Dispute Case].

141. FMTC 1.

142. (2020) Liao 07 Min Zhong 2004 Hao ((2020) 辽07民终2004号).

Similarly, in a more recent case, a Beijing court rejected an ex-husband's claim that the terms of the parties' divorce agreement were unreasonable because the amount of support for the ex-wife was extremely high. The court held the reasonableness of some terms of a divorce agreement can only be judged based on the totality of the parties' circumstances and the entirety of the agreement, and a party must first provide evidence of fraud, duress, or coercion that might make the agreement unfair or unreasonable before the court could consider the reasonableness of the agreement.[143]

8.6.2 Equal Division and Deviation

Chinese law does not explicitly provide that marital community property must be distributed equally between spouses upon dissolution of marriage. Over time, Chinese courts have developed a presumption that equal division is appropriate unless statutory factors, the rule of equity, or public order and good morals require uneven equitable distribution under special circumstances.

Chinese courts may penalize a party by making uneven division of marital property and award him/her a smaller portion of marital property or even no marital property if he/she has concealed, transferred, sold, destroyed, or wasted marital property, or falsified any debt in an attempt to misappropriate the other spouse's property; and if any aforementioned acts are discovered after the divorce, a new action may be brought for redistribution of marital property.[144]

True, accurate, and complete financial information is a prerequisite for equity and fairness in marital property distribution. Thus, Chinese courts penalize parties who fail to make full financial disclosure and conceal marital assets at the time of divorce. [145] In Guiding Case No. 66, *Lei v. Song*, the court awarded the husband a larger share of the parties' marital property than the wife, finding that the wife concealed and transferred the couples' marital retirement savings and other assets at the time of divorce.[146]

A spouse's concealment and unfair transfer of marital property prior to and/or during the divorce action are all sanctionable. In Guiding Case No. 66, *Lei v. Song*, the husband's wrongdoing occurred in the year prior to the

143. (2017) Jin 0102 Min Chu 17235 Hao ((2017) 京0102民初17235号).

144. The Civil Code art. 1092.

145. *See, e.g.*, FMTC 7; FMTC 23; FMTC 43.

146. Zhidao Anli 66 Hao: Lei Mou Mou Su Song Mou Mou Lihun Jiufen An [指导案例66号：雷某某诉宋某某离婚纠纷案] (Guiding Case No. 66: Lei Sue Song Divorce Dispute Case), Zuigao Renming Fayuan Guanyü Fabu Di Shisi Pi Zhidaoxing Anli De Tongzhi (Fa [2016] 311 Hao) [最高人民法院关于发布第十四批指导性案例的通知，(法[2016] 311号)] [The Supreme People's Court's Notification Regarding Publication of the Tenth Set of Guiding Cases (Law [2016] No. 311).

divorce action.[147] In *Zhang v. Yang*, the husband forged a divorce certificate to conceal, transfer, and dispose of marital property in the years preceding the divorce when the parties were separated. The Heilongjiang Province High People's Court affirmed the lower court's decision to award the wife a larger share of the parties' marital property because the husband concealed and transferred property in anticipation of the parties' divorce.[148]

The extent of sanctions against a party for nondisclosure and wrongful transfer of marital assets is subject to judges' discretion. Attempts to conceal assets sometimes warrant forfeiture of property. In the divorce action between Li and Ren, both Li and Ren concealed some marital assets and lied in their mandatory financial disclosure forms. The Shanghai court ordered each party to forfeit the assets that he/she failed to disclose.[149] In contrast, in *Huang v. Zhang*, the Chengdu court determined that a penalty was not necessary because although the husband transferred jointly owned stocks to the parties' son immediately before the wife commenced the divorce action, he did not personally benefit from the transfer. The court also justified its reluctance to punish the husband by the wife's extramarital affair.[150] Chinese courts quite consistently order an 80/20 or 70/30 split of marital assets and award the wrongdoer the smaller share in cases of concealment of marital assets. For example, a Shenzhen court divided a home acquired during the marriage 8:2 between Ou and Ton because Ton transferred marital funds to purchase the home through his mother so as to conceal assets from Ou.[151] A Hangzhou court awarded the wife 70 percent of the stocks that the husband concealed from her in the divorce action.[152]

Parties are incentivized by likely penalties on concealment of marital assets to make unfounded allegations of concealment against each other. In the divorce action between Li and Wei, the couple fought over more than several billion Chinese yuan of marital assets, including 14 companies and 66 real estate properties. Li and Wei accused each other of transferring and concealing assets from the other. Outside of the divorce action, they also instigated administrative and criminal investigations and unnecessary litigations against each other for the sole purpose of proving that the other party was secreting marital assets. After five years of protracted litigation, the SPC affirmed the lower court's findings and found no evidence of ill-intended transfer of

147. *Id.*
148. (2015) He Gao Min Shen San Zi Di 75 Hao ((2015) 黑高民申三字第75号).
149. (2020) Hu 0104 Min Chu 145 Hao ((2020) 沪0104民初145号).
150. (2021) Chuan 01 Min Zhong 1722 Hao ((2021) 川01民终1722号).
151. (2015) Shen Zhong Fa Min Zhong Zi Di 637 Hao ((2015) 深中法民终字第637号).
152. (2020) Zhe 0105 Min Chu 4575 ((2020) 浙0105民初4575号).

marital assets by either party.[153] The Guangzhou Intermediate People's Court expressed the court's frustration in *Deng v. Wu*:

> this action is a post-divorce action concerning marital property dispute brought by Wu for distribution of RMB12,600,000 marital assets that was allegedly concealed by Deng based on Wu's accounting of the parties' bank transactions for over a decade since 2008. Household expenditures are numerous and confusing. Therefore, adjudicators should not and are unable to audit the property transactions for the entire duration of a marriage, and therefore can only distribute the marital property that exists at the time of the divorce.

The Guangzhou court found that Wu offered no evidence of RMB12,600,000 that were still existent at the time of the parties' divorce action and, thus, denied her request.[154]

8.6.3 Marital Home

8.6.3.1 Evaluation

Evaluation of the value of the marital home is often the key issue in divorce actions in Chinese courts. Chinese courts generally rely on the price that the parties have agreed to as the basis for disposition of a marital home. If the parties cannot agree to the value of their marital home, the court may (1) allow them to set the value through bidding among themselves, if both parties seek the ownership of the home and agree to bidding; (2) allow the party who seeks ownership of the home to buy the other party out based on an appraisal value of the home; (3) distribute the sales proceeds after the sale of the home if neither party seeks ownership of the home.[155]

When the parties opt out of appraisals and agree to set the home value by bidding instead, the party who offers a higher price will receive the home and buy the other party out. For example, in *Zhu v. Pan*, the parties waived their right to appraise the marital home. At the trial, Zhu repeatedly stated that he wanted the home; the home's value was RMB600,000 and he was willing to pay Pan RMB300,000 for the home, whereas Pan stated that she believed the home's value to be RMB30,000 but she was more than happy to accept Zhu's offer. Thus, the court awarded the home to Zhu and ordered him to pay Pan RMB300,000 for her share in the home.[156]

Chinese courts typically set the valuation date as of the date of appraisal, which is usually immediately prior to the trial.[157] Disputes over the valuation date often arise in judicial supervision proceedings in cases where the retrial courts relied on the appraisals obtained in the original trial proceedings.

---

153. (2017) Zui Gao Fa Min Zhong 336 Hao ((2017) 最高法民终336号).
154. (2020) Yue 04 Min Zhong 24822 Hao ((2020) 粤01民终24822号).
155. The Marriage and Family Book Interpretations (I) art. 76.
156. (2015) Yu Gao Fa Min Shen Zi Di 02111 Hao ((2015) 渝高法民申字第02111号).
157. (2017) Wan Min Shen 1610 Hao ((2017) 皖民申1610号).

Home values may vary widely between the time of the original trial and the time of the retrial due to China's volatile real estate market. For instance, in *Geng v. Zhou*, the parties purchased their marital home for RMB352,685 with a mortgage of RMB210,000 in October 2012. Geng filed for divorce in 2014 and the court awarded 50–50 joint ownership of the parties because the home could not be sold due to resale restrictions on government-subsidized housing. Both parties appealed and the case was remanded for a new trial in 2017. The appraisal value of the home had risen to RMB2,295,207 by the time of the retrial in 2018. Zhou objected to the appraisal value. After the retrial, Zhou was awarded the home and ordered to pay Geng for her share of the home based on the appraisal value.[158] On appeal, Zhou objected to the valuation date, alleging that the home's value was inflated because of the undue delay of the trial. The Beijing High People's Court rejected Zhou's claim as the court found that the appraisal was proper.[159]

In *Di Yanjie v. Zhang Li*, the SPC addressed the issue of valuation date when the original appraisal had long expired at the time of the retrial. The original trial court ordered an appraisal for the parties' marital home in 2009. The date of valuation was January 13, 2009, and the expiration date of the appraisal was July 15, 2009. The trial court reserved the issues concerning the parties' home, as Di and Zhang could not accept the appraisal value and refused to pay the appraisal fee. Di appealed the trial court's disposition of the home. The case was remanded, and a new trial was held on January 29, 2010. At the retrial, Di and Zhang stipulated to the appraisal done in January 2009. The trial court then awarded Zhang the home and ordered him to pay half of the appraisal price to Di for her share of the home. Di appealed again and requested another retrial, arguing that the trial court should have ordered a new appraisal using the date of the retrial as the valuation date. The SPC rejected Di's request to reappraise the home as of the date of the retrial.[160]

If the parties cannot agree to the value of the home, or set the value by bidding or by appraisal, the court then compels the sale of the home through public auction and the mortgage holders have the right of first refusal to purchase the home. When Shi Wenhui and Lou Qi could not manage to co-own a former marital home in accordance with their divorce judgment, the Shanghai court ordered the home to be auctioned, as the parties could not agree to a price or an appraiser.[161]

158. (2017) Jing 0106 Min Chu 29772 Hao ((2017) 京0106民初29772号).
159. (2020) Jing Min Shen 419 Hao ((2020) 京民申419号).
160. (2015) Min Kang Zi Di 9 Hao ((2015) 民抗字第9号).
161. (2019) Hu 0112 Min Chu 2449 Hao ((2019) 沪0112民初2449号).

8.6.3.2 Premarital Funds

If prior to the marriage a spouse purchased a real property, paid the down payment with their premarital funds, and is the registered title owner of the property, but some mortgage payments were paid with marital funds during the marriage, the property remains the title spouse's separate property, the remainder of the mortgage also remains the title spouse's separate debt, and the non-title spouse is entitled to his/her share of the marital contribution to the home and its appreciation.[162]

Chinese courts use a simple formula to calculate a non-titled spouse's share in the title spouse's separate real property to which marital funds have been contributed:

Non-titled Spouse Share = Marital Contribution × [Present Appraisal Value / (Appraisal Value at the time of Marriage + Mortgage Interests Paid)] × 50%

Sun Hui v. Tan Feng, Tan Lingqi and Feng Meifang, shows how the formula is applied. Sun Hui was married to Tan Feng. Tan Lingqi and Feng Meifang are Tang Feng's parents. Tan Feng and her parents purchased a home before she married Sun. After the marriage, Tan Feng's parents lived in the home and Tan Feng paid for the mortgage of the home. Sun sought half of the appreciation of the home and reimbursement from Tan for half of the mortgage payments and other marital funds contributed to the home. First, the Shanghai court determined that two-thirds of the total sum of the mortgage payments that Tang Feng had paid during the marriage was a loan from Sun and Tang Feng to her parents, and the remaining one-third of the total mortgage payments were from marital funds, which amounted to RMB120,583.24. Second, the court determined the present value of the marital contribution based on the appreciation rate of the home. The appraisal value of the home at the trial was RMB6,105,000, the appraisal value of the home at time of marriage was RMB825,001.73, and the total of mortgage interest payments and other expenses was RMB45,001.73. Thus, the appreciation rate of the home was 7.017, equal to 6,105,000/(825,001.73 + 45,001.73). The present value of the marital contribution at the trial was RMB846,132.60, equal to 120,583.24 × 7.017. Considering that the wife, Tang Feng, was the primary caregiver of the parties' children, the court awarded Sun RMB380,000 as his share of the marital home, which was slightly less than one-half of the present value of the parties' marital contribution to the home.[163]

162. The Marriage and Family Book Interpretations (I) art. 78.
163. (2019) Hu 01 Min Zhong 14498 Hao ((2019) 沪01民终14498号).

8.6.3.3 Privatized Public Housing Benefits

While privately owned urban housing existed in the socialist era, the vast majority of urban residents received public housing assigned according to their status, seniority, and rank through the state socialist economy at nominal cost.[164] Many Chinese families still reside in assigned public housing units under the legacy of China's socialist economy. Whether the occupants of these housing units have full ownership, or the right to occupy with the option to purchase in the future, or merely the right to occupy depends on perplexing local rules and policies. Many of these public housing units were assigned by state-owned companies or governmental entities and then sold to the occupants of these units at steeply discounted prices.

In China's gradual housing privatization since the 1990s, home ownership is typically transferred to each public housing unit's occupants at deeply discounted prices, making home equity the largest component of household wealth held by the older generations.[165] Privatized public housing units, referred to as "housing reform home" (*fang gai fang*), have been at the center of contention in many divorce actions.[166]

Family homes that were assigned to or "rented" to one spouse prior to the marriage and later purchased with marital funds but registered in one spouse's name are marital community property.[167] In *Di Yangjie v. Zhang Li*, Di and Zhang were married in 1999. Zhang was assigned a residence owned by his employer and Zhang paid RMB20,000 prior to the marriage and then RMB10,000 after the marriage to acquire the residence when it was privatized. The residence was valued at RMB26,305.58 in 2002 when Zhang received the full ownership registration of the residence. The SPC held that despite that Zhang paid a portion of the purchase price prior to the marriage, the residence was Di and Zhang's marital residence because housing units, such as Di and Zhang's residence, were assigned and sold to employees in consideration of many factors, such as one's position, years of service, salary, and size of family; and the deeply discounted purchase price was a social benefit entitlement granted to both spouses, not just to the titled spouse.[168]

---

164. Tao Rong, *supra* note 5, at 177–79, discussing housing and other entitlements in China's transition from a socialist economy to a market economy.

165. Andrew G. Walder & Xiaobin He, *Public Housing into Private Assets: Wealth Creation in Urban China*, 46 Soc. Sci. Rsch. 85–99, (2014), a study on wealth transfer through urban housing privatization in China.

166. Ouyang Bo (欧阳波) Yin Shenfen Guanxi Chansheng Juzhuquan Jiufen Ying You Hunyin Jiating Fa Tiaozheng (因身份关系产生居住权纠纷应由婚姻家庭法调整) [Right of Occupancy Disputes Arising from Personal Status and Relationship Should Be Governed by Marriage and Family Law] Renmin Sifa (人民司法) [The People's Judicature], 24/2014, 29.

167. The Marriage and Family Book Interpretations (I) art. 27.

168. (2015) Min Kang Zi Di 9 Hao ((2015) 民抗字第9号).

It can take years for those who purchased their privatized public housing units to receive full private ownership titles. The uncertainty of home ownership inevitably affects the home value and makes it very difficult to divide the homes between divorcing spouses when they cannot agree to a price. Thus, in cases where the court is unable to determine the ownership of a residence because the parties have not yet received the full ownership of a disputed residence at the time of divorce, the court must decide the right of occupancy based on the circumstances of the parties and the parties may bring a new suit for distribution of the residence after the property's ownership is settled.[169] In *Han v. Zhang*, the parties' marital home was acquired through Zhang's employer with marital funds during the marriage. The home's purchase price was significantly discounted because Zhang's employer, a state-owned company, subsidized the purchase based on Zhang's years of service and seniority. The parties had the occupancy right but were waiting for ownership registration. The court of first instance awarded the home to Zhang with exclusive occupancy, and awarded Han half of the home's purchase price with an additional RMB10,000 for her to acquire another home. The court decided to give the home to Zhang because it was easier for Zhang to complete the ownership transfer and registration, as the home was assigned and sold to him as an employee of his company. The court reserved the issue of appreciation in value of the home until after Zhang acquires the registration of full ownership of the home. Han appealed. The appellate courts affirmed the original trial court's decision to reserve the issue of appreciation until the ownership was fully granted to Zhang and an appraisal could be conducted.[170]

Sometimes, housing subsidies are given in large lump sums to employees based on their past employment in the public sector or state-owned enterprises. These housing subsidy payments are marital property, as in Xiao's case. Xiao was a retired public-school teacher. He worked for the City of Chongqing public school system from 1950 to 1983. Xiao had six children from his first marriage. His first wife passed away in 1984. Xiao married Zhong in 1993. He died in 2003. In 2011, Xiao's estate received RMB51,324 for a housing subsidy from the City of Chongqing based on his past service as a city employee. Xiao should have received the payment in 1999. However, the payment was not disbursed to him until 2011. Xiao's children from his first marriage argued that the payment was earned prior to Xiao's second marriage to Zhong, and therefore was Xiao's premarital separate property but not his marital property. The court agreed with Xiao's children that the housing

169. The Marriage and Family Book Interpretations (I) art. 77.

170. (2016) Gan 01 Min Zhong 2642 Hao ((2016) 甘01民终2624号), and (2017) Gan Min Shen 1178 Hao ((2017) 甘民申1178号).

subsidy payment was Xiao's premarital property because it was based on his 33 years of employment prior to his marriage to the second wife.[171]

Urban housing benefits and entitlements available to city residents are treated as marital property as well. For example, in *Geng v. Zhou*, the Beijing courts ruled that the wife was entitled to the housing benefits, in the form of discounted purchase price, that the husband received as a veteran and a Beijing resident who had a Beijing household registration (*hukou*). The courts rejected the husband's argument that the marital home was his separate property because it was tied to his status as a veteran and registered resident of Beijing, and the wife, who did not have a Beijing household registration, would not have been eligible to purchase the home at the discounted price, which was a fraction of the market price of the home. The Beijing High People's Court upheld the lower court's decision that the home was the parties' marital property; and divided the equity equally between the parties based on the home's market value.[172]

However, if a couple purchased a privatized public housing unit with marital funds in one spouse's parent's name and titled the home in the parent's name, the home is not the parties' marital community property and the funds used to purchase the home are treated as a loan to the parent.[173] Thus, in *Xue v. Fu*, the court rejected the wife's claim that a home purchased with marital funds during the marriage was marital, as the home was titled in the husband's father's name and was purchased through a housing privatization program sponsored by the husband's father's employer.[174] Some employers and state entities allow parents to transfer their housing benefits or entitlements to their children. Therefore, if a couple purchases a spouse's parent's housing unit with marital funds in a spouse's name instead of in the parent's name, then the home is the spouses' marital community property.[175]

8.6.3.4 Rural Collective Entitlements

Rural residents of village collectives have three major entitlements: farmland tenure (*zenren tian*), residence allotment (*zhaiji di*), and ownership interests in village- or township-owned enterprises (*xiang zhen qiye*). Land in rural China

---

171. Zhang Huarong (张华荣), Fenpei Zhufang Butie Keyi Shuoji Jiwang (分配住房补贴可以溯及既往) [Distribution of Housing Subsidy Retroactively] Renmin Sifa (人民司法) [The People's Judicature] 06.2015, 107–09.

172. (2017) Jing 0106 Min Chu 29772 Hao ((2017) 京0106民初29772号), (2019) Jing 02 Min Zhong 8185 Hao ((2019) 京02民终8185号), and (2020) Jing Min Shen 419 Hao ((2020) 京民申419号).

173. The Marriage and Family Law Book Interpretation (I) art. 79.

174. (2020) Gan 01 Min Zhong 133 Hao ((2020) 甘01民终133号).

175. (2020) Jing 03 Min Zhong 6755 Hao ((2020) 京03民终6755号). *See also* (2017) 湘民再257号.

is owned and administered by "village economic collectives."[176] Membership in a village economic collective is determined by the village's residents' rural household registrations within the geographic boundary of the village. Rural households that are members of "village economic collectives" may lease a land tenure for farming for 30 to 70 years.[177] In addition to the farmland tenure, each household receives a residence allotment for housing.[178] Villagers' Committees periodically, but very infrequently, reallocate land among village households to adjust land distribution among households based on changes in household sizes due to births, deaths, and marriages. In recent years, commercial agriculture and urban expansion prompted large-scale land expropriation and large compensations for it were paid to rural residents. In addition to land, many villages own highly profitable village enterprises, in which every village member has an ownership interest.[179] Recent policy change allows village households to withdraw from their village collective economic organizations with compensation.[180] Consequently, rural residents' once-negligible entitlements in land and village enterprises, and other village collective entitlements have now become valuable property.

The case of Tang Xiaomao and Zhou Hongfang illustrates distribution of rural household residence allotment in a divorce action. Tang, Zhou, and Zhou's son from a previous marriage started living together in Tang's family home in 2002. All three of them jointly applied to Tang's Villager's Committee for a building permit to renovate and expand Tang's family home. A permit was issued to them. They rebuilt and expanded the Tang family home. Tang and Zhou married in September 2003 and moved in the newly renovated home in December 2003. In April 2004, Zhou and her son's household registrations were officially transferred to Tang's village and Zhou became a member of the village. In 2010, the village's land was expropriated. Based on the size of the expanded family home, Tang received three apartments from the government as land expropriation compensation. Tang claimed that the apartments were his premarital property because the home was his ancestral home, and the residence allotment was granted to his family and then him prior to the marriage. The courts rejected Tang's claim and found both the home and the residence allotment that the home sat on were marital property,

---

176. Zhonghua renmin gonghe guo tudi guanli fa (中华人民共和国土地管理法) [Land Management Law of the People's Republic of China] (promulgated on June 25, 1986, amended on Dec. 29, 1988, Aug. 29, 1998, Aug. 2008, 2004, and Aug. 26, 2019) [hereinafter the "Land Management Law"] art. 11.

177. The Land Management Law art. 13.

178. *Id.* art. 62.

179. Joel Andreas & Shaohua Zhan, *Hukou and Land: Market Reform and Rural Displacement in China*, 43(4) J. Peasant Studies 803, (2016).

180. *Id.* at 812; *see also* the Land Management Law art. 48.

as the parties rebuilt the home with joint funds and joint efforts and resided in the home as husband and wife.[181]

Similarly, in *Sun v. Guo*, the husband claimed that a resettlement apartment (*anzhi fang*) the parties received as land expropriation compensation was his separate property, as he received the land tenure prior to the marriage. The Beijing High People's Court rejected the husband's claim and held that the resettlement apartment and other related resettlement entitlements were all marital community property, in that both spouses' household registrations were registered to the land allotment.[182]

8.6.3.5 Multigenerational Homes

Intergenerational co-residence is common in China. Spouses often reside with the husband's parents in family homes that are jointly owned by the husband and his parents. Obviously, it would be unfair and impractical to force the husband's parents out of their family homes when the younger couple divorces. On the other hand, if the family home remains the husband's separate property, at the time of a divorce the wife could lose essentially her entire interest in the family's estate, which she might have made both financial and nonmonetary contribution to for years. Chinese courts must balance the competing interests of the family members in these cases.

The case of Ma, Huo and Liu illustrates how rural multigenerational marital homes are handled in Chinese courts. Ma and Liu were married in 1991 in a traditional wedding ceremony but never registered their marriage. The couple have two children. The couple lived with Ma's mother, Huo, and their children in Ma's ancestral home where the Ma family had lived for generations and was assigned to Ma's family members. In 2008, Liu and Ma rebuilt the home with Hou's help. Later, Huo moved to a smaller residence that Ma's older brother built for her adjacent to his home. Liu filed for divorce in 2018 after years of separation after Ma moved to a foreign country. She sought to stay in the family home. Since Ma and Liu's marriage was not legally registered, Liu's household registration was not transferred to Ma's village and her residency was not registered to the land allotment where the family home sits. Thus, Ma claimed that the family home was not marital property and was joint property of his family members who hold the land tenure of the allotment. The court rejected Ma's claim and found that the family home was Liu and Ma's marital property for several reasons: (1) according to the custom, Ma's older brother and mother are not members of Ma's household, as the brothers had established separate households after their marriages, and their mother, Huo, became a member of the older brother's household;

181. (2020) Su Min Shen 6048 Hao ((2020) 苏民申6048号).
182. (2020) Jing Min Shen 5033 Hao ((2020) 京民申5033号).

(2) the ownership and right to occupy the family home are severable from the rights to the land tenure of the allotment; and (3) the family home was built with Liu and Ma's joint efforts and marital funds during the marriage, and has been occupied by Liu, Ma, and their children. Thus, the court granted Liu and her younger daughter exclusive occupancy of the family home as Liu and her daughter have no other residence and Ma has been residing overseas for years. The court also ordered Liu to pay half of the appraisal value of the home to Ma, and ordered Liu and Ma each to pay RMB10,000 as compensation and support for Huo, as Huo helped them with building the home in 2008.[183]

8.6.3.6 Right of Occupancy

Chinese family law did not explicitly provide priority of a non-title spouse's marital rights over a titled spouse's ownership of a marital home. Thus, Chinese courts had to turn to property laws to construct a non-titled spouse's right to occupy a marital home that he/she does not own. Consider the Typical Case *Xin v. Yin*.[184] The plaintiff, Xin Guifang, was the paternal grandmother of the defendant, Yin Zhigang. Xin had lived in the family home for more than 30 years. The home was purchased, built, expanded, and jointly owned by her, her late husband, and her son. After he inherited his father and grandfather's interest in the family home, Xin's grandson, Yin, moved into the home. Xin then sued Yin for exclusive occupancy of the family home. Yin argued that he was the rightful owner of the family home as he inherited the home. The court held that Yin's interest was in the value of the home only, not in the possession or control of the home, and the grandmother, Xin, had both the right of ownership and the right of occupancy of the home because the home had been her marital home for more than 30 years, and therefore Xin was entitled to exclusive occupancy of the family home. The SPC explained that a person in possession of a property, whether by contracts or by operation of law, has the right of possession (*zhanyouquan*) and may seek the return, restoration, and protection of their right of possession under the Property Law. Following this logic, a spouse may acquire, through marriage, the right of possession of the marital residence and other marital or nonmarital property, regardless of the legal title of such property. The SPC pointed out that the purpose of the right of possession provisions is to "maintain and protect societal order and fairness."[185]

---

183. (2019) Ji 01 Min Zhong 7664 Hao ((2019) 冀01民终7664号) affirmed by (2019) Ji Min Shen 8171 Hao ((2019) 冀民申8171号).

184. FMTC 30.

185. FMTC 30. Zhonghua Renmin Gonghe Guo Wuquan Fa (中华人民共和国物权法) [The People's Republic of China Property Law] (promulgated Mar. 16, 2007, effective Oct. 1, 2007) [hereinafter Property Law], arts. 245, 241. *See also* Wang Mingsuo (王明锁), Lun Suoyouquan

Right of occupancy is now codified in the Civil Code. The Civil Code provides that the right of occupancy may be constructed by contract, personal status and relation, or wills.[186] Thus, a non-titled spouse can obtain the right of occupancy of his/her marital residence by agreements, such as divorce agreements;[187] based on the marriage;[188] or his/her spouse's will.[189] A person's right of occupancy to a residence cannot be transferred or inherited,[190] and terminates at the time set by the agreement or when the right holder dies.[191]

8.6.4 Other Marital Properties

8.6.4.1 Company Stock Holdings and Shares

Chinese courts may divide a spouse's interests between the spouses if the spouses cannot agree to a buyout price or it is difficult to set a buyout price of stocks, bonds, shares of investment funds, or shares in privately held joint stock limited companies.[192] When the parties' marital community property is invested in a limited liability company in one spouse's name, and the other spouse is not the company's shareholder, the shareholder spouse may transfer the entire investment or a part of the investment to the other spouse provided that the majority of the other shareholders agree to the transfer and expressly waive the right to purchase the shares, and the other spouse may then become a shareholder of the company. If the majority of the shareholders do not agree to the transfer of shares from the shareholder spouse to the other spouse, but agree to purchase the shares at the price that the spouses have agreed to, the court may distribute between the spouses the value of the spouses' shares sold to the other shareholders. If the majority of the other shareholders do not agree to transfer shares between the spouse or to purchase the shares

---

Zhanyouquanneng Yu Tawuquan Kongzhanquan Eryuanzhi Falü Tixi De Goujian (论所有权占有权能与他物权控占权二元制法律体系的构建) [On the Dual Legal System of Ownership Possession Right and Non-ownership Right of Possession and Control] Falü Kexue (法律科学) [Science of Law] 6, 14 (2009) (discussing titled owner's right of possession and non-titled persons' right of possession).

186. The Civil Code arts. 367, 368, 371; *see also* Pei Hua (裴桦), Fuqi Caichanzhi Yu Caichanfa Guize De Chongtu Yu Xietiao (夫妻财产制与财产法规则的冲突与协调) [The Conflicts between Marital Property Regime and Property Law Principals and Their Reconciliation] Faxue Yanjiu (法学研究) [Chinese J. L.] Vol. 4, 3–19 (2017) (discussing the conflicts between marital property regime provided in the Marriage Law and legal principals concerning contract and property in the Contract Law and the Property Law, and proposing solutions to reconcile the conflicts).

187. The Civil Code art. 367.

188. *Id.* art. 368.

189. *Id.* art. 371.

190. *Id.* art. 369.

191. *Id.* art. 370.

192. The Marriage and Family Book Interpretations (I) art. 72.

that non-shareholder spouse is entitled to, the court may order that shares be transferred to the non-shareholder spouse and said spouse may become a shareholder of the company.[193]

In divorce actions involving distribution of spouses' marital community property invested in partnerships, if one spouse is not a partner of the partnership and the spouses agree that the entire or a part of the spouses' investment in the partnership should be transferred to the non-partner spouse, the court may (1) allow the non-partner spouse to join the partnership upon the partners' unanimous consent; (2) distribute the proceeds from the sale of the non-partner spouse's interest in the partnership if the partners do not agree to transfer any portion of the partner spouse's interest to the non-partner spouse but agree to purchase the interest from the non-partner spouse under the terms that the spouses have agreed to; (3) distribute the investment withdrawn from the partnership if the partners do not agree either to transfer any portion of the partner spouse's interest to the non-partner spouse or to purchase the interest under the terms that the spouses have agreed to, but allow the partner spouse to withdraw the entire or part of the investment from the partnership, or (4) make the non-partner spouse a partner of the partnership if the partners do not agree to transfer any portion of the partner spouse's interest to the non-partner spouse, or to purchase the interest under the terms that the spouses have agreed to, or to allow the partner spouse to withdraw the entire or part of the investment from the partnership.[194]

If the spouses invested in a sole proprietorship company in one spouse's sole name, the court may distribute the spouses' marital community property invested in the sole proprietorship as follows: (1) award the ownership and control of the company to the spouse who wishes to manage the company, and compensation to the other spouse for their share based on the company's appraisal value; (2) award the ownership and control of the company to the spouse who offers the highest bid for the company, and compensation to the other spouse for their share based on the bid; and (3) dispose the company according to the Sole Proprietorship Company Law if neither spouse wishes to manage the company.[195]

In *Liu Yi v. Wang Junji*, Liu was not directly involved in a limited liability company that Wang started with his partners. Liu insisted on receiving the shares of the company instead of a cash buyout for the value of the shares. The SPC rejected her request and held that for the purpose of protecting the integrity of the company's partnership, a spouse who is not a limited liability company's shareholder may be compensated for the value of the shares that

193. *Id.* art. 73.
194. *Id.* art. 74.
195. *Id.* art. 75.

he/she is entitled to if the spouses could not come to an agreement on the distribution of the actual shares in the company.[196]

In *Li v. Wei*, the husband and wife owned and managed a conglomerate of nine companies. Three of these companies were jointly owned by Li and Wei with several other shareholders. Li had more shares than Wei in these three companies. Li sought to buy Wei out from these companies, alleging that Wei's continuing involvement in the companies would cause impasses in the companies' decision-making and cripple the business. The SPC found that the other shareholders did not object to equal distribution of the couple's shares between Li and Wei, Wei had been actively involved in the companies for many years and there was no evidence that Wei let the parties' acrimonious divorce affect the parties' business dealings. Therefore, the SPC rejected Li's request and affirmed the lower courts' decision to distribute Li and Wei's shares in the companies equally between them.[197]

8.6.4.2 Digital or Virtual Assets

The rise of e-commerce provided enormous opportunities for individuals to start small businesses and open online stores. Alibaba Group's Taobao e-commerce platform, a mass-selling site, is at the center of China's e-commerce boom. About one-third of the online businesses on Taobao are family businesses with all the employees being family members. The distribution of Taobao online stores, many of which are highly profitable, inevitably become a point of contention in divorces and succession disputes.[198]

Wang v. Wu was one of the first reported divorce cases involving Taobao online stores. Wang and Wu registered a Taobao baby and maternity products store in the wife, Wu's name. The store started by selling products that the wife, a flight attendant, brought back from her international trips. Wang, the husband, ran the daily operations of the store, first part-time and later full-time after the store earned a "Two Crown" rating and became very lucrative. At the time of divorce in 2011, Wu and Wang first agreed to divide the value of the store's inventory equally and transfer the store to Wang's name. After the divorce, Wu could not transfer the store to Wang because Taobao only allowed registered users to operate online store accounts and prohibited transfer of online store web addresses, linked payment accounts, and ratings. Wu then removed Wang's access to the online store and started running the store herself. Wang sued Wu to enforce the parties' agreement. The Beijing court found that Wang was the spouse who actually managed the store's

196. (2018) Zui Gao Fa Min Shen 796 Hao ((2018) 最高法民申796号).

197. (2017) Zui Gao Ma Min Zhong 336 Hao ((2017) 最高法民终336号).

198. Yehua Dennis Wei, Juan Lin & Ling Zhang, *E-Commerce, Taobao Villages and Regional Development in China*, 110(3) Geographical Rev. 380–405, 391, (2020).

operation and Wu's involvement was minimum. Thus, the court awarded the store to Wang. Online transaction regulations require that online merchants register with the e-commerce platforms with their true identities and must obtain commercial licenses required by relevant law or regulations. Thus, Taobao's user policy requires that a natural person must operate an online store with his/her true identity and may not sell, rent, or gift online stores to unregistered users. The court held that Wang and Wu's online store was marital community property, and the change in store registration from Wu to Wang was distribution of marital property and was not a "transfer" prohibited by Taobao for consumer protection. The court directed Taobao to change the store's registration to Wang.[199] After *Wang v. Wu*, Taobao revised its policy, in 2013, and now allows transfer of online store registration in connection with succession and divorce.[200] Other online retail platforms have adopted similar policies.

Although the Civil Code recognizes online stores and businesses as "virtual property," it does not define "digital property" or "virtual property."[201] Chinese courts and legal scholars generally agree that virtual and digital property includes online stores, social media and game accounts, and virtual items associated these accounts, such as game characters and virtual currency.[202] However, Chinese courts have been reluctant to divide Taobao online stores and other online accounts due to the difficulty in evaluation and appraisal.[203] Instead, following *Wang v. Wu*, Chinese courts usually award online stores or businesses to the spouse who is more involved in the online store's operation because not only he/she contributed more to the store but also the store's reputation and rating are directly attributed to his/her personal efforts and ability. Thus, in a widely publicized case, in 2018, the court awarded an online electronic store registered in the wife's name to the wife's

---

199. Zhu, *supra* note 10, Wang Mou Su Wu Moun Deng Lihun Hou Caichan Jiufen (王某诉吴某等离婚后财产纠纷) [Wang Mou Sue Wu Mou, Etc. Post-Divorce Property Dispute].

200. Liu Ting (刘婷), Hulianwang Shidai Beijing Xia Guanyu Lihun Anjian Zhong Wangzhan Fenge De Falü Wenti Yanjiu (互联网时代背景下关于离婚案件中网店分割的法律问题研究) [Analysis on Legal Issues of Distribution of Online Store in Divorce Actions in the Background of the Age of the Internet], Falü Shiyong (法律适用) [Nat'l Judges Col. L. J.] Issue 1 (2016), 89.

201. The Civil Code art. 127.

202. Nie lingmin (瞿灵敏), Xuni Caichan De Gainian Gongshi Yu Falü Shuxing – Jian Lun Minfa Zongze Di 127 Tiao De Lijie Yu Shiyong (虚拟财产的概念共识与法律属性—兼论《民法总则》第127条的理解与适用) [The Consensus on the Concept and Legal Attribute of Virtual Property—Additional Discussions on the Understanding and Application of the Civil Law General Provisions art. 127], Dongfang Faxue (东方法学) [Oriental Law].

203. Guo Yinghua, Xu Yanan (郭英华，徐亚男), Lihun Anjian Wangluo Xuni Caichan De Fenge—Yi Taobao Wangdian Weili (离婚案件网络虚拟财产的分割—以淘宝网店为例) [Division of Internet Virtual Assets in Divorce Cases—Taobao Online Stores as Examples], Chongqing Youdian Daxue Xuebao Shehui Kexue Ban (重庆邮电大学学报社会科学版) J. Chongqing Univ. of Posts & Telecommunications (Social Science Edition) V. 01.30 No. 5 (Sept. 2018).

mother. The mother made the $3,000 initial investment and grew the business to an enterprise that has more than $30 million annual gross revenue. In the wife's divorce action, the husband claimed that the online electronic store was registered in the wife's name and therefore was marital property subject to distribution between the couple. He also claimed that he created five WeChat, a Chinese social media platform, public accounts that generated clients for the online store. The wife's mother was joined in the divorce action. The parties settled the suit through mediation. The wife's mother was awarded the online store and WeChat accounts. In exchange, the husband received $50,000.[204]

8.6.4.3 Inheritance

The Civil Code provides that inheritance, bequests, or gifts received by either spouse during the marriage are community property unless the donor of a bequest or gift expressly specifies that the bequest or gift is given to a spouse individually.[205] If a spouse has vested interests in an estate during the marriage but the estate has not yet been distributed by the time of the divorce, the spouse's vested inheritance, although not yet received, is marital property. The spouses may preserve their right in the divorce action and bring a new suit for property distribution after the inheritance is distributed.[206] In *Liu v. Zhou and Zhao*, Zhou's father died in 2000 during the parties' marriage. Zhou and his brothers had a dispute over their father's estate. Zhou and Liu divorced in 2009 before Zhou's father's estate was settled and distributed. Zhou received a share in his father's home. Later, the home was expropriated, and Zhou and his second wife, Zhao received RMB520,000 in compensation. Liu sued for half of the compensation. The court found that Zhou's inheritance was vested but not distributed during his marriage to Liu and therefore it was Zhou and Liu's marital property. The court awarded Liu half of Zhou's inheritance in 2020, two decades after Zhou's father's death.[207]

Chinese courts generally tend to classify a spouse's inheritance that has been vested but not yet received during a long marriage as marital property. In the case of Liu, Xie, and He, Xie and He were a divorced couple; and Liu was He's father's second wife. He's mother died in 2014. He settled his mother's estate with his father and received 50 percent of his parents' marital residence in 2018. He then gifted his 50 percent interest in the residence back to

204. Jinri Shuo Fa, Nian Xiaoshou E 20,000,000 De Taobao Dian Jiujin Gui Shei? Xiaoliangkou Lihun, Xuni Caichai Fenge Yin Zhengyi (今日说法 | 年销售额2000万的淘宝店究竟归谁？小两口离婚，虚拟财产分割引争议) [Today's Legal Topic, Annual Sales Revenue 20,000,000 Taobao Online Store Belongs To Whom? Young Couple Divorce, Virtual Property Division Causes Dispute], https://www.sohu.com/a/304856951_235265.

205. The Civil Code art. 1602.

206. The Marriage and Family Book Interpretations (I) art. 81.

207. (2020) Ji 02 Min Zhong 544 Hao ((2020) 冀02民终544号).

his father without Xie's consent. He and Xie divorced in October 2019. Two months later, He's father gifted the entire residence to his new wife, Liu. Xie sued Liu for her share in the residence as half of the residence's value was He's inheritance from his mother. Xie contended that He's inheritance was marital property and inasmuch He had no right to gift his inheritance to his father, who in turn gifted it to Liu. The Chengdu court agreed with Xie. The court found He's interest in his parents' apartment was He and Xie's marital property and that He had no right to gift marital property to his father without Xie's consent. The court ruled that He's gift to his father was void and in turn He's father's gift to Liu was void as well.[208]

8.6.4.4 Appreciation of Separate Property

Even if an asset is a separate property, the income that it earns and the appreciation of its value during the marriage can be marital community property. Active appreciation (*shouyi*) that resulted from a spouse's efforts or contribution during the marriage is marital property. Active appreciation is fruits of the marital economic partnership and consequently belong to the marital community property regime.[209] In contrast, passive appreciation (*ziran zhengzhi*) accrued due to accumulation of interest, inflation, or market forces is independent of any efforts by either spouse and, therefore, is the titled spouse's separate property.

For example, the SPC rejected a wife's bid for a share in the appreciation of the husband's real estate development company because the wife made no contribution to the company's appreciation in value. The husband sold a tour company that he owned before the marriage and acquired the real estate development company. The new real estate development company was defunct at the time of the divorce. The SPC found that the parties did not dispute that the husband's real estate development company is the husband's separate property; and that the appreciation of the company, if any, would be solely due to the increase of price of land held by the company, which in turn is due to market force and not due to the husband's active efforts. Thus, the SPC upheld the lower courts' decisions not to award the wife any portion of the passive appreciation of the husband's company as it was not marital community property.[210]

8.6.4.5 Social Security Entitlements and Retirement Benefits

China's social security system consists of five different types of social security insurances and a fund (*wu bao yi jin*) for which both employees and employers

---

208. (2020) Chuan 01 Min Zhong 14641 Hao ((2020) 川01民终14641号).
209. The Marriage and Family Book Interpretations (I) art. 26.
210. (2020) Zui Gao Fa Min Shen 1003 Hao ((2020) 最高法民申1003号).

must make mandatory contributions: basic pension insurance (*jiben yanglao-jin*), unemployment insurance (*shiye baoxianjin*), medical insurance (*yiliao baox-ianjin*), work-related injury insurance, and maternity insurance (*gongshang shengyu baoxiangjin*); and a housing fund (*zhufang gongjijin*).[211] A spouse's entitlements and retirement benefits earned during the marriage are marital property. Thus, after a thorough review of the funds in the husband's basic pension insurance, medical insurance, and housing fund accounts, a Hunan court identified the premarital portion and marital portion of each account, and distributed the marital portion of the funds in these entitlement accounts between the husband and wife equally.[212]

Only vested interests and the actual savings in basic pension insurance accounts are marital property under the Civil Code.[213] If the titled spouse is not yet retired, the non-titled spouse's share in their spouse's basic pension insurance is limited to the actual contribution and interest accrued in the basic pension insurance account.[214] Thus, a non-titled spouse is not entitled to any portion of the titled spouse's future pension payments if the titled spouse is not retired.

As a form of compensation, Chinese employers typically make high matching contributions to employer-sponsored pensions, which usually become vested after 10 to 15 years of service.[215] Rural workers and urban workers who are self-employed, underemployed, or employed in informal sectors are under-covered by the basic pension insurance as they have little to no employer contributions to their basic pension insurance, and they have no access to private pensions.[216] As a result, there is often a substantial disparity in retirement benefits between the gainfully employed spouse who has both basic pension insurance and private employer-sponsored pension (*qiye yan-glaojin*), and the spouse who does not have any private pension. Some legal

211. Zhonghua Renmin Gongheguo Shehui Baoxian Fa (中华人民共和国社会保险法) [Social Insurance Law of the People's Republic of China] (Promulgated Oct. 28, 2010, effective from July 1, 2011, amended Dec. 29, 2018) Art. 2. For the history and development of China's social security system, see, *e.g.*, Qin Gao, Sui Yang & Fuhua Zhai, *Social Policy and Income Inequality during the Hu–Wen Era: A Progressive Legacy?*, 237 China Q. 82–107 (2019); and Qin Li & Alex He, *Popular Support for the Social Security System in Urban China: Evidence from a Cross-Sectional Survey in a Chinese City*, 35(3) J. Int'l & Compar. Soc. Pol'y 261–79 (Nov. 2018).

212. (2020) Xiang 07 Min Zhong 2199 Hao ((2020) 湘07民终2199号).

213. The Civil Code art. 1062(5), and the Marriage and Family Book Interpretations (I) art. 35.

214. The Marriage and Family Book Interpretations (I) art. 80.

215. Zhang Rongfang (张荣芳) Xinxing Fuqi Gongtong Caichan: Hunyin Qijian De Yang-lao Jin Quanyi (新型夫妻共同财产: 婚姻期间的养老金权益) [New Type of Marital Joint Property: Pension Rights during the Marriage] Faxue Pinglun (法学评论) [L. Rev.] Vol.2 08, Issue 2 (2018), 68.

216. *See, e.g.*, Jin Jiang, Jiwei Qian & Zhouyi Wen, *Social Protection for the Informal Sector in Urban China: Institutional Constraints and Self-selection Behavior* 47(2) J. Soc. Pol'y 335–57 (2018).

scholars have advocated non-titled spouses' rights to unvested benefits in private pensions.[217] However, the SPC has firmly held its stance not to distribute unvested private pension benefits at the time of divorce although at least a portion of the benefits are accrued during the marriage.[218] Thus, the Shanghai High People's Court refused to distribute the wife's employer-sponsored pension as marital property because she was not retired and her interest in the retirement account was not yet vested at the time of divorce.[219] Similarly, in a more recent decision, a Beijing People's Intermediate Court refused to divide a husband's employer-sponsored pension fund on the ground that the fund was not a basic retirement fund but a supplemental retirement fund, and the husband could not withdraw from the fund before his retirement.[220]

The non-titled spouse's loss of their share in unvested interests in the titled spouse's pensions can be significant. Chinese urban, rural, and migrant families' largest share of social benefits in household final income is from pensions.[221] In other words, the non-titled spouses, mostly wives, who are self-employed, underemployed, or employed in informal sectors, could lose a substantial portion of social benefits that were earned and accrued during their marriages because they are denied of any entitlement to unvested interests in their former spouses' pensions that they have contributed to during the marriage.

8.6.4.6 Post-Divorce Distribution of Undistributed Marital Property

It is well-settled law that if there is any marital property that was not distributed during a divorce, either party may bring a post-judgment action for distribution of the undistributed marital property.[222] Since most divorces are consensual and obtained by divorce registration, divorce agreements are often hastily signed without legal representation. As a result, post-divorce actions concerning marital property disputes (*lihun hou fuqi caichan jiufen*) are common. The post-divorce action for property distribution between Liu and Deng is a Typical Case where the parties divided all of their assets but two accounts in Deng's name in their divorce agreement in connection with their divorce

217. Zhang Rongfang, *supra* note 215, at 69. *See also* Chen Wei & Li Naizhong (陈苇, 黎乃忠), Xiandai Hunyin Jiating Fa De Lifa Jiazhi Quxiang—Yi Hunyin Fa Jieshi San Youguan Fuqi Caichan Guanxi De Guiding Wei Duixiang (现代婚姻庭家法的立法价值取向—以《婚姻法解释(三)》有关夫妻财产关系的规定为对象) [Modern Marriage Family Law's Legislative Value Choice—Marital Property Provisions in the Marriage Law Interpretations (III) as Subjects]. Jilin Daxue, Shehui Kexue Xuebao (吉林大学, 社会科学学报) [Jilin Univ. J. Soc. Sci. Ed.], 2013(1), 83.

218. The Marriage and Family Book Interpretations (I) art. 80.

219. (2017) Hu Min Shen 1439 Hao ((2017) 沪民申1439号).

220. (2020) Jin 03 Min Zhong 12213 Hao ((2020) 京03民终12213号).

221. Qin Gao, Sui Yang & Fuhua Zhai, *supra* note 211, at 95–98.

222. The Marriage and Family Book Interpretations (I) art. 83.

registration. After the divorce, Liu also discovered that Deng concealed RMB 2,325,920 from her. The Guangzhou People's Intermediate Court divided the undistributed marital funds in Deng's accounts in the post-divorce action concerning marital property dispute brought by Liu.[223]

A post-divorce action may be brought for distribution of marital property that was concealed and consequently was not distributed in the original divorce action. In Liu and Deng's case, Deng concocted a business loss to conceal RMB2,325,920 from Liu. Liu discovered his scheme after the divorce. The Guangzhou People's Intermediate Court distributed the funds that Deng concealed from Liu in Liu's post-divorce action for property distribution.[224] Similarly, in *Wu v. Yang*, Yang funneled more than RMB200,00 out of the couple's business and concealed the funds from Wu during the marriage. In a lawsuit that Wu brought against the couple's business partners for the missing funds, Wu found out that Yang misappropriated the funds. Wu and Yang were already divorced when Wu discovered Yang's concealment of the funds. He brought a post-divorce action immediately and the court distributed the funds between Wu and Yang.[225]

Chinese courts frequently bifurcate the divorce and property issues, and reserve all or some property issues to a post-divorce proceeding, particularly when the ownership of a real property is not yet settled,[226] or when the real property held in an estate is not yet distributed,[227] or when the parties co-own a family home with a spouse's parents. For example, in *Hu v. Long, Li, and Long*, Hu and Long lived with Long's parents and co-owned the family home with them. The court reserved the distribution of the family home to a post-divorce action in which Long's parents joined. Then, the court obtained the appraisal value, ascertained debts attached to the home and divided the equity of the home among Hu, Long, and Long's parents.[228]

§ 8.7 Divorce Relief (*lihun jiuji*)

Chinese law does not mandate equal distribution of marital property. The Civil Code requires that marital property distribution must ensure children's well-being and protect women's rights and interests.[229] Chinese courts must consider statutory factors and grant "divorce relief" (*lihun jiuji*) as equity

---

223. (2020) Yue 01 Min Zhong 24811 Hao ((2020) 粤01民终24811号).
224. *Id.*
225. (2020) Min 03 Min Zhong 1138 Hao ((2020) 闽03民终1138号).
226. The Marriage and Family Book Interpretations (I) art. 77.
227. *Id.* art. 81.
228. (2020) Chuan 07222 Min Chu 2538 Hao ((2020) 川0722民初2538号), affirmed in (2020) Chuan 07 Min Zhong 3501 Hao ((2020) 川07民终3501号).
229. The Civil Code art. 1087 (formerly the Marriage Law art. 39).

requires. Not to be confused with American-style alimony or spousal maintenance, divorce relief under Chinese matrimonial property law, albeit compensatory in its nature, is not support. Divorce relief is to equalize accrued financial gains between spouses and to compensate for a spouse's loss due to marital arrangements or marital misconducts, but is not to meet a spouse's financial needs after a divorce.

Chinese law provides three types of "divorce relief" (*lihun jiuji*):[230] (1) "domestic work compensation" (*jiawu laodong buchang*) for a spouse's unpaid domestic work, such as caring for the parties' children and elderly parents;[231] (2) "divorce damage" (*lihun sunhai peichang*) for emotional and physical injuries caused by a spouse's gross marital misconducts, such as adultery, bigamy, and domestic abuse;[232] and (3) "financial assistance" (*jingji bangzhu*) for support of a spouse that is indigent and is at risk of becoming homeless after the divorce.[233] Divorce relief payments in principle are paid in one lump sum, not by monthly payments.

8.7.1 Domestic Work Compensation

The deepened gendered division of labor at the workplace and at home in China's post-socialist economy prompted legal recognition of women's unpaid contribution to family life and its monetary value.[234] Although the 2001 Marriage Law provided compensation for a spouse's unpaid domestic work, it only allowed compensation for unpaid domestic work when spouses maintained a separate property regime during the marriage.[235] As a result, Chinese courts frequently declined to award compensation for domestic work when spouses did not opt-out of the community property regime. For example, in the case of Wang and Chen, the Haikou Intermediate People's Court rejected the wife's request for compensation for the care that she provided to the family, including her in-laws. The court held that the prerequisite of domestic work compensation was that the spouses had agreed to maintain a separate property regime during the marriage. Since Wang and Chen did not have a written agreement to keep their property or income separate, the

230. Sun Ruojun (孙若军), Lihun Jiuji Zhidu Lifa Yanjiu (离婚救济制度立法研究) [Divorce Relief System Legislative Studies], Faxue Jia (法学家) [The Jurist] No. 6, 2018, 1, 161–72, 161.

231. The Civil Code art. 1088 (formerly the Marriage Law art. 40).

232. The Civil Code art. 1091 (formerly the Marriage Law art. 46).

233. The Civil Code art. 1090 (formerly the Marriage Law art. 42).

234. Ma Yinan, Tong Yuanling & Panli Wangjing (马忆南, 童元玲, 潘丽, 王晶), Lihun Caichan Fenge Rugan Wenti De Shehui Xingbie Fenxi (离婚财产分割若干问题的社会性别分析) [A Social Gendered Analysis of Several Issues on Property Division in Divorce], Funü Yanjiu Luncong (妇女研究论丛) [Collection of Women's Studies], No. S2 Ser. No.77 (Dec. 2006), 42–46. *See also* Sun Ruojun, *supra* note 230, at 165–67.

235. The Marriage Law art. 40.

Haikou Court decided that the wife was not entitled to domestic work compensation according to the Marriage Law.[236] For the same reason, in *Wang v. Luo* the Wuhan Intermediate People's Court declined to award compensation for the wife's years of domestic work and household labor, although the court awarded the wife a larger share of marital property and compensations for physical and emotional harms that she had suffered from the husband's abuse.[237]

Basic-level courts, however, seemed to be willing to find ways to get around the legal technicality and awarded modest compensations for domestic labor contribution in cases where there was little marital property. *Zhang v. Li* was one of these rare cases. The parties had been separated when the wife, Zhang, abandoned the husband, Li, and their daughter, who was two years old at the time. Li raised the child alone. Twenty-four years later, Zhang reappeared and filed for divorce. The court found that the couple had maintained *de facto* separate property regimes as they had been living separate lives for more than 24 years. Considering that the husband raised the parties' child without the wife's contribution whatsoever, the court ordered the wife to pay the husband RMB20,000 as compensation for his contribution and sacrifice for the family.[238]

Some rural courts seemed to simply ignore the technical requirement of separate property regime and were willing to compensate women who had shouldered all responsibilities in childrearing, elderly care, and farming while their husbands worked in distant cities. In *Jiang v. Zhang*, a modest compensation was awarded to the wife for her contribution to the family. Jiang and Zhang were married for 14 years and had four children. During the marriage, Zhang, the wife cared for the parties' four children and her husband's parents in the parties' hometown. Jiang worked in factories as a migrant worker away from home for most of a year and was only able to visit his family occasionally. Later, Zhang accompanied the parties' oldest child to the City of Liuzhou so that the child could attend a good school and left the three younger children with Jiang's parents. To support herself and her children, Zhang sold vegetables in open markets and delivered produce to hotels. At the time of divorce, Zhang's income was about RMB10,000 per month and Jiang's income was about RMB5,000 per month. The parties had no assets or debts. Zhang sought RMB10,000 as compensation for her nonmonetary contribution to the family. Considering that Zhang had been the sole caregiver of the parties' four children and the husband's parents for years while her husband was away from home as a migrant worker, and that the husband had limited income,

---

236. (2020) Qiong 01 Min Zhong 1959 Hao ((2020) 琼01民终1959号); *see also* (2014) Hui Hai Fa Min Yi Chu Zi Di 913 Hao ((2014) 穗海法民一初字第913号).

237. (2014) E Wuhan Zhong Min Zhong Zi Di 00378 Hao ((2014) 鄂武汉中民终字第00378号).

238. (2014) Ying Zhan Min Yi Chu Zi Di 00388 Hao ((2014) 营站民一初字第00388号).

the court awarded the wife RMB5000 as compensation for her years of domestic service for the family.[239]

Similarly, in the tragic case of Zhu Weiming and Hu Limei, an Anhui court awarded the wife, Hu Limei, RMB70,000 compensation for her domestic work. Zhu and Hu were married in 1995 and had two children. Zhu left home to work as a migrant worker in 2002. Hu stayed in the village, farmed the family's land, and cared for the parties' children and Zhu's parents. In 2011, Hu was assaulted by Zhu's nephew and killed him in self-defense. Hu was sentenced to seven years' imprisonment. In 2013, Zhu filed for divorce. The court ordered Zhu to pay Hu RMB70,000 as compensation for her contribution to the family and support upon Hu's release. The court found the compensation was warranted because Hu sacrificed many years to care for the family and after her release from prison, she would have difficulty in supporting herself due to disability and lack of education.[240]

The Civil Code removed the prerequisite of separate property regime for domestic work compensation. It provides that a spouse who has spent considerably more effort on supporting children, taking care of the old, or assisting the other party in work and other responsibilities is entitled to compensation for unpaid domestic work and nonmonetary contribution to the family at the time of divorce.[241] In February 2021, a Beijing court awarded a stay-home mother RMB50,000 for her nonmonetary contribution to a five-year marriage. The case is the first domestic work compensation case after the Civil Code was enacted.[242] The decision went viral in China. The amount of award was ridiculed as being less than a fraction of a nanny's pay in Beijing. In response to the criticism, the Beijing court suggested that "after entering a marriage, one should balance family life and self-growth, focus on self-improvement, cherish employment opportunity, and maintain financial independence." In other words, the Beijing court's advice to Chinese women is, "Do not become a housewife."[243] Soon enough, a Chongqing court awarded a significant

239. (2017) Gui 13 Min Zhong 21 Hao ((2017) 桂13民终21号).

240. (2014) 芜中民一终字第00151号2014-05-21.

241. The Civil Code art. 1088.

242. Duo Zuo Jiawu, Lihunshi Ke Yaoqiu Buchang (多做家务，离婚时可要求补偿) [Do More Housework, Can Ask for Compensation at the Time of Divorce], http://fsqfy.chinacourt.gov.cn/article/detail/2021/02/id/5807660.shtml; Beijing Shi Fangshan Qu Fayuan Shiyong Minfa Dian Xingui Shouci Shenjie Lihun Jiawu Buchang An (北京市房山区法院适用民法典新规 首次审结离婚家务补偿案) [Beijing City Fanshan District Court Applying the Civil Code New Provision, Finalizing the First Divorce Domestic Work Compensation Case], https://tv.chinacourt.org/53553.html.

243. "Quanzhi Taitai Lihun Huo Wuwan Jiawu Buchang" Shang Resou, Zhushen Faguan Huiying ("全职太太离婚获5万家务补偿"上热搜，主审法官回应) ["Fulltime Housewife Got 50,000 Domestic Work Compensation" On Top Search List, The Presiding Judge Responds], https://news.sina.com.cn/s/2021-02-23/doc-ikftssap8186598.shtml.

domestic work compensation in the sum of RMB120,000 to a wife who cared for the parties' children and the husband's parents full time for more than ten years in the village, while the husband worked as a migrant worker away from home.[244]

8.7.2 Divorce Damages

Under the Civil Codes, courts may award victimized spouses compensatory "divorce damage" (*lihun sunhai peichang*) for emotional and physical injuries caused by marital misconduct, including (1) bigamy, (2) a spouse's cohabitation with a third-party, (3) domestic violence, (4) abuse or abandonment of a family member, or (5) any other gross misconduct.[245] Only an innocent spouse is entitled to damages for marital fault of their spouse.[246] A spouse that committed any marital misconduct is not entitled to divorce damages. Furthermore, claims for divorce damages can only be brought within a divorce action. Chinese courts do not allow lawsuits that only seek recovery of damages caused by marital fault, but not divorce.[247]

Divorce damages are not frequently awarded because most claimants for divorce damages fail to meet the burden of proof.[248] The amount of damage awarded is almost nominal, typically ranging from RMB5,000 to RMB10,000.[249] In practice, Chinese courts are more inclined to deviate from equal division and award a smaller share of marital property to the wrongdoer, instead of making an order for divorce damages.[250] For example, in *Wu v. Ye*, the trial court awarded Ye, the wife, 60 percent of the couple's marital property and 40 percent to the husband who emotionally and physically abused the wife. The trial court awarded the husband the title of the couple's

244. Liu Yang et al. (刘洋), Chongqing Yi Quanzhi Taitai Lihun Huopei Jinji Buchangjin (重庆一全职太太离婚获赔经济补偿金) [A Chongqing Full-time Wife Awarded Financial Compensation in Divorce], Remin Fayuan Bao (人民法院报) [People's Court Daily] (Apr. 29, 2021), https://www.chinacourt.org/index.php/article/detail/2021/04/id/6010243.shtml.

245. The Civil Code art. 1091 (formerly the Marriage Law art. 46).

246. The Marriage and Family Book Interpretations (I) art. 87.

247. *Id.*

248. Wei Chen, Lei Shi & Xin Zhang, The Divorce Damages System in China: Legislation and Practice, 30 Int'l J.L. Pol. & Fam. 105, 109 (2016). *See also* Chen Wei, He Wenjun (陈苇, 何文骏), Woguo Lihun Jiuji Zhidu Sifa Shijian Zhi Shizheng Diaocha Yanjiu—Yi Chongqing Shi Moumou Xian Jiceng Renmin Fayuan 2010–2012 Nian Bei Chouyang Diao Cha De Lihun Anjian Wei Duixiang (我国离婚救济制度司法实践之实证调查研究—以重庆市某基层人民法院 2010—2012 年被抽样调查的离婚案件为对象) [Empirical Survey on Our Country's Divorce Relief System's Judicial Practice—Chongqing City Moumou County Basic-Level People's Court 2010–2012 Sample Survey Divorce Cases], Hebei Faxue (河北法学) [Hebei Law Science], Vol. 32, No. 7, 19, 28–29 (July 2014).

249. Chen Wei et al., *supra* note 248, at 26.

250. Sun Ruojun, *supra* note 230, at 169.

marital home, ordered him to pay 60 percent of the home value to the wife for her interest in the home, and granted her exclusive occupancy of the home. In other words, the wife got to live in the home for free and received about RMB480,000 from the husband as her 60-percent share in the home's value. The Jiangxi Province High People's Court affirmed the lower court's decision, finding the award was appropriate because the husband was unfaithful, and he brutalized the wife during the marriage, including breaking her nose in one incident.[251] Although the court did not award the wife any divorce damages, which is customarily about RMB5,000 to 30,000, the wife, Ye, was much better off financially because she received free housing and at least RMB80,000 more than what she would have received in property distribution if the court had not deviated from equal division.

8.7.2.1 Domestic Violence

Domestic violence victims may seek damages for bodily and emotional harm in connection with a divorce action.[252] "Domestic violence" is defined as "beating, restraining, torturing, imprisoning or any other action that caused a family member physical or emotional injury," and continuing, frequent domestic violence conduct constitute "abuse."[253] In addition to civil remedies of damages and orders of protection, domestic violence victims may bring private prosecutions against their abusers.[254]

The SPC published detailed guidelines on the handling of financial compensations for domestic violence victims through property distribution as well as compensatory damages in divorce cases.[255] Compensatory damages for domestic violence must be awarded when there is clear evidence of either "bodily harm" or "mental injury" supported by policy reports, forensic reports, and medical records.[256] The amount of compensatory damage may include reasonable costs and expenses for treatment and rehabilitation, such as medical treatment expenses, nurse fees, travel expenses, and lost wages; loss of future income and future cost of care due to disability caused by the

251. (2020) Gan Min Shen 1614 Hao ((2020) 赣民申1614号).

252. The Civil Code art. 1091, and the Marriage and Family Book Interpretations (I) art. 86.

253. The Marriage and Family Book Interpretations (I) art. 1.

254. Marriage Law, art. 45; *see also* Zhonghua Renmin Gonghe Guo Xing Fa (中华人民共和国刑事诉讼法) [The People's Republic of China Criminal Procedure Law] (promulgated July 7, 1979, amended Mar. 14, 1997, effective Oct. 1, 1997) (the "Criminal Procedure Law") art. 204.

255. The DV Guidelines art. 53–62.

256. Zhonghua Renmin Gonghe Guo Qinquan Zeren Fa (中华人民共和国侵权法) [The People's Republic of China Tort Law] (promulgated Dec. 26, 2009, effective July 1, 2010) (the "Tort Law), art. 16, 22; *see also* DV Guidelines, art. 59.

bodily injuries; and burial cost.[257] The SPC's guidelines on compensatory damages have been carefully followed by Chinese courts.

Commenting on the Typical Case *Wang v. Jiang*, the SPC urged courts to award domestic violence victims compensatory damages, not only as a compensation for the victims but also as a preventative measure against domestic violence. In *Wang v. Jiang* the parties had a short marriage without children. Throughout the marriage, the husband, Jiang, drank excessively and physically abused the wife, Wang. In 2009, the wife left home after another beating by the husband and filed for divorce. The wife sought compensation for the emotional and physical injuries that she had suffered because of the husband's abuse. The court granted the wife a divorce, division of marital property, and compensatory damages for the emotional suffering inflicted by domestic violence.[258] Some critics, however, are skeptical as to whether compensatory damages would be effective in achieving these goals.[259]

Another Typical Case, *Zhang v. Chen*, hints at Chinese courts' willingness to forgo rigid procedural rules in consideration of fairness and substantive justice in domestic violence cases. Zhang and Chen were married in 2005. On May 26, 2008, Chen brutally assaulted Zhang and caused her serious injuries, including a broken nose and broken knees. Zhang was hospitalized due to the injuries. Soon after the incident, Chen filed for divorce on June 11, 2008. On August 5, 2008, Zhang brought a private prosecution criminal action against Chen. Zhang sought reimbursement of medical and travel expenses for her treatment of the injuries in the criminal case against Chen. Chen was convicted of assault and was ordered to reimburse Zhang roughly RMB3,000 for her out-of-pocket hospital expenses. Two years after the incident, on July 22, 2010, Zhang received a belated forensic medical report that detailed the extent of her injuries and disability that resulted from Chen's assault. On August 11, 2010, Zhang filed a civil suit for a total of RMB60,000 for additional medical expenses, home care expenses, and damages based on the new forensic medical report. On August 11, 2011, the court granted the parties' divorce and awarded Zhang compensatory damages for the domestic violence that Zhang suffered in Chen's hands. The trial court found that in Zhang's 2010 civil suit against Chen the statute of limitations started from August 5, 2008, because Zhang had known about her injuries when she brought a private prosecution action against Chen on August 5, 2008. The trial court also found that Zhang had been compensated for her injuries in the private prosecution action and

---

257. The Tort Law, art. 16. For a detailed review of determination of compensation for physical and emotional damages, *see* Mo Zhang, *Tort Liabilities and Torts Law: The New Frontier of Chinese Legal Horizon*, 10 RICH. J. GLOBAL L. & BUS. 415, 471–78 (2011).

258. FMTC 2.

259. Charles J. Ogletree, Jr. et al., *The Recently Revised Marriage Law of China: The Promise and the Reality*, 13 TEX. J. WOMEN & L. 251, 270 (2004).

the divorce action. The trial court thus dismissed Zhang's civil suit for additional damages on the ground that the one-year statute of limitation had lapsed.[260] The appellate court reversed, in that "limitation period for recovery of damages for apparent personal injury begins from the date the injury is inflicted. If the injury is not discovered at the time of injury but is later diagnosed after examination and is proven to be caused by the injurious act, limitation period begins from the date the condition of the injury is diagnosed."[261] The appellate court found that in Zhang's case the statute of limitations began running on July 29, 2010, when Zhang received the forensic medical report that had fully assessed the extent of her injuries. The appellate court awarded Zhang RMB48,664.31 for damages, including additional medical expenses, home care cost, and emotional damages. The appellate court did not consider that the divorce court had already awarded Zhang compensatory damages in the divorce action, during which Zhang's forensic medical report had been available, and that Zhang should have or could have offered the forensic medical report in her divorce action. It is unclear whether the trial court had computed its compensatory award based on Zhang's forensic medical report in the divorce action. It is clear, however, that the appellate court found the lower court's compensatory awards insufficient and thus awarded Zhang additional compensation despite some procedural defects in her actions.[262]

Claimants for recovery of damages caused by domestic violence bear the burden of proof of the abuse. A claimant must prove that their spouse's misconduct was intentional, the claimant suffered injury, and the claimant's injury was caused by their spouse's misconduct. The Hunan Province High People's Court found that Chen's husband, Han, physically abused her during the marriage, and Chen suffered severe mental illness. However, the court found that Chen failed to provide sufficient evidence to prove the causation between Han's domestic abuse and her mental illness. Therefore, the court affirmed the lower courts' decision to deny Chen's claim for damages resulted from Han's abuse of her.[263]

The amounts of compensatory damages for domestic violence vary and appear to be modest. According to a recent study on divorce cases heard by Beijing courts in 2014 and 2015, 26 percent of the awards made by Beijing courts were below RMB5,000, 26 percent were between RMB5000 and

260. Civil Procedure Law arts. 136, 137.

261. Zuigao Renmin Fayuan Guanyu Guanche Zhixing Zhonghua Renmin Gongheguo Minfa Tongze Ruogan Wenti De Yijian (最高人民法院关于贯彻执行中华人民共和国民法通则若干问题的意见) [The Supreme People's Court Judicial Opinions on Certain Issues Concerning the Implementation of the General Principles of the Civil Law of the People's Republic of China] (promulgated Apr. 2, 1988) (repealed), 1988 Sup. People's Gaz. 2, art. 168.

262. FMTC 31.

263. (2018) Xiang Min Shen 1416 Hao ((2018) 湘民申1416号).

RMB10,000, 39 percent were between RMB10,000 and RMB50,000, and 9 percent were over RMB50,000.[264]

8.7.2.2 Infidelity

A large fraction of the Chinese public believes that marital infidelity not only destroys families but also dismantles the moral fabric of society. Infidelity and concubinage, though widespread,[265] are regarded as immoral and unacceptable in Chinese society.[266] Marital fidelity is declared as a Chinese national virtue and is a legal obligation that requires all types of adulterous relationships be prohibited by law.[267] Although adultery is no longer a crime under Chinese law,[268] adultery may be nonetheless prosecuted as bigamy,[269] a crime that carries significant prison time under Chinese penal law.[270]

A Typical Case, *Zhou v. Zhang*, reflects China's effort to police marriages and to enforce monogamy through divorce damage awards. Zhou and Zhang were married in 2003 and have two children. They were divorced in July 2013 based on consent. After the divorce, Zhou found out that Zhang had an extramarital affair and had a daughter born in May 2013. Zhou sued Zhang for compensatory damages for emotional injury caused by Zhang's adultery. Zhou was awarded RMB15,000 as compensatory damages. The SPC explained that adultery is a violation of both the law and Chinese moral tradition, and therefore the adulterer must be punished and must compensate the injured spouse for emotional sufferings.[271]

Chinese courts have closely followed *Zhou v. Zhang*. For example, very recently a Jiangxi court granted the husband recovery for emotional damages inflicted by the wife's bigamy. The wife lived with another man openly as husband and wife and had a son with her new partner. The husband brought a post-divorce action against the wife and her new partner for recovery of emotional damages. The Chongqing High People's Court found that the wife

---

264. Huang Haitao (黄海涛), Fan Jiating Baoli Fa Zuowei Caipan Guize Zhi Shixiaoxing Fenxi (反家庭暴力法作为裁判规则之实效性分析) [Analysis on the Effectiveness of the Anti-Domestic Violence Law as Adjudication Rules], Renmin Sifa (人民司法) [The People's Judicature] 2019(7):4–9, 4.

265. Na Zhang et al., *Sexual Infidelity in China: Prevalence and Gender-Specific Correlates*, 41 Arch Sex Behav. 861, 864 (2012).

266. Alyssa Miller, *Punishing Passion: A Comparative Analysis of Adultery Laws in the United States of America and Taiwan and Their Effects on Women*, 41 Fordham Int'l L.J. 425, 435 (2018).

267. FMTC 12. *See also* the Civil Code art. 1043 para. 2.

268. Miller, *supra* note 266, at 434. Although adultery is rarely prosecuted, it remains a crime in 20 states in the United States; *see also* Jeremy D. Weinstein, *Adultery, Law, and the State: A History*, 38 Hastings L.J. 195, 218 (1986).

269. (2018) Zui Gao Fa Xin Shen 109 Hao ((2018) 最高法刑申109号).

270. The Criminal Law art. 258.

271. FMTC 12.

violated a spouse's duty to remain faithful and committed bigamy, and that the husband had no wrongdoing. Considering the severity of the wife's misconducts, harms caused by her actions, and the local standard of living, the court determined that it was appropriate to award the husband RMB30,000 as compensatory damages for emotional injuries that he suffered as the result of the wife's infidelity. The court, nevertheless, held that the husband had no standing to sue the wife's new partner for divorce damages.[272]

8.7.2.3 Violation of Public Order and Good Morals

To protect an innocent spouse's interest in marital property, Chinese courts often resort to the doctrine of public order and good morals (*gongxu liangsu*), an imported concept coined in the Civil Code.[273] *Li v. Yang* illustrates how Chinese courts apply the doctrine of public order and good morals in a Typical Case where the husband transferred marital assets to his mistress. Li and her husband, Song, had been married since 1998. Li and Song built a successful business together. In May 2011, Song met Yang and had an affair with her. Three months after they met, Song gave Yang RMB660,000. Later, Li discovered the affair and the bank transfer of RMB660,000 from Song to Yang. Li asked Yang to return the funds, but Yang refused. Li sued Yang for wrongful enrichment. Yang defaulted in the action that Li brought against her. The trial court ordered Yang to return RMB660,000 to Song and Li because Song had no right to dispose of any marital property without Li's consent, and, more importantly, Yang and Song's adulterous relationship violated public order and good morals (*gongxu liangsu*). The court held that Yang must not be allowed to unjustly enrich herself through her immoral relationship with Song and therefore Yang must repay Li the entire amount that Song gifted to her.[274]

In *Xia v. Zhou*, the court awarded Zhou RMB30,000 for emotional damages caused by Xia's violation of public order and good morals. Before they married, Xia and Zhou maintained a long-term, long-distance relationship

---

272. (2020) Yu Min Shen 2112 Hao ((2020) 渝民申2112号).

273. The Civil Code art. 153 para. 2 (providing that "any civil legal conduct contrary to public order and good morals shall be void"); *see* Zheng Xianwen (郑显文), Gongxu Liangsu Yuanze Zai Zhongguo Jindai Mingfa Zhuanxing Zhong De Jiazhi (公序良俗原则在中国近代民法转型中的价值) [The Public Order and Good Morals Principle's Significance in the Transformation of Chinese Modern Civil Law], Faxue (法学) [Law Sci.], Vol. 11, 87 (2017) (an overview of the adoption and application of "public order and good morals" in Chinese modern civil law codes and cases); *see also* Cai Chang (蔡唱), Gongxu Liangsu Zai Woguo De Sifa Shiyong Yanjiu (公序良俗在我国的司法适用研究) [A Study of Judicial Application of Public Order and Good Morals in Our Country], Zhongguo Faxue (中国法学) [China Legal Sci.], Vol. 6, 236 (2016) (a study of 699 published Chinese courts' decisions that relied on the principle of public order and good morals from 2007 to 2016, finding that the courts frequently rely on "public order and good morals" to rule against parties in adulterous relationships).

274. FMTC 23.

and had sex. A few months after the marriage, Xia gave birth to twins. Zhou believed that the children were his. When the children were about three years old, Zhou began to suspect that they were not his biological children. He did paternity tests and found that he was not the twins' biological father. Zhou filed for divorce and sought divorce damages for emotional injury caused by Xia's deceit. Xia was ordered to pay Zhou RMB30,000 for emotional damages and reimburse him the RMB44,000 that he paid for Xia's prenatal care, the medical expenses for the children's births, the children's living expenses, and the paternity tests. In addition, the court did not award Xia any marital property. The court found that Xia's egregious conduct warranted these compensations for Zhou.[275]

8.7.3 Post-Divorce Spousal Support

The Civil Code provides limited post-divorce spousal maintenance (*jingji bangzhu*) for a dependent spouse with extraordinary financial hardship at the time of divorce.[276] Post-divorce spousal support (*jingji bangzhu*) can be awarded *only* when a party is homeless, or at risk of becoming homeless, or unable to support him/herself at the poverty level of the region where he/she resides at the time of divorce. Chinese courts usually do no extend or increase a payor spouse's support obligation.[277] Post-divorce spousal support obligation terminates when the payee spouse remarries.[278]

The first basic principle of Chinese post-divorce spousal maintenance law is that both spouses have a mutual duty of financial support during the marriage; however, spousal support obligation terminates upon dissolution of the marriage. The second principle is self-responsibility, and every divorced person is expected to provide for his or her own maintenance. These principles resemble the tenets of post-divorce spousal maintenance laws in continental Europe.[279] Chinese post-divorce maintenance (*jingji bangzhu*) is unquestionably different from Anglo-American "spousal support," "maintenance," or "alimony," which is intended to mitigate adverse economic effects of a divorce on a less-moneyed spouse and to ensure that he/she could maintain the lifestyle that she/he had enjoyed during the marriage. In contrast to

275. (2020) Gan 10 Min Zhong 995 Hao ((2020) 赣10民终995号).

276. The Civil Code art. 1090.

277. Zuigao Renmin Fayuan Guanyu Guanche Zhixing Mingshi Zhengce Falu Ruogan Wenti de Yijian (最高人民法院关于贯彻执行民事政策法律若干问题的意见) [The SPC Opinions on the Application and Enforcement of Certain Policies and Laws in Civil Matters (1984)], art. 14. *See also* (2021) Ji 0323 Min Chu 175 Hao [(2021) 吉0323民初175号] art. 14.

278. *Id.*

279. French Civil Code art. 212, providing that spousal support obligation terminates after divorce; *see also* German Civil Code arts. 1569–1577, providing that the precondition of spousal maintenance is the spouse's inability to be self-sufficient.

spousal support, maintenance, or alimony, *jingji bangzhu* is not intended to address any financial consequences of the dissolution of the marital partnership. Under Chinese law, all economic effects of a divorce, such as compensation to a spouse's domestic work contribution to the marriage, are addressed through property division.[280] The sole purpose of *jingji bangzhu* is to prevent a dependent spouse from falling into extreme poverty immediately after the divorce.

Chinese law does not endorse the Anglo-American style of post-divorce maintenance, which is viewed as incentivizing parasitic behavior and divorce.[281] Nevertheless, divorcing couples' private agreements to pay substantial post-divorce maintenance are binding and enforceable. For instance, a Shanghai court enforced Mei and Luo's agreement under which Mei was obligated to pay Luo a total of RMB15 million for her support within two years of the divorce. Mei paid Luo RMB10 million pursuant to the agreement but later defaulted in RMB3.32 million by the time of Lou's enforcement action. The Shanghai court held that the support payment provisions in Mei and Lou's divorce agreement were legally binding and therefore enforceable. Thus, the court entered a judgment against Mei for RMB3.32 million with interests and penalty.[282] *Zhao v. Ma* is a case where the court enforced a much more modest support agreement. Ma and Zhao agreed in their divorce agreement that Zhao would pay Ma RMB2,000 per month for her support for life. Zhao failed to make the payments from December 2014 to March 2019. Zhao sued to enforce the agreement. The court compelled Ma to comply and held that spouses are free to enter agreements concerning post-divorce support and such agreements are legally binding and enforceable.[283]

Absent parties' agreement on post-divorce spousal maintenance, Chinese courts do not award post-divorce spousal maintenance or any maintenance beyond bare necessities. Post-divorce spousal maintenance award amount is determined based on the payee spouse's needs as well as the payor spouse's ability to pay and the local standard of living. Post-divorce spousal maintenance is not awarded when a spouse is able to support her/himself to the local standard of living. Therefore, in *Dong v. Zhang*, the courts declined to award the wife any post-divorce spousal support, as the marital property that she received was sufficient to maintain an average standard of living.[284] In contrast, in *Zhu v. Cai* the Dazhou City Intermediate People's Court increased the support amount for Zhou Zuzhen because Zhou was destitute. Zhou Zuzhen was 70 and Cai Zuze was 67 at the time of their divorce in 2020. Zhou and Cai

280. Marriage Law Explanatory Report ch. 4, arts. 29, 30, 42.
281. *Id.* ch. 4, art. 42.
282. (2020) Hu 0112 Min Chu 24358 Hao ((2020) 沪0112民初24358号).
283. (2019) Ji Min Shen 9882 Hao ((2019) 冀民申9882号).
284. (2016) Su 03 Min Zhong 1545 Hao ((2016) 苏03民终1545号).

are farmers in a mountainous region that was lifted out of extreme poverty very recently. They had been living together since 2008 and were married in 2015. Both parties were widowed and have adult children. Cai has a steady monthly income of RMB500. During the marriage, in addition to farming and housework, Zhou cared for Cai's parents and grandchildren. Zhou was represented by the local legal aid services. The trial court found that Zhou did not have any stable income and she would be homeless after the divorce. Thus, the court ordered Cai to pay RMB5,000 for her support. Zhou appealed. The Intermediate Court increased the support amount to RMB10,000, an amount that was sufficient for Zhou to secure housing.[285]

Chinese courts have developed a uniform approach in determining the form and duration of post-divorce spousal support. Generally, if the payee spouse is young and able to work but has temporary financial hardship, the award is usually a short-term or one-time cash assistance. If the spouse in need is old, ill, disabled, or unable to work and has no income after a long marriage, the payor party may be required to provide housing for the dependent spouse in addition to cash payments. Post-divorce spousal maintenance can be paid in the form of cash payments, labor, or housing. The case of *Yao v. Chen* is very similar to *Zhu v. Cai*. However, in *Yao v. Chen* the wife received RMB50,000 for her post-divorce support because the region has a slightly higher standard of living and the husband has better income. Both Yao and Chen were widowed. They were married for 13 years. Yao sued for divorce five times and the divorce was granted in his fifth action. Chen admitted that the couple had a tumultuous relationship but refused to end the marriage as she would not be able to support herself after the divorce. Yao was a schoolteacher and earned about RMB5139 a month. Chen objected to the divorce and sought post-divorce spousal support from Yao until she turned 70. Considering Chen's poor health and inability to hold stable employment, the court ordered Yao to pay Chen a total of RMB50,000 for her support in five yearly installments of RMB10,000 per year.[286]

Chinese courts usually do no extend or increase a payor spouse's support obligation.[287] For example, the court refused to increase the ex-wife's support amount from RMB4,000 per year to RMB12,000 per year in *Zhang v. Ren*. In this case, Zhang and Ren reached an agreement through the court's mediation in 2005 and Ren agreed to pay Zhang RMB4,000 per year for her support for her life. Ren fully complied with the agreement. In 2021, Zhang sought to increase the support amount. The court found that Ren had supported Zhang for many years, since 2005, that Ren was 81 years old and needed care and

285. (2021) Chuan 17 Min Zhong 5 Hao ((2021) 川17民终5号).

286. (2015) Gan Liu Zhong Min Zhong Zi Di 00809 Hao ((2015) 黔六中民终字第00809号).

287. The SPC Opinions on the Application and Enforcement of Certain Policies and Laws in Civil Matters art. 14.

support, that the parties had five adult children who could provide support for both parties, and that Zhang was not in any kind of financial hardship. The court held that whether post-divorce maintenance should be awarded is determined by both the payee's need of support and the payor's ability to support, and "in consideration of equity, Plaintiff, Zhang's request for an increase of maintenance to RMB12,000 per year must not be entertained."[288]

§ 8.8 Cohabitation

Although the Chinese society has become more tolerant to nonmarital cohabitation in contemporary China, researchers have found that the nonmarital cohabitation rate is actually very low in contemporary China.[289] Nevertheless, Chinese courts have developed a set of protocols in handling issues concerning property and children when a couple's cohabitation relationship has ended.[290]

When determining property distribution between cohabitation partners, Chinese courts consider the totality of the circumstances and equitable factors other than the titled ownership. With a few exceptions provided by law all property acquired during the marriage is marital property jointly owned by the spouses, whereas the source of funds used to acquire the property determines whether any property acquired during cohabitation is the cohabitants' joint property. Consider *Wang Li v. Zhang Wei*. Wang and Zhang had lived together since 2001. In 2002, they purchased a home for RMB30,000 in Zhang's name. They borrowed RMB13,000 from Qiu to purchase the home. They also borrowed additional loans in a total amount of RMB10,000 to pay for joint expenses. Wang and Zhang repaid Qiu when they were living together. Wang and Zhang still had some debts when they separated. Considering that Wang and Zhang had been living together as husband and wife for a long period of time, the court ruled that all income, assets, and debts acquired during their cohabitation period were the parties' joint property and liabilities. The court then divided the value of the home as well as the unpaid debts equally between the parties.[291]

Local courts in rural China often face difficult *de facto* marriage cases, in which the couple married in a traditional wedding ceremony and had lived as husband and wife for years without registering their marriage. A *de facto* marriage is not a legal marriage, and therefore the couple do not have any

288. (2021) Ji 0323 Min Chu 175 Hao ((2021) 吉0323民初175号).

289. Jia Yu & Yu Xie, *Cohabitation in China: Trends and Determinants*, 41(4) Population & Dev. Rev. 607–28 (Dec. 2015).

290. Chen Wei & Shi Lei, *Cohabitation in China: Legislation and Practice*, Int'l Surv. Fam. L. 55 (2017).

291. FMTC 26.

rights derived from a marriage. Nevertheless, Chinese courts tend to treat *de facto* marriages as a marriage instead of cohabitation. In the case of Liu Congde and Li Dan, Liu and Li were married in a traditional wedding ceremony but never registered their marriage. They lived together as husband and wife, operated an online store together, and had two children. Li was recovering from cancer when Li and Liu separated. Liu sued for custody of the parties' children and child support; and Li counterclaimed for partition of joint property, child custody, and support. Liu argued that he started the online store before the parties' relationship began and thus it was not joint property. The trial court found that Li and Liu operated the online store together as a family business and rejected Liu's claim that the online store was his personal property. The court also found that Li was a capable parent despite her poor health. The trial court divided the parties' joint assets, including the online store, equally between Li and Liu, awarded Li custody of the younger child and Liu custody of the older child, and ordered Liu to pay Li child support. Considering Li's poor health and financial hardship, due to her illness, the trial court ordered Liu to pay Li RMB30,000 for her maintenance (*jingji bangzhu*). Liu appealed. The trial court's decision was affirmed on appeal.[292] Clearly, the courts treated Li and Liu as if they were married.

292. (2019) Xiang 13 Min Zhong 1335 Hao ((2019) 湘13民终1335号).

Chapter 9

Parent-Child Relationship

Under Chinese law, a parent-child relationship can be created by genetic connections, adoption, marriage to a biological parent, and assumption of parental responsibilities. With respect to the laws of parent and children, China has adopted rules and principles widely accepted by the modern world and at the same time has retained established customs grown out of China's social and economic conditions. Central to Confucianism is filial piety, which speaks to life-long reverence, respect, and obedience to one's parents. Thus, the statutory scheme regulating parent and child relationship is comprised of two components—the protection, care, and support of minor children, and the protection, care, and support of elderly parents.

China has long adopted "the best interest of the minor child" standard as the guiding principle in its children's law. Applying the best interests of the child standard signifies a child-centered approach in legal matters concerning minor children. At the same time, Chinese law emphasizes the reciprocal nature of parent and child relationship—a sign of the tenacity of Confucian doctrine of filial piety and agrarian traditions. The Civil Code provides that parents have a duty to provide education for their minor children and their children have the right to education; and at the same time, parents have the right to discipline their children and the children have the duty to be educated and disciplined.[1] As the parent-child relationship continues in the child's adult life, parents and their childen have a reciprocal duty to care and support each other during their lifetimes—parents have the duty to support and care for their adult dependent children; and adult children have the duty to support and care for their elderly parents.[2] Striking similarities could be found between the 20th-century Chinese law concerning parent-child relationship and the laws of preindustrial New England. For instance, early Connecticut

1. The Civil Code art. 1068 para. 1.
2. *Id.* art. 26.

state law stressed "the reciprocal rights and duties, subsisting between parents and children":

> The duties of parents consist in affording their children maintenance, protection and education. . . . The power of parents over their children, is calculated to enable them to perform their duty and keep their children in obedience and subjection. . . . The duties of children to parents, are obedience and subjection during their minority, and honor, reverence, and respect during their lives. As they depended on the assistance and protection of their parents, during the feeble and defenseless period of infancy, so when their parents are reduced to a state of infirmity, by old age, it becomes the duty of children to yield the same assistance and protection. The statute law has therefore imposed upon children the same obligation to support their parents when reduced to want, as upon parents to support their children, under like circumstances"[3]

History of Western family life suggests that the child-centered family law emerged when preindustrial agrarian households began to decline, and modern conjugal families began to rise as family life became progressively more oriented around children.[4] Thus, we must note that laws concerning parent-child relations in highly industrialized, postmodern Western societies are naturally different from the laws of China, a society where nuclear, conjugal families just began to spread.

China's unique social and economic path to modernity contributes to some distinctive features in its laws concerning parent-child relationship. For example, under Chinese law, a parent-child relationship can be created not only by biological conception or legal adoption but also by a kinfolk caregiver's assumption of parental responsibilities and establishment of custodial relationship with a child. In rural China, many children still live in multigenerational, polymorphous households full of various kinfolk. With a large labor force migrating between their rural home bases and manufacturing centers in the last 30 years, grandparents, adult siblings, parents' siblings, and other family members frequently serve as minor children's primary caregivers in the absence of the biological parents. Recognizing the agrarian childrearing tradition and the high frequency of absentee biological parents, Chinese law confers parental rights and duties to grandparents, adult siblings, and any other kinfolk caregivers as *de facto* parents.

We must also note the diversity of social, economic, and cultural conditions in a vast country like China when considering laws concerning children. Shared custody favored by U.S. lawyers and judges has gained interest and preference from urban, middle-class Chinese families. Thus, shared child custody is endorsed by Chinese courts. However, most Chinese parents that just came out of extreme poverty very recently, shared custody, even regular overnight visitations, could be difficult to achieve due to a lack of stable housing and great geographic distance between the separated parents.

---

3. 1 Zephaniah Swift, A System of the Laws of the State of Connecticut 204–06 (1795).
4. William L. O'Neill, Divorce in the Progressive Era 4–5 (1967).

§ 9.1 Establish Parent-Child Relationship

9.1.1 Biological Parents

Under Chinese law, parental rights and obligations are presumptively correlated with genetic connections: biological parents have rights and obligations toward their children regardless of their marital status.[5]

9.1.1.1 Biological Parentage

When there are legitimate reasons to dispute biological parentage, a presumptive parent or adult child may bring an action for determination of parentage.[6] Mere speculation is not sufficient for a court to order a paternity test. Thus, the Heilongjiang Province High People's Court upheld the lower court's decision not to order a genetic test when a photo was the only evidence that a husband relied on to support his suspicion of his daughter's paternity.[7] In addition, paternity can be established or disproved by genetic testing or circumstantial evidence if the presumptive father refuses to take the test in child support proceedings.[8]

Only a presumptive parent or an adult child has the standing to bring a paternity suit. Therefore, Chinese courts have consistently rejected a third party's request for a court-ordered paternity test in inheritance disputes in that a third party does not have the standing for a paternity suit and that allowing a paternity suit after a father's death is a violation of the father's and the child's privacy.[9] Thus, in *Yi v. Ou and Ou*, the Guangzhou City Intermediate People's Court declined to order a DNA test to determine whether the deceased was a daughter's biological father.[10] Similarly, in *Xu v. Wang*, an inheritance dispute, the Beijing No. 3 Intermediate Court held that for protection of a minor and the privacy of her and her late father, a paternity test should not be ordered over the minor's objection. The court further held that the court must draw negative inference from the minor's objection to a paternity test and drew the conclusion that the minor was not the deceased's biological child.[11]

5. The Civil Code art. 1071.

6. *Id.* art. 1073.

7. (2017) Hei Min Shen 2894 Hao ((2017) 黑民申2894号).

8. Zhong Fusheng (钟富胜), Shengfu Ju Zuo Qingzi Jianding Qingxing Xia Falü Zeren Panding (生父拒做亲子鉴定情形下法律责任判定) [The Determination of Legal Liability When Biological Father Refuses Paternity Test], Renmin Sifa (人民司法) [The People's Judicature] 2015(16), 50–53.

9. Dai Zhenkui Xiang Qiong (代贞奎, 向琼), Caipan Jicheng Quan Jiufen Buyi Qinzi Guanxi Jianding Wei Yiju (裁判继承权纠纷不以亲子关系鉴定为依据) [Adjudication of Inheritance Right Should Not Be Based on Paternity Test], Renmin Sifa (人民司法) [The People's Judicature] 2017(14), 54–56.

10. (2021) Yue 01 Min Zhong 377 Hao ((2021) 粤01民终377号).

11. (2020) Jing 03 Min Zhong 14672 Hao ((2020) 京03民终14672号).

Presumptive fathers' challenges to paternity are generally permitted in child support actions. Chinese courts do not hesitate in allowing a presumptive father to test his paternity without considering the child's privacy and feelings. For example, in Typical Case *Zhang v. Jiang*, the court ordered a DNA test for the husband and the child when the husband suspected that he was not the child's biological father, although the child was six years old and had known the husband as his only father.[12]

Minor children do not have the standing to bring a suit for determination of paternity. For example, a Jiangsu court dismissed a paternity action brought by a minor child, through his mother, to determine the mother's ex-husband was not his father as the child did not have standing to bring the action.[13]

Paternity can be established or disproved by genetic testing or circumstantial evidence if the presumptive father refuses to take the test in child support proceedings. For example, in *Jian v. Deng*, the Fujian courts determined that Deng was the child's biological father by circumstantial evidence and ordered Deng to pay child support although he refused to take a paternity test. The child's mother and Deng had a relationship but broke up not long before the mother married another man. The mother later admitted to her ex-husband that the child was not his child. As a result, the mother and her ex-husband divorced. Her divorce agreement stated that the ex-husband was not obligated to pay child support because the ex-husband is not the child's biological father. The mother sought child support from Deng. Deng disputed the paternity and refused to submit to a paternity test. Thus, the courts imputed Deng as the child's biological father based on Deng's refusal of a DNA test and other circumstantial evidence. The presiding judges indicated that there was overwhelming evidence of the relationship between Deng and the child's mother that led the court to find that Deng was the child's father. Thus, the court found that it would be in the child's best interest to make the decision without a DNA test since the court could not force Deng to take a DNA test and the two-year-old child needed a father to support and care for him.[14]

---

12. Yong Gongkai Cu Gongzheng Jianshe Hexin Jiazhi "Zhuti Jiaoyu Huodong Hunyin Jiating Jiufen Dianxin Anli (用公开促公正 建设核心价值" 主题教育活动 婚姻家庭纠纷典型案例) ["Promote Justice Construct Core Value through Transparency" Focused Education Campaign: Family and Marriage Disputes Typical Cases] (Dec. 4, 2015) [hereinafter FMTC], 45.

13. Liu Gan (刘干), Lihun Hou Yu Fouren Qinzi Guanxi De Su De Xuanze (离婚后欲否认亲子关系的诉的选择) [Choice of Actions in Denying Paternity after Divorce], Renmin Sifa (人民司法) [The People's Judicature] 2017(26), 76–78.

14. Zhong Fusheng (钟富胜), Shengfu Ju Zuo Qingzi Jianding Qingxing Xia Falü Zeren Panding (生父拒做亲子鉴定情形下法律责任判定) [The Determination of Legal Liability When Biological Father Refuses Paternity Test], Renmin Sifa (人民司法) [The People's Judicature] 2015(16), 50–53.

9.1.1.2 Reproductive Technology

Reproductive technology has unsettled genetic-connection-based parentage in recent decades. The use of assisted reproductive technology is tightly regulated in China. Only married couples are permitted to use artificial insemination.[15] Children born during the parents' marriage, through artificial insemination and with both parents' consent are the parents' biological children of marriage.[16]

Surrogacy is illegal in China. Despite the prohibition of surrogacy, many Chinese couples use surrogacy to have children, either in China or abroad. Disputes over parentage and custody of children born of surrogacy have made it into Chinese courts in recent years. When determining parentage of children born of illegal surrogacy, Chinese courts first consider a child's genetic connection with the potential parents. For example, when a surrogate mother hired by a married couple refused to surrender a child born from the husband's sperm and a donor's egg, the Chinese court ordered the surrogate mother to turn over the child to the husband and his wife because the child was the husband's biological child, and the surrogate mother had no biological connection with the child.[17] However, children born of surrogacy do not always have genetic connections with their parents. For instance, in one of the early surrogacy cases, a couple's child was born of surrogacy using donor sperm and egg. In 2008, the wife sought a declaration that she was not the child's parent. Since the wife did not have any genetic connection with the child, the court had to declare that the child was not the wife's child. By the same logic, the child was not the husband's child either.[18] As a result, the child was put in a very peculiar and vulnerable legal limbo. Without clear statutory rules to follow, Chinese courts now turn to the principle of the best interest of the child in determining parentage and custody of children born through surrogacy.[19] In China's first surrogate

15. Weisheng bu renlei fuzhu shengzhi jishu guanli banfa (卫生部人类辅助生殖技术管理办法) [The Ministry of Health Regulations on Human Assisted Reproductive Technology Management] (promulgated on Feb. 10, 2001, effective from Aug. 1, 2001).

16. The Marriage and Family Book Interpretations (I) art. 40.

17. Yang Chengming, Pan Kun (杨成铭, 潘坤), Feifa Daiyun Zhong De Qingzi Guanxi Rending Guize Yanjiu—Ping Dianxing Feifa Daiyun Qinzi Jiufen An (非法代孕中的亲子关系认定规则研究—评典型非法代孕亲子关系纠纷案) [A Study on the Rules Concerning Parent-Child Relationship Determination in Illegal Surrogacy—Commentary on Representative Cases of Parent-Child Relationship Determination Related to Illegal Surrogacy], Falü Shiyong (法律适用) [Nat'l Judges Col. J.] Issue 24 (2020), 6.

18. *Id.* at 5.

19. Zhu Xiaofeng [朱晓峰], Feifa Daiyun Yu Weichengnian Ren Zuida Liyi Yuanze De Shixian [非法代孕与未成年人最大利益原则的实现] [Illegal Surrogate Pregnancy and the Realization of the Best Interest of the Child Principle], Qinghua Faxue [清华法学] (Tsinghua Univ. L. J.) Vol. 11, No. 1, 120–33. Hou Weiqing [侯卫青], Daiyun Zinü Jianhuquan Jiufen Zhong De Liyi

child custody case in 2014, the Shanghai courts determined the children's parentage based on their genetic connections with the potential parents. The case involved twins who were conceived with the husband's sperm and an unknown donor's egg and were carried by a gestational surrogate. The wife and husband raised the twins as their marital children. After the husband's death, the paternal grandparents sought custody of the children, claiming that the twins were not the wife's children. The courts in Shanghai ruled that the wife was in fact the children's stepparent and had the same parental rights and duties as their biological parents because her spouse was the children's biological parent, and she raised the children and had a parent-child relationship with the children since their births.[20]

9.1.2 Stepparents

When a biological parent of a child marries someone other than the child's other biological parent, that spouse becomes the child's stepparent. Under Chinese law, a formal adoption is not required to create a legal parent-child relationship between a stepparent and a stepchild. A legal parent-child relationship is created, by operation of law, between a stepchild and their stepparent when the stepparent assumes parental responsibilities and establishes a custodial relationship (*fuyang guanxi*) with the child.[21]

Divorce or a biological parent's death does not necessarily terminate the parent-child relationship between a stepparent and a stepchild. A stepparent cannot be compelled to continue the legal parent-child relationship with their stepchild after the divorce or after the biological parent's death. However, he/she may be entitled to custody of the stepchildren that he/she has an established custodial relationship (*fuyang guanxi*) if he/she chooses to.[22] When determining whether to award a stepparent custody of his/her stepchild, Chinese courts give more weight to a stepparent's established custodial relationship with the child than biological connections. For instance, the Shanghai court granted custody of two children to the children's biological

Hengliang Ji Falü Lujin Xuanze—Yi Quanguo Shouli Daiyun Zinü Jianhuquan Jiufen An Wei Li [代孕子女监护权纠纷中的利益衡量及法律路径选择—以全国首例代孕子女监护权纠纷案为例] [Evaluation of Rights and Interests and Legal Solution in Surrogate Birth Children Custody Disputes], Qingshaonian Fanzui Wenti, 2017 Nian Di Yi Qi [青少年犯罪问题, 2017年第一期] (Adolescences Crime Issues, 2017, vol. 1), 4–14.

20. (2015) Min Shaomin Chu Zi Di 2 Hao, 2015 Hu Yi Zhong Shaomin Zhong Zi Di 56 Hao, (2015 闵少民初字第2号, 2015沪一中少民终字第56号), Shanghai Shi Gaoji Renmin Fayuan Shenpan Weiyuanhui 2016 Nian 10 Yue 8 Ri Taolun Tong Guo [上海市高级人民法院审判委员会2016年10月8日讨论通过] (discussed and approved at the Shanghai High People's Court Adjudication Committee on Oct. 8, 2016).

21. The Civil Code art. 1072 para. 2.

22. The Marriage and Family Book Interpretation art. 54.

father's wife, not the children's biological grandparents in a case where the children were born through surrogacy after the husband's death. The Shanghai Court's reasoning was that the wife was the children's stepparent who had cared for them since their births, and therefore it was in the best interest of the children to grant her custody of the children despite lack of genetic connections between her and the children.[23] Similarly, in *Fu Youngji v. Zhao Qihong*, a girl's biological father and stepfather both sought custody of her after her mother's death. The court awarded the girl's custody to the stepfather because the stepfather had cared for, supported, and raised the child since she was five, whereas the child's biological father did not have a close relationship with her.[24]

Stepparents and stepchildren who have a legal parent-child relationship enjoy the same legal rights as biological parents and children,[25] including the rights to support and to inherit from each other.[26] In turn, stepchildren have the same filial support obligation to their stepparents who have raised them and have had an established custodial relationship with them.[27] Stepparents and stepchildren must not abuse or discriminate against each other.[28]

9.1.3 *De Facto* Parents: Grandparents, Older Siblings, and Other Kinfolk

In traditional as well as contemporary China, children are often raised in multigenerational households. Three-generation co-residence remains relatively prevalent both in urban and rural China. Chinese families heavily rely on intergenerational family support not only for old-age care of elderly parents but also for childcare of young children. With women's high labor force participation rate of 85 percent, grandparents become the most important childcare providers. Grandparents providing childcare on a full-time basis is common in China, even when their adult children's families are intact or when they and their adult children maintain separate households. In regions with large migrant labor forces, many young children's sole caregivers are their grandparents instead of their migrant-worker parents. Migrant workers, including the ones immigrated to foreign countries, often leave their children to the care of the grandparents. The grandparents become full-time surrogate parents of these "left-behind children" (*liushou er'tong*).[29] The strong

23. *Supra* note 20.
24. (2016) Qian 04 Min Zhong 283 Hao ((2016) 黔04民终283号).
25. The Civil Code art. 1072 para. 2.
26. *Id.* art. 1127.
27. *Id.* art. 1072 para. 2.
28. *Id.* art. 1072 para. 1.
29. Esther C.L. Goh, *Grandparents as Childcare Providers: An In-depth Analysis of the Case of Xiamen, China*, 23 J. Aging Studies 60–68, 64–65 (2009).

and close bond between grandparents and grandchildren is recognized in the Civil Code. Courts are required to consider grandparents' role as their grandchildren's primary caregivers in child custody decisions.[30] Grandparents are given first preference in guardianship appointment.[31] When a child's parents are deceased or unable to support or care for their child, grandparents and grandchildren assume a parent-child relationship and have reciprocal duty to support and care. Both paternal grandparents and maternal grandparents have the rights and obligations to raise their minor grandchildren whose parents are deceased or are unable to care for them. Adult grandchildren, in turn, have a duty to support and care for their grandparents if their parents are deceased or are unable to support them.[32]

Older siblings have similar roles as grandparents in the upbringing of their younger siblings. Older siblings are at the second level of preference for guardianship appointment for minor children.[33] When their parents are deceased or incapacitated, older siblings have an obligation to support and care for their younger siblings, and the younger siblings in turn are obligated to support their elder siblings who have assumed parental roles and raised them.[34] If an elderly older sibling does not have any other source of support, younger siblings, who have the financial ability to support, must support their elderly older siblings even if the older siblings have not assumed parental roles in their upbringing.[35]

9.1.4 Adoption

Adoption creates a legal parent-child relationship where there had not been one before.

9.1.4.1 Adoption Registration

Adoption of a child is a quasi-judicial registration process in China. An adoption becomes effective when the adoption registration is completed.[36] An adoption should be registered where an orphan is located, or where an adoptee's birth parents or guardians reside.[37]

30. The Marriage and Family Book Interpretations (I) art. 47.
31. The Civil Code art. 27 (1).
32. *Id.* art. 1074.
33. *Id.* art. 27 (2).
34. *Id.* art. 1075.
35. The Elderly Protection Law art. 23.
36. The Civil Code art. 1105 para. 1.
37. Zhongguo Gongmin Shouyang Zinü Dengji Banfa (中华人民共和国民政部中国公民收养子女登记办法) [Measures for Registration of Adoption of Children by Chinese Citizens] (May 12, 1999) art. 4.

Adoptions must be consensual. The consent of a minor over eight years of age must be obtained when he/she is adopted.[38] When a minor is placed for adoption by birth parents, both parents' consent must be obtained; and if one parent is unknown or missing, the known parent's consent must be obtained.[39] If a birth parent's whereabouts are unknown, the adoption registration agency must notify the parent by publication though regional newspapers and may register the adoption if the birth parent does not respond within 60 days after the date of publication.[40] In the case of *Chen Sheng and Wang Qiupu v. Chen Shan and Wang Rigui*, the Guangdong Province High People's Court canceled the adoption of a child on the ground that the adoption was registered without the birth parents' consent. In this case, Wang Qiupu and Wang Rigui are sisters. Rigui and her husband left their son in the care of Qiupu and her husband for years since the child was very young. The child considered Qiupu and her husband his parents. When Rigui tried to get her son back, Qiupu and her husband registered the adoption of Rigui's son by falsely claiming that the child was an orphan. The court held that although the court was sympathetic to Qiupu and her husband's feelings for the child, the adoption must be rescinded as it was obtained without the birth parents' knowledge or consent.[41] However, only birth parents have the standing to challenge an adoption on the ground of lack of consent. Thus, in *Gu v. Xiangtan City Civil Affairs Bureau*, the Hunan courts denied Gu's request to rescind an adoption, as Gu failed to prove that he was the child's birth father.[42]

Adoption registration agencies must conduct an adoption evaluation before approving and registering an adoption.[43] After an adoption application is submitted, the agency must schedule an adoption trial period (*shouyang ronghe qi*) during which the prospective adoptive child will live with the prospective adoptive parents in their home for at least 30 days. The adoption evaluators must examine and report each prospective adoptive parent's reason for the adoption, moral and personality traits, education, health, financial and housing conditions, marital and family status, household members' opinions on the adoption, childrearing plan, relationship with the neighbors, environment of the community, and relationship with the prospective adoptive child during the adoption trial period.[44]

---

38. The Civil Code art. 1104.

39. *Id.* art. 1097.

40. *Id.* art. 1105 para. 2. *See also* Measures for Registration of Adoption of Children by Chinese Citizens art. 7; and Minzheng Bu Shouyang Dengji Gongzuo Guifan (收养登记工作规范) [The Ministry of Civil Affairs Adoption Registration Protocols] (Sept. 1, 2008) art. 17.

41. (2017) Yue Xing Shen 907 Hao ((2017) 粤行申907号).

42. (2017) Xiang Xing Shen 801 Hao ((2017) 湘行申801号).

43. The Civil Code art. 1105 para. 5.

44. Minzheng Bu Shouyang Pinggu Banfa (民政部收养评估办法) [The Ministry of Civil Affairs Measures for Adoption Evaluation] (Dec. 31, 2020) art. 8.

9.1.4.2 Who May Be Adopted?

A minor may be adopted under the following circumstances: (1) he/she is an orphan who has lost both parents; (2) the birth parents are unknown; or (3) the birth parents are unable to care for the child due to extraordinary hardships.[45] An orphan is a minor whose parents are deceased or are declared deceased by a court.[46]

Persons or entities that may place a minor for adoption (*songyang ren*) include (1) an orphan's guardian; or (2) child welfare agencies; or (3) a minor child's birth parents.[47] If both parents do not have full legal capacity and pose real dangers to the minor, then the minor's legal guardian may place the minor for adoption.[48] Kinfolk placement is preferred under Chinese law. A child's legal guardian is usually one of their grandparents or adult siblings.[49] Before a minor is placed for adoption by a legal guardian, the minor's legal guardian must obtain the consent of the persons who have a support obligation to the minor, and if such persons do not consent to the minor's adoption, the legal guardian must be replaced.[50] Persons who have support obligations to a child whose parents are deceased or unable to provide support include the child's grandparents and siblings.[51]

9.1.4.3 Who May Adopt?

Adoptive parents must have the ability to care, educate, and protect the adoptee; have no disease that medical science defines as not suitable for adopting any child; and have no criminal history that may be detrimental to a child's upbringing.[52] An adoptive parent must be at least 30 years old.[53] In addition, a nonmarried, single adoptive parent must be at least 40 years older than the adopted child if the adoptive parent and the adopted child are of different sexes.[54]

An adoptive parent can only have no more than one child before adopting a child.[55] An adoptive parent that has no children may adopt two children,

---

45. The Civil Code art. 1093.
46. Minzheng Bu Guayu Zai Baili Shouyang Dengji Zhong Yange Qufen Guer Yu Chazhao Bu Dao Sheng Fumu De Qiying De Tong Zhi (民政部关于在办理收养登记中严格区分孤儿与查找不到生父母的弃婴的通知) [The Ministry of Civil Affairs' Notice on Strictly Distinguish Orphans and Abandoned Infants Whose Birth Parents Cannot Be Located] (Aug. 11, 1992).
47. The Civil Code art. 1094.
48. *Id.* art. 1095.
49. *Id.* art. 27.
50. *Id.* art. 1096.
51. *Id.* art. 1074.
52. *Id.* art. 1098(2).
53. *Id.* art. 1098(5).
54. *Id.* art. 1102.
55. *Id.* art. 1098(1).

and an adoptive parent with one child can only adopt one child.[56] However, the limit on the number of children that can be adopted by one adoptive parent may be exempted if the adopted child is an orphan or is disabled, or if the child is placed for adoption by a child welfare agency because the child's parents are unknown.[57] If an adoptive parent is an overseas Chinese and the adopted child's lineal relative by blood within the third degree of relationship, the adopted parent is also exempted from the limit on the number of children in their household.[58]

China encourages kinship adoption. When a child is adopted by their stepparent or lineal relatives by blood within the third degree of relationship, the adoptive parent is exempted from certain restrictions.[59] When a husband and wife are to adopt a child, they must do so jointly, except when the adopted child is the biological child of one of the spouses.[60] If one spouse is deceased and the surviving spouse is placing their child(ren) for adoption, the deceased spouse's parents have the priority to adopt their grandchild(ren).[61] A stepparent may adopt his/her stepchild with the consent of the child's birth parents.[62]

9.1.4.4 Effects of Adoption

Upon the adoption, the adopted child's legal parent-child relationship with their adoptive parents as well as their legal relationship with the adoptive parents' close relatives begins; and their legal relationship with their birth parents and their family ends.[63] In other words, the adopted child becomes a member of the adoptive parents' family and has the same legal rights and duties as a biological child. An adopted child's household registration must be changed to their adoptive parents' household.[64] An adopted child may use the family name of the adoptive father's or the adoptive mother's, or keep their birth name.[65] Adoption information must be kept confidential upon the request of the adopter or the person who placed the child for adoption.[66]

If an adoption is invalid, it is then invalid *ab initio*.[67] Most adoptions in China had been informal before a formal adoption system was put in place in

56. *Id.* art. 1100 para. 1.
57. *Id.* art. 1100 para. 2.
58. *Id.* art. 1099 para. 2.
59. *Id.* arts.1099, 1103.
60. *Id.* art. 1101.
61. *Id.* art. 1108.
62. *Id.* art.1103.
63. *Id.* art. 1111.
64. *Id.* art. 1106.
65. *Id.* art. 1112.
66. *Id.* art. 1110.
67. *Id.* art. 1113.

the early 1990s. *De facto* adoptions incurred prior to the 1992 Adoption Law are valid and binding. In a case concerning biological child's interests in his birth parents' land tenure, the SPC held that the child was not entitled to any interests in his birth parents' land tenure in that the child's legal parent-child relationship was terminated by his adoption in 1982, finding that the child was adopted in 1982 and the adoption was a valid and binding *de facto* adoption. The SPC also held that the adoption was not terminated by the adoptive parents' deaths, and the legal parent-child relationship between an adoptive parent and his/her adoptive child survives the death of either.[68]

Informal adoptions remain common after the Adoption Law was enacted in 1992. Consequently, Chinese courts are often asked to affirm *de facto* adoptions (*shishi shouyang*) that have never been registered with the Civil Affairs Bureau in disputes related to filial support and inheritance. *Liu Shixian v. Liu Nan* is a Typical Case concerning *de facto* adoption. Liu Nan was an abandoned orphan. Liu Shixian and Liu Guishu found her and brought her home in 1992. The couple raised Liu Nan as their child. Liu Nan called Liu Shixian "laohan" (dad) and Liu Guishu "mama" (mom). The Lius' family, their friends, and neighbors all considered Liu Na as the Lius' daughter. However, the Lius never registered the adoption formally with the Civil Affairs Bureau. Liu Guishu passed away in 2015. Liu Shixian then sought a declaratory judgment to declare that Liu Na's adoption was invalid. The lower courts found that Liu Na's adoption a *de facto* adoption and denied Liu Shixian's claim. However, the Chongqing High People's Court reversed and held that although the adoption was a *de facto* adoption, it was nonetheless invalid as the adoption was not registered pursuant to the Adoption Law. The Chongqing High People's Court further held that adoptions occurred after the enactment of the 1992 Adoption Law must be registered to be legally valid and binding.[69]

9.1.4.5 Termination of Adoption

Adoptions may be terminated by agreement or by a court order. Upon termination of the adoption, the child's legal relationship with his/her adoptive parents dissolves and his/her legal relationship with the birth parents resumes.[70]

An adoption may not be terminated before the adopted child reaches majority, except when the adoptive parents and the person who placed the child for adoption have agreed to terminate the adoption. The adopted child's consent must be obtained before an adoption is terminated if the adopted

68. (2016) Zui Gao Fa Xing Shen 4181 Hao ((2016) 最高法行申4181号).
69. (2017) Yu Min Zai 273 Hao ((2017) 渝民再273号).
70. The Civil Code art. 1117.

child is over eight years old.[71] If an adoptive parent has failed to financially support the adopted child, or has abused, neglected, or otherwise harmed the adopted child, a court may terminate the adoption upon the request of the person who placed the child for the adoption.[72]

If the relationship between an adoptive parent and his/her adult adopted child has deteriorated to the extent that they can no longer reside in the same household, the adoption may be terminated by the adoptive parent and the adoptive child's agreement or by a court order.[73] For example, a Shanghai court had to terminate an adoption because the adoptive father insisted that he never wanted to adopt his adopted daughter, he could not stand seeing her or living with her, and he did not want to have any contact with her. The court found that the adoptive father was incapacitated but had a sound mind, and therefore the court had to respect his wishes.[74] In contrast, in *Liu v. Liu* a Henan court rejected an adoptive father's request to terminate an adoption. The adoptive father was 80 years old. He claimed that his adopted daughter was not treating him well and sought to terminate the adoption. The father testified that his daughter hit him with an onion three times. The court found no evidence of the daughter's maltreatment of the father. Instead, the court found that the adopted daughter had been taking care of the father and his late wife, paid for their medical care, and provided monthly financial support. Last, the court found that the adoptive father's nephew interfered with the adopted daughter's relationship with her adoptive father and the suit to terminate the adoption was brought in the context of a bitter dispute over the adoptive mother's estate. Thus, the court declined to terminate the adoption.[75]

Termination of the adoption does not necessarily end an adult adopted child's support obligation to their adoptive parents. After termination of the adoption, an adult adopted child must continue supporting his/her adoptive parents who are no longer able to work and have insufficient income. Furthermore, if the termination of the adoption is due to an adult adopted child's maltreatment of the adoptive parents, the adult child must compensate the adoptive parents for the financial support that they have provided to the child.[76] For instance, in *Liu v. Liu*, the adoptive mother requested termination of the adoption because the relationship between her and her adopted daughter had deteriorated. The court found that the mother and

71. *Id.* art. 1114 para. 1.
72. *Id.* art. 1114 para. 2.
73. *Id.* art. 1115.
74. (2021) Hu 02 Min Zhong 1178 Hao ((2021) 沪02民终1178号).
75. (2021) Yu 07 Min Zhong 674 Hao ((2021) 豫07民终674号).
76. The Civil Code art. 1118 para. 1.

daughter had a good relationship until the daughter dropped out of college, moved in with a divorcee, and had a child with him out of wedlock. The daughter harassed her adoptive mother for money and brought two people to her home to attack her verbally. The court terminated the adoption and ordered the adopted daughter to pay her adoptive mother RMB100,000 as compensation for the support that she had received from her adopted mother from the date when she was adopted to the date when the adoption was terminated.[77]

The birth parents may be required to compensate the adoptive parents the financial support provided to their child during the adoption if the adoption is terminated upon the birth parents' request, except where the termination of adoption is due to the adoptive parents' maltreatment of the child.[78] In *de facto* adoption cases, Chinese courts sometimes require the birth parents to reimburse the adopted parents for the child's expenses incurred during the adoption. For instance, in the case of Ou, a 13-year-old child, Ou, found out that she was adopted and returned to her birth family. Ou's adoptive family and birth family live in the same village. Ou's birth parents gave Ou to the adoptive parents three days after she was born because they wanted to have a son. The adoptive parents registered Ou in their household but did not register the adoption. The adoptive parents paid the fine levied under the "one child" policy and raised Ou. When Ou was about 13 years old, she found out that she was adopted and returned to her birth family. The court found that the *de facto* adoption was not legally binding because it was not registered, and thus Ou's birth parents could take her back. In addition, the court held that in consideration of fairness, the birth parents must reimburse Ou's adoptive parents for Ou's expenses and the fine in the sum of RMB65,000.[79]

9.1.4.6 International Adoption

Foreign nationals that qualify to adopt under the laws of their country of origin may adopt children in accordance with Chinese law.[80] China is a signatory country of the Convention of 29 May 1993 on Protection of Children and Co-operation in Respect of Intercountry Adoption (the "Hague Adoption Convention"). Therefore, international adoption of children in China follows the Hague process.

---

77. (2016) Jin 0108 Min Chu 263 Hao ((2016) 晋0108民初263号).
78. The Civil Code art. 1118 para. 2.
79. (2019) Qian 26 Min Zhong 547 Hao ((2019) 黔26民终547号).
80. The Civil Code art. 1109.

§ 9.2 Parental Rights and Duties

9.2.1 Minor Children

Parents have the duty to provide their minor children maintenance, education, and protection.[81] If a parent fails to support their minor children or dependent adult children, the children are entitled to seek support from the parent.[82] Parents are responsible for their minor children's living expenses, educational cost, medical expenses, and any other reasonable expenses.[83] The support obligation for children is extended beyond natural parents. Any person who has accepted a child as a member of his or her family and has established a custodial relationship (*fuyang guanxi*) with the child has the duty to provide the child financial support. Therefore, the stepparent, grandparent, or sibling who has assumed a parent-child relationship and established a custodial relationship with a child is obligated to support the child if the child's biological parents are unable to support the child.[84]

Children have the right to education and parents have the duty to educate and discipline their minor children. All parents are obligated to ensure that their children receive an education suitable to their age, ability, and aptitude, and again the obligation is extended to any person who has an obligation to support the child.[85] Parents' duty to provide their children education is fulfilled by sending a child to school as mandated by the PRC Compulsory Education Law. It is an offence for any parents to fail to send their child to school without any reasonable cause.[86]

Parents are their minor children's guardians.[87] Both parents have the full authority to conduct juridical acts on the behalf of their minor child and the duty to protect their minor child's person, property, and other lawful interests.[88] Inasmuch, parents are their children's legal representatives and are liable for any damages to third persons caused by their minor children.[89] For discussions of parents' authority and duty as guardians of their minor child, see subsection 11.2.1. For discussions of parents' liability for their minor children's acts to third persons, see § 11.3.

---

81. *Id.* art. 26.
82. *Id.* art. 1067.
83. The Marriage and Family Book Interpretations (I) art. 42.
84. The Civil Code arts. 1072, 1074, 1075.
85. *Id.* art. 26.
86. Zhonghua Renmin Gongheguo Yiwu Jiaoyu Fa (中华人民共和国义务教育法) [the People's Republic of China Compulsory Education Law] (promulgated on June 29, 2006, effective on Sept. 1, 2016) (hereinafter the Compulsory Education Law) arts. 59, 60.
87. The Civil Code art. 27.
88. *Id.* art. 34 para. 1.
89. *Id.* art. 1069.

Parents' guardianship (*jianhu*) and custody (*fuyang*) of their children are clearly distinguished under Chinese law. Parents' custody of their children entails the routine childcare and support in day-to-day life, whereas parents' guardianship of children affords them the authority and duty to conduct juridical acts on behalf of their children and to be fully responsible for the children's person and property. In other words, parents' guardianship of their minor children under Chinese law essentially amounts to "legal custody" in Anglo-American laws. The Anglo-American concept of "legal custody" is not unknown to Chinese courts. For example, in *S v. Tan*, the Beijing court awarded residential custody of the child to the mother and at the same time affirmed the father's guardianship and parental rights, considering that the child would eventually relocate to the United States. In the case, the father, S, was an American citizen living and working in Beijing. The mother was a native of Beijing. The parents were married in Beijing. The family had always lived in Beijing during the marriage. The court found that it was in the child's best interest to award the mother residential custody because the child was only four years old and had been living with the mother for over two years since the parties' separation. Considering that the child would attend school and live in the United States, the trial court and the Beijing No. 3 Intermediate People's Court specifically affirmed the father's guardianship of the child.[90]

A parent's guardianship of his/her child may be terminated when the parent has failed to perform his/her duty as the child's guardian or when a parent has neglected, abused, or caused harm to the child. The SPC published ten Typical Cases of termination of a parent's guardianship,[91] where the parent physically abused,[92] sexually assaulted,[93] abandoned,[94] swindled,[95] or nearly murdered his or her child.[96] When a child's parents' guardianship is terminated, the child is placed in the care of their new guardians, usually their grandparents or close family members,[97] or child welfare institutions run by the local Civil Affairs Bureau if a child does not have any family members who are willing or able to care for him/her.[98]

90. (2015) San Zhong Min Zhong Zi Di 08588 Hao ((2015) 三中民终字第08588号).

91. Zuigao renmin fayuan guanyu qinhai weichennian ren quanyi bei chexiao jianhuren zige dianxin anli (最高人民法院关于侵害未成年人权益被撤销监护人资格典型案例) [Termination of Guardianship for Violation of Minor's Rights and Interests Typical Cases] (May 31, 2016) [hereinafter TGTC].

92. TGTC 1, TGTC 5.

93. TGTC 2, TGTC 8, and TGTC 10.

94. TGTC 3, TGTC 4, TGTC 7.

95. TGTC 9.

96. TGTC 6.

97. TGTC 3, TGTC 6, TGTC 7, and TGTC 9.

98. TGTC 1, TGTC 2, TGTC 4, TGTC 5, and TGTC 10.

9.2.2 Adult Children

Parents who are able to provide must provide care and support for their disabled adult children.[99] In the Typical Case, *Han v. Zhang*, Han was a mentally disabled adult under the care and custody of his mother, Liu, since his biological parents' divorce. Zhang attempted to abandon Han. The trial court held that Zhang, as Han's stepfather, had the duty to care and support Han because during the marriage between a biological parent and a stepparent, a parent as well as a stepparent has the obligation to support their dependent adult child.[100]

A parent is, however, not responsible for an adult child who can work and support themselves but chooses not to. Thus, the Shanghai courts rejected an 18-year-old's request for support from his 70-year-old father. The courts found that child was healthy and capable of working, and it was his fault that he failed to graduate from high school in Shanghai. The Shanghai court refused to compel the father to pay for the child's international high school in Singapore.[101]

9.2.3 Filial Support

Chinese families shoulder the care for the elderly and infirm members of the family. Central to the Chinese system of old-age support is the norm that adult children, especially sons, support their parents; that is, they provide financial support and daily care for their elderly parents. Tapping into the deep-seated sense of duty to support ones' parents and family members, Chinese government pushed to create a strong family-support mechanism as an essential part of its social-welfare system. Filial support (*shanyang*) obligation has been enshrined in Chinese law since the 1950 Marriage Law. Retaining filial obligation in the Civil Code also signifies China's policy that caring for the elderly is not the state's duty but a private, family affair despite of the tremendous expansion of social benefits in Chinese society.

Parents and adult children have a statutory duty to financially support each other if either the parents or the adult children are unable to provide for themselves. Adult children must provide support, assistance, and protection to their parents.[102] Specifically, adult children must provide adequate housing,[103] and medical care, and living assistance.[104] They must provide emotional care

99. The Civil Code art. 1067 para. 1.

100. FMTC 14.

101. (2021) Hu 02 Min Zhong 1931 Hao ((2012) 沪02民终1931号).

102. The Civil Code art. 26 and art .1067; and the Elderly Persons' Rights and Interests Protection Law art. 14.

103. The Elderly Protection Law art. 16.

104. *Id.* art. 15.

and have the obligation to visit their parents regularly.[105] In rural China, adult children must farm and manage their parents' farm or forest land tenures if the parents are no longer able to farm.[106]

Chinese law does not set any specific standards for determination of filial support amount. Adult children must support their parents based on the parents' needs and their own financial ability. A court may compel adult children to provide filial support to indigent parents who are unable to work or support themselves (*shenghuo kunnan*), including farming their land tenures.[107] However, filial support may be ordered even if an elderly parent is financially independent.[108]

In the Typical Case *Li v. Zi, et al.*, Li is a widow over 80. She is unable to support herself. Her six children refused to support her despite repeated pleas and mediation by the relatives. Li had no choice but suing her children. The court ordered Li's six children to each pay Li RMB200 (a total of RMB1200) per month for her living expenses and to share Li's medical expenses equally.[109] In *Qiu Guixia v. Li, et al.*, Qiu is the mother of the four defendants. Qiu's only income was a RMB55 monthly minimum rural social security income from the government. Qiu asked the court to order her four children each to pay RMB150 per month for her support and to share her medical expenses. The court found that Qiu was unable to support herself and her requests were modest and reasonable. Thus, the court ordered each of Qiu's children to pay Qiu RMB150 (a total of RMB600) per month and allocated Qiu's medical expenses among her children based on their respective financial ability.[110]

In some cases, filial support is ordered for parents who are financially independent. For example, in *Liu v. Liu Jia and Liu Yi*, the father, Liu, was 77 years old when he sued his son, Liu Jia, and daughter, Liu Yi, for support. The children argued that Liu did not need any support from them as Liu had medical insurance and ample income to support himself. The court found that Liu's monthly income was RMB4000, Liu Jia's monthly income was RMB6500, and Liu Yi had no income but was employable. Based on Liu and his children's respective income, the court ordered Liu Jia to pay RMB900 per month and Liu Yi to pay RMB500 per month for Liu's support.[111]

In *Li v. Li Jia and Li Yi*, the father, Li, has two sons, Li Jia and Li Yi. The father was 65 years old at the time of the action. Li received nearly RMB200,000 for

105. *Id.* art. 18.
106. *Id.* art. 17.
107. The Civil Code art. 1067 para. 2.
108. FMTC 8.
109. FMTC 19.
110. FMTC 49.
111. FMTC 8.

land expropriation compensation. After his land was expropriated, the father lived with Li Jia temporarily in Chongqing. The court found that Li's pension is RMB605 a month, which is RMB600 below the average urban resident standard of living in Chongqing. The court also found that although Li received a significant amount of cash, he needed it to secure housing. Thus, the court ordered Li Jia and Li Yi to each pay RMB300 per month for Li's support and share Li's medical expenses when the actual expenses are incurred.[112]

Filial support obligations can be satisfied by cash payment, goods, or labor, whichever may be practical. *Zhu Shaochang v. Zhu Zhengfang, Zhu Zhengde and Zhu Lixiang* was a very difficult case where all parties were elderly and living in extreme poverty. At the time of the father's filial support action in 2015, the father was over 80 and his children were all over 60 years old. A filial support order for the father was entered in 2007. The father sought to increase the support amount in 2015 due to the increase in cost of living. By 2015, Zhu's children were receiving filial support from their own children because of their age and financial hardship. Considering the children's circumstances and the father's needs, the trial court ordered the children to each pay RMB500 per year for their father's living expenses, provide him 200 kg of rice per year, farm their father's land tenure allotment, and share their father's medical expenses equally.[113]

Filial support may be nonmonetary. In recent years, Chinese courts have increasingly added visitation in filial support orders as the courts recognize that elderly parents not only need financial support but also emotional support from their children as in the case of Chen. Mr. Chen had two sons and three daughters. His wife and sons all passed away. Mr. Chen lived with his youngest daughter. Mr. Chen wanted to see his two older daughters more often and would like them to contribute to his medical expenses. The court ordered the daughters to visit Mr. Chen at least once a month and visit him more if he was hospitalized. Commenting on Chen's case, the SPC stressed filial piety and reiterated Chinese courts' intent to enforce it through filial support orders.[114]

With their parents' consent, adult children may enter filial support agreements to determine each child's share of support obligation. Such agreements are legally binding and enforceable. In *Lu, etc. v. Li, etc.*, Lu's three sons entered a filial support agreement for Lu and her husband's support. The second son stopped paying support, as he felt that the parents favored his brothers when dividing the family's assets. The second son was ordered to pay support arrearage and comply with the filial agreement.[115]

112. FMTC 35.
113. FMTC 41.
114. EPTC 4.
115. FMTC 46.

Parents who depend on their adult children's financial support and care are susceptible to their children's manipulation, exploitation, and sometimes abuse. Recognizing elderly parents' vulnerability and their financial dependence on their adult children, the Elderly Persons Rights and Interests Protection Law makes specific provisions to protect elderly parents from physical, emotional, and financial abuse.[116] Adult children must respect their parents' rights to marry and shall not interfere with the parents' marital affairs; and adult children's obligation to support their parents does not terminate because of any changes in the parents' marital relationship.[117]

116. The Elderly Protection Law arts. 22, 25.
117. The Civil Code art. 1069; and the Elderly Protection Law art. 21.

Chapter 10

Parents and Minor Children

Under Chinese law, parents (fathers and mothers) have equal parental rights and the duty to protect the best interest of their minor children. Parental rights and duties are almost entirely separated from marital status. Laws governing the relationship between parents and their biological children of marriage are applicable to parents and their nonmarital or nonbiological children, including adoptive children and stepchildren.[1] Children born out of wedlock, adoptive children, and stepchildren enjoy the same rights and bear the same obligations as biological children born of their parents' marriage.

Parents have the duty to provide their minor children with maintenance, education, and protection.[2] If a parent fails to support their minor children, the children are entitled to seek support from the parent.[3] Parents are responsible for their minor children's living expenses, educational costs, medical expenses, and any other reasonable expenses.[4] A biological parent who does not reside with their biological child has an obligation to pay for the child's living and educational expenses until the child turns 18.[5] All parents, regardless of their marital status or living arrangements, must support their children financially. Child support obligation is extended beyond biological parents. Stepparents, grandparents, or siblings who establish a custodial relationship with a child have the same support obligation as biological parents.[6]

A minor's parents are his or her guardians.[7] Parents, as legal guardians, have the duty to educate and discipline their minor children. All parents are obligated to ensure that their children receive an education suitable to their

1. The Civil Code art. 1072.
2. *Id.* art. 26.
3. *Id.* art. 1067.
4. The Marriage and Family Book Interpretations (I) art. 42.
5. The Civil Code art. 1671.
6. *Id.* arts. 1072, 1074, 1075.
7. *Id.* art. 27.

age, ability, and aptitude, and again the obligation is extended to include any person who has an obligation to support the child.[8] In connection with parents' duty to educate and discipline their minor children, Chinese law imputes children's misconduct to their parents as a failure to supervise and discipline minor children. Parents are liable for any damages to others caused by their minor children.[9]

§ 10.1 Child Custody

The most contentious family law disputes in Euro-American jurisdictions often relate to how custodial rights over minor children will be divided between separating parents. Child custody battles are far less frequent or complicated in China, probably because child custody rules are relatively straightforward: there is a strong presumption of joint legal custody and sole residential custody for young children.[10] Residential custody of children two years of age and younger is with their mothers, and children eight years of age or older decide with which parent they will live. The best interest of the child standard applies in child custody and visitation disputes.[11]

Parents' guardianship (*jianhu quan*) of their minor children does not terminate after the parents' divorce, regardless of which parent has residential custody and directly cares (*zhijie fuyang*) for the children.[12] After divorce, both parents continue to have equal rights and duties to support, educate, and protect their children.[13] In other words, parents have equal and joint guardianship of their children although the parent with whom the children resides will provide direct care (*zhijie fuyang*). Both parents have the obligation to facilitate the children's relationship with both parents. Neither parent may unilaterally change a child's name. If a child's name was unilaterally changed by a parent, the child must resume the use of their original name. A parent cannot refuse to pay child support because of the change of a child's name.[14]

Sole residential custody is the norm when parents are separated. The residential parent has direct custody (*zhijie fuyang*) of the children and is responsible for their routine care. Nonresidential parents have visitation rights.[15] Nevertheless, shared residential custody is an option if it is in the child's best interest.[16] In the event that neither parent wants residential custody of

8. *Id.* art. 26.
9. *Id.* art. 1069.
10. *Id.* art. 1084 paras. 1, 2.
11. *Id.* art. 1084 para. 3.
12. *Id.* art. 1084 para. 1.
13. *Id.* art. 1084 para. 2.
14. The Marriage and Family Book Interpretations (I) art. 59.
15. The Civil Code art. 1086.
16. The Marriage and Family Book Interpretations (I) art. 48.

the children, the court will place child custody on one parent.[17] Residential custody arrangements do not affect either parent's decision-making authority over their child's upbringing.

§ 10.2 Guardianship of a Minor

10.2.1 Types of Guardians

There are three types of guardians in Chinese law: statutory guardian (*fading jianhu ren*), voluntary guardian (*yiding jianhu ren*), and designated guardian (*zhiding jianhu ren*). A statutory guardian assumes guardianship of a ward by operation of law. A voluntary guardian is appointed by a person's directive. A designated guardian is appointed by a local community organization, usually an Urban Residents' Committee or Villagers' Committee, or a court.[18]

Parents, including biological parents, stepparents, and adoptive parents are their minor children's statutory guardians.[19] Where both parents of a minor are deceased or cannot act as the minor's guardian, one of the following persons, if capable of acting as a guardian, may act as the minor child's guardian in the following order: (1) paternal or maternal grandparents; (2) adult brothers or sisters; or (3) other individuals or organizations willing to act as a guardian, after obtaining the approval from the Urban Residents' Committee, Villagers' Committee, or Civil Affairs Bureau at the place of the minor's domicile.[20]

Parents who are the guardians of their child may designate a guardian for their child by wills.[21] Since both parents are a minor child's statutory guardians regardless of their marital status or child custody arrangement, a parent's guardianship designation by a will has no effect if the other parent survives him/her.[22] The Civil Code is silent on whom parents may appoint as their child's guardian, or whether parents may exclude anyone from being appointed as the child's guardian, or whether the parents may appoint more than one guardian.[23]

---

17. The Marriage and Family Book Interpretations art. 60.

18. Rebecca Lee, *Guardianship of the Elderly with Diminished Capacity: The Chinese Challenge*, 29 INT'L J.L. POL. & FAM. 1, 4 (2015).

19. *Id.* art. 26.

20. *Id.* art. 27.

21. *Id.* art. 29.

22. Liu Diqi (柳地奇), Yizhu Zhiding Jianhu Zhidu Yu Gongzheng Shiwu (遗嘱指定监护制度与公证实务) [Appointment of Guardian by Will System and Notary Practice], Zhongguo Gongzheng (中国公证) (China Notary J.), 2018(02):18–21, 19–20.

23. Meng Qinguo, Tang Ruilun (孟勤国, 唐瑞), Lun Yizhu Zhiding Jianhu De Wanshan—Yi Minfa Dian Hunyin Jianting Bian De Bianzhuan Wei Zhongdian (论遗嘱指定监护的完善—以民法典《婚姻家庭编》的编纂为重点) [On Refining the Guardianship Appointment by

10.2.2 Duties and Responsibilities of a Guardian

As the guardians of their minor children, parents are fully responsible for the care and protection of their children's person, property, and other lawful rights and interests.[24] A temporary guardian may be appointed for a minor child in the event when both of his/her parents are temporarily unable to perform their duty.[25] Parents are the legal representatives of their children and represent their children in performing juridical acts.[26] Inasmuch, parental authority is derived from parents' guardianship of their children.

A guardian has a fiduciary duty to act in the best interest of the ward.[27] Thus, parents may not dispose of their child's property unless the disposition benefits the child.[28] A minor over the age of eight is "a person with limited civil legal capacity" (*xianzhi minshi xingwei nengli ren*), who must carry out most judicial acts through their guardian but may independently perform some juridical acts.[29] The Civil Codes provides that if a protected person has limited legal capacity, his/her guardian must consult with him/her, according to his/her mental capacity, before making any decision that may affect his/her interests.[30] Thus, parents of a child over eight years old must consult with the child and consider the child's wishes when making major decisions that affect the child's welfare. A parent who has failed to discharge the duties of guardianship or has violated his/her child's lawful rights and interests is legally liable for breach of his/her fiduciary duty.[31]

As their child's guardians, parents and/or a person whom the parents have entrusted their child's care to are liable to third persons for damages caused by the child's actions.[32] However, if a parent has fulfilled his/her guardianship duty and has not been negligent, his/her liability for the damages might be reduced.[33] If a child has his/her own assets, the child must pay

Will—Drafting the Civil Code, Marriage and Family Book as Focus], Hebei Faxue (河北法学) [Hebei Law Science], Vol. 37, No. 5, 14–25, 19–20 (May 2019).

24. The Civil Code art. 34 para. 1.

25. *Id.* art. 34 para. 4.

26. *Id.* art. 23.

27. *Id.* art. 35.

28. *Id.* art. 35 para. 1.

29. *Id.* art. 16.

30. *Id.* art. 35 paras. 2 and 3.

31. *Id.* art. 34 para. 3.

32. *Id.* art. 1188 para. 1, and art. 1189. For a review of a guardian's third-party liability under Chinese law, see Sun Yuhong (孙玉红), Woguo Jianhu Ren Zeren Guifan De Fansi Yu Zai Jiedu (我国监护人责任规范的反思与再解读) [Rethinking and Re-Interpreting Our Country's Guardian Liability Regulation], Falü Kexue (法律科学) [Legal Science] Issue 1 (2016), 104–10.

33. The Civil Code art. 1188 para. 1.

for the damages that he/she has caused to a third person with his/her own assets first; and if the child does not have sufficient assets to satisfy the liability, his/her parents as the guardians are liable for the remaining amount.[34]

The most common scenario of a guardian's third-party liability is when a minor child has caused damages to a third party. For example, in *Liu v. Li and Zhang*, Liu and Zhang's son, Zile, was four years old when he accidentally hit Liu with his tricycle in a playground in Beijing. Liu was 69 years old at the time of the accident. She fell and broke her hip. The Beijing No. 2 Intermediate People's Court affirmed the lower court's findings that Zile was negligent when he was riding the tricycle, and that Zile's parents had no grounds to reduce their liability. Zile's parents were ordered to pay for Liu's medical treatment and care in the sum of RMB121,165.17.[35] Critics of parents' third-party liability rule criticized the rule in two aspects. First, a minor child is unable to discern the nature of their act, and therefore their actions lack the required mental condition of "intention" or "negligence." Thus, the critics argue that minor children should not be held liable for negligence. Second, a parent should only be held liable when he/she is negligent for having failed to exercise his/her duty to prevent his/her child from causing harm to third persons.[36]

10.2.3 Removal of Guardian

Upon application of a concerned party, a court must remove a guardian and appoint another guardian in the best interest of the ward if the guardian has committed any of the following misconducts: (1) having caused serious harm to the ward's physical and mental health; (2) having neglected the duty of guardianship or refused to delegate part or all of the duty of guardianship to another person when unable to perform the duty of guardianship, and endangered the ward's well-being; or (3) any other conducts that have severely harmed the ward's lawful rights and interests.[37] Thus, a parent's guardianship of his/her child may be terminated by a court when the parent has failed to perform his/her duty as the child's guardian or when a parent has neglected, abused, or caused harm to the child.

Concerned parties could be rights groups, local community organizations, or social welfare agencies, such as a Urban Residents' Committee, a Villagers' Committee, a school, a medical institution, a Women's Federation, a Disabled

34. *Id.* art. 1188 para. 2.
35. (2021) Jing 02 Min Zhong 1692 Hao ((2021）京02民终1692号).
36. Sun Yuhong, *supra* note 32.
37. The Civil Code art. 36 para. 1.

Persons' Federation, an organization for the protection of minors, an organization for seniors, and a Civil Affairs Bureau.[38] The Civil Affairs Bureau has the duty to file a removal application in court if a guardian has committed any misconduct that warrants a removal.[39]

Termination of a parent's guardianship of their child does not terminate their support obligation.[40] A parent's guardianship may be reinstated by a court, except where the guardian has committed an intentional crime against the child.[41]

10.2.4 Guardianship versus Custody

Parents are their minor children's guardians.[42] Parents' guardianship (*jianhu*) and custody (*fuyang*) of their children are clearly distinguished. Parents' custody of their children entails the routine childcare and support in day-to-day life, whereas parents' guardianship of children affords them the authority and duty to conduct juridical acts on behalf of their children and to be fully responsible for the children's person and property.

When a child's parents are separated, the parents' separation does not affect each parent's rights and responsibilities as their child's guardian. However, custody of the child must be assigned between the parents for the child's daily care. For instance, in *Xiang v. Cai*, the mother had residential custody of the parties' two children after the parties' divorce. The mother remarried and planned to immigrate to Germany with her new husband. She petitioned for sole guardianship of the children as the children were going to live with her in Germany. The court held that

> with respect to minor children, their parents are their statutory guardians. Parents' guardianship of their children is based on a legal parent-child relationship, and both parents have equal rights of guardianship of their children, which no one can remove or restrict. After the spouses' divorce, the party who lives with the children has no right to deprive the other of their guardianship of their children, except where a court decides to terminate their guardianship due to their criminal act, abuse or any other acts that are harmful to the children.

Thus, court rejected the mother's petition, finding that the father did not commit any wrongdoing that could justify any restrictions or termination of his guardianship.[43]

---

38. *Id.* art. 36 para. 2.
39. *Id.* art. 36 para. 3.
40. *Id.* art. 37.
41. *Id.* art. 38.
42. *Id.* art. 27.
43. (2016) Xiang 1224 Min Chu 1280 ((2016) 湘1224民初1280号).

§ 10.3 Best Interests of the Child

The best interests of the child standard applies in child custody disputes. Courts must consider the parents' specific circumstances in determining custody and visitation issues.[44] Like the laws of most American states, Chinese law directs courts to consider a list of statutory factors. When determining residential custody (*zhijie fuyang*) of a child over two years old, Chinese courts must consider the following circumstances and give preference to the parent (1) who is unable to have any more children; (2) who has been residing with the children and change of children's residence will not be beneficial to the children's welfare; (3) who does not have any other children whereas the other parent has children other than the child in dispute; or (4) whom it is beneficial for the children to reside with because the other parent has long-term contagious disease or other serious illness that makes it unsuitable for the children to reside with him/her, or because there are other factors that render it inappropriate or detrimental for the children to reside with him/her.[45]

Preference is also given to the parent whose parents have been the primary caregivers of the children and can continue caring for them.[46] The preference favoring grandparents grew out of necessity and concern for the stability of children's lives after their parents' separation. With a large population of migrant workers, China has many children raised by grandparents in rural areas. Middle-class working parents also heavily rely on grandparents for childcare of young children. Thus, it is not only necessary but also beneficial for the children to remain in an established custodial environment with the grandparents who have been their primary caregivers. For example, in *Chen v. Jiang*, at the time of the divorce, Chen, the mother, agreed that Jiang, the father, would have custody of their daughter. However, Jiang went to Xinjiang to work and left his one-year-old child with Chen's parents in Sichuan. Chen and Jiang both visited the child but left the child in the maternal grandparents' care. Six years later, Chen sought a change of custody and child support for the child. Considering the close bond between the child and the maternal grandparents, the Sichuan court changed the child's custody to Chen and ordered Jiang to pay child support.[47]

Chinese courts are allowed considerable discretion in child custody determinations and need not strictly apply the statutory preferences when the best interest of the child standard requires flexibility. Commenting on a Typical Case, *Chen v. Liang*, the SPC reiterated that the best interest of the child is paramount in child custody determinations. In *Chen v. Liang*, the trial court

44. The Civil Code art. 1084 para. 3.
45. The Marriage and Family Book Interpretations art. 46.
46. *Id.* art. 47.
47. (2021) Chuan 15 Min Zhong 738 Hao ((2021) 川15民终738号).

awarded custody of a boy to his unwed mother. The child's parents, Chen, the father, and Liang, the mother, were not married. The child was born in 2011. He resided with his mother and his paternal grandparents in his father's family home while his father worked as a migrant worker in another city. The parents ended their relationship in March 2014, and the mother left the father's family home. The child first stayed with the paternal grandparents, and then moved in with his mother in March 2015. Later on, the father returned home from his job and sought custody of the child on the ground that the paternal grandparents had been the child's primary caregivers. Breaking from the long-standing preference for grandparents who have been and can continue to be a child's caregivers, the trial court awarded custody to Liang, an unwed single mother. The court found that although the paternal grandparents had been the child's primary caregivers, the child had resided with his mother since March 2015 and had been doing well under Liang's care, and therefore it would be in the child's best interest to grant the mother custody of her son.[48]

"The best interest of the child" standard by its nature is vague and offers little guidance in contentious child custody disputes. American courts turn to a checklist of statutory factors and judges' discretion, which potentially invites significant bias and inconsistent decision-making. Chinese judges share similar concerns. The Xiaozhou District People's Court, a basic-level trial court in the city of Zhuhai in Guangdong Province, did an in-depth survey of 52 family matter judges throughout China. The study found that the judges focus on a few factors, listed in the following table, in making child custody decisions:[49]

Factors	Do you consider this in your child custody decisions	Percentage Among Interviewees
The child's gender	Yes	80.77%
	No	17.31%
	Other	1.92%
The preference of a child over 10	Yes	98.08%
	No	1.92%
	Other	0

48. FMTC 20.

49. Guangdong Sheng Zhuhai Shi Xiangzhou Qu Renmin Fayuan Diaoyan Zu (广东省珠海市香洲区人民法院调研组) [Guangdong Province Zhuai City Xiangzhou District People's Court Research Department], Guanyu Jiashi Shenpan Zhong Ertong Quanyi Baohu Wenti De Diaoyan (关于家事审判中儿童权益保护问题的调研) [Research Report on the Protection of Children's Rights and Interests in Family Matter Adjudication].

Factors	Do you consider this in your child custody decisions	Percentage Among Interviewees
A parent's family of origin	Yes	71.15%
	Not much	28.8%
	Not at all	0
The likelihood of a parent's compliance with visitation	Yes	82.69%
	Not much	17.31%
	Not at all	0

Although 94.23 percent of the judges that were interviewed indicated that their decisions were grounded in the best interest standard, the judges felt that the children's perspectives are often overlooked when they narrowly focus on a few factors in their decision-making process due to the vagueness of the best interest of the child standard. They also indicated that they would consider their decisions from the parents' perspective. For example, 48.08 percent of them indicated that they often balance the parents' interests in child custody and other ancillary issues, such as property division and marital fault, 38.46 percent of them would do so occasionally and only 13.46 percent of them would consider child custody completely separately from the parents' interests. In fact, 59.62 percent of the judges who were interviewed indicated that they would award custody of the children to the parent who did not commit any marital misconduct. Furthermore, the judges indicated that they would consider the impact of their custody decisions on future litigations between the parents. 30.77 percnet of the judges would split siblings to appease the parents and avoid protracted litigation; 69.23 percent of them would consider the totality of the circumstances in deciding whether to split siblings between the parents, and none of the judges being interviewed believed that separating siblings would be detrimental to the children's well-being. Most alarmingly, 34.62 percent of the interviewees would consider awarding custody to a parent who might abduct the child if he/she were not awarded custody in hopes of preventing parental abduction.[50]

Based on the outcome of the study, the Xiaozhou District People's Court called for independent legal representation for children in high conflict custody disputes, and more resources for the courts to engage mental health professionals.[51] The Xiaozhou court's study echoes the legal field's call for

50. *Id.*
51. *Id.*

court-appointed legal representation for children and protection of vulnerable children in custody proceedings.[52]

Protections of children's best interest in divorce registration (*xieyi lihun*) process are also called for. Most concerning is that there is no guarantee that a child's voice is heard in the divorce registration process. Chinese courts are required to inquire and consider the wishes of a child over the age of eight in proceedings concerning the child's welfare. However, children could be completely ignored in their parents' out-of-court divorce registrations. The marriage registration authority does not review the content and merit of a divorce agreement. Thus, parents are free to make deals without any judicial supervision. For instance, not too few parents bargain away their children's right to child support for a quick divorce. Parents' unfettered power to barter the support, custody, and sometimes property of their children poses a serious risk of parents prioritizing their own interests over the best interest of their children.[53]

10.3.1 Tender Years Doctrine

The Civil Code expressly provides that in principle, mothers should have residential custody (*zhijie fuyang*) of children younger than two after divorce.[54] However, a father may have residential custody (*zhijie fuyang*) of a child who is younger than two if the parents agree to such custody arrangement and the arrangement is not detrimental to the child's welfare.[55] Furthermore, the father may have residential custody (*zhijie fuyang*) of a child younger than two under the following circumstances: (1) the mother has long-term contagious disease or other serious illness that makes it unsuitable for the child to reside with her; (2) the mother has failed to support the child, and the father requests that the child reside with him; or (3) there are other reasons that it is not appropriate for the child to reside with the mother.[56]

In *Wei v. Pang*, the court followed the "tender years doctrine" codified in the Civil Code and awarded the mother custody of the parties' infant son. Pang Mengyin and Wei Ziteng were married in a traditional wedding

52. Zuo Xiaoqing (邹小琴), Xieyi Lihun Zhong Weichengnian Zinü Liyi Baohu Zhidu De Fansi Yu Wanshan (协议离婚中未成年子女利益保护制度的反思与完善) [Rethinking and Refining the Protection of Minor Children's Rights and Interests in Consensual Divorces] Renmin Sifa (人民司法) [The People's Judicature] 08.2014, 80–81.

53. *Id.* at 78–89; *see also* Qian Xiaofang (钱晓芳), Lun Fuyu Jiufen Zhong Weichengnian Zinü Minshi Quanyi De Sifa Baozhang (论抚育纠纷中未成年子女民事权益的司法保障) [On Judicial Protection of Minor Children's Civil Rights and Interests in Custody and Support Disputes] Renmin Sifa (人民司法) [The People's Judicature] 15.2010, 88.

54. The Civil Code art. 1084 para. 3.

55. The Marriage and Family Book Interpretations art. 45.

56. *Id.* art. 44.

ceremony in 2017 but never registered their marriage. At the time of the wedding ceremony, Pang was 20 and Wei was 18, and neither of them had reached the legal age of marriage. Pang moved back to her natal home with the parties' son after an argument in 2020. When Pang and Wei separated, their son was barely one year old. Wei sought custody of his son. The court awarded Pang residential custody of the child and ordered Wei to pay child support, holding that child should be raised by his mother as he was younger than two and there was no evidence that his mother was unfit.[57] Similarly, in *Yu v. Du*, the court awarded the custody of the parties' infant daughter to the mother simply because the child was younger than two.[58]

10.3.2 The Child's Preference

Chinese courts are required to consider the preference of children over eight years old in custody determinations.[59] For instance, in *Zeng v. Jiang*, the court interviewed the parties' 14-year-old daughter and 11-year-old son, and both children wished to live with their mother. The court awarded the mother residential custody of both children according to the children's preference.[60]

In the case of *Su v. Chen*, the parties were married in 2002 and had triplets. Soon after the girls were born, Chen, the father, left home for work as a migrant worker. Su stayed home and cared for the children. Due to the extended periods of separation during the marriage, Su and Chen's marital relationship broke down and they agreed to divorce in 2017. However, they could not agree to the custody of the three children. Su wanted residential custody of all three children. Chen wanted the custody of at least one child and insisted that his family was entitled to at least one child to continue the family's bloodline. The court interviewed the children and the children expressed strong preference not to be separated and to stay with their mother, who had been their primary caregiver since their births. Customarily, the court would have separated the sisters. However, in this case the court decided that the children should stay together and remain in the mother's residential custody because of the children's preference to stay together with their mother. The court found that it must respect the children's preference as the children's wish to stay with their mother was reasonable and separating the triplets would cause irreparable emotional harm to all three children. At the same time, the court ruled that the parents should have joint custody (*gongtong fuyang quan*) of the children and the children remain members of both parents' families despite that they would continue residing with the

57. (2021) Ji 06 Min Zhong 823 Hao ((2021) 冀06民终823号).
58. (2021) Jin 02 Min Zhong 34 Hao ((2021) 晋02民终34号).
59. The Civil Code art. 1084 para. 3.
60. (2016) Yue 04 Min Zhong 2324 Hao ((2016) 粤04民终2324号).

mother. The presiding judges of the case explained that many parents seek residential custody because of the misunderstanding that their children are no longer members of their family if they do not have residential custody and, consequently, their family bloodlines will end. Thus, they suggested that judges should explain to parents that they have joint custody (*gongtong fuyang quan*) of their children and the legal parent-child relationship does not terminate just because one parent has primary residential custody (*zhijie fuyang quan*), and courts' child custody decisions should serve the best interest of the children, not parents' desire to continue their family bloodlines.[61]

Chinese law does not provide mechanisms, such as court-appointed children's attorneys or guardian *ad litem*, to safeguard children's interests in custody and visitation proceedings. Consequently, young children are left to represent themselves, sometimes in complicated custody matters.[62] Chinese judges have expressed concerns about children's lack of maturity or being manipulated, exploited by parents in custody proceedings.[63] The Typical Case *Guo v. Jiao* is a good example. Guo and Jiao were divorced in 2012. Jiao, the father had residential custody of the parties' daughter. Guo, the mother, had visitation. A year after the divorce, Guo alleged that Jiao interfered with visitation and failed to care for the child. She petitioned for a change of child custody. The trial court interviewed the child, who was four years old at the time of the interview. The child indicated that she wished to live with her "mother." The trial court then changed the child's custody to Guo. Jiao appealed. At the appeal, the intermediate court interviewed the child again and found that the child considered Jiao's second wife, not the biological mother Guo, as her "mother" and she lacked the maturity to form or express reasonable preferences. Commenting on *Guo v. Jiao*, the SPC cautioned Chinese courts to assess the child's maturity when considering a child's preference.[64] As many Chinese

61. Huang Demei, Chen Xiaojin (黄德梅, 陈小鑫), Gongtong Fuyang Moshi De Yingyong (共同抚养模式的应用) [Joint Custody Model's Application] remin sifa (人民司法) [The People's Judicature] 08.2018, 33–34.

62. FMTC 3; *see also* Zhao Li & Ding Yu (赵莉 丁钰), Lihun Anjian Zhong Sheji Weichengnian Zinü (离婚案件中涉及未成年子女抚养权归属存在的问题及对策—以南京市六家基层法院四年(2011–2014年) 离婚纠纷案件判决书为样本) [Issues and Solutions in Divorce Cases Concerning Minor Children Custody—Use Divorce Disputes Judgments of Six Nanjing City Basic Level Courts in Four Years (2011–2014) as Specimens], Zhonghua Nuzi Xueyuan Xuebao (中华女子学院学报) [China Women's University Journal] Vol. 1, 24–34 (2016) (found that children were interviewed by the court in 63 percent of the 167 cases surveyed and that in most cases custody was awarded according to the child's wishes and preferences).

63. *See supra* note 49.

64. *See, e.g.*, FMTC 3 (where a four-year-old had to express her preference in a custody dispute); FMTC 25 (where an eight-year-old had to decide whether she wanted to stay with her abusive stepmother).

judges have advocated, Chinese courts need to institutionalize a mechanism to ensure a child's true voice is heard and their best interest is fully represented in high-conflict child custody proceedings.

10.3.3 Domestic Violence

Chinese courts generally do not award residential child custody to a parent that has a history of domestic abuse of the other parent or the child.[65] Chinese judges are keenly aware of the harms that domestic violence inflicts on a child. They overwhelmingly call for mental health services in cases involving children and domestic violence, not only to assist the children in coping with the trauma but also to assist the courts in custody determination.[66]

In Typical Case *the Matter of Luo*, the court found that the child's correspondence with the mother and the forensic medical report of the child's injuries were clear evidence of the father's physical and verbal abuse of the child. Thus, the court changed the child's custody from the father to the mother within a week after the mother filed a custody petition and a personal protection order for the child against the father.[67]

Kim Lee Li v. Yang Li is a high-profile domestic violence case widely reported by Chinese media. The husband, Yang Li, is a Chinese businessman, and runs a multibillion-dollar English-learning business. The wife, Kim Lee Li, is a stay-home mother. The couple met in the U.S. in 1999 and had their first child in 2002. They married in Nevada in 2005. Kim is a U.S. citizen. They had two more daughters born of the marriage. In 2006, Yang beat Kim over some files that Kim deleted from a computer. Yang and Kim divorced in 2010. On August 30, 2011, Yang again brutally assaulted Kim and severely injured her. Kim reported the incident on WeChat, a Chinese social media platform. On April 12, 2012, Kim went to the police and reported that Yang had been harassing her and made death threats. Kim also sought a personal safety protection order, residential custody of her daughters, and compensation for damages caused by Yang's assaults. The Beijng Chaoyang District People's Court issued a personal safety protection order for Kim, awarded her residential custody of all three children and compensatory damages in the sum of

65. The SPC reiterated the policy in recent years; *see* Dibaci Quanguo Mingshi Shangshi Shengpan Gongzuo Huiyi (Mingshi Bufen) Jiyao (第八次全国法院民事商事审判工作会议（民事部分）纪要) [The Eighth National Conference on Courts' Adjudication in Civil and Commercial Matters (Civil Matters) Memorandum] Nov. 30, 2016, https://www.chinacourt.org/article/detail/2016/11/id/2361616.shtml; *see also* the DV Guidelines, arts. 63, 65.

66. *See supra* note 49.

67. DVTC 1.

RMB50,000.[68] The child custody award to Kim was novel in two aspects. First, Chinese courts tend to favor a parent who is better off financially and can provide a higher standard of living for the children. In this case, Yang is one of the wealthiest persons in China, and Kim was an unemployed housewife. Yang would have been favored because of his superior financial status. Second, Chinese courts tend to separate siblings between the parents. Yang would have had custody of at least one child. The chief trial judge, Liu Li explained that the court followed the SPC guidelines on handling of domestic violence matters in the Lis' case and weighed Yang's history of domestic abuse against all other factors. Judge Liu indicated that the court awarded custody to Kim for the protection of the children, who had witnessed Yang's brutal assault of Kim and had to intervene to protect their mother. Considering Yang's considerable wealth, the court ordered him to pay Kim RMB100,000 per year per child for the children's support. Furthermore, Judge Liu emphasized that post-divorce personal protection orders are important measures to protect domestic violence victims because divorces do not necessarily end domestic violence but rather provoke more "breakup violence" against the victims in many cases.[69]

§ 10.4 Visitation

The nonresidential parent has visitation rights, and the residential custodial parent has the obligation to facilitate the nonresidential parent's visitation with the children. The parents can arrange visitation by agreement. If the parents cannot reach an agreement, the court must make a visitation order.[70]

The visitation dispute in *Zhang Yanru v. Zhang Zhenjie* is quite common. The parents agreed that the father, Zhang Zhenjie, should have residential custody of the parties' daughter, and the mother should have visitation after their divorce. However, the Zhangs' divorce agreement did not have a visitation schedule. After the divorce, the father took his daughter to his parents' house in the countryside to live with them. The mother demanded he send the daughter to her for visitation once a week for a day from the morning to the evening. The father refused. The mother then sued for visitation with her daughter. At the time of the visitation proceeding, the child was about four years old. The court ordered the father to facilitate the mother's bi-weekly

68. Liu Li (Presiding Chief Judge) (刘黎 (审判长)), Lihun Anjian Zhong Jiating Baoli De Rending Yu Chuli (离婚案件中家庭暴力的认定与处理) [Determination and Handling of Domestic Violence in Divorce Cases], Renmin Sifa (人民司法), 22/2013, 77–78.

69. *Id*. at 78–80.

70. The Civil Code art. 1086.

visitation with the daughter on the first Sunday of each month from 9:00 am to 6:00 pm and the third Sunday of each month from 9:00 am to 6:00 pm.[71]

Chinese courts consider the child's age, daily routine, and the parents' living conditions when determining a visitation schedule. For example, in *Lao v. Wang*, the parents' divorce judgment omitted to include a visitation schedule for the father. Having failed to reach an agreement with the mother, the father brought an action for visitation. A Shanghai court then ordered biweekly visitation for the father on alternate Saturdays from 9:00 am to 7:00 pm and directed the parties to arrange holiday visitations for the father and the school-aged child. The court indicated that overnight visitation was not appropriate due to the father's living conditions at the time of the proceeding.[72] In *Peng v. Wang*, a Hangzhou court determined that the nonresidential parent's visitation on alternate Saturdays from 9:00 am to 6:00 pm, consecutive five days during the child's winter break, and consecutive eight days during the child's summer break were appropriate for a school-aged child.[73] School-aged children have demanding schedules in China. Thus, the amount of visitation time ordered by Chinese courts may appear very limited by American standards. Nevertheless, noncustodial parents may have more generous visitation time when it is appropriate. For example, in *Li v. Hou*, the court ordered that the mother should have parenting time with the child from 6:00 pm on Friday to 6:00 pm on Sunday every week because the child was not attending school yet, and the mother was away to attend graduate school in another city during the week.[74]

Custodial parents' improper interference with child visitation, ranging from parental kidnapping to occasional denial of visitation, has forever plagued the world. Chinese courts have been struggling with thorny issues of custodial parents' interference with noncustodial parents' visitation or access rights, and have been searching for effective visitation enforcement mechanisms.[75] In *Han v. Yang*, Han, the mother was awarded weekly over-

71. (2021) Ji 04 Min Zhong 928 Hao ((2021) 冀04民终928号).

72. (2020) Hu 0104 Min Chu 30632 Hao ((2020) 沪0104民初30632号).

73. (2021) Zhe 0108 Min Chu 859 Hao ((2021) 浙0108民初859号).

74. (2021) Yun 0326 Min Chu 390 Hao ((2021) 云0326民初390号).

75. For Chinese judges' discussions on problems in visitation enforcement and proposed solutions, see Wang Jian (王 剑), Tanwang Quan Ji Qi Qiangzhi Zhixing Ruogan Wenti Chutan (探望权及其强制执行若干问题初探) [Preliminary Discussions of Several Issues on Visitation Right and Its Enforcement], Shangdong Sheng Wulian Xian Renming Fayuan (山东省五莲县人民法院) [Shangdong Province Wulian County People's Court], Li Maofu (李茂富), Lun Tanshiquan Anjian Zhixing Nan De Yuanying Ji Duice (论探视权案件执行难的原因及对策) [On the Causes of the Difficulties in Visitation Right Enforcement Cases and Countermeasures], Jiangxi Sheng Lepin Shi Renming Fayuan Wang (江西乐平市人民法院网) [Jiangxi Province Lepin City People's Court Website]; Zhang Haitao & Zhao Rongrong (章海涛 赵容容), Qiantan Tanshiquan De Qiangzhi Zhixing (浅谈探望权的强制执行) [A Brief Discussion of Visitation Right

night visitation with the parties' daughter and the father, Yang, was ordered to facilitate the visitation. Yang failed to comply with the visitation order. Han then sought to enforce visitation. Yang alleged that Han was unable to ensure the child's safety because of her religion and her work schedule. He asked the court to reduce visitation to bi-weekly and to suspend Han's visitation in the event Han's child support payments were late. The court found that Yang's actions were frivolous and directed Yang to comply with the visitation order. However, the court seemed to have no effective means to compel Yang's compliance.[76]

Whether child support and visitation rights are independent or may be conditioned upon each other has been debated around the world.[77] Some jurisdictions view the obligations of support and visitation as exclusive issues,[78] and the others allow termination of support or denial of visitation as a measure to coerce compliance.[79] Commenting on the Typical Case *He v. Jiang*, the SPC made it clear that a noncustodial parent's access or visitation rights should not be conditioned upon child support payment. In *He v. Jiang*, He and Jiang were divorced in 2010. The parties had one child by marriage. He, the father, owed child support arrears and did not want to pay certain medical expenses for the child. Jiang refused to allow He to visit the child before He paid the arrears and medical expenses in full. He sought enforce-

---

Enforcement], Zhongguo Fayuan Wang (中国法院网) [Chinese Courts Website], https://www.chinacourt.org/article/detail/2016/04/id/1839427.shtml.

76. FMTC 29.

77. For discussions of interdependent issues of child support and visitation, see Carolyn Eaton Taylor, *Making Parents Behave: The Conditioning of Child Support and Visitation Rights*, 84 COLUM. L. REV. 1059 (1984); Alison Kitch, *Conditioning Child Support Payments on, Visitation Access: A Proposal*, 5 INT'L J.L. & FAM. 318 (1991); John E.B. Myers, *"I Won't Pay Child Support, but I Insist on Visitation." Should Visitation and Child Support Be Linked?* 45 MCGEORGE L. REV. 695 (2014).

78. *See, e.g.*, MINN. STAT. ANN. § 518.612); K.S.A. § 23-2717; TEX. FAM. CODE ANN. § 153.001; FLA. STAT. ANN. § 61.13(4)(a); Appert v. Appert, 80 N.C. App. 27, 39–40, at 341 S.E.2d 342, 349 (1986) (visitation and child support rights are independent rights accruing primarily to the benefit of the minor child and that one is not, and may not be made, contingent upon the other); Sampson v. Johnson, 846 A.2d 278, 287 (D.C. 2004) (a father's visitation rights cannot be conditioned upon compliance with a support order); Carter v. Carter, 198 W. Va. 171, 177, 479 S.E.2d 681, 687 (1996) (the right of a noncustodial parent, to visit that child may not ordinarily be made dependent upon the payment of child support by that parent); Lalonde v. Lalonde, 2005 CanLII 16637 (ON SC), http://canlii.ca/t/1kt84 (the issue of the father's outstanding child support payment is not tied to his access rights.

79. *See, e.g.*, N.Y. DOM. REL. LAW § 241 (McKinney) (Custodial parent's wrongful interference with, or withholding of, the noncustodial parent's visitation rights would justify suspension of alimony or child support); Rohr v. Rohr, 709 P.2d 382, 383 (Utah 1985) (when the noncustodial parent's refusal to pay child support is contumacious, or willful and intentional, and not due to inability to pay, visitation rights may be reduced or denied, if the welfare of the child so requires).

ment of visitation. The trial court ordered visitation for He and the child and directed Jiang to facilitate the visitation. The SPC held that custodial parents may not interfere with visitation for any financial reasons because fostering a noncustodial parent's relationship with their child is in the child's best interest.[80]

If a parent's visitation is not in their children's best interests, their visitation may be suspended by a court, and the parent's visitation may resume when the reason for suspension no longer exists.[81] A parent's visitation may be suspended or restricted in cases of domestic violence, substance abuse ,or any other circumstances that may endanger a child's well-being. In *Li v. Luo,* the court awarded the mother custody of the children and placed restrictions on the father's visitation based on the father's long history of alcohol abuse and domestic violence. The trial court found that the father beat the mother and the children whenever he was intoxicated and that the father not only caused the children physical and emotional harm but also might pass his violent behavior on to the children. Thus, the court ruled that in the best interest of the children, the father should not have custody of the children and his visitation should be restricted.[82]

§ 10.5 Relocation and Parental Abduction

On principle, Chinese courts do not condone parents' unilateral removal of children, and do not tolerate parental abduction of children. To illustrate: in *Pan v. Li,* the parties had agreed in their divorce settlement that the father should have residential custody of the child and the mother should have liberal visitation. The child lived with his father in Fuzhou and had visitation with the mother after the divorce. Six months after the divorce, during a visit, the mother removed the child from Fuzhou and took him to her parents' house in another city. The mother's parents refused to turn the child over to the father when he went to their house to retrieve his child. The mother and her parents had retained the child for months and refused to return the child before the father paid them RMB100,000. The father then brought an action for a residential custody order based on the parties' divorce agreement and the return of his child. The mother counterclaimed for residential custody of the child on the ground that the child had been living with her. The mother's bid for custody was resonantly rejected by the courts of Fuzhou. The Fuzhou courts found the mother's action not only violated the parties' custody agreement but more importantly jeopardized the child's well-being. The court

80. FMTC 21.
81. The Civil Code art. 1086 para. 3.
82. DVTC 4.

ordered the mother to return the child to the father's custody. Despite her abduction of the child, the court allowed the mother to have bi-weekly unsupervised visitation with the child, holding that the mother's visitation right was a legal right that could not be terminated.[83]

Chinese law does not require a parent to obtain either the other parent's consent or the court's permission to change the legal residence of their minor child. Nor does Chinese law set any standard for allowing a minor child's relocation. As a result, some parents had gained advantage in custody disputes by removing and concealing children in cases like *Liu v. Wang*. In *Liu v. Wang*, the mother, Wang, was awarded residential custody of the son in the parties' divorce action. Soon after the divorce, the mother relocated from Inner Mongolia, where she and Liu lived during the marriage, to Shanxi Province, where her natal family lived. At the time of the relocation, the parties' son was six. After the mother and the son left Inner Mongolia, the father traveled to Shanxi five times and finally found the mother and the child four years later. The father requested visitation with the child, but the mother refused. The father then sought a visitation order to allow his son to spend the winter and summer breaks with him in Inner Mongolia. A basic-level court in Shanxi heard the parents' testimonies, and then interviewed the child in private. The child was ten at the time of the interview. The child told the court that he did not like the father because the father made a scene at his school and embarrassed him; and that the child did not want to spend his entire vacation time with the father away from his cousin who he considered as his little brother and the mother's second husband who he considered as his "father." The court found that the father's actions caused the child great embarrassment at school and among his friends, and the child was now resentful toward the father and refused to see him. The court decided that at the time the court had to respect the child's preference and feelings, and therefore could not order visitation between the son and father.[84] It is difficult to discern whether the court considered many factors other than the child's preference in this acrimonious case, such as the severe alienation between the father and son due to the mother's removal and concealment of the child, or possible influence or manipulation that the mother and her family members might have exerted on the child. However, it is evident that the Chinese court had carefully considered the child's feelings and wishes in its decision, and the child's voice was heard.

Recognizing the harm of parental abduction of children, the newly amended Minors Protection Law makes it illegal for parents to remove or retain children to gain child custody.[85] The new law affords Chinese courts

83. (2016) Min 0111 Min Chu 1017 Hao ((2016) 闽0111民初1017号), affirmed by (2016) Min 01 Min Zhong 2346 Hao ((2016) 闽01民终2346号).

84. (2019) Jin 0404 Min Chu 501 Hao ((2019) 晋0404民初501号).

85. The Minors Protection Law art. 24.

a sound statutory basis to protect children from parental abduction. The protections provided in the new Minors Protection Law are available to "foreign nationals and persons without nationality who are under the age of 18 within the territory of China."[86] Thus, the Minors Protection Law protects children who are wrongfully removed by their parents to China to gain advantage in custody disputes, regardless of their nationality. In other words, the Minor Protections Law has made international parental abduction of children to or from China illegal in China. Any person that has violated the Minor Protections Law and caused a child severe harm is subject to civil and/or criminal penalty.[87]

§ 10.6 Modification of Custody

Child custody and visitation arrangements may be modified by the parents' agreement.[88] Upon a parent's application for modification, the court may change custody under the following circumstances:

(1) The residential custodial parent is unable to care for the children due to serious illness or disability;
(2) The residential custodial parent has neglected, abused, or caused harm to the children's well-being;
(3) The child is over eight and wishes to reside with the nonresidential custodial parent; or
(4) There are any other reasons that warrant change of custody.[89]

There must be a substantial change of circumstances to justify a change of custody. Usually, the change of the child's actual residence from the residential custodial parent to the nonresidential custodial parent may be a sufficient reason for change of custody. For example, in *Li v. Zhen*, Li and Zhen were married in a traditional ceremony but did not register their marriage. They lived together for about a year and had a son. When the child was about one month old, Zhen moved back to her parents' home and left the child with Li. A year later, the parties entered a custody agreement, providing that Zhen would have residential custody of the child. However, Zhen never picked up the child from Li, and the child continued living with Li. Li sued for change of custody when the child was about three years old. The court changed the child's residential custody from Zhen to Li and ordered Zhen to pay child support to Li. The court found that the child had been living with Li, and Li

86. *Id.* art. 131.
87. *Id.* art. 129.
88. The Marriage and Family Book Interpretations art. 56.
89. *Id.* art. 57.

could provide the child with a better environment as he had steady income and gainful employment, while Zhen lacked the ability to care for the child, as she was unemployed and was remarried with more children. The court also found that Zhen did not offer sufficient evidence to prove her allegation that Li took the child to Xinjiang and prevented her from retrieving the child. Thus, the court held that it was in the best interest of the child to change residential custody to Li.[90]

However, a child's actual residence with one parent alone does not warrant a change of custody. As the Lanzhou Intermediate People's Court held in *Zhao v. Fang*, in determining a change of custody, courts must consider the benefits for the child's well-being and interest as well as both parents' parenting ability and environment. In *Zhao v. Fang*, the divorce court awarded the mother custody of the child. However, the father refused to release the child to the mother and kept the child with him for more than a year. Then, he sought a change of custody. The Lanzhou court found that it would be in the child's best interest for her to live with her mother as she was a three-year-old girl, and her mother could better care for her, although the child had been living with her father and her brother and had a stable custodial environment since her parents' divorce. Thus, the Lanzhou court declined to change the child's custody from the mother to the father and ordered the father to turn the child over to her.[91]

Nor can child custody be changed or modified when a child's residence was changed due to a parent's wrongful retention or removal of the child. For example, in *Liang v. Zhu*, a Guangdong court declined to change the child's custody for lack of change of circumstances. The father, Liang, was awarded custody of the parties' one-year-old son in the parties' divorce action. A year after the divorce, the mother removed the child from Guangdong to Hunan under the false pretense of seeking medical treatment for the child. She refused to return the child to the father and sought a change of custody. The court rejected her request and ordered her to return the child to the father in Guangdong as the court found no change of circumstances.[92] Interference of visitation alone is not sufficient for a change of custody. In *Zhang v. An*, the father sought change of custody because the mother refused to allow visitation between the father and the child. The Beijing High People's Court held that change of custody is warranted only when a statutory circumstance occurs, and it was in the child's best interest for her to remain in the mother's custody.[93]

90. (2020) Gui 13 Min Zhong 1797 Hao ((2020) 桂13民终1797号).
91. (2019) Gan 01 Min Zhong 2948 Hao ((2019) 甘01民终2948号).
92. (2019) Gan 01 Min Zhong 2948 Hao ((2019) 甘01民终2948号).
93. (2016) Jing Min Shen 2920 ((2016) 京民申2920号).

§ 10.7 Child Support

Parents have the duty to provide their minor children maintenance, education, and protection.[94] If a parent fails to support their minor children or dependent adult children, the children are entitled to seek support from the parent.[95] Parents are responsible for their minor children's living expenses, educational cost, medical expenses, and any other reasonable expenses.[96] When the parents do not live in the same household, a nonresidential parent is responsible for all or a part of the financial support that their children need; and if the parents are unable to agree to the duration and amount of child support, a court must issue an order for the child's support.[97]

10.7.1 Children's Right to Support

Child support is an obligation owed to the child but not to the residential parent. Therefore, the child, not the custodial parent, has the standing to bring legal actions against the noncustodial parent for child support in Chinese courts. If a parent fails to provide financial support for a child during the parents' marriage, the child may bring a legal action for support against the parent.[98] After their parents' divorce, a child may seek an increase of child support.[99] Since a minor child is not legally competent to bring their own suit, child support proceedings are usually brought by the child through the custodial parent acting as their legal representative.[100]

10.7.1.1 Parentage and Custody

Children have an inherent right to child support from their parents, including their biological parents and adoptive parents.[101] They also have a right to child support from stepparents,[102] and child support from grandparents and siblings when their biological parents are unable to support them.[103] When the parents do not live in the same household, a nonresidential parent who does not reside with their children remains responsible for all or a part

---

94. The Civil Code art. 26.
95. *Id.* art. 1067.
96. The Marriage and Family Book Interpretations (I) art. 42.
97. The Civil Code art. 1085.
98. The Marriage and Family Book Interpretations (I) art. 43.
99. *Id.* art. 55.
100. *See, e.g.*, FMTC 4; FMTC 6; FMTC 9; FMTC 10; FMTC 16; FMTC 18.
101. The Civil Code art. 1067 and art. 1071 para. 1.
102. *Id.* art. 1072 para. 2.
103. *Id.* art. 1074 para. 1 and art. 1075 para. 1.

of the financial support that their children need.[104] At the same time, a child loses the right to support from an adult when their parent-child relationship is ended. Thus, a child is not entitled to receive financial support from their adoptive parents when the adoption is terminated. Nor is a child entitled to support from a stepparent when the stepparent's marriage with the child's biological parent is dissolved. Last, when a child is found not to be a person's biological child, the presumptive legal parent-child relationship between him/her and the presumptive parent ends, and consequently the child is no longer entitled to any support from the presumptive parent.

When the parents are separated and the child lives with one parent, the nonresidential parent has the obligation to provide financial support to their child regardless of the legal disposition of the custody of the child.[105] In *Yang v. Cai*, there was a child custody proceeding brought by the mother in Australia, where the child and the father resided, and a child support proceeding brought by the father in Beijing, where the mother lived. The mother argued that a Beijing court's child support order was not proper because the Australian court had not determined the custody of the child. She also argued that although the child had been living with the father, the father should not be treated as the custodial parent for child support purpose. The Beijing High People's Court held that "the prerequisite for a court to order child support is not whether there is a child custody order but rather whether a parent is fulfilling his/her duty to support the child." Thus, the court declined to stay the child support proceeding brought by the father in Beijing and affirmed the lower courts' child support order.[106]

10.7.1.2 Parents' Marital Status

Once a child's biological or adoptive parentage is established, a nonresidential parent must provide reasonable financial support for their child's upkeep, regardless of the parents' marital status.[107] Parents' divorce is not a prerequisite for a court to order child support. If one parent or both parents fail to support a minor child, the child is entitled to a court order for their support.[108] Thus, in *Fu (minor) v. Fu*, the court ordered the father to pay child support where the parents were separated since the child's birth but had no plan for a divorce.[109]

104. *Id.* art. 1085.
105. *Id.* art. 1085.
106. (2018) Jing Min Shen 3505 Hao ((2018) 京民申3505号).
107. The Civil Code art. 1067 para. 1 and art. 1071 para. 2.
108. The Marriage and Family Book Interpretations (I) art. 43.
109. FMTC 16.

Children born out of wedlock enjoy the same right to support as children born of marriage.[110] For example, in *Gao v. Shen*, the Beijing No. 2 Intermediate People's Court ordered the biological father of a child born out of wedlock to pay child support after his paternity was established.[111] In *He (minor) v. Zhou*, He's parents were married in a traditional wedding ceremony in 2006 but did not register the marriage legally. He was born in 2007. He's mother, Zhou, abandoned He and her father when He was about three years old. Zhou later remarried. After He's father located Zhou, He sued Zhou for a lump sum payment for 18 years of child support. Zhou claimed that she had no money to pay child support. The trial court ordered Zhou to pay RMB1,800 per year for child support, commencing on December 31, 2015, until 2025. The SPC remarked that parents' child support obligation is a mandate by law and Chinese tradition that cannot be avoided for any reason, such as a parent's lack of financial resource or the parents' marital status.[112]

A biological parent's marriage to a third party does not prevent a child born out his/her extramarital affair from receiving support from him/her. To illustrate. In *Mao v. Wang*, Mao's husband, Yang, had a child with Wang. Mao sued Wang for unjust enrichment, alleging that Yang purchased a home for Wang with marital funds and paid child support for Wang and Yang's child. The Chongqing court found that Yang paid Wang monthly support for his child. The court held that the child had the same right to support from his father as a child born of a marriage. Therefore, the court denied Mao's request for repayment from Wang, finding that the payments from Yang to Wang were not for Wang's enrichment but for the support of their child.[113] In the Typical Case entitled "Sister-in-law Sues Older Brother-in-law for Child Support," the child's biological parents had an affair while being married to third parties. The mother was married to the child's biological father's brother and the biological father was married to another woman. After the child was born, the biological father denied paternity and refused to pay for the mother and the child's medical expenses and the One-Child-Policy fine (as the child was the mother's second child) or provide any financial support for the child. The mother sued the biological father for child support. The court ordered a paternity test and established the biological father's paternity. The trial court held, and the SPC agreed, that a child's biological parents have an obligation to provide financial support for the child regardless of their marital status. The trial court awarded the mother custody of the child and ordered the biological father to pay child support and all expenses related to the child's birth.[114]

110. The Civil Code art. 1071 para. 1.
111. (2019) Jing 02 Min Zhong 10545 ((2019) 京02民终10545号).
112. FMTC 45.
113. (2017) Yu Min Shen 1084 Hao ((2017) 渝民申1084号).
114. FMTC 38.

10.7.1.3 Parents' Agreement Concerning Child Support

Absent fraud or duress, parents' agreements on child support are legally binding and enforceable. But a child's claim for support may not be restricted by their parents' agreement concerning child support. The child support amount agreed on by the parents may be increased by a court to meet the child's reasonable needs.[115] Parents may agree to waive a nonresidential parent's child support obligation. However, a court may not approve such waiver if it is apparent that the residential custodial parent is unable to meet the child(ren)'s needs without the nonresidential parent's financial contribution.[116]

A noncustodial parent's child support obligation may not be waived by agreement if such waiver is not in the child's best interest. Nor can a custodial parent profit through any child support agreement.[117] In *Fu (minor) v. Fu*, Liu and Fu were married and have a child born in 2011. When Liu and Fu separated in May 2012, they executed a separation agreement, providing that the child would reside with the mother, Liu, and the father, Fu, would pay child support. The parents also agreed that Fu must pay a penalty if he missed any child support payments. Fu stopped paying child support. The child, represented by his mother Liu, sought child support arrears and penalty for Fu's breach of the separation agreement. The court awarded the child support arrearage but not the penalty. The court found that Fu's child support obligation was statutory not contractual, and thus his failure to pay child support was not a basis for penalty for breach of contract. The court held that parents' child support agreements are enforceable if such agreements are consistent with the law and the child's best interest. However, child support, the SPC commented, is intended for the support and protection of a child after his/her parents' separation and is to benefit a child, not to punish a parent or to enrich another parent. Thus, custodial parents should not be allowed to profit from child support through so-called breach penalty.[118]

Absent fraud or duress, parents' agreements on child support are legally binding, and enforceable. For example, a parent's alleged lack of understanding of the agreement is not a sufficient ground to set aside or modify the agreement. In *R v. B*, the father, B, was an Irish citizen who had lived in China for over a decade. R was B's daughter. In B's divorce agreement with R's mother, B agreed to pay RMB5,000 per month for R's support until R turned 18. After the divorce, B refused to pay the agreed amount for R's support. He claimed that he signed the agreement under duress, and he did not understand the divorce agreement because he could not read Chinese. In addition,

115. The Civil Code art. 1085 para. 2.
116. The Marriage and Family Book Interpretations (I) art. 52.
117. FMTC 4.
118. *Id.*

B claimed that he could not afford to pay RMB5,000 per month for child support. The Chinese court found that there was no evidence of duress or fraud, and at the minimum, B could read the number "5000" in the agreement. In addition, the court found that B's after-tax income was over RMB250,000 per year and he was more than capable to pay RMB5,000 for child support, and that RMB5,000 per month was a reasonable amount based on the child's reasonable needs and the cost of living in Shanghai, where the child lived.[119]

10.7.1.4 Reimbursement of Child Support: Fraudulent Paternity

There is no presumption of legitimacy of a child born of marriage under Chinese law. A child born of marriage is not presumed to be the husband's child. Therefore, Chinese courts do not hesitate to stop a husband's child support in so-called fraudulent parentage (*qizhaxin fuyang*) cases, where a husband has raised a child born of his wife's extramarital affair as his own. Following a SPC's advisory issued in 1992, Chinese courts have even ordered reimbursement of child support and compensation for damages inflicted on the husband by the wife's breach of the legal duty of fidelity and deceit of the child's paternity.[120]

In the Typical Case *Zhang v. Jiang*, the court continued to follow the SPC's 1992 advisory. Zhang and Jiang were married in 2004. During the marriage, Jiang gave birth to a son in 2008. In 2014, Zhang did a paternity test and found that he was not the son's biological father. Zhang filed for divorce and sought reimbursement of child support and compensatory damages for emotional injury from Jiang. Jiang was ordered to reimburse Zhang for the child support that Zhang had provided to the child from 2008 to 2014, and to pay Zhang RMB30,000 as compensatory damage for emotional harm inflicted on Zhang by her affair and concealment of the child's paternity. The SPC opined that a husband and wife have a legal duty to remain faithful to each other, as adultery causes very serious emotional injuries, and such emotional injuries must be compensated. The SPC explained that Zhang suffered emotional damage upon learning the child was not his biological child and thus the court supported his request for emotional damages. The SPC further explained that

119. (2018) Yue 06 Min Zhong 2839 Hao ((2018) 粤06民终2839号).

120. Zuigao Renmin Fayuan Guanyu Fuqi Guanxi Cunxu Qijian Nanfang Shoupian Fuyang Fei Qinsheng Zinü Lihun Hou Kefou Xiang Nüfang Zhuisuo Fuyang Fei De Fuhan (最高人民法院关于夫妻关系存续期间男方受欺骗抚养非亲生子女离婚后可否向女方追索抚养费的复函) [The Supreme People's Court's Response Regarding Whether a Husband Who Was Defrauded to Raise Non-Biological Child May Have the Wife Repay Child Support after the Divorce] [1991] Min Ta Zi Di 63 Hao ([1991]民他字第63号). See Han Deqiang, Ran Chao (韩德强, 冉超), Qizha Xing Fuyang Wenti De Sanwei Jiegou (欺诈性抚养问题的三维解构) [Three-Dimensional Analysis on Fraudulent Child Custody Issue], Renmin Sifa (人民司法) [The People's Judicature], 02.2020, 20.

Zhang had no legal obligation to support the child, as he was not the biological father of the child; hence, Zhang was entitled to reimbursement for the financial support that he had provided for the child.[121] In similar cases, U.S. courts have been more inclined to impose equitable estoppel to protect the status of a child in an already recognized and operative parent-child relationship,[122] "which is in the child's best interests to protect."[123] In contrast, neither the SPC's commentary nor the courts' decisions in *Zhang v. Jiang* indicate any consideration of the child's interest.

Following the SPC's directives, the court in *Li v. Shi* ordered a mother to reimburse her ex-husband child support and to pay him emotional damages for having concealed her daughter's paternity from him for 17 years. Li and Shi started dating in October 1998, got married in November 1999, and had a daughter born in June 2000. They divorced in June 2009. After the divorce, Li had residential custody of the daughter and cared for the child without any financial support from Shi until November 2014 when the daughter moved to Shi's residence. Li religiously paid monthly child support to Shi after the daughter started living with Shi. On February 10, 2017, Li did a DNA test and found out he was not the daughter's biological father. Li sought reimbursement of child support and compensatory damages from Shi. The court found that Shi concealed the paternity of the daughter for over 17 years, violated the duty of fidelity as well as public order and good morals, and caused Li immense anguish, as Li had raised the child and had a good relationship with the child. The court ordered Shi to repay Li RMB200,000 for child support and RMB50,000 for emotional damages. The presiding judge of this case, Judge Kong, explained that the amount of reimbursement and damages were based on Shi's financial ability to repay Li and to continue supporting the child. Judge Kong indicated that Shi would not have been ordered to repay Li's child support if Li had known the child's paternity and had willingly supported her despite that she was not his biological child.[124]

Similarly, in *Nie and Fan v. Zhao*, Nie and Fan were married, and Fan had an extramarital affair with Zhao. A child was born to Fan. When the child was 12, Nie and Fan found out the child was Zhao's biological child after a DNA

121. FMTC 45.

122. Fung v. Fung, 238 A.D.2d 375, 375–76, 655 N.Y.S.2d 657, 658–59 (1997).

123. Shu Jun Zhu v. Bin Pan, 55 Misc. 3d 1209(A), 57 N.Y.S.3d 677 (N.Y. Sup. Ct. 2017); *see also* Fung v. Fung (citing Matter of Ettore I. v. Angela D., 127 A.D.2d 6, 14, 513 N.Y.S.2d 733); Golser v. Golser, 115 A.D.2d 695, 698, 496 N.Y.S.2d 521; Shu Jun Zhu v. Bin Pan, 55 Misc. 3d 1209(A), 57 N.Y.S.3d 677 (N.Y. Sup. Ct. 2017).

124. Kong Xiangfeng (Trial Judge) (孔祥凤,一审承办人) and Zhu Qijia (朱齐家), Fei Qinzi Guanxi De Fuyang Fei Fanhuan He Jinshen Sunhai Peichang (非亲子关系的抚养费返还和精神损害赔偿) [Repayment of Child Support and Emotional Damage Compensation in Non-Biological Parent-Child Relationship], Renmin Sifa (人民司法) [The People's Judicature], 14.2020. 39–40.

test. Nie and Fan sued Zhao for 12 years of child support. The Beijing court ordered Zhao to repay Fan's husband RMB50,000 for child support because Zhao was the child's biological father.[125]

10.7.2 Child Support Amount

Child support includes a child's reasonable expenses, including housing, food, clothing, and education.[126] A nonresidential parent's child support amount must be determined based on the child's actual needs, each parent's respective financial ability, and the cost of living at the place where the child resides.[127]

Chinese courts must first consider a child's reasonable needs when determining child support amount.[128] For instance, in *Li v. Zhang*, each parent was ordered to pay RMB750 per month based on their child's actual living and educational expenses. Li and Zhang's daughter was 15 years old, but she had started the first year in college. The daughter's college expenses, including room and board, were about RMB1500 a month. Thus, the court determined the parents' child support amount based on their daughter's financial needs.[129]

Chinese courts must balance between the child's needs and other factors, particularly the parents' respective financial ability and the cost of living at the place where the child resides. For example, in *Li v. Li*, a Shanghai court ordered a father to pay RMB10,000 per month for his daughter's support until the child graduated from college, based on the high standard of living that the child had enjoyed prior to her parents' divorce, her high educational cost, the cost of living in Shanghai, and the parents' financial ability.[130]

If a parent has regular income, his/her child support amount may be 20 to 30 percent of his/her monthly or yearly income for one child, and the amount may be adjusted upward but no more than 50 percent for two children.[131] For instance, in *Gao v. Shen*, the nonresidential parent's monthly income was over RMB10,000. Considering the cost of living in Beijing and the parent's income, the Beijing No. 2 Intermediate People's Court ordered the nonresidential parent to pay RMB4,000 per month for the child's support, which is slightly higher than 30 percent of his monthly income.[132] In *Zhang v. Wu*, the Sichuan Province High People's Court affirmed that the husband's child support amount of RMB800 per month determined by the lower courts

125. (2015) San Zhong Min Zhong Zi Di 16166 Hao ((2015) 三中民终字第16166号).
126. The Marriage and Family Book Interpretations (I) art. 42.
127. *Id*. art. 49.
128. *Id*. art. 49 para. 1.
129. (2013) An Min Chu Zi Di 1378 Hao ((2013) 安民初字第1378号).
130. (2020) Hu 0112 Min Chu 7424 Hao ((2020) 沪0112民初7424号).
131. The Marriage and Family Book Interpretations (I) art. 49 para. 2.
132. (2019) Jing 02 Min Zhong 10545 Hao ((2019) 京02民终10545号).

was appropriate. The husband Wu's monthly income was RMB4,704. The wife requested the husband to pay RMB1411 per month, which amounted to 30 percent of his income, for child support. Considering the cost of living in Chengdu and the husband's additional obligation to share half of the child's educational and medical expenses, the courts determined that RMB800 per month was a more appropriate amount.[133] In *Zeng v. Jiang*, the father's monthly income was RMB5,000 per month, and considering the high cost of living in Zhuhai, the Zhuhai court set his child support amount at RMB1200 per month for each of his two children, which amounted to approximately 50 percent of his monthly income.[134]

If a parent does not have regular income, his/her child support amount may be determined based on the average standard of living in the region where he/she resides, the average income of his/her profession, or the special circumstances in a case.[135] Commenting on Typical Case *Fu (minor) v. Fu*, the SPC suggested that the child support amount must be based on a child's actual financial needs, including clothing, food, housing, transportation, education, and health care, as well as the parents' income, expenses, financial obligations, socioeconomic status, and ability to meet their respective child support obligation. In *Fu (minor) v. Fu*, both parents were rural residents and did not have regular income. The mother asked RMB1500 per month for the child's support from the father. The trial court ordered the father to pay RMB400 per month based on the average standard of living in the region.[136] Consistent with *Fu (minor) v. Fu*, in *Zhang v. Liu*, a Shandong court calculated the payor parent's annual child support amount based on the Shandong Province average rural resident annual income because the payor parent was a rural resident and had no regular income.[137] Similarly, in *Pang v. Wei*, a Hebei court ordered the father, a farmer, to pay RMB587 per month for his son's support based on 25 percent of the year 2020 Hebei Province average rural residents annual income of RMB28,201.[138]

10.7.3 Payment Methods

Child support may be paid periodically or in a lump sum if a payor parent's financial circumstances allow it.[139] In practice, many parents agree to lump sum child support payments as part of their divorce settlement. However,

---

133. (2015) Chuan Min Shen Zi Di 621 Hao ((2015) 川民申字第621号).
134. (2016) Yue 04 Min Zhong 2324 Hao ((2016) 粤04民终2324号).
135. The Marriage and Family Book Interpretations (I) art. 49.
136. FMTC 16.
137. (2016) Lu 14 Min Zhong 1766 Hao ((2016) 鲁14民终1766号).
138. (2021) Jin 06 Min Zhong823 Hao ((2021) 冀06民终823号).
139. The Marriage and Family Book Interpretations (I) art. 50.

Chinese courts rarely order lump sum child support for obvious reasons. First, the child support amount needs to be modified when there is a substantial change of circumstances, such as an increase in a child's financial needs. Second, most parents do not have the ability to pay a lump sum for years of child support. Third, lump sum advance payments for child support may not be necessary and appropriate in certain cases. Residential custodial parents often prefer assets in lieu of periodical child support payments in divorce settlements. However, once the assets are turned over to a residential custodial parent as child support, it becomes difficult for the court and the nonresidential parent to shield the assets from the custodial parent's creditors or to prevent the custodial parent's misuse or mismanagement of the assets. In other words, advance payments of child support could put a child's financial security at risk. Thus, Chinese courts do not normally award lump sum child support payments. For example, in *Shen v. Gao*, the Beijing court rejected the custodial parent's request for a lump sum payment of child support for a three-year-old and ordered monthly child support payments based on the child's actual needs and the noncustodial parent's modest income.[140]

Nonetheless, when the best interest of child requires that a parent pay child support in advance, Chinese courts do make lump sum child support orders. In *Yang v. Shi*, the Shenyang court ordered the mother to pay child support in one lump sum with her share of marital property. Yang and Shi had a daughter. The mother, Yang, resided in New Zealand. The child resided with her father in Shenyang. In the divorce action, Yang indicated that she would withhold child support if the father interfered with her visitation with the parties' daughter. The father, Shi, argued that Yang should be ordered to pay all future child support in advance in one lump sum because he would not be able to collect child support from Yang if she failed to pay child support. Considering the difficulty to collect child support from the mother due to her residency abroad, the court ordered the mother to pay a lump sum child support in the sum of RMB216,000, which amounted to RMB1500 per month until the child turned 18. The court deducted the child support amount from the mother's share in the parties' marital home. Judge Zhang, one of the presiding judges in *Yang v. Shi*, remarked that the court was concerned that the mother would use her superior financial position to withhold child support and gain leverage in future child custody disputes because the mother had threatened to condition her child support payments on the satisfaction of her visitation demands. Considering the child's best interest, the court order the mother to pay child support in a lump sum in advance as security for the child's financial needs.[141]

140. (2019) Jing 02 Min Zhong 10545 Hao ((2019) 京02民终10545号).

141. (2018) Liao 01 Min Zhong 1616 Hao ((2018) 辽01民终1616号). *See also* Zhang Zhongxing, Li Guojun (张忠星 李国军), Queding Fuyang Fei Geifu Fangshi Ying Youxian Kaolü Zinü

A nonresidential parent's noncompliance with a child support order does not always warrant a lump sum advance payment of child support. For example, in *Zhou v. Zhou*, the Shenzhen Intermediate People's Court found that a lump sum advance payment of child support was not necessary, as the father eventually complied with the child support order and purged his child support arrears. The court also found that the father did not have the ability to pay in a lump sum, as his child support amount was RMB8,000 per month per child.[142] A Beijing court made a similar decision in *Xu v. Xu*, where the father had accrued a significant amount of child support arears and had not been paying support regularly. The Beijing court found the father's noncompliance did not warrant a lump sum advance payment because he did not have the ability to pay.[143] However, the Chaozhou Intermediate People's Court found that it was necessary to compel a father to make a lump sum advance payment for all future child support because he persistently refused to pay child support and he was living in Thailand for business.[144]

Chinese courts may also order child support be paid with a payor parent's assets if the payor parent does not have any income or is missing.[145] In *Zhang v. Zhi*, a Beijing court ordered the father to liquidate some of his assets to pay child support, finding that the father did not have any income after he quit his job but he had ample assets available for the child's support.[146] In *Zhou v. Chen*, the father was serving a seven-year prison sentence. The court found that he would not have any income to pay child support during his incarceration and thus awarded the mother a portion of the father's marital share in the parties' marital assets as child support.[147] In *Zhou v. Liu*, the husband, Liu had been declared missing for about ten years. The wife filed for divorce and requested that a portion of the husband's share in the marital property be used to support the parties' son. The court granted the wife's request.[148]

10.7.4 Duration of Child Support

Usually, a nonresidential parent's support obligation terminates when the child turns 18, or when the child is over 16 years old and has become self-sufficient.[149]

Quanyi (确定抚养费给付方式应优先考虑子女权益) [The Determination of Child Support Payment Method Must Prioritize the Children's Rights and Interests], Renmin Sifa (人民司法) [The People's Judicature], 32.2018, 34–35.

142. (2018) Yue 0307 Min Chu 13129 Hao ((2018) 粤0307民初13129号).
143. (2015) Chao Min Chu Zi Di 22985 Hao ((2015) 朝民初字第22985号).
144. (2020) Yue 51 Min Zhong 80 Hao ((2020) 粤51民终80号).
145. The Marriage and Family Book Interpretations (I) art. 51.
146. (2020) Jing 0101 Min Chu 17383 Hao ((2020) 京0101民初17383号).
147. (2014) Zhu Dou Fa Heng Min Chu Zi Di 32 Hao ((2014) 珠斗法横民初字第32号).
148. (2017) Yue 0305 Min Chu 16032 Hao ((2017) 粤0305民初16032号).
149. The Marriage and Family Book Interpretations (I) arts. 52, 53.

However, a noncustodial parent may be responsible for a child's prenatal care, birth, and post-majority support under certain circumstances.

10.7.4.1 Prenatal Care and the Birth

Chinese courts may order support for the care of the mother and child during the pregnancy, birth, and after the birth. Thus, a Shanghai court ordered the child's biological father to reimburse the mother half of her out-of-pocket expenses for prenatal care and birth.[150] Similarly, in *Xie v. Guo*, the parties were not married and had a child in common. The parties separated when the mother was pregnant with the child. The mother sought child support and reimbursement for expenses incidental to the child's birth. The court ordered the child's father to reimburse the mother 70 percent of the expenses that she had paid for the child's prenatal care during the pregnancy, medical expenses for the birth, and childcare expenses after the child's birth.[151]

10.7.4.2 Pre-Majority Support

A parent's child support obligation generally terminates when a child turns 18. However, if a child has turned 18 but has not yet graduated from high school, the child support continues until the child graduates from high school. In *Zhao v. Zhao*, the child turned 18 but had not graduated from a trade school, which was equivalent to a high school. Thus, the father was ordered to pay support until the child's graduation.[152] Parents may stop child support payments if the child is over 16 and is able to support him/herself with their employment earnings to the level of the local average standard of living. [153]

10.7.4.3 Retroactive Support

A parent's child support obligation is retroactive to the date when he/she has stopped providing support for the child. For example, in *Zhang v. Zhang*, the child's parents had been separated in January 2009. The child had resided with the mother since the parents' separation. The father did not pay child support from January 2009 to October 2015, when the child, through the mother, brought the action for child support. The father was ordered to pay child support a total of RMB67,500 for child support arrears, including at the rate of RMB800 per month for the period from January 2009 to April 2015, and at the rate of RMB1500 per month from May 2015 to September 2015. Furthermore, he was ordered to pay RMB1,500 per month commencing in October

150. (2015) Pu Shao Min Chu Zi Di 237 Hao ((2015) 浦少民初字第237号).
151. (2021) Liao 10 Min Zhong 53 Hao ((2021) 辽10民终53号).
152. (2019) Jing 03 Min Zhong 220 Hao ((2019) 京03民终220号).
153. The Marriage and Family Book Interpretations (I) art. 53.

2015.[154] Similarly, Jiang and Pan, a married couple, separated in October 2014. The parties' daughter had been living with Pan since the separation. Jiang did not pay any child support. In July 2015, Pan, on behalf of the child, sued Jiang for child support. The Beijing Haidian District People's Court determined that (1) the father's child support arrearage accrued from the parties' separation in October 2014 to the date of the child support action in July 2015 was a total of RMB7400, and (2) the father child support amount should be RMB1000 per month, commencing in August 2015 until the child turned 18.[155]

10.7.4.4 Post-Majority Support

Chinese parents are expected to contribute to their children's college expenses. However, Chinese law does not explicitly require any parent to pay educational expenses for an adult child. A nonresidential parent's support obligation terminates when the child turns 18, or when the child is over 16 years old and has become self-sufficient.[156] However, Chinese culture expects parents to pay for their children's college expenses. Because of the conflict between the custom and the law, Chinese courts are often asked to decide whether an adult child is entitled to financial support from the parents to pay for reasonable educational and living expenses while attending college. In *Li Pailin, Li Ning v. Li Tao*, an adult child and his mother brought an action together against the child's father for college education expenses. Li Ning and Li Tao divorced in 2008, when their son, Li Pailin was 14 years old. The parties' divorce settlement agreement provided that Li Ning would have custody of Li Pailin and that Li Tao would be fully responsible for Li Pailin's college and wedding expenses in exchange for paying no child support before the child started college. In September 2012, Li Pailin started college, however Li Tao refused to pay for Li Pailin's college expenses despite Li Ning and Li Pailing's repeated requests. The court ordered Li Tao to pay Li Pailin's college tuition and living expenses. The SPC explained that divorced parents' agreements to pay for their child's college expenses are enforceable as such agreements conform with the societal expectation that parents should pay for a child's college education and this social norm does not violate any law or public policy.[157]

However, the SPC did not clarify whether a parent can be compelled to pay college expenses absent an agreement to pay. Since Chinese law does not require post-majority support absent the parents' agreement, a Changchun Basic-level court rejected a son's request for college expenses from his father. The court held that the son had no legal claim for support from the father

154. (2015) Hu Yi Zhong Shao Min Zhong Zi Di 72 Hao ((2015) 沪一中少民终字第72号).
155. (2016) Jing 01 Min Zhong 618 Hao ((2016) 京01民终618号).
156. The Marriage and Family Book Interpretations (I) arts. 52, 53.
157. FMTC 34.

and the father had no legal obligation to support him because the son was an adult capable of working. The court, however, commented that although the father had no legal obligation to help the son with his college expenses, "according to China's current social norm, the father has a moral obligation" to help pay for his son's college. The Changchun City Intermediate People's Court agreed, stating that:

> This Court believes that it is understandable that the appellee (the father) is unwilling to pay child support as the appellant (the son) has reached majority. The appellant can pay tuition, room and board, and living expenses by various means such as applying for state student loans, or work-study. In addition, although the appellant is an adult and person with full civil legal capacity, his complaint was still written from the perspective of his mother, as if she were his legal representative. [This Court] hopes that after the conclusion of this case the appellant will reimagine his life as an adult and make efforts to achieve his own life goals. If the appellee could provide appellant with some support to his best ability, the tension within the family will certainly ease, and the appellant will certainly appreciate his father's affection.[158]

10.7.5 Modification

Child support may be modified if the best interest of a child requires it or there is a significant change of circumstances. Modification of child support has three legal bases under Chinese law. First, the parents' agreement concerning child support does not restrict a child's ability to seek more child support. Thus, when a child's needs cannot be met with the support amount that the parents have agreed to, the child is entitled to an increase in support. Second, parents' child support agreements that are entered in good faith and are fair and reasonable are usually legally binding and may not be modified. However, some substantial change of circumstances may justify modification of the agreement. Third, substantial change of circumstances necessitates the modification of a child support order.

10.7.5.1 Child Support Increase

Child support amount may be increased under the following circumstances: (1) the original amount is not sufficient to maintain the child's standard of living to the level of local average standard of living; (2) the child's actual need is more than the original amount due to the child's medical or educational needs; and (3) any other reasonable reasons for an increase.[159]

Child support may be increased if a child's actual need is more than the original amount due to the child's medical or educational needs. Li's daughter is disabled and requires medical treatment for eye disease. The child had to undergo an expensive procedure by a specialist in Beijing. The procedure

158. (2021) Ji 01 Min Zhong 958 Hao ((2021) 吉01民终958号).
159. The Marriage and Family Book Interpretations (I) art. 58.

was successful and prevented the child from becoming completely blind. The mother asked the father to reimburse her some of the medical expenses and an increase in child support to pay for the continuing medical treatment and care for the child. The SPC found that the child's medical expenses and ongoing treatment and care warranted an increase of the father's child support.[160] Similarly, in *Wang v. Xie*, the court ruled that the mother should pay RMB900 per month for the child's living expenses although the parties' divorce agreement did not require her to pay for the child's living expenses. The father, Wang, was the residential custodial parent of the parties' daughter. Wang and Xie agreed in their divorce settlement agreement that the parents would share the child's educational expenses equally and the father would be solely responsible for the child's living expenses and medical care. The child was two years old at the time of the divorce. Eight years later, Wang brought an action for an increase in child support in a Chongqing court. Based on the child's increased financial needs and the mother's financial ability, the Chongqing courts increased the mother's support obligation.[161]

In *Ma (minor) v. Ma*, the court was asked to increase the noncustodial parent's child support to pay for a middle-class child's extraordinary education and medical expenses. The parents had agreed that the father should pay RMB1,500 per month for child support for the parties' daughter. Later, the mother paid RMB13,422 for the child's medical expenses and RMB11,105 for the child's educational expenses. On behalf of the child, the mother sought reimbursement of the child's medical and educational expenses and an increase in child support. The court held that in addition to monthly basic child support, which includes a child's ordinary living, educational, medical, and other expenses, a child's extraordinary educational and medical expenses must be shared by the parents as well. The court found that the medical treatment for the child's eyes was necessary and the child's chess lessons were reasonable because both parents supported the child's interest and training in chess prior to the divorce. Thus, the father was ordered to reimburse the mother one-half of the child's out-of-pocket medical and educational expenses. Considering the child's reasonable needs, the court also increased the father's child support amount from RMB1,500 per month to RMB2,500 per month. Commenting on *Ma (minor) v. Ma*, the SPC affirmed that child support amount should be based on the child's reasonable needs and the child's best interest as well as the parents' respective financial ability and overall fairness of their support obligation. While recognizing the financial needs of children

---

160. (2017) Zui Gao Fa Min Sheng 3980 Hao ((2017) 最高法民申3980号).

161. Chen Jian, Cao Juan Zi (陈健, 曹鹃), Zinu Qingqiu Zengjia Fuyang Fei De Fading Tiaojian (子女请求增加抚养费的法定条件) [The Statutory Grounds for Children's Request to Increase Child Support], Renmin Sifa (人民司法) [The People's Judicature], 11.2020, 50–52.

in wealthy and middle-class families, the SPC further cautioned the lower courts not to award excessive child support, which would finance "extravagant" lifestyles for the child and the custodial parent.[162]

Increase in child support is necessary when the initial amount is no longer sufficient to maintain the child's standard of living to the level of local average standard of living. In *Yu (minor) v. Yu*, the court increased the child support amount based on the increased cost of living in the region where the child resided and the child's actual needs. At the time of the divorce in 2008, the father made a lump sum payment of RMB23,000 as advanced child support to satisfy his support obligation. The court found that the father's payment of RMB23,000 would equal to approximately RMB62.5 per month until the child turns 18 while the average monthly living cost per person is RMB419 per month in the region where the child resided. Clearly, the father's child support payment was insufficient to maintain the child's standard of living at the regional average. In addition, the child was admitted to a magnet school for gifted children, and the tuition for the school was RMB3,600 per year. Considering the cost of living in the region and the child's educational needs, the court held that the father's child support amount should be increased to RMB1,000 per month. The SPC declared that Chinese courts should apply the principal of "the best interest of a child," which is widely followed around the world and consistent with Chinese traditional values of caring for children and the elderly in determining issues related to child support. The SPC remarked that child support orders and agreements may be adjusted if the best interest of the child warrants a modification.[163]

Clearly, Chinese courts would award child support increases to meet a child's needs. On the other hand, modification is warranted only when it is "necessary" (*bi yao*). In *Li v. Li*, through the court's mediation, the parents agreed that the mother should have residential custody of the child and a larger share of the parties' marital property in exchange for child support. The agreement was incorporated in the parties mediated divorce decree. Less than a year after the divorce, the mother sought child support from the father. The trial court entered a support order against the father. On the appeal, the Shenyang City Intermediate People's Court found that there was no change of circumstance that would necessitate modification of the parents' agreement as the mother waived child support in exchange for a significant amount of property and she had ample resource to support the child. Furthermore, the court found that the mother's suit for child support modification was not only meritless but also in bad faith as she entered an agreement that she had no intention to abide and her action was a violation of good faith.

162. FMTC 6.
163. FMTC 10.

The Intermediate Court held that child support agreements, particularly the agreements that were reached after courts' mediation, should not be readily modified without showing any of the statutory circumstances; and that allowing easy modification of support agreements would undermine the public's confidence that the courts will uphold and enforce a fair, reasonable agreement.[164]

10.7.5.2 Child Support Reduction

A parent seeking a reduction of child support obligation must show substantial change of circumstances that can justify the reduction. Temporary unemployment or loss of income are not sufficient reasons for child support reduction. For example, the Shanghai courts denied a father's request for a reduction of child support due to unemployment, finding that the father had the ability to obtain gainful employment and had sufficient assets to support the child while looking for another job.[165] Similarly, in *Liu v. Liu* the Shanghai No.1 Intermediate People's Court affirmed the lower court's decision to reject the father's request for a child support reduction due to decrease in his income, finding that the father's income decrease was temporary and seasonal.[166] Similarly, the Shanghai courts declined to reduce a father's child support although his companies were not as profitable as they used to be, and ordered the father to pay RMB45,000 per month per child as he had agreed to in the divorce settlement agreement. The court found that the father still had sufficient assets and the earning capacity to pay the agreed child support amount.[167]

On the other hand, if a parent's financial circumstances have deteriorated substantially, Chinese courts would consider child support reduction. In *Deng v. Deng*, the father had complied with the divorce agreement and paid RMB3500 per month for child support even after he was laid off. He sought a reduction of child support after his six-month severance pay ended. The Shanghai No. 2 Intermediate court affirmed the trial court's decision to reduce the father's support amount to RMB355. The court found that the father had always paid child support, his unemployment was involuntary, he had been looking for a job, and he indeed could not afford to pay RMB3500 per month for child support.[168]

---

164. Guo Xiaojuan, Zhang Zhongxing (郭晓娟, 张忠星), Biangeng Fuyang Fei Ying Fuhe Fading Tiaojian (变更抚养费应符合法定条件) [Modification of Child Support Must Meet the Statutory Requirements], Renmin Sifa (人民司法) [The People's Judicature], 22.2015, 107–08.
165. (2015) Hu Yi Zhong Shao Min Zhong Zi Di 26 Hao ((2015) 沪一中少民终字第26号).
166. (2015) Hu Yi Zhong Shao Min Zhong Zi Di 28 Hao ((2015) 沪一中少民终字第28号).
167. (2015) Hu Yi Zhong Shao Min Zhong Zi Di 8 Hao ((2015) 沪一中少民终字第8号).
168. (2014) Hu Er Zhong Shao Min Zhong Zi Di 36 Hao ((2014) 沪二中少民终字第36号).

10.7.6 Child Support Enforcement and Collection

Child support enforcement is a complex issue that affects not only the welfare of children and their parents but also a country's social welfare system. With an increasing number of separated families, child support collection cases have started to fill Chinese courts' dockets. Consequently, Chinese courts have toughened on child support collections.

10.7.6.1 Standing to Collect Child Support Arrears

Both a child and his/her custodial parent have the standing to bring a child support enforcement proceeding. The SPC held in *Chen v. Feng* that a custodial parent, who had supported the child financially, had the standing to bring enforcement proceedings against the payor parent based on the parties' mediation agreement.[169]

10.7.6.2 Statute of Limitations

Statute of limitations do not apply in actions for payment of child support.[170] In *Liu v. Liu*, the Dongguan City Intermediate People's Court held that pursuant to Article 196 of the Civil Code, statute of limitation does not apply in an action for child support brought by an adult child and affirmed the lower court's decision to order the child's father to pay child support arrearage accrued from the parents' separation in 2009 to the date of the action and monthly child support thereafter until the child's 18.[171]

Prior to the Civil Code, Chinese courts followed a well-established rule that if the subject child is a minor child or an incapacitated adult child, statute of limitations does not apply. However, a three-year statute of limitation starts once a child reaches majority.[172] Thus, in *Peng v. Liu*, a Shanghai court held that statute of limitation for child support did not start to run until a child reached majority as child maintenance was an obligation derived from personal status and a durational obligation that would continue until the child's 18. The court ordered the child's father to reimburse the mother in the sum of RMB163,000 for child support arrears accrued retroactively from 2001 to 2018 when the action for child support was brought; and to pay RMB2,400 per month for the child's support until the child turned 18.[173]

---

169. *Id*.
170. The Civil Code art. 196(3).
171. (2020) Yue 19 Min Zhong 11754 Hao ((2020) 粤19民终11754号).
172. The Civil Code art. 188 para. 1.
173. (2019) Hu 0120 Min Chu 11847 ((2019) 沪0120民初11847号).

Similarly, in enforcement proceedings, the SPC held in *Chen v. Feng* that statute of limitations does not apply in a child support enforcement proceeding brought by the custodial parent, Chen, in 2019 for collection of child support arrears accrued from 2002 to 2012 in that the child was a minor at the time when the enforcement proceeding was initiated, as Feng's child support obligation was continuing and all previous collection proceedings were ongoing as well. In *Chen v. Feng*, the parties had a mediation agreement, providing that Feng should pay Chen RMB7000 per month for the parties' second child starting from November 2000. The child was born in 1996. Feng did not pay any child support from November 2000 to November 2001. Thus, Chen sued him to collect the child support arrears. As of July 9, 2003, when the enforcement proceeding was concluded, Chen collected RMB107,346. In May 2012, Chen brought another enforcement proceeding for Feng's child support arrears in the sum of RMB798,000 accrued since November 2002. The parties agreed to stay the enforcement until after Feng liquidated some of his stockholdings to satisfy the arrears. Feng again did not pay after the settlement. In 2019, Chen brought another enforcement proceeding to collect Feng's child support arrears. Feng argued that he was not liable for any child support arrearage as the child had reached majority and Chen's enforcement proceeding was time barred. The SPC and the lower courts rejected Feng's arguments.[174]

10.7.6.3 Mediation

The SPC encourages courts to mediate and reach amicable resolutions in child support cases. The Typical Case *Chen (minor) v. Chen* is an exemplary example. In the *Chen* case, the child's parents were divorced in 2008. After the divorce, the child resided with the mother and the father paid RMB3,000 a year for child support. After the mother died in 2009 the child went to live with the maternal grandparents. The father stopped paying child support after the mother passed away. In 2014, the child started high school and brought an action for child support arrears and an increase of child support. Through the court's mediation, the father agreed to pay RMB7,000 per year until the child graduated from high school, and an additional RMB28,000 for the child's college education when the child began college. The SPC commended the *Chen* court for its exemplary handling of the case. First, in considering the financial circumstances of the child, the court waived court fees and made it possible for the child to bring the suit. Second, the court focused on mediation instead of adjudication and facilitated an amicable resolution. Third, the court helped repair the child and the father's relationship and

174. (2020) Zui Gao Fa Zhi Jian 66 Hao ((2020) 最高法执监66号).

encouraged a positive, loving relationship between the child, the father, and the child's maternal grandparents. The court asked the father to be grateful to the child's maternal grandparents for their efforts to care for and provide for the child, and at the same time the court asked the child to forgive her father and to understand her father's financial burden of raising two younger children from his second marriage. The court's follow-up investigations showed the child is doing well academically and socially, and all parties are satisfied with the outcome of the case.[175]

10.7.6.4 Enforcement Measures

Enforcement measures to recover support include advance enforcement, attachment, seizure, garnishment, income execution, fine, and imprisonment.[176] In addition to the conventional enforcement measures, China's social credit system (*xingyong tixi*) is a powerful child support collection tool.[177] Chinese courts' successes in child support collections by placing parents who owe child support on the List of Dishonest Persons have been widely reported.[178] For example, in Typical Case *Sun v. Peng*, Sun and Peng were divorced in 2013 in Beijing. Peng was ordered to pay child support, but he never complied with the order. In 2015, Sun brought an enforcement proceeding against Peng for child support arrearage. When the judge called Peng to notify him of the enforcement proceeding, Peng pretended that he was his brother and told the judge that his whereabouts were unknown. Peng did not show up for

---

175. FMTC 18.

176. Civil Procedure Law arts. 106(1), 241, 242, 243, 245.

177. The List of Dishonest Persons Subject to Enforcement is a reporting system stabled in 2013 pursuant to Zuigao Renmin Fayuan Guanyu Gongbu Shixin Beizhixingren Mingdan Xinxi De Ruogan Guiding (最高人民法院关于公布失信被执行人名单信息的若干规定) [Several Provisions of the Supreme People's Court on Issuance of List of Dishonest Persons Subject to Enforcement] (promulgated July 1, 2013, amended Jan. 16, 2017) 2017 Sup. People's Ct. Gaz. 6. The purpose of the "List" is to carry out "credit punishment." Judgment debtors on the List of Dishonest Persons Subject to Enforcement are prohibited from engaging a wide range of financial activities, from buying first-class train tickets to applying for loans. The List is circulated among government authorities, agencies, financial institutions and published online. *See* the SPC White Papers: Judicial Transparency by People's Courts, V. Disclosure of Enforcement Information.

178. *See, e.g.*, Ye Tao & Wang Haifeng (聂涛,王海峰), Anhui Jieshou: Shengfu Jüfu Fuyangfei Chuchu Shouxian Jifukuan (安徽界首：生父拒付抚养费,处处受限急付款) [Anhui Jieshou: Biological Father Who Had Refused to Pay Child Support Rushed to Pay Due to Constant Restrictions], Renmin Fayuan Xinwen Chuanmei Zongshe (人民法院新闻传媒总社) [The People's Court Press and Media Office], http://jszx.court.gov.cn/main/ExecuteNewsletter/89603.jhtml, and Du Fanfei (杜凡非), Jüjue Zhifu Fuyangfei De Ta, Zhudong Lai Fayuan Huan! Qian! Le! (拒绝支付抚养费的他主动来法院还!钱!了!) [He Who had Refused to Pay Child Support Voluntarily Came to the Court to Pay Money!], http://jszx.court.gov.cn/1100/ExecuteNews/120607.jhtml.

the enforcement hearing. At the hearing, the judge called Peng again and put Peng on the speaker when Peng took the call. Both Sun and the child identified Peng by his voice immediately. The judge warned Peng of the consequences of his failure to pay child support, including being put on the List of Dishonest Persons Subject to Enforcement and criminal charges. Peng ignored the judge's warning. The judge then put Peng on the List of Dishonest Persons and garnished payments from Peng's bank accounts. Peng purged the support arrearage within days after putting on the dishonest people blacklist.[179]

179. FMTC 9.

Chapter 11

Domestic Violence

The U.S. Centers for Disease Control and Prevention reported that about one in five women and about one in seven men in the United States report having experienced severe physical violence from an intimate partner in their lifetime.[1] China reports similar widespread violence behind closed doors at home. Cases where the victims suffered severe injuries or loss of life have been prosecuted criminally in China. Recovery of damages caused by bodily and emotional harm inflicted by domestic violence has been available under Chinese law for nearly two decades.[2] Pilot programs on combatting domestic violence were installed in local courts as early as in 2008.[3] It was, however, not until the promulgation of the Anti-Domestic Violence Law in 2016 that China formally established a civil protection system under which domestic violence victims can seek civil protection orders as well as criminal prosecution against violent acts perpetrated by a family member or an intimate partner.

§ 11.1 Definition of Domestic Violence

The Anti-Domestic Violence Law defines "domestic violence" as a family member's battery, restraining by force, torture, imprisonment by force, pattern of degrading and threatening, and any other acts causing physical and psychological harm to another family member.[4]

The SPC Guide for Trying Marriage Cases Involving Domestic Violence (the "DV Guide"), although not an official set of judicial interpretations, is

1. U.S. Centers for Disease Control and Prevention, Preventing Intimate Partner Violence 1 (2020).

2. The Marriage Law art. 45; and the Criminal Procedure Law of the People's Republic of China (the "PRC Criminal Procedure Law") art. 204.

3. Jue Jiang, *The Family as a Stronghold of State Stability: Two Contradictions in China's Anti-Domestic Violence Efforts*, 33 Int'l J. L., Pol'y Fam., 228–51, 229, (2019).

4. The Anti-Domestic Violence Law art. 2.

widely used as guidelines in family matters by Chinese courts. The DV Guide adopted a similar definition of domestic violence and defined four forms of domestic violence: (1) physical violence, (2) sexual violence, (3) psychological violence, and (4) economic control.[5]

§ 11.2 Personal Safety Protection Order

A personal safety protection order proceeding may be commenced as an independent action or in conjunction with another family matter action. A person that has suffered domestic violence or is at risk of domestic violence perpetrated by a member of his/her family or household is entitled to a personal safety protection order.[6] The petition must be in writing.[7] The Basic-Level court at the place where a petitioner resides, or where a respondent resides, or where a domestic incident occurs has the jurisdiction to issue a personal safety protection order.[8] A personal safety protection order expires in six months. However, a court may extend, modify, or vacate an order before its expiration.[9] The SPC's Provisions Concerning Several Issues on the Application of Law in the Handling of Personal Safety Protection Order Cases (the "Personal Safety Protection Order Rules") sets out detailed rules in personal safety protection order proceedings in Chinese courts.[10]

11.2.1 Members of Family or Household

"Domestic violence" is defined as violence perpetrated by a family member against another family member.[11] Thus, the petitioner and respondent must have a family relationship. The Anti-Domestic Violence Law expanded the protection to members of a common household.[12] The SPC Personal Safety Protection Order Rules specifies that personal safety protection orders may be issued against family members as well as people who live in the same residence and are related by marriage, or have a guardianship, custody or

5. The DV Guide art. 3.
6. The Anti-Domestic Violence Law art. 23.
7. *Id.* art. 24.
8. *Id.* art. 25.
9. *Id.* art. 30.
10. Zuigao Renmin Fayuan Guanyu Banli Renshen Anquan Baohu Ling Anjian Shiyong Falü Ruogan Wenti De Guiding (最高人民法院关于办理人身安全保护令案件适用法律若干问题的规定) [the SPC's Rules Concerning Several Issues on the Application of Law in the Handling of Personal Safety Protection Order Cases] (promulgated by the Sup. People's Ct., June 7, 2022, effective Aug. 1, 2022) (hereinafter the "Personal Safety Protection Order Rules").
11. *Id.* art. 2.
12. *Id.* art. 37.

foster-care relationship.[13] The SPC widened the definition of "family members" and extended personal safety protection to victims who have not been protected under a narrow definition of "family members." In its recent publication of Typical Cases concerning personal safety protection orders, the SPC clarified that a victim may petition a court for a personal safety protection order against a person with whom the victim has or had a relationship through guardianship, foster care, cohabitation, or a previous marriage, and with whom the victim lives in the same household.[14]

A divorced spouse may petition for personal safety protection orders against his/her former spouse. In the *Matter of Zhong*, the court issued a personal safety protection order for Zhong against Chen, Zhong's ex-husband. After the parties were divorced, Chen had refused to leave the marital residence and demanded to eat and sleep with Zhong as though they had not been divorced. Chen attempted to restrict Zhong's social life by beating, disparaging, and threatening her. After he was removed from the marital residence by the police, Chen used his visitation with the parties' children to stalk, harass, and intimidate Zhong. The court found that Chen's behavior constituted typical "break-up violence" and was likely to escalate to more serious crimes. Thus, the court issued a personal safety protection order enjoining Chen from harassing, stalking, threatening, and assaulting Zhong, and ordered him to stay at least 200 meters away from Zhong, Zhong's home, and Zhong's workplace. In addition, the court forbade Chen from visiting the children at Zhong's residence.[15] Similarly, a Jiangsu court issued a personal safety protection order that prohibited the ex-husband from harassing, stalking, or having any contact with the ex-wife, the parties' children, and the ex-wife's close relatives.[16]

A victim may seek a personal safety protection order to enjoin someone with whom they have or have had a "dating" and cohabitation relationship. In *Wu Personal Safety Protection Order Petition Case*, Wu, the petitioner, and Yang, the respondent lived together for nearly ten years. After their breakup, Yang harassed, stalked, and physically and verbally assaulted Wu at her residence

---

13. The Personal Safety Protection Order Rules art. 4.

14. Zuigao Renmin Fayuan Gongbu Shiqi Jiating Baoli Dianxing Anjian (最高人民法院公布十起家庭暴力的典型案例) [the Supreme People's Court Published Ten Domestic Violence Typical Cases], 2015 Sup. People's Ct. Gaz. 2. Zuigao Renmin Fayuan Fabu She Jiating Baoli Fanzui Dianxing Anjian (最高法发布涉家庭暴力犯罪典型案例) [the SPC Published Crimes Involving Domestic Violence Typical Cases] (Mar. 4, 2015) [hereinafter CVTC] 3.

15. Zuigao Renmin Fayuan Gongbu Shiqi Jiating Baoli Dianxing Anjian (最高人民法院公布十起家庭暴力的典型案例) [the Supreme People's Court Published Ten Domestic Violence Typical Cases], 2015 Sup. People's Ct. Gaz. 2. [hereinafter DVTC] 6.

16. Zuigo Renmin Fayuan Renshen Anquan Baohu Ling Shi Da Dianxing Anli (最高人民法院人身安全保护令十大典型案例) [the SPC Ten Important Personal Safety Protection Order Typical Cases] (Nov. 25, 2020) [hereinafter PSPOTC] 3.

and her workplace. Wu sought help from the police on numerous occasions. Yang completely disregarded the police's warnings. Finally, a Chengdu court issued a stayaway order against Yang.[17]

Personal safety protection orders may be issued to minor children against their parents. A parent, the child's school, and community-based groups may petition for a personal safety protection order on behalf of the child. A parent may petition for a personal safety protection order on behalf of his/her child. In Typical Case *Li and Tang Personal Safety Protection Order Petition Case*, the mother, who was the nonresidential custodial parent, discovered that the child was physically abused by the father. After the mother intervened, the father escalated his abuse of the child. The court issued a personal safety protection order for both the child and the mother and changed the child's custody to the mother.[18] A protected child's school and community-based organizations may petition on the child's behalf as well. For example, in the Typical Case of *Lin Personal Safety Protection Order Petition Case*, the child's school sought a protection order on behalf of the child after the child disclosed to her teacher that she was molested by her father. The court issued the order and placed the child in her grandparents' custody.[19] Similarly, in the Typical Case *Zhu Personal Safety Protection Order Petition Case*, the child was physically abused by his father and stepmother, and the child's school intervened. The school sought help from the local Women's Federation. The local Women's Federation represented the child and petitioned for a personal safety protection order against the father and stepmother. The court issued the order and ordered the local Women's Federation, Urban Residents' Committee, and police to supervise the parents' compliance of the order.[20] The child, however, remained in the father and stepmother's custody because China lacks any state facility for child placement.

Community-based organizations may intervene on behalf of an elderly person and seek a protection order on his/her behalf. In the Typical Case of *Luo Personal Safety Protection Order Case*, Luo was an elderly man and was subject to his adopted son's constant physical and verbal abuse. After the son threatened to kill him, Luo complained about the incident to his village's Villagers' Committee. The Villagers' Committee petitioned for a personal protection order on Luo's behalf. The court evicted the adopted son from Luo's home and issued a stay away order. [21]

17. PSPOTC 8.
18. PSPOTC 4.
19. PSPOTC 6.
20. PSPOTC 5.
21. PSPOTC 7.

11.2.2 Expedited Procedure

A court must conduct an evidentiary hearing and determine whether to issue a personal safety protection order within 72 hours, or within 24 hours in case of an emergency, after a petition for a personal safety protection order is made.[22] *Chen v. Zhang* is one of the earliest cases where a personal protection order was issued in Chinese courts. At the parties' divorce case hearing, the court found that Zhang instituted unreasonable rules in the household to exert control over the wife, and that Zhang often berated his wife and beat her when she "disobeyed" his "house rules." Having observed the husband's controlling behavior throughout the case in court, the judge immediately issued a personal protection order barring the husband from assaulting, threatening, stalking, and harassing the wife and their adult daughter.[23]

Lawmakers intended to provide expeditious relief to victims. Thus, Chinese courts are required to conduct an evidentiary hearing and determine whether to issue a personal safety protection order within 72 hours, or within 24 hours in case of an emergency, after a petition is made.[24] The accelerated procedure is a double-edged sword. In many cases, the courts do not have sufficient evidence to issue a personal safety protection order because the victims have very little time to collect and present evidence after a petition is filed. Twenty-four to 72 hours is not nearly enough time to put together a case, particularly when most of the petitioners do not have legal representation and are still processing their trauma. Consequently, Chinese courts heavily rely on police reports as evidence, because the petitioners do not have sufficient time to collect and present their own evidence. However, the police reports are often limited due to the police's lack of training and legal authority to collect evidence expeditiously.[25] Although the Anti-Domestic Violence Law requires the police to investigate and collect evidence in domestic violence incidents, there is no guidance as to the police's authority to search, investigate, and collect evidence at the scene in a private home. Consequently, without explicit statutory authority to search and collect evidence at the scene of a domestic violence incident, the police often misses the opportunity to preserve evidence in domestic violence cases.[26]

---

22. The Anti-Domestic Violence Law art. 28.

23. DVTC 3.

24. Anti-Domestic Violence Law art. 28.

25. Zhang Hai, Chen Aiwu (张海，陈爱武), Tamen De Renshen Anquan Baohu Ling Yuanhe Bei Fayuan Caiding Bohui—Jiyu Caidingshu De Zhagen Lilun Yanjiu (她们的人身安全保护令缘何被法院裁定驳回 - 基于裁定书的扎根理论研究) [Why Their Personal Safety Protection Order Was Rejected by the Court—Grounded Theoretical Research Based on the Ruling], Hebei Faxue (河北法学) [Hebei Law Science], Vol. 39, No. 4, 185–200, 195–96 (Apr. 2021), 42–43.

26. Wang Yiming (王一明), Lun Gongan Jiguan Chuzhi Jiabao Anjian Chengxu De Wanshan (论公安机关处置家暴案件程序的完善) [On Improving Disposal Regulations of Public Security

Recognizing these obstacles that many domestic violence victims face, the SPC Personal Safety Protection Rules allows the court to question respondents by video, telephone, email, or other means of telecommunication and to issue ex parte personal safety protection orders.[27] In addition, the SPC has eased evidentiary rules, and Chinese courts may allow a wide range of evidence in personal safety protection order proceedings.[28] Furthermore, the court may issue personal safety protection orders when there is sufficient evidence that the petitioner is at risk of domestic violence.[29]

11.2.3 Basis for Issuing or Denying a Personal Safety Protection Order

The court must issue a personal safety protection order if it finds (1) the respondent is clearly identified; (2) the relief sought is sufficiently stated; and (3) the petitioner has suffered domestic violence or faces credible risk of domestic violence.[30] Grounds for issuance of a personal safety protection order include all forms of domestic violence, including physical violence and psychological violence.[31] Repeated threats of violence cause a victim psychological harm and pose a credible risk of physical harm, and therefore are grounds for issuance of a personal safety protection order.[32] Deprivation of food, clothing, or housing, and infliction of bodily or psychological harm by constant disparaging, defaming, threating, stalking, or harassing are also "domestic violence" that warrant personal safety protection orders.[33]

In personal safety protection order petition cases, Chinese courts generally followed the evidentiary standards in civil matter. The courts' rigidity in upholding evidentiary requirements has created significant procedural barriers for the petitioners.[34] It is always difficult to collect evidence of domestic violence as the events occur in private. The expedited procedure makes it even more difficult for petitioners to collect, organize, and present evidence as the evidentiary hearing must be held within 24 to 72 hours after a petition is filed. Consequently, petitioners often have to resort to their own testimo-

---

Organ in Anti-domestic Violence Law] J. Liaoning Police College No. 1 (Ser. No. 107) Jan. 2018, 41–45, 41–43.

27. The Personal Protection Order Rules art. 7.

28. *Id* art. 6 (1)–(11).

29. *Id* art. 6.

30. The Anti-Domestic Violence Law art. 27.

31. *Id*. art. 2.

32. PSPOTC 2.

33. The Personal Safety Protection Order Rules art. 3.

34. Zeng Jianfei, Jin Cong (曾建飞 金 丛), Renshen Anquan Baohu Ling Zhidu Ruogan Wenti Yanjiu (人身安全保护令制度若干问题研究) [A Study on Several Issues in the Personal Safety Protection Order System], Renmin Sifa (人民司法) [The People's Judicature], 2017(7), 15–20, 15–16.

nies and circumstantial evidence. Because of a lack of direct evidence, such as eyewitnesses, it is extremely difficult for a petitioner to prove that his/her injuries were caused by the respondent's violent act.[35] Chinese courts' strict compliance with evidentiary rules was a contributing factor to the rejection of a considerable fraction of personal safety protection order petitions.[36] The Personal Safety Protection Order Rules has eased the petitioner's evidentiary burden. It allows a variety of documentary evidence and testimonies, including minor children's testimonies, in personal safety protection order proceedings.[37]

It is important to remove procedural barriers that confront domestic violence victims to afford them justice and protection. It is equally important to treat the respondents with neutrality, respect, and consistency. Given the enormous barriers that confront domestic violence victims, legal reformers in the United States have been most concerned with expansion of the judicial system's responsiveness to the alleged victims and have reduced the level of procedural justice accorded to alleged batterers. In recent decades, some have begun to question the wisdom of this approach as an emerging body of social science research shows that the likelihood of a person's perception of fair process improves their compliance with court orders issued in civil and criminal cases.[38] Chinese courts have reported a high compliance rate of personal safety protection orders. For example, a Hunan basic level court reported that among a total of 46 personal safety protection orders that the court issued in the three years following the promulgation of the Anti-Domestic Violence Law, there were only two cases of violation, and the respondents resumed compliance after being verbally reprimanded by the court upon the petitioners' request.[39] The high compliance rate may be because Chinese courts do not compromise their evidentiary standards and afford respondents a level of procedural fairness that promotes compliance of the order. Thus, although the SPC permits ex parte personal safety protection orders, it has not made ex parte orders readily available.[40]

35. Zhang Hai et al., *supra* note 25, at 196–98.

36. *Id.* at 187–200. The study found about 38 percent of the petitions in the study were rejected.

37. The Personal Safety Protection Order Rules art. 6 (1)–(11).

38. Deborah Epstein, *Procedural Justice: Tempering the State's Response to Domestic Violence*, 43 Wm. & Mary L. Rev. 1843, 1845–46 (2002).

39. Liu Qun, Xu Zhengxing (刘群, 许振兴), Renshen Anquan Baohu Ling Anjian Banli Zhong De Kunjing Ji Qi Jiejue (人身安全保护令案件办理中的困境及其解决) [The Difficulties in Handling Personal Safety Protection Order Cases and Solutions], Renmin Sifa (人民司法) [The People's Judicature], July 2019, 10–14, at 10.

40. The Personal Safety Protection Order Rules art. 7.

Frivolous petitions for personal safety protection orders are frequently denied. Abuse of personal safety protection orders to gain leverage in divorce actions is rampant in Chinese courts. A spouse who has committed acts of domestic violence is penalized in marital property distribution and is liable for compensatory damages in a divorce action. Motivated by these financial gains, some litigants do not hesitate to make false accusations and file frivolous petitions for personal protection order.[41]

11.2.4 Protective Measures

Under the Anti-Domestic Violence Law, Chinese courts may grant a wide range of protection measures, including to exclude the respondent from the petitioner's residence. A personal safety protection order may (1) prohibit the respondent from committing any act of domestic violence; (2) prohibit the respondent from harassing, stalking, or having contact with the petitioner; (3) remove the respondent from the petitioner's residence; and (4) order any other measures for the petitioner's protection.[42] The court may prohibit the respondent from disparaging, defaming, or threatening the petitioner and his/her close relatives by telephone calls, text massages, instant messengers, or emails.[43] In addition, the court may order the respondent to stay away from the petitioner's and the petitioner's close relatives' residence, school, workplace, and any other places where the petitioner and/or the petitioner's close relatives engage in routine life, education, and employment activities.[44]

11.2.5 Service and Enforcement

Personal protection orders must be served on the respondents.[45] A personal protection order takes effect when it is served on the respondent. Respondents may file an objection to the order and seek a reconsideration within five days after the service.[46]

Personal safety protection orders must be served on local police, Urban Residents' Committees, Villagers' Committees, and Women's Federation as well. These agencies must provide assistance in enforcing personal safety protection orders.[47]

---

41. Zhang, *supra* note 25, at 195–96.
42. The Anti-Domestic Violence Law art. 37.
43. The Personal Safety Protection Order Rules art. 10(1).
44. *Id.* art. 10(2).
45. *Id.* art. 32.
46. *Id.* art. 31.
47. *Id.* art. 32.

11.2.6 Consequences of Violations of Protection Orders

Violation of a personal safety protection order can result in detention and fine.[48] For example, in the Hong Violation of Personal Safety Protection Order Case, the victim, Bao, and Hong were dating and living together. Hong beat Bao and injured her. Bao broke up with Hong and moved out. After the breakup, Bao harassed and stalked Bao. Bao reported Hong's stalking of her to the police. The police reprimanded Hong. Bao also obtained a personal safety protection order against Hong. However, Hong ignored the order and continued harassing and stalking Bao. The court found that Hong was in violation of the personal safety protection order against him, and Hong was detained for 15 days and fined RMB1000 for the violation.[49]

Chinese law lacks specific procedural protections for victims who have petitioned for personal safety protections orders during the personal protection order proceedings. Fortunately, some local courts have developed some techniques to address these issues. For example, a Hunan court implemented protocols for petitioners' confidential information protection, control of respondents' intimidations during the hearings, and post-order follow-up visits.[50]

§ 11.3 Civil Damages

Domestic violence victims may seek compensatory damages for physical and/or emotional harm as well as economic loss caused by their batterers' violent acts in divorce actions and civil suits. For discussions on compensatory damages for domestic violence in divorce actions, see § 8.7.2.

A tort action may be brought contemporaneously with the divorce action or with a petition for a personal safety protection order, or in an independent action. A civil action is filed in the general civil division of a court of first instance. Civil suits are frequently used in China to redress domestic violence. A claimant's civil suit does not preclude them from asserting claims for relief in a divorce action, or vice versa. For example, in Typical Case *Zhang v. Chen*, the wife was brutally assaulted by her husband and suffered serious injuries, including a broken nose and broken knees. The wife was hospitalized due to the injuries. The husband was convicted of assault and was ordered to reimburse Zhang roughly RMB3,000 for her out-of-pocket hospital expenses in the wife's private prosecution criminal action against him. The wife was awarded compensatory damages for the domestic violence that she suffered in the divorce action. Additionally, the wife filed a civil suit for a

48. *Id.* art. 34.
49. PSPOTC 10.
50. Liu et al., *supra* note 39, at 10.

total of RMB60,000 for additional medical expenses, home care expenses, and damages based on new evidence of her injuries. In the civil suit, the wife was awarded RMB48,664.31 for damages for additional medical expenses, home care cost, and emotional damages.[51]

Claimants of domestic violence primarily rely on their own testimonies and circumstantial evidence and offer little evidence to prove that their injuries were caused by the alleged violent acts.[52] As a result, they are often unsuccessful in getting civil damages due to lack of sufficient evidence of domestic violence.[53]

§ 11.4 Criminal Liabilities

Chinese courts show a propensity in employing subjective justice in criminal cases involving domestic violence. Domestic violence crime charges can be brought against a victim's family members and anyone that has a custodial, guardianship, or cohabitation relationship with the victim.[54] The SPC called for lenient sentencing for domestic violence victims who injured or killed their abusers in self-defense and more severe punishment for abusers that caused severe injuries or death of their victims. The SPC contends that in cases where a domestic violence victim killed or injured their abuser in self-defense, lesser charges and lenient sentences could prevent domestic violence and diffuse "social conflicts."[55]

For example, in the Wong assault case, Wong's husband, Hu, had abused Wong for years. On the night of the incident, Hu brought his mistress, Yang, home. Wong objected. Hu then started beating Wong, first with a broomstick and then with a coat hanger. Wong tried to get away from Hu, but Hu went after her. Wong grabbed a paring knife to defend herself. Wong stabbed Hu in the chest during the parties' struggle. She immediately took Hu to the hospital. Hu died from the stabbing wound. The trial court found that Wong accidentally killed Hu in self-defense and that Wong took immediate action to save Hu. Considering Hu's history of domestic abuse and adultery and that Hu attacked Wong first, the trial court sentenced Wong for three years

51. FMTC 31.

52. Huang Haitao (黄海涛), Fan Jiating Baoli Fa Zuowei Caipan Guize Zhi Shixiaoxing Fenxi (反家庭暴力法作为裁判规则之实效性分析) [Analysis on the Effectiveness of the Anti-Domestic Violence Law as Adjudication Rules], Renmin Sifa (人民司法) [The People's Judicature] 2019(7):4–9, 5–6.

53. A study on 196 cases involving domestic violence in Beijing's intermediate courts found that the courts found sufficient evidence to establish allegations of domestic violence in about 10 percent of the 196 cases in the study. *Id.* at 7.

54. CDVTC 4.

55. FMTC 22.

imprisonment with five years of probation, which essentially allowed Wong to stay out of prison.[56] In the Zhu Chao Cun Abuse Case, Zhu and Liu were married in September 1998. In November 2011, Zhu and Liu were divorced. However, they continued living together after the divorce. Zhu had beaten Liu and injured her numerous times. One day, Zhu and Liu had an argument over their daughter's education. During the argument, Zhu beat Liu with a belt and denigrated Liu by claiming that their daughter was not his biological child, and Liu took a knife and killed herself. Zhu was held responsible for Liu's suicide and was sentenced to five years' imprisonment. The SPC explained that Zhu's long history of domestic violence was the direct cause of Liu's death and, thus, an aggravating factor in his sentencing.[57]

Lenient treatment is also extended to persons who defended their family members against abuse. Chang Lei, a man who killed his father with a cleaver when trying to protect his mother, was sentenced to three years of imprisonment with five years of probation. Chang's father was an alcoholic and had been verbally and physically abusive to Chang's mother and Chang for years. On August 29, 2012, Chang's father was drunk and started berating Chang's mother. Chang's mother went into Chang's room to hide from Chang's father. The father followed her into the room and started beating her and Chang. Then, Chang's father got a cleaver from the kitchen and threatened to kill Chang and Chang's mother. Chang grabbed the cleaver from his father. Chang's father then attacked Chang's mother and beat her viciously. Chang was enraged and struck his father with the cleaver repeatedly. Later, Chang took his father to the hospital and surrendered himself to the police. Chang's father died the next day. Chang received a lenient sentence because Chang and Chang's mother suffered severe domestic violence in his father's hands for years and Chang killed his father to defend his mother.[58]

In contrast, domestic abusers are given harsher sentences for violent crimes against family members. In Yu Zheng Ying murder case, Yu, who had beaten his daughter to death, received a life sentence and avoided the death penalty only because he cooperated with the law enforcement.[59] Similarly, in Xu Hong Tao Murder Case, Xu was executed for killing his father and for his abuse of his elderly parents. Xu's physical abuse of his parents was so severe that his mother was too afraid to go home. The SPC remarked that the death penalty was appropriate in Xu's case as Xu's heinous crime violated the moral standard and tradition of Chinese people.[60]

56. FMTC 22.
57. CDVTC 4.
58. DVTC 3.
59. DVTC 2.
60. DVTC 1.

§ 11.5 Challenges

11.5.1 Infrastructure Deficiencies

As China's civil protection order system is still under construction, there are institutional insufficiency and flaws that contribute to difficulty in assisting victims to obtain and enforce personal safety protection orders in China. Two major infrastructure deficiencies are the lack of supporting law enforcement mechanisms and the lack of a comprehensive, community-based service network.

11.5.1.1 Law Enforcement

Domestic violence victims' first contact with the justice system is usually law enforcement. The Chinese police force is not well equipped in handling domestic violence cases. First, the police force lacks training in handling domestic violence incidents.[61] More importantly, the police's ability to intervene and assist has severe institutional constraints. The Anti-Domestic Violence Law requires the police to dispatch officers, stop the violence, investigate, collect evidence, and examine injuries, but the Chinese police do not have any operational protocol to follow in handling domestic violence incidents. As a result, frontline police officers are often at a loss about what they can do and what they are expected to do. The most pressing issue is the lack of statutory authorities on whether the police can arrest an abuser at the scene of a domestic violence incident or under what circumstances arrests may be made.[62] Although there is not any express statutory basis for Chinese law enforcement to make arrests in domestic violence incidents, the SPC has suggested that it would be appropriate for the police to arrest an abuser. In a Typical Case, *Chen Personal Safety Protection Order Petition Case*, the wife, Chen, called the police when her husband brutally assaulted her at home. The police arrested the husband and detained him for ten days. While the husband was detained, the court conducted a hearing and quickly issued a personal safety protection order for Chen.[63]

---

61. Gao Yang (高扬), Jingcha Ganyu Jiating Baoli De Kunjing Yu Kexing Xing Duice—Yi Liaoning Diqu Shizheng Yanjiu Wei Jichu (警察干预家庭暴力的困境与可行性对策—以辽宁地区实证研究为基础) [The Predicament and Countermeasures of Police Interfering with Domestic Violence—Based on Empirical Study of Liaoning Province], Liaoning Jingcha Xueyuan Xuebao (辽宁警察学院学报), J. Liaoning Police Col., Jan. 2017, No. 1 (Ser. No. 101), 68–74, 68–71.

62. Wang Yiming, *supra* note 26, at 41–43.

63. PSPOTC 1.

11.5.1.2 Insufficient Community-Based Service Network

Last but not the least, the judicial system and law enforcement lack institutional service infrastructure needed for domestic violence victims and their minor children involved in domestic violence incidents. China has not yet established a comprehensive child protection system for emergency placement and care of at-risk children.[64] Community-based victim's rights advocacy and service groups are indispensable to implementing laws combatting domestic violence. "There is a broad consensus that the most effective response to domestic violence is a coordinated community response, in which the court's efforts are part of a continuum of services offered by the justice system and social services communities. Courts can best function as part of a coordinated community response when they are aware of the variety of specialized services provided by domestic violence agencies."[65] China has yet to integrate its various components—judicial system, law enforcement, state agencies, and community support groups—into a powerful anti-domestic violence coalition.

11.5.2 Policy Deficiencies

The civil aspects of China's domestic violence laws, and the performance of state actors, including the courts, law enforcement, and state agencies, have received some scorching criticism from legal scholars, rights activists, the media, and the public. The critics contend: (1) Chinese judicial system and law enforcement are indifferent to domestic violence victims, evidenced by reports of wife beating and killing after the victims had sought protection but were not given any; (2) state actors have suppressed the victims to maintain "social stability," evidenced by insignificant penalty on the abusers, and considerable number of cases resolved by mediation and reconciliation; (3) domestic violence victim's rights activism is suppressed.[66]

Under Chinese law, personal safety protection orders are temporary measures to enjoin abusers' violent acts and to create a "space" to shield victims from future violence.[67] Civil damages are not punitive penalties but compensation for loss caused by physical or emotional harms inflicted by the violence. In other words, the civil personal safety protection order system

64. Wang, *supra* note 26, at 41–43.

65. Michigan Judicial Institute, Domestic Violence Benchbook: a Guide to Civil & Criminal Proceedings (4th ed.).

66. For a review of scholarly studies on Chinese authorities' handling of domestic violence, see Jue Jiang, *The Family as a Stronghold of State Stability: Two Contradictions in China's Anti-Domestic Violence Efforts*, 33 Int'l J. L., Pol'y & Fam. 228–51 (2019).

67. Liu et al., *supra* note 39, at 12.

and civil damages are in its nature nonpunitive. Inasmuch, a civil protection order has limited punitive effects, and limited power in preventing domestic violence. Chinese civil justice system's inherent lack of punitive effects on domestic violence does not equate to institutional, systemic, and societal indifference to victims of domestic violence.

While "saving and repairing the marital relationship" or "maintaining social harmony" may be primarily for Chinese government's political interest, these policy goals are not contrary to the interests of Chinese families. Many Chinese litigants consider civil domestic violence matters as private family matters, and prefer mediation, settlement, or reconciliation for reasons such as privacy.[68] In the United States in the 1980s, criminalization and state intervention, including mandatory arrests and no-drop prosecutions, became the norm, driven by growing demands for meaningful state responses to domestic violence through punishing offenders and rescuing survivors.[69] Some advocates for domestic violence survivors have since found that not all survivors wanted to see their partners arrested and prosecuted. Mandatory state intervention policies are now recognized as potentially alienating women and men who wish to live free of violence, but on their own terms.[70] Some even argued that mandatory state intervention in domestic violence cases actually constitutes a form of state violence.[71] Similarly, many Chinese families prefer to live free of violence on their own terms, even if it means forgiving a family member's wrongdoing.[72] Thus, high rate of settlement, mediation, or withdrawal in cases concerning domestic violence does not necessarily indicate Chinese courts' suppression of victim rights.

The Chinese legal system faces significant institutional challenges in combatting domestic violence as the work has just begun. Unrealistic expectations, however, are not helpful. Failures in individual cases do not always indicate the failure of a system. The sad reality is that neither the law enforcement nor the judicial system can guarantee the safety of every domestic violence victim in China, or in the United States, or anywhere else in the world.

---

68. *See, e.g.*, Kimberly D. Bailey, *It's Complicated: Privacy and Domestic Violence*, 49 Am. Crim. L. Rev. 1777, 1794–1800 (2012).

69. Sabrina Balgamwalla, *Trafficking Rescue Initiatives as State Violence*, 122 Penn St. L. Rev. 171, 183 (2017).

70. *Id.* at 173–74. *See generally* Deborah Epstein, *Procedural Justice: Tempering the State's Response to Domestic Violence*, 43 Wm. & Mary L. Rev. 1843 (2002); Leigh Goodmark, *Autonomy Feminism: An Anti-Essentialist Critique of Mandatory Interventions in Domestic Violence Cases*, 37 Fla. St. U. L. Rev. 1 (2009); Tara Urs, *Coercive Feminism*, 46 Colum. Hum. Rts. L. Rev. 85 (2014).

71. Linda G. Mills, *Killing Her Softly: Intimate Abuse and the Violence of State Intervention*, 113 Harv. L. Rev. 550 (1999).

72. A local court reported that upon the petitioner's request, the court did not fine or detain a respondent for violation of a protection order; and the parties had no further domestic incidents. Liu et al., *supra* note 39, at 10.

Chapter 12

International Aspects of Chinese Family Law

Chinese family law is internationalized as China ascends on the world's stage. Throughout China's long history of emigration, Chinese diasporas settled around the world. In recent years, a significant number of Chinese diasporas are returning to China with their families. China has gradually become a destination of immigration as well. Skilled and unskilled workers across the globe are attracted by the opportunities offered by China's nonstop economic growth. While women from China constitute the major proportion of foreign wives in affluent Asian regions, such as South Korea, Taiwan, and Hong Kong, more and more foreign brides are marrying into China from its bordering countries and the former Soviet Union.[1] With the rapid globalization of the Chinese population, China has eased foreign litigants' access to Chinese courts, developed a coherent framework of conflicts of law, and adopted bilateral treaties and international conventions on civil matters to facilitate international cooperation in family matters.

China, now a leading force in globalization, has granted foreign litigants' easy access to its courts. Foreign litigants can commence actions and participate in legal proceedings in Chinese courts entirely through virtual means. For example, on February 24, 2020, Gao logged on the "Hebei Mobile Court," the Hebei Province court system's remote court access app, and appeared for the last hearing in his divorce action at the Sanhe City People's Court. Gao resides in the United States. Gao's spouse, Wang resides in China. Wang filed for divorce in November 2019, also through the Hebei Mobile Court app in the Sanhe court. The Sanhe court conducted mediation and evidentiary hearings in Gao and Wang's divorce action all through the mobile app. On

1. Elena Barabantseva, *Losing Self to Discover National Citizenship: Contestations over Parental Rights among the post-Soviet Foreign Wives in China*, Geopolitics (June 2019), https://doi.org/10.1080/14650045.2019.1620208.

February 24, 2020, the court held the last appearance and pronounced Gao and Wang's divorce judgment.[2] The ease and convenience of access to Chinese courts has expanded the reach of Chinese family law and judicial system across the globe.

China has made significant progress in developing a coherent system of conflicts of law in the past 30 years.[3] The PRC Civil Procedure Law (the "Civil Procedure Law")[4] and the PRC Law on the Applicable Laws to Foreign-Related Civil Relations (the "Law on Applicable Laws")[5] set forth four major sets of conflicts of law rules: (1) rules setting out the conditions under which a Chinese court will have jurisdiction to hear a dispute containing foreign-related elements; (2) once jurisdiction is confirmed, rules to identify the laws of a country that will be applied to solve the dispute; (3) rules to determine the circumstances in which a foreign court judgment will be recognized and, if necessary, enforced; and (4) special civil procedure rules for proceedings concerning foreign-related matters.

Bilateral and international treaties are now an integral component of Chinese family law. China is a member country of the Hague Conference on Private International Law, and a signatory of the Hauge Convention on the Service Abroad of Judicial and Extrajudicial Documents in Civil or Commercial Matters, Convention on the Taking of Evidence Abroad in Civil or Commercial Matters, and Convention on Protection of Children and Co-operation in Respect of Intercountry Adoption.[6] China's two Special Administrative Regions, Hong Kong and Macao, are also signatories of the Hague Convention on the Civil Aspects of International Child Abduction.[7] China has also entered bilateral treaties with many countries on judicial assistance, cooperation in civil and commercial matters, and recognition and/or enforcement of foreign judgments.[8]

2. Sanhe Shi Renmin Fayuan (三河市人民法院) [Sanhe City People's Court], Sanhe Fayuan "San Ge Ling" Quan Liucheng Wangshang Shenli Yiqi Kuaguo Lihun An (三河法院 "三个零" 全流程网上审理一起跨国离婚案) [Sanhe Court Heard a Cross-border Divorce Case Using "Three Zero" Online Procedure Entirely] (Feb. 27, 2020), http://shsfy.chinacourt.gov.cn/article/detail/2020/02/id/5299650.shtml.

3. Qingkun Xu, *The Codification of Conflicts Law in China: A Long Way to Go*, 65 Am. J. Comp. L. 919, 920 (2017).

4. Zhonghua Renmin Gonghe Guo Minshi Susong Fa (中华人民共和国民事诉讼法) [The People's Republic of China Civil Procedure Law] (promulgated Apr. 1, 1991, amended on Oct. 28, 2007, Aug. 31, 2012, and June 27, 2017).

5. Zhonghua Renmin Gonghe Guo Shewai Minshi Guanxi Falü Shiyong Fa (中华人民共和国涉外民事关系法律适用法) [The People's Republic of China Law on the Applicable Laws to Foreign-Related Civil Relations] (promulgated on Oct. 28, 2010, effective from Apr. 1, 2011).

6. HCCH Authorities (Per Party), https://www.hcch.net/en/states/authorities.

7. *Id.*

8. The Ministry of Foreign Affairs maintains a database of bilateral and multilateral treaties: http://treaty.mfa.gov.cn/Treaty/web/index.jsp.

§ 12.1 Foreign-Related Civil Matters

In civil cases involving some foreign elements, Chinese courts must first decide whether a case is a "foreign-related civil matter" (*shewai minshi anjian*) that concerns any foreign-related civil relationship (*shewai minshi guanxi*). A civil relationship is a foreign-related civil relationship when (1) at least one party is a foreign national or stateless person; or (2) at least one party's habitual residence is outside the territory of the PRC; or (3) the subject matter is outside the territory of the PRC; or (4) the legal facts that created, changed, or terminated the civil relationship in question occurred outside the territory of the PRC; or (5) there are any other foreign-related circumstances.[9]

A person's habitual residence is the place where the person intends to be his/her home and has continuously lived for more than one year at the time of the creation, change, or termination of a foreign-related civil relationship. However, if a person's presence at a place is only for medical treatment, oversea employment, or governmental affairs, such place is not the person's habitual residence regardless, even if the person's presence at such place is for more than a year.[10] Chinese courts often rely on a party's Chinese border entry and exit records to determine whether their habitual residence is in China. For example, a Guangxi court found a defendant father's habitual residence was in China because his Chinese border entry and exit records showed that the longest period when he had continuously lived in Taiwan was 11 months and 25 days.[11] Similarly, in a divorce action, the Chinese court found the defendant's habitual residence was in China as his Chinese border entry and exit records indicated that he had never continuously lived outside of China for more than a year.[12]

If a matter is not a foreign-related civil matter despite that it involves some foreign elements, Chinese courts need not to consider special provisions concerning foreign-related matters. For instance, in *Tang Fei v. Xing Shanhu*, the plaintiff wife brought the divorce action in the county where she resided, arguing that the defendant resided in the United States and therefore the court at the place of her habitual residence should have jurisdiction over the

9. Zuigao Renmin Fayuan Guanyu Shiyong Zhonghua Renmin Gonghe Guo Shewai Minshi Guanxi Falü Shiyong Fa Ruogan Wenti De Jieshi (Yi) (关于适用《中华人民共和国涉外民事关系法律适用法》若干问题的解释(一)) [the Supreme People's Court Interpretations on Some Issues Concerning the Application of the People's Republic of China Law of the Applicable Laws to Foreign-Related Civil Relations (I)] (promulgated by the Sup. People's Ct., Dec. 10, 2012, amended and effective Dec. 23, 2020) 2021 Sup. People's Ct. Gaz. 10 [hereinafter the "Applicable Laws Interpretations"] art. 1.

10. Civil Procedure Law Interpretations art. 4.

11. (2016) Gui 03 Min Zhong 2111 Hao ((2016) 桂03民终2111号).

12. (2019) Liao 06 Min Xia 18 Hao ((2019) 辽06民辖18号); *see also* (2019) Liao 06 Min Xia 19 Hao ((2019) 辽06民辖19号).

parties' divorce. The SPC found that the defendant, Xing Shanhu, traveled between China and the United States frequently, and his habitual residence remained in China despite his extended periods of stay in the United States. Thus, the SPC held that the divorce between Tang and Xing was not a foreign-related matter and the special jurisdiction rule that permits a plaintiff to bring an action at the place of the plaintiff's habitual residence in a foreign-related civil matter did not apply. The SPC ordered the divorce action to be transferred to the court at the defendant's habitual residence pursuant to the general jurisdictional rules applicable to domestic civil matters.[13]

If a matter is a foreign-related civil matter, Chinese courts must apply special rules of jurisdiction, choice of law, and enforcement designed for foreign-related matters. For instance, in divorce actions between a Chinese national and a non-Chinese national, Chinese courts must apply laws governing foreign-related matters to determine whether the court has proper jurisdiction, and whether the laws of China or another country should apply, as divorces between a Chinese citizen and a foreign national are foreign-related civil matters. In addition, Chinese courts must follow special civil procedural rules governing civil actions concerning foreign-related civil matters in these divorce actions between Chinese citizens and foreigners.

§ 12.2 Jurisdiction

In foreign-related civil matters concerning marriage and family, Chinese courts' jurisdiction can be seized based on either party's habitual residence,[14] either party's Chinese nationality,[15] location of disputed property in China,[16] or the parties' choice of forum in property disputes.[17] Specifically, Chinese courts take jurisdiction in foreign-related family matter disputes under the following circumstances:

(1) Where one party's habitual residence is in China, one party resides outside of China;[18]
(2) Where both parties are Chinese nationals, reside outside of China permanently, and the court of the foreign country where both parties habitually reside has declined jurisdiction over the parties' divorce;[19]

13. (2020) Zui Gao Fa Min Xia 83 Hao ((2020) 最高法民辖83号).
14. Civil Procedure Law arts. 17, 21, 22.
15. Civil Procedure Law Interpretations arts. 13, 14.
16. Civil Procedure Law art. 33.
17. *Id.* art. 34. *See also* Civil Procedure Law Interpretations art. 529.
18. Civil Procedure Law arts. 17, 22(1).
19. Civil Procedure Law Interpretations arts. 13, 14.

(3) Where China is the habitual residence of a child or ward under guardianship;[20]
(4) Where the parties' assets subject to a post-divorce property division action are located in China;[21]
(5) Where the real property in dispute is located in China;[22]
(6) Where China is a decedent's habitual residence at the time of death or where the majority of the decedent's estate is located;[23] or
(7) Where the parties designated Chinese courts as the forum by written agreement in property disputes.[24]

Chinese courts may decline jurisdiction for *forum non conveniens*.[25] Chinese courts may also retain jurisdiction in parallel proceedings when it is deemed appropriate,[26] especially in divorce actions where one party is a Chinese citizen living abroad and another party is a Chinese citizen residing in China.[27]

12.2.1 Territorial Jurisdiction

Generally, Chinese courts have personal jurisdiction over a person whose habitual residence is within the territory of the PRC in any legal actions concerning personal relations, such as marriage and parentage.[28] However, Chinese courts' jurisdiction deviates from the general rules in certain foreign-related family matters involving non-Chinese nationals or Chinese nationals who do not reside in China.

12.2.1.1 Habitual Residence

Chinese courts may take jurisdiction in foreign-related family matters when either the defendant or the plaintiff resides in China. However, if the plaintiff resides in China but the defendant does not, Chinese courts' jurisdiction is limited to actions concerning personal status, whereas Chinese courts have broad jurisdiction in actions concerning personal status as well as property if the defendant's habitual residence is in China but the plaintiff's habitual residence is outside of China.

If a defendant resides in China, the Chinese court at the place where the defendant's household registration or habitual residence is located has

20. *Id.* art. 10.
21. *Id.* art. 17.
22. Civil Procedure Law art. 33(1).
23. *Id.* art. 33(3).
24. *Id.* art. 34, and Civil Procedure Law Interpretations art. 34.
25. Civil Procedure Law Interpretations art. 530.
26. *Id.* art. 531 para. 1.
27. *Id.* art. 15.
28. Civil Procedure Law arts. 17, 21, 22.

jurisdiction in actions concerning personal status and property disputes.[29] For example, in *Huang v. Zhuo*, the plaintiff husband's habitual residence was New York and the defendant wife's habitual residence was Fuzhou. Therefore, the Fuzhou court held that based on the defendant wife's habitual residence in Fuzhou it had proper jurisdiction over the parties' divorce as well as their financial disputes.[30]

If a Chinese court's jurisdiction is acquired based on the plaintiff's habitual residence in China, the court's jurisdiction is limited to the parties' personal status, such as divorce or child custody.[31] For instance, in *Yang v. AMI*, the husband was a citizen of the Republic of Benin living in Benin, whereas the wife maintained her household registration and lived in Mei County with the parties' daughter. Since the defendant husband resided outside of China, the Mei County People's Court, as the court of the plaintiff wife's habitual residence, had personal jurisdiction to adjudicate the parties' divorce and ancillary personal status issues, such as child custody and support.[32]

As Chinese courts may exercise jurisdiction based on a plaintiff's habitual residence when the defendant resides outside of China, a Chinese court at the place of the plaintiff's habitual residence may determine and enforce filial support, spousal support, and child support against an obligor defendant that resides outside of China.[33] For instance, in *Liu v. Wong*, based on her habitual residence in Guangdong a Guangdong court took jurisdiction in a mother's action for child support against a father, who lived in Malaysia. The court entered a default child support order against the father.[34]

Some Chinese courts took jurisdiction in some filial support actions brought by Chinese parents against their adult children who reside outside of China. For instance, in the *Support Matter of Deng Kuanling*, the mother, Deng Kuanling resided in Guangdong and her son resided in Macao. The Guangdong court found that it had proper jurisdiction to make a filial support order for the mother because the plaintiff mother's habitual residence was in Guangdong.[35] In some instances, such as in *Yan v. Yan*, Chinese courts' imposition of jurisdiction could be overreaching. In the *Yan* case, an elderly father sued for filial support in Chongqing against his daughter, who lived in California. At the time of the filial support proceeding, the father had been living in the United States for more than six years. However, the father alleged that

29. *Id.* arts. 17, 21.
30. (2015) Gu Min Chu Zi Di 2457 Hao ((2015) 鼓民初字第2457号).
31. Civil Procedure Law art. 22.
32. (2014) Mei Xian Fa Min Yi Chu Zi Di 169 Hao ((2014) 梅县法民一初字第169号).
33. Civil Procedure Law Interpretations art. 9.
34. (2016) Yue 0606 Min Chu 13061 Hao ((2016) 粤0606民初13061号).
35. (2020) Yue 06 Min Zhong 19 Hao ((2020) 粤06民终19号).

his permanent residency in the United States would expire in four years, and he would eventually have to return to China when his U.S. permanent residency expired. The daughter objected to the Chongqing court's jurisdiction on the ground that neither party's habitual residence was in China. Nevertheless, the Chongqing court rejected the daughter's jurisdictional objection and held that Chongqing was the father's habitual residence and the place of his household registration and consequently the Chongqing courts had proper jurisdiction to determine and enforce filial support for the father.[36]

12.2.1.2 Chinese Nationals Living Abroad: Common Nationality

Chinese courts have jurisdiction in divorce actions where one party habitually resides in China and the other party resides overseas, whether permanently or temporarily, as Chinese courts' jurisdiction is based on either party's habitual residence in actions concerning personal status. Thus, a divorce action may be brought by either party in the Chinese court at the place where one party's habitual residence is in China if the other party is living abroad.[37] As in *Chen v. Huang*, where the parties had been separated for more than three years after the wife left the husband in China and immigrated to New York, the Chinese court took jurisdiction in the divorce action brought by the husband in China because the husband's habitual residence was in China.[38]

Chinese courts may take jurisdiction in divorce actions based on the parties' common Chinese nationality when both parties are living abroad. Whether Chinese courts may take jurisdiction based on the parties' common Chinese nationality depends on the parties' overseas residency status. Generally, Chinese courts retain jurisdiction over Chinese nationals who maintain their habitual residence in China and are living abroad temporarily, whereas Chinese courts have limited jurisdictional power over *huaqiao*,[39] Chinese diasporas who have settled and acquire legal permanent residency in their host countries.

---

36. (2014) Zhong Qu Fa Min Chu Zi Di 09494 Hao ((2014) 中区法民初字第09494号).

37. Civil Procedure Law Interpretations art. 15.

38. (2017) Yue 0704 Min Chu 642 Hao ((2017) 粤0704民初642号).

39. *Huaqiao* are defined as oversea Chinese citizens who have acquired legal long-term or permanent residency in a foreign country and have continuously resided abroad for over two years; and Chinese citizens who have not yet acquired legal long-term or permanent residency in a foreign country but have lived in a foreign country legally for over five years. Chinese students and workers who are studying or working overseas are not *huaqiao*. *See* Guowu Yuan Qiaowu Bangongshi Guanyu Jieding Huaqiao Waiji Huaren Guiqiao Qiaojuan Shenfen De Guiding (Guo Qiao Fa [2009] 5 Hao) (国务院侨务办公室关于界定华侨外籍华人归侨侨眷身份的规定 (国侨发 [2009] 5号) [State Council Oversea Chinese Office Provisions Concerning Status Definition of Oversea Chinese, Chinese Foreign Nationals, Returning Oversea Chinese and Family Members of Oversea Chinese (Guo Qiao Fa [2009] 5 Hao)].

If both parties in a divorce action are living abroad temporarily, the Chinese court at the place where either party last resided may exercise jurisdiction over the parties' divorce.[40] In such cases, Chinese courts' jurisdiction hinges on that the parties' habitual residence is in China and their residency abroad is only temporary. Thus, the Wuhai Intermediate People's Court affirmed the lower court decision to take jurisdiction in a divorce action where both parties were attending school in Japan as international students. The court found that both parties' residence in Japan was temporary, and the plaintiff's habitual residence was in Wuhan. Thus, the court held that the Wuhai courts had jurisdiction over the parties' divorce.[41]

Chinese courts may take jurisdiction in divorce actions where both parties are Chinese nationals living abroad with foreign permanent residency (*huaqiao*) if the courts of the country where they reside have declined jurisdiction.[42] However, Chinese courts' jurisdiction is predicated on the courts of the country where the parties reside having declined jurisdiction. To illustrate: in *Wang v. Tian*, the Chinese court dismissed the divorce action between two Chinese nationals who had obtained permanent residency in Germany because the German courts had not declined jurisdiction.[43] Similarly, in *Hu v. Yang*, the Shenzhen Intermediate People's Court affirmed the lower court's dismissal of a husband's suit for a declaratory judgment to declare the marriage void for lack of jurisdiction in that both parties' habitual residence was in Hong Kong. The court held that the Shenzhen courts can only take jurisdiction based on the parties' common nationality when Hong Kong courts have declined jurisdiction.[44]

12.2.1.3 Guardianship: The Ward's Habitual Residence

The court at the place of a ward's habitual residence may take jurisdiction over appointment or change of guardianship.[45] In other words, guardianship disputes may be brought in the place of a minor child's habitual residence in China. Thus, a Shanghai court heard two grandparents' dispute over the guardianship of their grandson, whose habitual residence was in Shanghai, although he was a Canadian citizen and lived in Canada intermittently.[46] In *P v. W*, the Beijing court held that it had jurisdiction to hear the parents' dispute over their child's guardianship in that the child had lived in Beijing for over a year and Beijing had become her habitual residence. The parents, P and

40. Civil Procedure Law Interpretations art. 16.
41. (2016) E 01 Min Xia Zhong 166 Hao ((2016) 鄂01民辖终166号).
42. Civil Procedure Law Interpretations arts. 13, 14.
43. (2018) Shan 0103 Min Chu 86 Hao ((2018) 陕0103民初86号).
44. (2017) Yue 03 Min Zhong 8694 Hao ((2017) 粤03民终8694号).
45. Civil Procedure Law Interpretations art. 10.
46. (2015) Min Min Yi (Min) Te Zi Di 39 Hao ((2015) 闵民一（民）特字第39号).

W, were German citizens of Chinese origin. The child was a German citizen born in Germany. The parents were never married to each other. The child was born in 2006 in Germany and had lived in Germany until 2012. The father moved in with the mother and the child in 2009 and lived with them in Germany until 2011. The mother and the child relocated to Beijing in 2012 after the German court awarded the mother sole guardianship of the child. In May 2016, the mother brought an action in Beijing for an order to affirm her sole guardianship of the child and for child support from the father. The father objected to the Chinese court's jurisdiction on the ground that neither party or the child were Chinese nationals and had no habitual residence in China. The Beijing No. 1 Intermediate Court affirmed the lower court's decision to retain jurisdiction, holding that the Beijing court had proper jurisdiction in the parents' guardianship dispute as the child had been continuously living in Beijing for more than four years and Beijing was her habitual residence.[47]

Chinese courts usually take jurisdiction over guardianship and custody issues concerning a child whose parents' divorce is heard in a Chinese court even if the child's habitual residence is not in China, unless there are compelling reasons, such as *forum non conveniens*, for the court to decline jurisdiction. For example, in *Lu v. Sun*, the father lived in China and the mother lived in California with their five-year-old daughter. The father brought a divorce action in China based on his habitual residence. The mother appeared in the Chinese court and sought custody of the parties' child and child support. The Chinese court granted the divorce and ordered child support and custody of the child to the mother although the child's habitual residence was in California.[48] Similarly, the Beijing court awarded child custody and support to the mother in *Zhang v. Chu*, where the mother concealed her pregnancy and the birth of the parties' child in the parties' divorce action in the Beijing court. During the divorce action, the mother moved to the United States, gave birth to the child in New York, and resided in New York with the child after the child's birth. The father had always resided in Beijing and learned about his child after the divorce action the Beijing court had ended. The mother brought a post-judgment action against the father for custody and support in the Beijing court. The Beijing court exercised continuing jurisdiction in the post-divorce action and entered a child custody and support order. The court held that it was in the child's best interest to award the mother residential custody of the child because the child had resided in the United States with the mother for her life and the mother had been her sole caregiver.[49]

47. (2016) Jing 01 Min Xia Zhong 288 Hao ((2016) 京01民辖终288号).
48. (2016) Wan 0123 Min Chu 6 Hao ((2016) 皖0123民初6号).
49. (2017) Jing 0105 Min Chu 59332 Hao ((2017) 京0105民初59332号).

12.2.1.4 Foreign Nationals

Chinese law does not require Chinese courts to decline jurisdiction in family matters concerning foreign nationals who reside in China. Nor does it require Chinese courts to take jurisdiction in these matters. Some provincial High People's Courts, such as Shanghai High People's Court, implemented local jurisdictional rules that restrict foreign nationals' access to Chinese courts' jurisdiction in foreign-related family matters. Chinese courts generally are reluctant to take jurisdiction over contested family matter disputes between non-Chinese nationals despite that they live in China. For instance, pursuant to the Shanghai High People's Court rules, Shanghai courts must decline jurisdiction in divorce actions between non-Chinese nationals who reside in China but did not register their marriage in China, unless the parties agree to submit to Shanghai courts' jurisdiction.[50] In the *Matter of Yirguenda Shawhailu*, a court in Zhejiang Province rejected a divorce action brought by an Ethiopian citizen, who resided in Zhejiang, for lack of jurisdiction, finding that neither party's habitual residence was within the geographic area under the court's jurisdiction. The court did not address whether Shawhailu could file for a divorce after he had established his habitual residence in Zhejiang.[51] In *Zheng v. Wang*, the Shenyang courts declined to take jurisdiction in a divorce action between two German nationals residing in Shenyang, indicating that Chinese courts generally do not take jurisdiction over family disputes between foreign nationals living in China unless the parties agree to submit to Chinese courts' jurisdiction.[52]

12.2.2 Exclusive Jurisdiction

Chinese courts have exclusive subject matters jurisdiction in disputes concerning (1) real properties located in China[53] and (2) the estate of a decedent whose habitual residence at the time of the death is in China or the majority of whose estate is in China.[54]

12.2.2.1 Real Property

Chinese law adopted the rules of the *lex situs* that a real property is governed by the courts and the law of the country in which the property is situated. The

50. Shanghai Shi Gaoji Renmin Fayuan Yinfa Lian Wenti Jieda De Tongzhi (上海市高级人民法院关于印发《立案问题解答》的通知) [Shanghai City High People's Court's Notice on the Publication of Case Acceptance Questions and Answers] Hu Gao Fa Li (2001) 1 Hao (沪高法立(2011)1号).

51. (2017) Zhe 0702 Min Chu 16568 Hao ((2017) 浙0702民初16568号).

52. (2017) Liao 01 Min Zhong 11236 Hao ((2017) 辽01民终11236号).

53. Civil Procedure Law art. 33(1).

54. *Id.* art. 33(3).

Chinese court at the place where a real estate is located has *in rem* jurisdiction over disputes concerning a real property located in China.[55] Thus, in *Huang v. Cui*, the Chinese court had proper jurisdiction to determine the parties' respective share in the real properties that they acquired during their cohabitation as the disputed real properties were in China although neither party lived in China.[56]

Chinese courts at the place where the major assets are located have jurisdiction in post-judgment property disputes over marital assets, particularly real property, that have not been distributed by foreign courts.[57] For example, in *Wang v. Xue*, the parties were divorced in Australia. However, the Australian court did not make any decision regarding their properties in Shanghai. After the divorce, Wang brought a post-judgment property dispute action in the Shanghai court for division of the parties' movable and immovable properties located in Shanghai. The Shanghai court divided the properties between Wang and Xue.[58] Similarly, in *Lu v. Wang*, a Texas court distributed the parties' marital property in Texas but did not distribute three real estate properties that the parties owned in China. Lu brought a post-divorce property dispute action in Shanghai where the parties resided after their divorce in Texas. The Shanghai court distributed the properties between the parties.[59]

Disputes over distribution of marital joint real property incidental to divorces are not real estate disputes but rather disputes over marital relations and personal status. Therefore, a Chinese court's jurisdiction over property distribution in connection with a divorce is determined by either party's habitual residence, but not by the location of the disputed real property.[60] As such, Chinese courts may retain jurisdiction over property located outside of China in divorce actions brought in Chinese courts. In practice, however, Chinese courts often decline to take jurisdiction over foreign real properties mostly due to *forum non conveniens* or lack of competent evidence.

12.2.2.2 Inheritance Disputes

Inheritance disputes are under the jurisdiction of the court at the place of a decedent's residence at the time of the death or the court at the place where most of the decedent's estate is located.[61] For example, in *the Matter of Lei*, the decedent passed away in 1976 in the Philippines, where he had lived for many years before his death. The property in dispute was a family home that

---

55. *Id.* art. 33(1).
56. (2020) Ji Min Zhong 225 Hao ((2020) 吉民终225号).
57. Civil Procedure Law Interpretations art. 17.
58. (2017) Hu 0112 Min Chu 33072 Hao ((2017) 沪0112民初33072号).
59. (2017) Hu 0109 Min Chu 1880 Hao ((2017) 沪0109民初1880号).
60. (2020) Zui Gao Fa Min Xia 14 Hao ((2020) 最高法民辖14号).
61. Civil Procedure Law art. 33(3).

the decedent owned in Xiamen, Fujian Province. There was no other property in the decedent's estate. Since the only asset in the decedent's estate was the family home in Xiamen, China, the Xiamen court had jurisdiction of the inheritance dispute between the decedent's children over the home in Xiamen.[62]

12.2.3 Choice of Forum

The Civil Procedure Law provides that parties to a foreign-related contract or any property disputes may, by mutual agreement, choose a foreign country court to adjudicate the dispute, provided that the parties' choice of forum does not violate Chinese courts' exclusive jurisdiction.[63] Choice of forum clauses in divorce agreements, prenuptial agreements, or any marital agreements concerning property are enforceable under Chinese law.

However, parties may not designate a chosen jurisdiction in matters concerning personal status, such as divorce or child custody. Chinese law only permits parties' choice of forum in property disputes arising from cohabitation, dissolution of marriage, or termination of adoption.[64] For example, in *Mao v. Duan*, the parties agreed in their divorce settlement agreement that the Yunyan District People's Court should have jurisdiction over any disputes arising from the parties' divorce settlement agreement. After the divorce, the husband brought a post-divorce property dispute action in the Yunyan District People's Court. The Yunyan District People's Court declined jurisdiction, finding that the parties' choice of forum clause was unenforceable because it was part of the parties' divorce agreement that contained provisions related to the parties' personal relations and status, including the parties' marriage, child custody, visitation, and privacy. The appellate court, the Guiyang City Intermediate People's Court, reversed the Yunyan district court's ruling, and held that the choice of forum clause in the parties' divorce agreement was enforceable in the post-divorce property dispute action in that the action was a property dispute and did not involve claims related to personal relations or status.[65] Similarly, in a post-divorce property dispute action, the Changsha City Intermediate People's Court reversed the lower court's decision and upheld the parties' choice of forum clause in their divorce settlement agreement.[66]

In property disputes in connection with cohabitation or divorce, parties may, by written agreement, select the courts where either party resides; where the disputed property is located; or where an agreement concerning the

62. (2014) Xia Min Zhong Zi Di 1059 Hao ((2014) 厦民终字第1059号).
63. Civil Procedure Law art. 34. *See also* Civil Procedure Law Interpretations art. 529.
64. Civil Procedure Law Interpretations art. 34, and Civil Procedure Law art. 34.
65. (2021) Qian 01 Min Xiao 25 Hao ((2021) 黔01民辖25号).
66. (2021) Xiang 01 Min Xia Zhong 251 Hao ((2021) 湘01民辖终251号).

cohabitation, marriage, or adoption was entered or performed, provided that that the parties' choice of forum conforms with Chinese courts' hierarchical jurisdiction and exclusive jurisdiction.[67] For instance, in *Ma v. Bao*, the Shengyang City Intermediate People's Court upheld the parties' choice of forum clause in their postnuptial agreement on the wife's support in the event of a divorce. The court found that the parties' choice of forum clause designated exclusive jurisdiction to the courts at the place of the wife's residence and that such clause did not violate any law and was therefore enforceable.[68]

Choice of forum agreements may not contradict Chinese courts' exclusive jurisdiction. Therefore, a decedent's heirs and/or testamentary beneficiaries may not choose foreign courts to adjudicate any dispute over the decedent's properties in China if the decedent's last residence was in China or the property in dispute is located in China, as actions concerning succession are under the exclusive jurisdiction of the court at the place of the decedent's residence at the time of their death or at the place where most of the estate is located.[69]

A choice of forum clause is unenforceable if it is inconsistent with the courts' hierarchical jurisdiction. For instance, in *Ma v. Zhang*, the parties agreed that any disputes related to the parties' Agreement of Support and Testamentary Gift should be heard in the Jinan Intermediate People's Court. The Jinan Intermediate People's Court found that the parties' dispute was not within intermediate courts' hierarchical jurisdiction and thus the choice of forum clause was not enforceable. Thus, the Jianan Intermediate People's Court transferred the case to a lower court within its jurisdiction.[70]

Choice of forum agreements must be in writing and unambiguous. If it is not possible to ascertain which court should have jurisdiction under a choice of forum agreement because the agreement is too ambiguous or otherwise flawed, the jurisdiction will be determined in accordance with the relevant provisions of the Civil Procedure Law.[71] For example, in *Chen v. Jian*, Chen and Jian were divorced in Guangzhou. The parties' divorce agreement provided that Jian must transfer the parties' home in Guangzhou to Chen, and either party may bring an action of property dispute at "the present place." When Chen sued Jian for breach of the divorce agreement in Chongqing, the Chongqing Court held that phrase "the current place" was too vague, and as a result, the party's choice of forum clause was unenforceable. The court ruled that the court of the place where the defendant resided had jurisdiction over the parties' dispute.[72]

---

67. Civil Procedure Law Interpretations art. 34, and Civil Procedure Law art. 34.
68. (2021) Liao 01 Min Xia Zhong 360 Hao ((2021) 辽01民辖终360号).
69. Civil Procedure Law art. 33(3).
70. (2019) Lu 01 Min Xia Zhang 548 Hao ((2019) 鲁01民辖终548号).
71. Civil Procedure Law Interpretations art. 30.
72. (2018) Yu Min Xia 64 Hao ((2018) 渝民辖64号).

12.2.4 Parallel Proceedings

China's long-held approach to parallel proceedings is that a Chinese court may accept a case if one party brings an action in a Chinese court while the other party has brought a suit on the same dispute in a foreign court.[73] If both parties are Chinese citizens residing in a foreign country, and one party brings a divorce action in the foreign country where he/she resides, and the other party brings a divorce action in China, the Chinese court may retain jurisdiction over the parties' divorce.[74] Chinese courts are not required to decline jurisdiction unless a foreign court has rendered a final judgment and the judgment has been recognized in China.[75]

Chinese courts' retention of jurisdiction in parallel divorce proceedings is constrained by Chinese courts' limited jurisdiction over nonresident Chinese nationals or non-Chinese nationals. Chinese courts can only take jurisdictions in divorce actions when at least one party's residence abroad is temporary and his/her habitual residence remains in China, or when the courts of the country of the parties' permanent residence have declined jurisdiction. *Wang v. Lin* illustrates Chinese courts' handling of parallel divorce actions. In *Wang v. Lin*, the husband was a Canadian citizen, the wife was a Chinese citizen and a permanent resident of Canada. Both parties had lived in Canada with their children as a family for years. The marital assets were in Canada. A month after the wife brought a divorce action in Canada, the husband commenced divorce action in Fuzhuo, China, where the wife resided before she immigrated to Canada. The Fuzhou court dismissed the husband's action for lack of jurisdiction. The court held that on principle, a divorce action between two parties who do not reside in China must first be brought in the country where the parties reside, and Chinese courts that do not have jurisdiction before the courts in the country of the parties' habitual residence have declined to exercise jurisdiction. Thus, the Fuzhou court dismissed the divorce action brought by the husband while the parties' Canadian divorce action was pending.[76] Clearly, Chinese courts do not encourage forum shopping.

12.2.5 *Forum Non Conveniens*

Chinese courts may decline jurisdiction for *forum non conveniens*. A Chinese court may dismiss an action and defer jurisdiction to a foreign court if all of the following criteria are met: (1) the defendant requests that the case be heard in a more convenient foreign country court with proper jurisdiction,

73. Civil Procedure Law Interpretations art. 531 para. 1.
74. *Id.* art. 15.
75. *Id.* art. 531 para. 2.
76. (2015) Gu Min Chu Zi Di 1711 Hao ((2015) 鼓民初字第1711号).

or has made other jurisdictional objections; (2) the parties do not have any agreement that Chinese courts should have jurisdiction; (3) Chinese courts do not have exclusive jurisdiction; (4) the dispute does not concern the interests of the Chinese state or a Chinese citizen, legal person, or other organization; (5) the material facts of the dispute did not occur in China, Chinese law does not apply, and a Chinese court will have great difficulties in adjudicating the factual and legal issues of the case; and (6) a foreign country's courts have proper jurisdiction, and is a more convenient forum.[77]

When it is evident that a custody dispute should be heard in the courts of the foreign country that is a minor child's habitual residence and home, Chinese courts have consistently declined jurisdiction for *forum non conveniens*. For example, in *T v. Peng*, the Guangzhou court dismissed the father's action for visitation on the ground of *forum non conveniens* because the child's habitual residence was in Michigan and Michigan courts were clearly the most appropriate forum to hear and determine custody and visitation issues related to the child. In this case, the parents were divorced in Guangzhou in 2017. The Guangzhou court awarded the mother residential custody of the child, and weekly visitation for the father. After the divorce, the father moved to California and the mother relocated to Michigan in 2018. The father could not have his weekly visits with the child after both parties moved to the United States. The father brought an action to enforce his visitation right in the Guangzhou court, where the initial custody and visitation orders were issued. The court dismissed the father's action on the ground of *forum non conveniens*, and ruled that Michigan, instead of Guangzhou, had proper jurisdiction to hear the custody and visitation issues concerning the child in that the child had been living in Michigan for over a year and her habitual residence was now in Michigan. The father appealed. On the appeal, the Guangzhou City Intermediate Court affirmed the lower court's decision to dismiss the action.[78]

Similarly, in *Zhen v. Wang*, the Shenyang City Intermediate Court affirmed the lower court's decision to dismiss the divorce action brought by the mother as the child's habitual residence was in Germany. Zhen and Wang immigrated from China to Germany and were married in Germany in 2001. They had a daughter born in 2011 in Germany. The family's home was in Germany. The parents and the child were all German citizens. The family went to Shenyang in 2016 and planned to stay there for a year. The mother brought a divorce action in Shenyang at the end of the family's stay and wanted to remain in China with the child. The father objected to the Shenyang court's jurisdiction and sought a dismissal of the action. He argued that Germany was a more

77. Civil Procedure Law Interpretations art. 530.

78. (2020) Yue 0104 Min Chu 14065 Hao ((2020) 粤0104民初14065号).

appropriate and convenient jurisdiction. The court of first instance granted the father's request for dismissal and held *inter alia* that Germany, which was the child's habitual residence and home country, was the most appropriate jurisdiction for the protection of the child's well-being. The Shenyang City Intermediate Court affirmed the lower court's decision on appeal.[79]

Chinese courts also apply the doctrine of *forum non conveniens* in property disputes. In *Hong v. Ling*, the defendant husband sought dismissal of a post-divorce property dispute action brought by the wife in Shanghai for *forum non conveniens*. The Shanghai court dismissed the action on *forum non conveniens* grounds, finding that Taiwan was a more convenient forum because most of the disputed properties were in Hong Kong and Taiwan, where both parties' habitual residence was located and where their divorce was settled and granted.[80]

Chinese courts follow the statutory criteria rigorously when determining *forum non conveniens*, and do not easily defer jurisdiction to another forum. In *M v. S*, the Nanjing City Intermediate People's Court rejected a wife's request to defer its jurisdiction to the Reading Crown Court in England. The wife argued that England was a more convenient jurisdiction as the parties' minor children resided in England with the wife, and the parties' marital properties were all in England, and the English court had proper jurisdiction over child custody and support, spousal maintenance, and marital property. The Nanjing court held that the divorce action should not be dismissed on *forum non conveniens* grounds because the action was properly brought by the plaintiff husband in Nanjing where he was a habitual resident, and it was not burdensome for the Nanjing court to hear the case, as the husband only sought a divorce without any auxiliary relief.[81] *Zhu v. Chen* is another example. Chen, the defendant husband objected to the Suzhou court's jurisdiction on *forum non conveniens* ground, arguing that Taiwan was a more appropriate jurisdiction because he and the parties' child both resided in Taiwan. The court rejected his objection in that the wife was a Chinese citizen and her habitual residence was in Suzhou.[82]

12.2.6 The Hague Convention on International Child Abduction

The Hague Convention on the Civil Aspects of International Child Abduction (the "Hague Abduction Convention" or "Abduction Convention") was created to prevent international parental child abduction by felicitating international corporation in securing prompt return of children who are wrongfully

79. (2017) Liao 01 Min Zhong 11236 Hao ((2017) 辽01民终11236号).
80. (2020) Hu 0115 Min Chu 34125 Hao ((2020) 沪0115民初34125号).
81. (2018) Su 01 Min Xia Zhong 1073 Hao ((2018) 苏01民辖终1073号).
82. (2019) Su 05 Min Xia Zhong 137 Hao ((2019) 苏05民辖终137号).

removed or retained by their parents.[83] Pursuant to the Hague Abduction Convention, the courts of the country where a child's habitual residence is located have exclusive jurisdiction to adjudicate custody and access issues concerning the child. The Convention requires its member countries not to take jurisdiction over the children that are wrongfully removed or retained by their parents and return them to the country of their habitual residence so that the courts of the child's habitual residence may make custody or access determinations. After taking effect in 1984, the Convention has expanded its membership to include an impressive diverse group of nations, and has succeeded in strengthening global cooperation in combating international parental child abduction.[84]

Although an active member of the Hague Conference, China has not yet joined the Hague Abduction Convention. As a result, there have been serious concerns of parental child abduction to China. For instance, the State of Michigan outright bans Michigan courts from allowing children to travel or relocate to China if one parent does not consent to the trip or relocation.[85] The international legal community has urged China to join the Abduction Convention.[86] The Abduction Convention's good intention and success in strengthening international cooperation in child custody and access are widely recognized in China. However, there are some strong reservations about China's joining the Hague Abduction Convention.[87] First, there are serious concerns that

83. Elisa Perez-Vera, Explanatory Report, Convention on the Civil Aspects of International Child Abduction, Hague Conference on Private International Law, III Actes et documents de la Quartorzi me session 426, 435 (1980).

84. Convention of 25 October 1980 on the Civil Aspects of International Child Abduction Status Table, https://www.hcch.net/en/instruments/conventions/status-table/?cid=24.

85. Michigan law, MCL 722.27(a)10, mandates that "a parenting time order shall contain a prohibition on exercising parenting time in a country that is not a party" to the Hague Convention unless "both parents provide the court with written consent to allow a parent to exercise parenting time in a country that is not a party to the Hague Convention." Michigan Court of Appeals interpreted MCL 722.27(a)10 as to preclude any court from "granting parenting time in a country that is not a party to the Hague Convention, unless the other parent agrees in writing." Elahham v. Al-Jabban, 319 Mich. App. 112, 128, 899 N.W.2d 768, 779 (2017).

86. Hans Van Loon (汉斯·范鲁), Guoqu Sanshi Nian Guoji Sifa Zhi Fazhan—Zhongguo, Haiya Guoji Sifa Huiyi Yu Shijie (过去三十年国际私法之发展—中国、海牙国际私法会议与世界) [Private International Law's Development in the Past 30 Years—China, Hague Private International Law Conference and the World], Guoji Fa Yanjiu (国际法研究) [Chinese Rev. of Int'l L.], 2018(05):80–86, 84.

87. Wu Yong (吴用), Haiya Guoji Youguai Ertong Minshi Fangmian Gongyue Pingjia – Jianlun Woguo Jiaru Gongyue De Kexing Xing (海牙《国际诱拐儿童民事方面公约》评介——兼论我国加入公约的可行性) [Commentary on Hague Convention on the Civil Aspects of International Parental Abduction of Children – Additional Discussion on the Possibility of Our Country Join the Convention], Zhongguo Qingnian Zhengzhi Xueyuan Xuebao (中国青年政治学院学报) [J. China Youth Univ. for Pol. Sci.] Vol. 6 (2013), 37.

domestic violence victims are not adequately protected under the Abduction Convention and that it is unwise to compel separation between the children and their primary caregivers for the sake of jurisdictional convenience of the left-behind parents.[88] Having realized that most taking parents are primary-caregiver mothers, often fleeing from domestic abuse,[89] women's rights advocates who had pushed for Taiwan and China's participation in the Abduction Convention recently started calling for a pause, due to concerns of the well-being and safety of taking parents and their children's in international child removal cases.

Second, the Hague Abduction Convention does not provide a uniform framework for resolving jurisdictional disputes in international parental child removal cases. For instance, the well-settled exception provided in Article 12 of the Convention alone has been interpreted and applied inconsistently among common law jurisdictions in the U.S., Australia, Canada, and the UK.[90] The lack of uniform interpretation, application, and implementation of the Abduction Convention sometimes create more problems than the Convention can solve.

Third, the Hague Abduction Convention is not a panacea in preventing parents' unilateral removal of children.[91] In the Hague Abduction Convention member countries, it often takes months and even years to get a decision in Hague Abduction Convention return cases.[92] Globally, the overall return rate in Hague Abduction Convention cases was merely 45 percent, and the average number of days taken to reach a final resolution of a Hague Convention return application was 254 days in 2015.[93] In the case of the U.S., the overall return rate of children who were abducted to the U.S. was only 43 percent, and the average time taken to resolve a return application received by

88. *See, e.g.*, Merle H. Weiner, *International Child Abduction and the Escape from Domestic Violence*, 69 Fordham L. Rev. 593 (2000).

89. The Hague Conference on Private International Law Permanent Bureau, Part I—A statistical analysis of applications made in 2015 under the Hague Convention of 25 October 1980 on the Civil Aspects of International Child Abduction—Global report, 8 (2018).

90. Du Huanfang (杜焕芳), Qiangzhi Jiaohuan Guoji Youguai Ertong De Sifa Cailiang—Yi Haiya Gongyue Di 12 Tiao Di 2 Kuan Wei Fenxi Duixiang (强制交还国际诱拐儿童的司法裁量—以海牙公约第12 条第2 款为分析对象) [Judicial Discretion in Compulsory Return of International Parental Abduction Children—The Hague Convention Article 12 (2) as the Analytical Subject], Zhengfa Luntan (政法论坛) [Trib. Pol. Sci. & L.], Vol. 32, No. 3 (May 2014), 25–34. *See also* Wu Yong, *supra* note 87, at 38.

91. Thalia Kruger, International Child Abduction: The Inadequacies of the Law (2011).

92. Wu, *supra* note 87, at 38.

93. The Hague Conference on Private International Law Permanent Bureau, Part I—A statistical analysis of applications made in 2015 under the Hague Convention of 25 October 1980 on the Civil Aspects of International Child Abduction—Global report, 3 (2018).

the U.S. Central Authority was 208 days in 2015.[94] In 2018, 174 (or 58 percent) of the 300 U.S. children abducted to Convention countries were returned to the U.S., whereas 58 (or 56 percent) of the 104 U.S. children abducted to non-Convention countries were returned.[95] Nor is there much evidence that the Hague Abduction Convention has any significant deterrence effect against parental abduction among its member countries. In fact, more U.S. children were abducted to Hague Convention countries than to non-Hague Convention member countries. The U.S. Central Authority reported that 404 U.S. children were abducted to or wrongfully retained in another country in 2018. Three hundred (or 74 percent) of these 404 children were abducted to Hague Abduction Convention member countries, whereas 104 (or 26 percent) of them were abducted to non-Convention countries.[96] There has been a steady increase of incoming abduction to the U.S. as well. Specifically, the number of incoming return applications for children who were abducted to the U.S. was 254 in 1999, 345 in 2003, 329 in 2008, and 379 in 2015. In 2015, the U.S. received more return applications than any other Hague Abduction Convention member country.[97] These data suggest that the Hague Abduction Convention has not been effective in returning children expeditiously or in deterring parental child abduction.

Last, the Hague Abduction Convention does not adequately address the issue of visitation and access.[98] In many international child removal cases, the root problem is to afford the left-behind non-primary-caregiver parents meaningful access to their children. The Convention lacks an adequate mechanism to address access issues, and consequently is not effective in resolving the conflicts.

Absent the Hague Abduction Convention, Chinese courts adjudicate international child removal disputes pursuant to China's internal laws and its bilateral treaties with various countries. In *Huang v. Zhuo*, the child was born in New York on July 22, 2012. The parents were Chinese immigrants who attended graduate schools in the U.S., lived in the U.S. for years, and became U.S. permanent residents. The father, Huang, was gainfully employed as an engineer. However, the mother had difficulties in adjusting to life in New York and could not find any employment. The mother returned to China with the child when the child was about one and a half years old, on December 10, 2013. The father consented to the trip as he believed the mother and the child were

94. The Hague Conference on Private International Law Permanent Bureau, Part III—A statistical analysis of applications made in 2015 under the Hague Convention of 25 October 1980 on the Civil Aspects of International Child Abduction—Global report, 147 (2018).

95. The U.S. Department of State, Annual Report on International Child Abduction (2019), 6.

96. *Id.*

97. *Id.*

98. Wu, *supra* note 87, at 38.

going to China for a short visit with the mother's family. However, as soon as the mother and child arrived in China, the mother retained the child and refused to return to the United States. The father filed for divorce and sought custody of the child in August 2014 in a Fuzhou court. The Fuzhou court eventually awarded the mother residential custody of the child and liberal visitation for the father. The court held that considering the child's young age and the mother's role as the child's primary caregiver, it would be in the best interest of the child for him to remain in the mother's custody and it would be detrimental to the child's well-being to change his environment.[99]

Recognizing pervasive parental abduction of children in custody disputes, the newly amended Minors Protection Law makes it illegal for parents to remove or retain children to gain child custody.[100] The new law affords Chinese courts a sound statutory basis to curb parental abduction of children. The protections provided in the new Minors Protection Law are applicable to "foreign nationals and persons without nationality who are under the age of 18 within the territory of China."[101] Thus, the Minors Protection Law protects children who are wrongfully removed by their parents to China to gain advantage in custody disputes, regardless of their nationality. In other words, international parental abduction of children to or from China is illegal pursuant to the Minor Protections Law.

§ 12.3 Choice of Law

Once a Chinese court takes jurisdiction of a matter with foreign elements, the court must identify which country's law should be applied in its adjudication of the matter. In other words, in foreign-related family matters, Chinese courts must determine which country's law is to be applied and if a foreign country's laws should be applied, how the foreign country's law should be applied.

The governing laws in a foreign-related family matter should be selected first according to the parties' choice of law agreement. Absent the parties' agreement on governing law, Chinese courts must determine applicable laws according to statutory provisions on choice of law set forth in the Law on Applicable Laws or any other laws.[102] Absent the parties' agreement or

---

99. (2015) Gu Min Chu Di 2457 Hao ((2015) 鼓民初字第2457号).

100. Zhonghua Renmin Gongheguo Weichengnian Ren Baohu Fa (中华人民共和国未成年人保护法) [the People's Republic of China Minors Protection Law] (promulgated on Sept. 4, 1991, amended on Dec. 19, 2006, amended on Oct. 26, 2012, amended on Oct. 17, 2020, effective June 1, 2021) [hereinafter the "Minors Protection Law"] art. 24.

101. *Id.* art. 131.

102. Law on Applicable Laws art. 2 para. 1.

statutory provisions on governing law, the laws of the country that has the closest connection to the subject matter should be applied.[103]

12.3.1 Parties' Choice of Law

Parties may choose the governing law applicable to their foreign-related civil relationship.[104] Parties' choice of law agreements are generally enforceable, absent a showing of violation of Chinese law.[105] Parties' ability to choose applicable law is limited in family matters. Choice of law is permitted only in matters concerning spouses' property relationship,[106] or in divorce settlement agreements.[107]

Chinese courts must apply the governing law stipulated by marital property agreements. For instance, in a contract dispute between a married couple and their business partner, the Chinese court held that the laws of Macau should apply in determining whether the couple should be jointly liable for a debt owed to their business partner, in that at the time of their marriage in Macau, the couple entered into an agreement that the "common marital property regime" under Macau law should govern their marital property relationship.[108]

If the parties have an agreement on governing law, and such agreement is made before the conclusion of the trial in the court of first instance, the court must allow the agreement and apply the law of the country chosen by the parties' agreement.[109] Thus, in *L. v. Li*, the Chinese court applied Chinese law in a post-divorce property dispute between a Chinese citizen and a Canadian citizen over properties in China as the parties expressly agreed to apply Chinese law during the litigation.[110] Similarly, the Guangzhou court applied Chinese law in a post-divorce property dispute between Guan, a South African citizen and Chen, a Chinese citizen based on the parties' agreement to apply Chinese law.[111]

If the parties have consistently relied on the laws of the same country and neither party has raised any objection, the court may deem that the parties have chosen to apply that country's law.[112] For example, in *Liao v. Wu*, Liao was a permanent resident of Hong Kong and Wu was a Chinese citizen. Liao

---

103. *Id.* art. 2 para. 2.
104. *Id.* art. 3.
105. Law on Applicable Laws Interpretations arts. 4, 6.
106. Law on Applicable Laws art. 24.
107. *Id.* art. 26.
108. (2016) Yue 2071 Min Chu 9256 Hao ((2016) 粤2071 民初9256 号).
109. Law on Applicable Laws Interpretations art. 6 para. 1.
110. (2021) Liao 06 Min Zhong 690 Hao ((2021) 辽06民终690号).
111. (2021) Yue 01 Min Zhong 533 Hao ((2021) 粤01民终533号).
112. Law on Applicable Laws Interpretations art. 6 para. 2.

brought a suit in a Guangdong court for her share in the properties that the parties acquired during their cohabitation. Because of Liao's Hong Kong resident status, the parties' property dispute was a foreign-related civil matter. Thus, the Guangdong court must determine whether to apply Chinese law or Hong Kong law. The court ruled that Chinese law should apply, in that both parties cited and relied on Chinese law in their pleadings and neither party raised any objection to the application of Chinese law.[113]

12.3.2 Marriage

In determining the validity of a foreign marriage, Chinese courts must first decide (1) whether the spouses were eligible to marry under the applicable law and (2) whether the manner in which the marriage was entered conformed with the applicable law.

Eligibility to marry is governed by the laws of (1) the country of the parties' common habitual residence; or (2) the country of the parties' common nationality if the parties do not have a common habitual residence; or (3) the country of a party's habitual residence if the parties do not have a common habitual residence or a common nationality; or (4) the country where the marriage was celebrated if the parties do not have a common habitual residence or a common nationality.[114] Thus, in *Cai v. Lin*, the Guangdong Province High People's Court held that Australian law should apply to determine the validity of the parties' marriage because the marriage was celebrated in Australia, and the parties did not share a common habitual residence or a common nationality at the time of the marriage.[115]

When the validity of a marriage is determined by the law of the parties' habitual residence, the place of their habitual residence is the place where they resided at the time of the marriage.[116] In *Xie v. Huang*, the decedent married his wife in China in a traditional ceremony in the 1960s. After the wedding ceremony, the couple had lived as husband and wife in China and had five children born of the marriage. They later moved to Hong Kong. The lower court ruled that the decedent's marriage was not valid under the laws of Hong Kong, where the decedent and his wife resided at the time of his death. The Quanzhou City Intermediate People's Court reversed the lower court's decision and held that Chinese law should be applied in determining the validity of the decedent's marriage because the decedent's and his wife's habitual residence immediately prior to and at the time of the marriage was

113. (2020) Yue 01 Min Zhong 23814 Hao ((2020) 粤01民终23814号).
114. Law on Applicable Laws art. 21.
115. (2018) Yue Min Zhong 745 Hao ((2018) 粤民终745号).
116. Law on Applicable Laws Interpretations art. 13.

in China. The court further held that although the decedent's marriage was never registered, it was valid pursuant to Chinese law that recognizes *de facto* marriages entered before 1994.[117]

When the parties did not share a common habitual residence at the time of the marriage, the laws of the country of the parties' common nationality should be applied to determine their eligibility to marry.[118] In *Lin v. Zhang*, the Chinese court held that the decedent's marriage to Lin entered in the United States was invalid, as the parties were not eligible to marry pursuant to Chinese law, which was the law of the country of their common nationality. The Chinese court found that Lin and the decedent did not have a common habitual residence; however, they were both Chinese nationals at the time of the marriage. Thus, the Chinese court applied Chinese law pursuant to Article 21 of the Law on Applicable Laws, and found that the decedent and Lin were not eligible to marry each other under Chinese law because they were first cousins. Therefore, the court held that the U.S. marriage of Lin and the decedent was invalid pursuant to Chinese law, which prohibits blood relatives within third degree of kinship from marrying each other.[119]

The manner in which a marriage is entered is governed by the laws of the place where the marriage was entered, or the laws of the place of a party's habitual residence or nationality.[120] For example, in *Lim v. Lim*, the Fuzhou court found that the date of the Lims' marriage was the date of the parties' Buddhist wedding ceremony held in Malaysia because Malaysian law recognizes the validity of marriages entered and celebrated according to Buddhist tradition.[121]

Chinese law is silent on the validity of same-sex marriages entered in foreign countries in accordance with foreign laws. Same-sex marriages in which both spouses are Chinese nationals are presumably invalid because Chinese law is the law of the country of a couple's common habitual residence and common nationality, and Chinese law should govern when the Chinese court decides the validity of same-sex marriages between Chinese nationals.[122] However, Chinese courts might have to recognize foreign same-sex marriages in which at least one spouse is not a Chinese national and China is not the spouses' common habitual residence.[123]

---

117. (2017) Min 05 Min Zhong 6970 Hao ((2017) 闽05民终6970号).
118. Law on Applicable Laws art. 21.
119. (2019) Min 01 Min Zhong 1631 Hao ((2019) 闽01民终1631号).
120. Law on Applicable Laws art. 22.
121. (2020) Min 01 Min Zhong 1811 Hao ((2019) 闽01民终1811号).
122. Law on Applicable Laws art. 21.
123. For in-depth discussions of the validity of same-sex marriages in China, see Yin Liu, *China's Non-Recognition of Foreign Same-Sex Unions*, 34 INT'L J. L., POL'Y & FAM., 204–24 (2020).

12.3.3 Spousal Personal Relations

Spousal personal relations are governed by the law of the spouses' common habitual residence, or the law of the country of the spouses' common nationality if the spouses do not have a common habitual residence.[124] The choice of law rules on spousal personal relations must be distinguished from the choice of law rules on marriage. The choice of law rules on spousal personal relations are used to select laws applicable to the rights and duties arising from a valid marriage, whereas the choice of law rules on marriage deal with laws governing the validity of a marriage.

To illustrate: in *Qin v. Fu, etc.*, Qin married the decedent in Japan. The defendants, Fu, etc., were the decedent's children from her first marriage. The decedent's children objected to Qin's right to inherit the decedent's estate and alleged, *inter alia*, that the marriage of Qin and the decedent was not valid and that Qin was not the decedent's intestate heir. The Shanghai court found that Qin and the decedent were both Japanese citizens and their common habitual residence was in Japan. Thus, the Shanghai court held that (1) the court should apply Japanese law to determine the validity of Qin and the decedent's marriage because the couple's common habitual residence was Japan at the time of the marriage and Japanese law should apply pursuant to the choice of law rules concerning the validity of a marriage; and (2) if the marriage was entered in conformity with Japanese law and was therefore valid under Japanese law, then the court should apply Japanese law to determine whether Qin, as the decedent's spouse, was the decedent's intestate heir because Japan was the couple's common habitual residence and country of common nationality and Japanese law should be applied pursuant to the choice of law rules concerning spousal personal relation.[125]

Similarly, in the matter of *Hu and Ji, etc.*, the habitual residence of the wife, Hu, and the husband, Herbert, was France. Herbert was an Irish citizen. The wife passed away after her mother died and before her mother's estate was distributed. The wife's mother's estate was in Beijing. The Beijing court held that Herbert and his late wife's marital status and rights, including Herbert's right to inherit from his late wife, were governed by French law, which was the law of the place of the couple's common habitual residence.[126]

12.3.4 Spousal Property Relationship

Spouses may choose, by written agreement, the laws of the place where a party's habitual residence or nationality is, or the laws of the place where

---

124. Law on Applicable Laws art. 23.
125. (2017) Hu 02 Min Zhong 3070 Hao ((2017) 沪02民终3070号).
126. (2019) Jing 0102 Min Chu 10175 Hao ((2019) 京0102民初10175号).

the majority of the parties' property is located as the governing law of their property relationship.[127] Absent such agreement, the laws of the place of the parties' common habitual residence, or if the parties do not share a common habitual residence, the laws of the place of their common nationality shall apply.[128]

Choice of law clauses in prenuptial agreements, post-nuptial agreements, divorce agreements, or any other interspousal agreements concerning property are legally binding and enforceable as long as the governing law chosen is the law of a country that is a party's habitual residence, or nationality, or where the majority of the parties' property is situated. If the parties have a valid choice of law agreement, Chinese courts must apply the laws of the country designated by the parties in disputes related to spousal property relationship. For example, in *You Minzhu v. Zhang Tianshou*, the Shenzhen court held that Chinese law should be applied in the interpretation and enforcement of the parties' spousal support agreement entered in Hong Kong because the parties stipulated to apply Chinese law.[129]

When a prenuptial agreement or any other type of interspousal agreement concerning property fails to include a choice of law clause, the choice of law rules on spousal property relation apply. Thus, in *Cai v. Lin*, the Guangdong court determined that Chinese law should apply in the determination of the parties' property relation, including the validity and enforceability of their prenuptial agreement, because China had the closest connections with the parties' financial life during the marriage, finding that most of the parties' assets were in China and their financial activities were conducted mainly in China, and that the parties did not have a common habitual residence or a common nationality.[130] Similarly, in *Sun v. Dong*, the Shanghai court found that the parties' divorce settlement agreement entered in their Australian divorce action did not have a choice of law clause, and the parties had no common habitual residence but both had Chinese citizenship. Thus, the Shanghai court held that the law of China, which is the country of the parties' common nationality, should apply in determining the enforceability of the parties' divorce settlement agreement. The court further found that the parties' Australian divorce settlement agreement was legally binding and enforceable as it was entered voluntarily without fraud or duress.[131]

Whether a married couple's assets or debts are marital is an issue concerning "spouses' property relation." Thus, the laws of the place of a couple's common habitual residence, or common nationality determine the nature of

127. Law on Applicable Laws art. 24.
128. *Id.*
129. (2018) Yue 0303 Min Chu 10674 Hao ((2018) 粤0303民初10674号).
130. (2018) Yue Min Zhong 745 Hao ((2018) 粤民终745号).
131. (2017) Hu 02 Min Zhong 10660 Hao ((2017) 沪02民终10660号).

their marital property regime. For example, the Shanghai People's High Court affirmed in *Pan v. Yang* that absent a choice of law agreement between the parties, the laws of the jurisdiction of the parties' common habitual residence should be applied in the parties' post-judgment property distribution action in the Shanghai court, and therefore Nevada law should be applied because Nevada was the parties' common habitual residence.[132] Similarly, in *Li v. Lei*, the Jiangxi Province High People's Court held that Chinese laws should be applied to determine whether a loan was a couple's marital debt, finding that the couple's habitual residence was in China although they were both permanent residents of Hong Kong.[133]

When the parties do not have a choice of law agreement, a common habitual residence, or a common nationality, the laws of the jurisdiction that has the closest connection with the spouses' property relationship should apply.[134] Thus, in *Lin v. Zhou*, having found that the parties did not share a common habitual residence or a common nationality, the Fuzhou court held that New York law should be applied to determine whether the parties' New York co-op apartment was their marital property, in that New York had the closest connection with the parties' marriage and the disputed property, which was located in New York.[135]

12.3.5 Cohabitation Property

The choice of law rules governing married couple's property relations are not applicable in property disputes between unmarried cohabitation partners. Instead, the law of the place where the real property is situated applies in disputes over real property between unmarried intimate partners.[136] Moreover, the law governing movable property is the law chosen by the parties' agreement or the law of the place where the movable property is located at the time of the dispute if the parties do not have any agreement on choice of law.[137] For example, in Huang and Cui's cohabitation property division case, Huang was a Korean citizen and Cui was a Chinese citizen, and all of their joint real property and personal property were in China. Therefore, Chinese law should be applied in the determination of their respective interest and share in the property that they acquired during cohabitation.[138]

---

132. (2018) Hu Min Shen 888 Hao ((2018) 沪民申888号).
133. (2018) Gan Min Zhong 407 Hao ((2018) 赣民终407号).
134. Law on Applicable Laws art. 2.
135. (2017) Min 01 Min Zhong 3992 Hao ((2017) 闽01民终3992号).
136. Law on Applicable Laws art. 36.
137. *Id*. art. 37.
138. (2020) Ji Min Zhong 225 Hao ((2020) 吉民终225号).

12.3.6 Divorce

There are two sets of choice of law rules concerning divorces: the rules on consensual divorces[139] and the rules on contested divorces.[140]

12.3.6.1 Consensual Divorce

In a consensual divorce, the governing law should be selected in the following order: (1) the laws of the country of a party's habitual residence, or the laws of the country of a party's nationality, whichever is elected by the parties' agreement; (2) the laws of the country of their common habitual residence if the parties do not have a choice of law agreement; (3) the laws of the country of the parties' common nationality should govern if the parties do not have a choice of law agreement or a common habitual residence; (3) the laws of the country where the authority handling the divorce is located if the parties do not have a choice of law agreement, or a common habitual residence, or a common nationality.[141]

12.3.6.2 Contested Divorce

The laws of the country where the court is located should govern in contested divorce actions.[142] Thus, Chinese substantive law as well as procedural rules should be applied not only to dissolution of the marriage but also to ancillary issues in contested divorce actions in Chinese courts. *Jin v. Zhang* was a divorce action brought by a South Korean national, against her husband, a Chinese national in Jinling. The wife resided in South Korea, and the husband and the parties' child resided in Jiling, China. Having ascertained the court's jurisdiction based on the husband's habitual residence in China, the Jiling court determined that Chinese law should be applied in the action, as the law of the forum of the divorce action should govern pursuant to Article 27 of the Law on Applicable Laws. The court then dissolved the parties' marriage, distributed their property, and determined child custody and support according to Chinese law.[143]

12.3.7 Parents and Children: Custody, Guardianship, and Support

When claims related to parent-child relations are brought independent of a divorce action, Chinese courts must follow the choice of law rules governing

139. Law on Applicable Laws art. 26.
140. *Id.* art. 27.
141. *Id.* art. 26.
142. *Id.* art. 27.
143. (2016) Ji Min Zhong 156 Hao ((2016) 吉民终156号).

child custody, guardianship, and support provided respectively in Article 25, Article 29, and Article 30 of the Law on Applicable Laws.

12.3.7.1 Parent-Child Personal Relations: Custody and Visitation

Article 25 of the Law on Applicable Laws provides that personal and property relationships between a child and his/her parent are governed by "the law of common habitual residence; or, if no common habitual residence, the laws of the place of one party's habitual residence or nationality, whichever better protects the protected person's rights and interests."[144] To illustrate: in *Du v. Li, etc.*, Du was married to the defendants' father. After Du's husband died, Du brought an action for filial support from the defendants who were her husband's adult children. Du was a citizen of Myanmar. The defendants were Chinese citizens. Du and all the defendants lived in a border town in Yunnan, China. The court held that pursuant to Article 25 of the Law on Applicable Laws, Chinese law should apply in Du's suit for filial support because China was the country of Du and her stepchildren's common habitual residence.[145]

12.3.7.2 Maintenance: Child Support

Article 29 of the Law on Applicable Laws provides that maintenance (*fuyang*) is governed by the laws of the country of a party's habitual residence, or of the country of a party's nationality, or of the country where the main property is located, whichever best protects the protected person's rights and interests. Maintenance within the meaning of Article 29 includes financial support for parents, children, and spouses. It should be noted that Article 25 dictates which country's laws should be applied to decide whether there is any support obligation between a parent and a child, whereas Article 29 determines which country's law should be applied to decide the amount and duration of an obligor's maintenance obligation.[146]

To illustrate: in *Sun etc. v. Li*, Li had two children born out of wedlock in Germany. Li later married the children's mother. Li was a Chinese citizen, and the children were German citizens, and the family had lived in Germany for some years after the children's births. Li divorced the children's mother in Germany. The German court did not make any support provisions for the children in the divorce judgment as the children were not born of the marriage. After the divorce, Li, the children's mother, and the children moved to China. The children then brought a child support action, through their mother, against Li in Beijing, where both Li and the children had lived for

144. Law on Applicable Laws art. 25.
145. (2020) Yun 3102 Min Chu 1912 Hao ((2020) 云3102民初1912号).
146. (2014) Er Zhong Shao Min Zhong Zi Di 08865 Hao ((2014) 二中少民终字第08865号).

over a year after their relocation to China. Li objected to the Beijing court's jurisdiction and argued that German law should apply if the court were to exercise jurisdiction. The Beijing court found that the children's habitual residence was indeed in Beijing. Thus, the court held that it had jurisdiction over the children's support issue based on the children's as well as Li's habitual residence in Beijing. The court further held that (1) pursuant to Article 25 of the Law on Applicable Laws, Chinese law should be applied to determine Li's paternity and whether Li had any obligation to support the children if his paternity was established; and (2) pursuant to Article 29 of the Law on Applicable Laws, Chinese law should be applied to decide Li's child support amount and duration if his paternity was established. The Beijing court found that Li was the children's biological father based on the paternity test results and ordered him to pay child support pursuant to Chinese law, under which nonmarital children enjoy the same rights to support as marital children.[147]

12.3.7.3 Maintenance: Filial Support

Maintenance for filial support of elderly parents is governed by the law of the country of a party's habitual residence or nationality, whichever better protects the rights and interests of the protected party.[148] Chinese courts' jurisdiction over parents' filial support (*shanyang*) claims is generally obtained based on the parents' habitual residence in China. As a result, Chinese law would inevitably apply in filial support proceedings in Chinese courts because Chinese law not only is the law of the country of the plaintiff parents' habitual residence but also favors the elderly parents' interests, as in *Deng v. Huang, etc.* In the *Deng* case, the 81-year-old mother sued her children for filial support, as her only income was RMB500 per month in public assistance. The Chinese court applied Chinese law on filial support and ordered her children, including her son, whose habitual residence was in Macao, to each pay her financial support in the sum of RMB1200 per month.[149]

Chinese courts may rely on the children's Chinese nationality and/or habitual residence in China to apply Chinese filial support law. In *Cui v. Pu*, the Chinese court entered a filial support order for an elderly mother, who was a North Korean citizen living in China. The court held that pursuant to Article 29 of the Law on Applicable Laws, Chinese law should apply to determine the mother's support, as the mother's habitual residence was China and her children were all Chinese citizens.[150]

---

147. *Id.*
148. Law on Applicable Laws arts. 25, 29.
149. (2019) Yue 0605 Min Chu 15154 Hao ((2019) 粤0605民初15154号).
150. (2018) Ji 24 Mn Chu 128 Hao ((2018) 吉24民初128号).

Chinese courts may apply Chinese law based on the parents' Chinese nationality and the parties' close connections with China to order their adult children to pay filial support. For example, in *Yan v. Yan*, the Chongqing court ordered an adult daughter, who was a U.S. citizen residing in California, to pay her father filial support according to Chinese law. The court found that although the father had been living in the U.S. for more than six years, he was a Chinese citizen and he intended to return to China in a few years. The Chongqing court held that Chinese law should be applied in determining the daughter's filial support obligation in that the father was a Chinese citizen and China was the place that had the closest connection with her support obligation.[151]

12.3.7.4 Guardianship

Article 30 of the Law on Applicable Laws provides that guardianship should be governed by the laws of a party's habitual residence or nationality, whichever better protects the rights and interests of the ward.[152] Chinese courts differ in whether Article 25 or Article 30 should be applied in guardianship and custody disputes concerning minor children. The Guangdong court consistently applied Article 30 in child custody disputes.[153] In contrast, the Beijing No. 1 Intermediate People's Court applied Chinese law pursuant to Article 25 in a guardianship dispute between a minor child's parents. The Beijing court held that parental guardianship of a minor child was a parent-child personal relationship within the meaning of Article 25 of the Law on Applicable Laws. Therefore, the Beijing court applied Chinese law pursuant to Article 25 because the parents did not have a common habitual residence, China was the mother and child's habitual residence and Chinese law best protected the child's best interest.[154] Similarly, the Chongqing court applied Chinese law pursuant to Article 25 of the Law on Applicable Laws in a grandparents-visitation case, where the grandparents were Chinese citizens living in China and the minor child resided in New Zealand with his mother. The Chongqing court believed it was "lawful" to apply Chinese law in the case because the grandparents were Chinese citizens and Chinese law offered better protection for their relationship with their grandson. The Chongqing court ordered visitation for the grandparents.[155]

151. (2017) Yu 05 Min Xiao Zhong 196 Hao ((2017) 渝05民辖终196号).

152. Law on Applicable Laws art. 30.

153. (2016) Yue 0606 Min Chu 13061 Hao ((2016) 粤0606民初13061号); and (2018) Yue 06 Min Zhong 2839 Hao ((2018) 粤06民终2839号).

154. (2016) Jing 01 Min Xia Zhong 288 Hao ((2016) 京01民辖终288号).

155. (2018) Yu 05 Min Zhong 1121 Hao ((2018) 渝05民终1121号).

12.3.7.5 Minor Children

Chinese courts are likely to apply Chinese law in child custody, guardianship, and support proceedings where the subject child's habitual residence is in China because laws in the jurisdiction of a minor child's habitual residence are given preference in matters concerning the child's custody, guardianship, and support.

For example, in a divorce action between a Chinese citizen and a Benin citizen, the Guangdong court applied Chinese law and ruled that it was in the child's best interest for the child to remain in her mother's custody and continue living with her mother in Guangdong, where she had lived for her life.[156] In a child custody and support action against a Hong Kong resident, the Zhuhai court held that the Zhuhai court had jurisdiction over the child's custody and support issues because the child's habitual residence was in Zhuhai, China, and that Chinese law should apply pursuant to Article 25 of the Law on Applicable Laws because the child's habitual residence was in China and Chinese law could better protect her interest under the circumstances of the case.[157] In a guardianship dispute concerning a minor child who is a Canadian citizen and lived in Canada intermittently, the Shanghai court asserted its jurisdiction based on the child's habitual residence in Shanghai and affirmed the child's maternal grandmother's guardianship of the child by applying Chinese law.[158]

In cases where a child's habitual residence is not in China, Chinese courts have consistently applied Chinese law in the support proceeding against the noncustodial parent who resides in China. In these cases, it is evident that it would be in the best interest of the child as well as judicial economy for the court to apply Chinese law and to deliver financial support to the child in a timely manner. For example, in *Lin v. Lin*, the child resided in Macau with her mother, and the father resided in Guangdong. The father had not paid any child support since 2012. The child, through her mother, brought a child supporting proceeding against the father for child support arears and increase in support. The Chinese court applied Chinese law pursuant to Article 29 of the Law on Applicable Laws, ordered the father to pay child support arrears, and increased his support amount based on the child's needs.[159] Similarly, in *Ding v. Ding*, the father resided in Wuhan, and the mother and child resided

156. (2014) Mei Xian Fa Min Yi Chu Zi Di 169 Hao ((2014) 梅县法民一初字第169号). *See also* (2016) Yue 0606 Min Chu 13061 Hao ((2016) 粤0606民初13061号), where the father left for his country of origin and abandoned the mother and child in China; the mother was awarded custody and child support in the father's default.

157. (2019) Yue 04 Min Zhong 866 Hao ((2019) 粤04民终866号).

158. (2015) Min Min Yi (Min) Te Zi di 39 Hao ((2015) 闵民一（民）特字第39号).

159. (2016) Yue 0705 Min Chu 1719 Hao ((2016) 粤0705民初1719号).

in Australia. The Wuhan court ordered the father to pay child support according to Chinese law and determined his child support amount based on the financial affidavit that he submitted to the Australian court.[160]

12.3.8 Proof of Foreign Law

The parties must provide proof of foreign law if they have chosen the foreign law as governing law by agreement. Absent any choice of law agreement, Chinese courts, not the parties, bear the burden to ascertain foreign laws.[161] Chinese courts must conduct their own research on foreign law. The courts may appoint legal experts, such as the Chinese Politics and Law University Foreign Law Institute, to conduct research and provide expert opinions on foreign laws.[162] The courts may also consider relevant foreign law material or source presented by the parties, including testimony. If the parties have agreed opinions on foreign law, the court may accept the parties' joint opinions. If the parties differ in their opinions on foreign law, the court must conduct a hearing on applicable foreign law.[163]

Several Chongqing judges explained how they researched and applied foreign law in a foreign divorce judgment recognition case. After receiving a petition for recognition of a Maryland default divorce judgment, the judges first researched Maryland law on the finality and effects of default divorce judgments rendered by Maryland courts. They started with Maryland Rule 2-613 on Westlaw (govt.westlaw.com), as the Maryland divorce judgment in front of them stated that the judgment should take effect pursuant to "Maryland Rule 2-613." The Chongqing judges found that a Maryland divorce judgment becomes final if no appeal is taken within 30 days after the judgment is entered under Rule 2-613. They then researched Maryland case law. Relying on *Das v. Das*[164] and *Franklin Credit Management Corp. v. Fred Nefflen*,[165] the Chongqing judges found that a final judgment may be vacated or modified for "fraud, mistake, irregularity," "newly-discovered evidence," or "clerical mistakes" pursuant to Maryland Rule 2-535. As there was no evidence of any appeal or action to vacate or modify the Maryland default divorce judgment in front of them, the judge concluded that the Maryland default divorce

---

160. (2019) E 01 Min Zhong 3105 Hao ((2019) 鄂01民终3105号).

161. Law on Applicable Laws art. 10 para. 1.

162. Sun Wen (Presiding Trial Judge) (孙 雯 (一审承办法官)), Tongguo Zhuanjia Tujng Chaming Waiguo Fa De Yunzuo 通过专家途径查明外国法的运作 [The Process of Using Expert to Investigate Foreign Country Law], Renmin Sifa (人民司法) [The People's Judicature], 32.2017, 75–77.

163. Law on Applicable Laws Interpretations art. 16.

164. Das v. Das, 754 A.2d 441 (Md. App. 1999).

165. Franklin Credit Mgmt. Corp. v. Fred Nefflen, 57 A.3d 1015 (2012), 208 Md. App. 712.

judgment was final and conclusive pursuant to Maryland law and therefore, should be recognized by the Chongqing court.[166]

When a Chinese court is unable to obtain proof of applicable foreign laws by reasonable means or when a party has failed to provide evidence of foreign laws pursuant to the court's order, Chinese law should apply.[167] In *Zhou v. Lin*, the Fuzhou court held that New York law should apply in determining whether a married couple's New York co-op apartment was marital property. The court ordered the plaintiff to pay the expert fees for obtaining information on New York law from New York pursuant to a U.S.-China bilateral judicial assistance treaty. The plaintiff did not pay the fees. As a result, the Fuzhou court could not obtain sufficient information about New York law. The court held that the court had to apply Chinese law due to the court's inability to ascertain New York law and ruled in the defendant's favor.[168]

§ 12.4 Foreign Court Judgments and Orders

There are two criteria for recognition and enforcement of a foreign court civil judgment: (1) the judgment must be final and conclusive; and (2) recognition and enforcement of the judgment must not violate China's law, sovereignty, national security, and public interest.[169] When a foreign court judgment meets both criteria, Chinese courts must recognize and enforce, if necessary, the judgment pursuant to the recognition and enforcement provisions of the treaty between China and the country where the judgment is originated, or pursuant to reciprocity.[170] Reciprocity is interpreted as a foreign jurisdiction's willingness to enforce Chinese judgments either evidenced by its precedents of recognition and enforcement of Chinese judgments (*shishi huhui*) or by the foreign jurisdiction's internal law that requires recognition and enforcement of Chinese judgments (*falü huhui*). In recent years, Chinese courts have enforced foreign court judgments based on foreign courts' precedents of enforcing Chinese judgments as evidence of reciprocity. There also have been commercial and civil cases where Chinese courts had declined to recognize or

166. The Judges Handled the Maryland Default Divorce Judgment Case Illustrated the Process of Their Research and Determination of Maryland Law on Default Divorce Judgment. *See* Cao Ke, Song Shuang, Du Dongan (曹柯, 宋爽, 杜东安), Waiguo Falü Chaming De Lujing He Fangfa (外国法律查明的路径和方法) [Means and Methods of Investigation of Foreign Law], Renmin Sifa (人民司法) [The People's Judicature] 31.2018, 50–53.

167. Law on Applicable Laws art. 10, and Law on Applicable Laws Interpretations art. 15.

168. (2017) Min 01 Min Zhong 3992 Hao ((2017) 闽01民终3992号).

169. Civil Procedure Law arts. 281, 282.

170. *Id.* art. 281; Civil Procedure Law Interpretations art. 542.

enforce a foreign judgment for lack of reciprocity.[171] However, Chinese courts' recognition and enforcement of a foreign divorce judgment do not require bilateral treaties or reciprocity between China and the country from which the divorce judgment is originated.

12.4.1 Application Process

A party to a foreign court judgment or order may apply for recognition and enforcement of the judgment or order within two years after the judgment or order has become final. If the parties only apply for recognition but do not apply for enforcement at the same time, the period of application for enforcement shall be recalculated from the effective date of the Chinese court's recognition of the foreign court judgment or order.[172] An application for the recognition and enforcement of a judgment or order entered by a foreign court must include (1) a written application; (2) the original or certified copy of the foreign judgment or order; (3) the Chinese translation of the judgment; (4) proof of service, if the foreign court's judgment or order is a default judgment or order; and (5) any other documentation required by any relevant international treaty concerning the recognition and enforcement of the foreign judgment in China.[173] After the Chinese court has recognized a foreign court judgment or order, either party may seek enforcement and execution pursuant to Chinese law.[174]

Applications for recognition of foreign divorce judgments concerning Chinese nationals must include evidence that the defendant was summoned and served, and the foreign divorce judgment is final and conclusive and has taken legal effect.[175] The original or certified copy of the foreign divorce judgment must be notarized by the notary of the country where the judgment was

---

171. Li Shuangli, Zhao Qianxi (李双利, 赵千喜), Lun Chengren He Zhixing Waiguo Fayuan Panjue Shenqing Zhi Sifa Shen Cha—Yi Zhong Mei Liangguo De Lifa He Sifa Anli Wei Fenxi Duixiang (论承认和执行外国法院判决申请之司法审查—以中美两国的立法和司法案例为分析对象) [On Judicial Discretion in Recognition and Enforcement of Foreign Country Court Judgment], Falu Shiyong (法律适用) [National Judges College Journal] Issue 5, 2018, 28–30.

172. Civil Procedure Law Interpretations art. 545, and Civil Procedure Law art. 239.

173. Civil Procedure Law Interpretations art. 541.

174. *Id*. art. 544.

175. Zuigao Renmin Fayuan Guanyu Zhongguo Gongmin Shenqing Chengren Waiguo Fayuan Lihun Panjue Wenti De Guiding (最高人民法院关于中国公民申请承认外国法院离婚判决程序问题的规定) [Provisions on the Procedural Issues Concerning Chinese Citizens' Application for Recognition of Foreign Country Court Divorce Judgments] (promulgated by the Sup. People's Ct., July 5, 1991, effective Aug. 13, 1991), 1991 Sup. People's Ct. Gaz.3 [hereinafter the "Provisions Concerning Chinese Citizens' Application for Recognition of Foreign Court Divorce Judgment"] arts. 8, 9.

entered and legalized by the Chinese embassy or consulate stationed in that country.[176]

12.4.2 Treaty Partners

When a foreign judgment is originated from a jurisdiction that has an international treaty with China with respect to recognition and enforcement of each other's civil judgments, the judgment will be subject to the recognition and enforcement procedure prescribed in the treaty.[177] For example, Spain and China have a treaty to recognize and enforce each other's divorce judgment.[178] Thus, in the *Matter of Wang Jianqiong*, following the Spain-China bilateral treaty, the Wenzhou court recognized a Spanish divorce judgment, including provisions on child custody, support, marital property, and visitation upon Wang's application for recognition and enforcement of the judgment.[179]

Chinese courts not only afford recognition of foreign divorce judgments originated from a treaty partner but also enforcement. In *Dogancay Irina v. Dogancay Metin*, the Shanghai court recognized and enforced a Belarus child support order pursuant to the treaty between China and Belarus. In this case, the couple were married in Belarus and had a child. In 2018, they were divorced in Minsk, Belarus, and the Minsk court ordered the father to pay child support. The father did not comply with the Minsk court's order. In 2019, the mother brought a child support enforcement proceeding against the father in a Minsk court. The father, a Turkish citizen, was living and working in Shanghai at the time. Therefore, the Minsk court transmitted the mother's application to the Shanghai court pursuant to the judicial assistance treaty between Belarus and China. The Shanghai court accepted the case and conducted a trial. The court found that the Minsk court's child support order met the requirements for recognition and enforcement of a judgment pursuant to the Belarus-China treaty. Therefore, the court held that the child support order issued by the court of Minsk, Belarus, should be recognized and enforced according to the treaty and ordered the father to comply with the Minsk court's child support order. When he failed to comply, the court garnished

176. *Id.* art. 10.

177. Treaty status can be found in Ministry of Foreign Affairs' treaty database at: http://treaty.mfa.gov.cn/Treaty/web/index.jsp.

178. Zhonghua Renmin Gonghe Guo He Xibanya Wangguo Guanyu Minsh, Sangshi Sifa Xiezhu De Tiao Yue (中华人民共和国和西班牙王国关于民事、商事司法协助的条约) [The People's Republic of China and the Kingdom of Spain Judicial Assistance in Civil and Commercial Matters] (effective Jan. 1, 1994).

179. (2016) Zhe 03 Xie Wai Ren 14 Hao ((2016) 浙03协外认14号).

the ex-husband's bank accounts in Shanghai to satisfy his child support arears and monthly support that was ordered by the Minsk court.[180]

12.4.3 Recognition of Foreign Divorce Judgments Concerning Chinese Nationals

12.4.3.1 Chinese Courts' Recognition Is Required

A divorce judgment dissolving a marriage between two Chinese nationals or between a Chinese national and a non-Chinese national is not final or valid under Chinese law before it is recognized by a Chinese court.[181] For instance, in a collection action against a husband and his late wife's estate, the SPC held that the marriage between the decedent and her husband was not dissolved in China because the parties' New York divorce judgment had not been recognized by a Chinese court.[182] Similarly, the Tianjin People's High Court held that a man's second marriage was void because he failed to obtain a Chinese court's recognition of his Canadian divorce judgment and as a result his first marriage was not dissolved under Chinese law before he remarried in China.[183]

The requirement of Chinese courts' recognition of foreign divorce judgments concerning Chinese citizens is an exercise of China's sovereignty over its own citizens.[184] Thus, it is not applicable to marriages between non-Chinese nationals. Since an order of recognition of foreign divorce judgment is only required for marriages in which at least one party is a Chinese national, Chinese courts do not entertain any application for recognition of a foreign court divorce judgment when neither spouse is a Chinese citizen.[185] For instance, in *Xu v. Li*, Xu and Li were both residents of Hong Kong, and they were divorced in New York. The Shenzhen court dismissed Xu's appli-

---

180. (2020) Hu 02 Xie Wai Ren 5 Hao ((2020) 沪02协外认5号), and (2020) Hu 02 Xie Wai Ren 4 Hao ((2020) 沪02协外认4号); *see also* (2020) Hu 02 Zhi 1210 Hao ((2020) 沪02执1210号).

181. The Provisions Concerning Chinese Citizens' Application for Recognition of Foreign Court Divorce Judgment art. 20.

182. (2016) Zui Gao Fa Min Shen 436 Hao ((2016) 最高法民申436号). *See also* (2015) Su Min Zhong Zi Di 00085 Hao ((2015) 苏民终字第00085号).

183. (2016) Jin Min Shen 1888 Hao ((2016) 津民申1888号).

184. Huang Haitao, Li Xiaolong (Presiding Judge at Second Instance), Wang Xiangyu (黄海涛, 李晓龙 (二审承办法官), 王湘羽), Weijing Chengren Zhi Waiguo Panjue De Xiaoli Fenxi (未经承认之外国判决的效力分析) [Analysis on the Effect of Foreign Judgment That Is Not Recognized], Renmin Sifa (人民司法) [The People's Judicature], 22.2013, 28–32, 30.

185. Zuigao Renmin Fayuan Guanyu Renmin Fayuan Shouli Shenqing Chengren Waiguo Fayuan Lihun Panjue Youguan Wenti De Guiding (最高人民法院关于人民法院受理申请承认外国法院离婚判决有关问题的规定) [Regulations on the People's Courts' Acceptance of Application for Recognition of Foreign Country Court Divorce Judgment Cases] (promulgated by the Sup. People's Ct., Dec. 1, 1999, effective Mar. 1, 2000, 2000 Sup. People's Ct. Gaz.2) art. 2.

cation for recognition of the New York divorce judgment because neither spouse was a Chinese citizen.[186] In *Zhang v. Xi*, the Shenyang court dismissed Zhang's application for recognition of Canadian divorce judgment, as both parties were Canadian citizens.[187] The dismissal of applications for recognition does not suggest that Chinese courts do not recognize foreign divorces between non-Chinese nationals. Instead, as a Wenzhou court held in the case of Yu Heping, a final foreign divorce judgment dissolving a marriage between non-Chinese nationals is final and valid in China without the need for Chinese courts' recognition, as it does not concern China's sovereignty, national security, or public interest. Therefore, the Wenzhou court ruled that the Dutch court divorce judgment between two Dutch citizens did not need the recognition of the Chinese court; and the parties were free to remarry, as their marriage had been dissolved by the Dutch divorce judgment.[188] Similarly, a Wuhan court held in *Yang v. Gu* that the parties, who were a U.S. citizen and a Canadian citizen, were free to marry after the Quebec court entered a final divorce judgment that dissolved their marriage.[189]

12.4.3.2 Criteria for Chinese Courts' Recognition

If there is a treaty on recognition and enforcement of civil judgments between China and the country from which the divorce judgment is originated, Chinese courts must follow the treaty procedure to recognize and enforce the divorce judgment. If there is no such treaty, generally, Chinese courts afford recognition of a foreign court divorce judgments, except when (1) the judgment is not final; (2) the court entered the judgment without jurisdiction; (3) the judgment was entered in the defendant's default and without lawful service of process; (4) there is a prior valid final judgment dissolving the parties' marriage; or (5) the judgment violates China's sovereignty, national security, or public interest.[190] Reciprocity is not required for Chinese courts' recognition of foreign divorce judgments.[191]

China is a signatory country of the Hague Convention on the Service Abroad of Judicial and Extrajudicial Documents in Civil or Commercial Matters (the "Hague Service Convention"). Service of process in China must be effectuated through the central authorities in compliance with the Service Convention. However, Chinese courts seem to be willing to recognize foreign divorce judgments when the defendant has had actual notice of the

186. (2019) Yue 03 Min Chu 4167 Hao ((2019) 粤03民初4167号).
187. (2019) Liao 01 Xie Wai Ren 9 Hao ((2019) 辽01协外认9号).
188. (2018) Zhe 03 Xie Wai Ren 13 Hao ((2018) 浙03协外认13号).
189. (2018) E 01 Xie Wai Ren 12 Hao ((2018) 鄂01协外认12号).
190. Provisions Concerning Chinese Citizens' Application for Recognition of Foreign Court Divorce Judgment art. 12
191. *Id*. art. 1.

foreign divorce action and accepted the service although the service of process might not have been compliant with the Hague Service Convention. For instance, in Wang Jiaxin's case, Wang's ex-wife, Feng, obtained a default divorce judgment against Wang in New York. Wang applied in the Chinese court for recognition and enforcement of the New York default divorce judgment obtained by his ex-wife. The court granted Wang's application without inquiring how Wang was served in the New York divorce action or whether the service of process was in compliance with the Hauge Service Convention. Obviously, Wang had actual notice of the New York divorce action and accepted the service.[192] Similarly, in *Yang v. L*, L obtained a default divorce judgment against Yang in Kansas, and subsequently Yang applied in the Wuhan court for recognition of the Kansas divorce judgment. The Wuhan court found that Yang, a life-long Wuhan resident, was served by mail but did not appear or answer in the divorce action in Kansas. Nevertheless, the Wuhan court granted Yang's application for recognition of the Kansas default divorce judgment despite that Yang was not served in compliance with the Hague Service Convention.[193]

12.4.3.3 Effect of Chinese Courts' Recognition

Chinese courts' recognition of foreign divorce judgments concerning Chinese nationals is limited to dissolution of marriage.[194] Separate post-judgment actions must be commenced if the parties have any dispute over ancillary issues, such as property divisions or child custody and support.[195] If one or both parties are Chinese nationals, the foreign divorce judgment must be recognized in China before any post-judgment action concerning property, children, or any other ancillary issues can be brought in a Chinese court. For example, in *S v. Dong*, the Chinese court dismissed a post-judgment property dispute action for properties in China that were not distributed in the parties' Australian divorce action because the Australian divorce judgment had not been recognized by a Chinese court before commencing a post-judgment property dispute action.[196] In *Wayneneer v. Zhen*, a Hangzhou court dismissed

192. (2020) Lu 11 Xie Wai Ren 1 Hao ((2020) 鲁11协外认1号).

193. (2019) E 01 Xie Wai Ren 23 Hao ((2019) 鄂01协外认23号).

194. Rules on Recognition of Foreign Divorce Judgment art. 2.

195. Jilin Sheng Yanbian Chaoxian Zizhizhou Zhongji Renmin Fayuan Keti Zu (吉林省延边朝鲜族自治州中级人民法院课题组) [Jilin Province Yanbian Korean Autonomous District Intermediate People's Court Research Group], Shenqing Chengren Dahan Minguo Fayuan Lihun Panjue Xiaoli Anji De Shenli Qingkuang Ji Fenxi (申请承认大韩民国法院离婚裁判效力案件的审理情况及分析) [Report and Analysis on the Adjudication of Application for Recognition of Divorce Judgments Issued by the Courts of the Republic of Korea], Renmin Sifa (人民司法) [The People's Judicature], 25.2020, 69.

196. (2018) Zhe 0212 Min Chu 5611 Hao ((2018) 浙0212民初5611号).

the ex-husband's post-judgment property dispute action because he failed to first obtain the court's recognition of the parties' Washington divorce judgment before commencing the post-judgment action.[197]

12.4.4 Foreign Judgments Concerning Property Distribution

Parties to a foreign court divorce judgment may bring a post-judgment property dispute action in the Chinese court with proper jurisdiction to enforce the judgment or to seek division of properties located in China. When determining the effect and enforceability of a foreign court's divorce judgment with respect to the parties' property distribution, Chinese courts must apply the law of the place of the parties' common habitual residence or nationality,[198] or the law of the place that had the closest connections with the parties' marriage.[199]

Chinese courts are likely to apply the law of the country where the divorce judgment was originated in post-judgment property disputes between non-Chinese nationals, because the country where the divorce judgment was entered is usually the country of the parties' common habitual residence or common nationality. To illustrate: in *Pan v. Yang*, the couple were married in Hong Kong and divorced in Nevada. The Nevada court determined that two apartments that the parties acquired in Shanghai were the couple's marital property, and awarded both apartments to Pan. Because Yang refused to transfer the titles of the apartments to Pan, Pan had to bring a post-judgment property dispute action in Shanghai to enforce the Nevada court's order. The Shanghai People's High Court affirmed the lower courts' decision that (1) Nevada law should be applied to determine the parties' property relation because the parties' common habitual residence was in Nevada; (2) the parties' Nevada divorce judgment was entered according to Nevada law and was final and enforceable under Nevada law; and (3) the Shanghai court must recognize the Nevada divorce judgment and enforce its provisions concerning the parties' property distribution. The court rejected Yang's argument that pursuant to the Supreme People's Court's Regulations on Procedural Issues Concerning Chinese Citizens' Application for Recognition of Foreign Country Court Divorce Judgment, Chinese courts may not recognize or enforce property provisions in a foreign court divorce judgment. The Shanghai High People's Court held that "the Supreme People's Court's Regulations on Procedural Issues Concerning Chinese Citizens' Application for Recognition of Foreign Country Court Divorce Judgment only regulates Chinese citizens'

---

197. (2016) Zhe 0103 Min Chu 8721 Hao ((2016) 浙0103民初8721号).
198. Law on Applicable Laws art. 24.
199. *Id.* art. 2.

actions and is not applicable in the present case where both parties are American citizens."[200]

Chinese courts apply Chinese law in recognition and enforcement of property settlement agreements in connection with a foreign court divorce judgment between two Chinese nationals because China is the country of the parties' common nationality. In *Chen v. Guan*, the parties were both Chinese nationals residing in South Africa. They divorced in South Africa and entered a divorce settlement agreement providing that their real property in China should be sold, and the net sales proceeds should be divided between them equally. After the divorce, Guan refused to comply with the agreement. Chen first applied for Chinese court's recognition of the parties' South African divorce judgment, and then brought a post-judgment property dispute action to enforce the parties' divorce agreement. The Chinese court held that Chen and Guan's divorce agreement was part of a valid foreign court divorce judgment and was "legally binding and enforceable as it does not violate Chinese law, under which martial property agreements between spouses in connection with a divorce are legally binding and enforceable." Although the court did not explain the basis for its choice of Chinese law, the court emphasized that the parties were both Chinese nationals and the disputed property involved third parties in China and was purchased under complex local housing rules.[201]

In practice, it is often cumbersome for a foreign court to dispose of properties located in China, particularly real properties regulated by complex local housing rules concerning the purchase, transfer, and sale of these properties. When issues related to properties located in China are not addressed in a foreign divorce judgment, Chinese courts generally allow the parties to bring a post-judgment property dispute action to distribute the properties that were not disposed of in their foreign divorce action. For example, in *Lu v. Wang*, the parties brought a post-judgment property dispute action in a Shanghai court for distribution of the parties' properties that were not disposed of in their Texas divorce, including the parties' various complex business and real estate holdings in Shanghai.[202] In *Wang v. Xue*, in the parties' divorce action in Australia, the Australian court did not distribute a home that the parties purchased with their parents through various housing programs of the City of Shanghai. After their divorce in Australia, Wang brought a post-judgment property dispute action for distribution of the home in a Shanghai court. The court divided the home between the parties and their parents.[203] Similarly,

200. (2018) Hu Min Shen 888 Hao ((2018) 沪民申888号); *see also* (2016) Hu 0105 Min Chu 21844 Hao ((2016) 沪0105民初21844号).

201. (2021) Yue 01 Min Zhong 533 Hao ((2021) 粤01民终533号).

202. (2017) Hu 0109 Min Chu 1880 Hao ((2017) 沪0109民初1880号).

203. (2017) Hu 0112 Min Chu 33072 Hao ((2017) 沪0112民初33072号).

in *Yu v. Wei*, a Fuzhou court divided the parties' subsidized housing unit acquired through the husband's military service after the Australian court dissolved the parties' marriage but deferred the disposition of the parties' housing unit in China to Chinese courts.[204] As shown by these cases, Chinese courts are clearly the most convenient and appropriate forum for adjudicating complex real estate interests and housing benefits that are unique to China.

12.4.5 Foreign Judgments Concerning Children

When a foreign court judgment concerning children can be recognized and enforced pursuant to an international treaty to which China is a party, Chinese courts must recognize and enforce the judgment according to the treaty.

Absent any bilateral or multilateral treaty, Chinese courts must follow the procedure prescribed in Chinese law to determine whether and how a foreign court order concerning a child may be enforced in China. Chinese courts must first ascertain that they have proper jurisdiction to hear the dispute arising from the foreign court order. Chinese courts have broad jurisdiction in foreign-related family matters based on one parent's Chinese nationality or habitual residence in China, and consequently may exercise jurisdiction over his/her children regardless of where the children's habitual residence may be. Chinese courts' broad jurisdictional power, thus, can be translated into a broad power in enforcing foreign courts' orders concerning children, even if a parent's presence in China is only transient. If the Chinese court takes jurisdiction over a dispute arising from a foreign court's orders related to a child, the court will determine applicable law in the dispute and decide on the merit of the dispute according to the applicable law. For example, if a parent wrongfully removes a child to China, the Chinese court may assert jurisdiction over the parent based on his/her Chinese nationality and order the child's return to the other parent by applying the law of the country of the parents and child's common habitual residence.

If a child's habitual residence is in China when a dispute related to a foreign custody order arises, Chinese courts will likely apply the law of the jurisdiction where the foreign custody order is originated to determine the validity of the order, and apply Chinese law to determine how the order should be enforced in the best interest of the child. In *Jawad Shaikh v. Wang Xueying*, the child was born out of wedlock in Malta in 2015. On May 13, 2018, the mother and the child left Malta without the father's knowledge or consent. Eventually, the left-behind father located the mother and the child in Cangzhou, China. Armed with a paternity determination from the Malta court, the father sought weekly access rights to the child. The Cangzhou court first

204. (2019) Min 01 Minzhong 5433 Hao ((2019) 闽01民终5433号).

established the father's paternity based on the Malta paternity order. Then, the Cangzhou court applied Maltese law to determine the parents' respective parental rights. The court found that the mother had *de facto* guardianship of the child pursuant to Maltese law and her departure from Malta with the child did not violate Maltese law. Finally, the court held that the father was entitled to visitation with the child and the mother had the duty to facilitate the visitation pursuant to Chinese law. The court found that weekly visitation for the father and the child was unrealistic and might be disruptive to the child's life because the father and child lived in two different countries. Thus, the court entered an access order for the father, directing the mother to make the child available for visitation with the father on the first weekend of every month. The court did not specify where the visitation should take place.[205] The Cangzhou court did not explicitly explain its application of Maltese law and Chinese law in this case. However, it was clear that the Cangzhou court found Maltese law should be applied to determine the father's paternity and the parents' respective parental rights and duty prior to the child's departure from Malta, as Malta was the child's habitual residence at the time; and Chinese law should be applied to determine the child's custody and visitation, as the child's habitual residence had changed to China when the father brought the action for custody and visitation.

The case of Xin Wang and Weihua Feng illustrates the complexity of enforcement of foreign court child custody orders in China. Xin Wang, the father, and Weihua Feng, the mother, were both Chinese citizens. They both went to the United States for graduate school and were married in the United States in 2010. After the marriage, the couple lived in California and their son was born in May 2012. In September 2012 when the child was about four months old, the mother traveled to Shanghai alone to visit her dying maternal grandmother. She had to extend her stay to care for her mother after her maternal grandmother's death. By December 2012, the mother was ready to return to California, but the father refused to provide the mother the documents that she needed from him to obtain a spousal visa for her to return to the United States. In January 2013, the father filed for a divorce in San Diego, California, and sought sole legal custody of the child. Eventually, in September 2013, the mother managed to obtain a tourist visa to return to the United States to defend herself in the divorce action and to be reunited with her child. After a long, protracted litigation, the San Diego court entered an order dated July 23, 2014, giving the mother permission to relocate with the child to Shanghai and granting the father two two-week visits with the child in Shanghai and two two-week visits in California every year. The San Diego court's decision was, *inter alia*, based on the court's observation of the

205. (2019) Ji 0903 Min Chu 4219 Hao ((2019) 冀0903民初4219号).

mother's greater commitment to co-parenting. The father appealed and the trial court's decision was affirmed on appeal in November 2015. In addition, the parties stipulated to San Diego court's exclusive and continuing jurisdiction over the child. The mother and the child relocated to Shanghai in August 2014. In 2015, the father had two visits with the child in Shanghai pursuant to the San Diego court's order. However, the mother refused to facilitate the father's 2015 visits with the child in California because the father had moved to Shanghai by December 2014. Starting from February 2015, the father petitioned in the San Diego court repeatedly for his visits with the child in California, and for change of custody based on the mother's failure to comply with the visitation order. On July 3, 2015, the mother brought a post-judgment child custody dispute action in a Shanghai court after the court recognized the parties' Californian divorce judgment. The Shanghai court issued a restraining order prohibiting both parents and the child from leaving China during the pendency of the child custody proceeding. The mother informed the San Diego court of the Shanghai court's restraining order and the child custody proceeding that she initiated in Shanghai. She did not appear in the San Diego court for the hearing held for the father's petitions on July 14, 2015. In both the Shanghai court and the San Diego court, the mother argued that it would be in her son's best interest to remain in her care and custody, and that it did not make any sense to force her son to have visitation with the father in San Diego because the father had moved back to Shanghai and was not living in San Diego. On July 20, 2015, the San Diego court awarded the father sole legal and physical custody of the child and sanctioned the mother for her repeated failure to produce the child for his visits with the father in California on the dates specifically ordered by the San Diego court. On December 16, 2015, the father and his parents abducted the child from his daycare by force and retained the child in his home in Shanghai. The Shanghai court was fully briefed on the history of the parties' custody and visitation proceedings in California and conducted an evidentiary hearing. In March 2016, the Shanghai court granted the mother residential custody of the child and ordered four ten-day visits per year for the father. The Shanghai court did not specify the location of the father's visits. In the meantime, the mother appealed the San Diego court's decision to change the child's custody to the father. Seven months after the Shanghai court awarded custody to the mother, the California appellate court affirmed the San Diego trial court's custody award to the father. As a result, the child is subject to two conflicting child custody orders, one from the Shanghai court and one from the California court.[206]

206. (2015) Hong Shao Min Chu Zi Di 41 Hao (2015) 虹少民初字第41号, *In re* Marriage of Xin Wang & Weihua Feng, No. D068610, 2015 WL 7428927 (Cal. Ct. App. Nov. 23, 2015), and *In re* Marriage of Xin Wang & Weihua Feng, No. D068610, 2016 WL 6123923 (Cal. Ct. App. Oct. 20, 2016).

The Wang and Feng case illustrates the "enforceability conundrum" in international relocation cases, where the court of initial jurisdiction has no guarantee of enforcement of its visitation order because it will eventually have to concede jurisdiction to the courts at the child's new home state and habitual residence.[207] The conflicting custody orders in the Wang and Feng case were the results of the jurisdictional conflict between the child's former habitual residence, San Diego, and his new habitual residence, Shanghai. Pursuant to Chinese law, the Shanghai court had proper jurisdiction to hear the mother's application for modification of the father's visitation as Shanghai was the habitual residence of the child and the mother, and the place of the father's household registration and country of nationality. On the other hand, the San Diego court's jurisdiction hinged on the parties' stipulation to "exclusive continuing jurisdiction based on Child's undisputed American citizenship and habitual residence in the U.S.," and that the "[m]other conceded the court's jurisdiction several times and invoked the court's powers to enforce support payments."[208] However, neither the parties' choice of court agreement nor a party's concession may confer jurisdiction over child custody to a court, as subject matter jurisdiction over a child custody proceeding cannot be conferred by the parents' agreement or concessions.[209] The California court faulted the conflict to China's nonparticipation in the Hague Abduction Convention. The blame was misplaced. Indeed, the father could have enforced his access rights pursuant to the Convention if China were a signatory member of the Convention. However, the Convention was irrelevant as the child's relocation was lawful and China's internal law required the Shanghai court to enforce the father's visitation rights, which was exactly what the Shanghai court did. In fact, the Shanghai court's exercise of jurisdiction was consistent with the Convention's principle that the court of a child's habitual residence should have exclusive jurisdictional power to make custody and access decisions. The Shanghai court's modification of the California court order was within its jurisdictional power, and unarguably the Shanghai court was best situated to hear Wang and Feng's visitation dispute after Shanghai had become the habitual residence of the child and his parents. To avoid jurisdictional conflicts exhibited in the Wang and Feng case, Chinese courts typically defer jurisdiction to the court at the place of the child's new habitual residence, where the evidence of the child's well-being is more readily available, and enforcement of access is more practical. Deferring jurisdiction over child custody and visitation to a child's new habitual residence is a wise approach.

---

207. *In re* Marriage of Condon, 62 Cal. App. 4th 533, 561, 73 Cal. Rptr. 2d 33, 52 (1998).

208. *In re* Marriage of Xin Wang & Weihua Feng, No. D068610, 2016 WL 6123923, at 5 (Cal. Ct. App. Oct. 20, 2016).

209. 24A Am. Jur. 2d *Divorce & Separation* § 809. *See also* Cal. Fam. Code § 3422 (West), and Civil Procedure Law Interpretations arts. 34, 529.

§ 12.5 Special Rules of Civil Procedure in Foreign-Related Civil Matters

Special rules of civil procedure apply in foreign-related civil matters in Chinese courts.[210]

12.5.1 Foreign Litigants

In general, foreign nationals suing or being sued in Chinese courts need to engage PRC-qualified attorneys as their litigation representative (*susong daili ren*).[211] A foreign national may be represented by an attorney of their country of origin as their personal litigation representative, but not in the capacity of an attorney.[212] In other words, a foreign national's non-Chinese attorney may appear in Chinese court as their personal agent. Having foreign attorneys present at proceedings in the Chinese court may be necessary to ensure that the foreign parties' interests are protected.

A foreign party's appointment of litigation representative must be in writing and must be attested by a Chinese judge or a Chinese notary.[213] If a foreign party does not reside in China, he/she may appoint Chinese attorneys by power of attorney. A power of attorney for appointment of legal counsel must be notarized in the appointing party's country and authenticated or legalized by the Chinese embassy or consulate in that country.[214] Alternatively, it may be attested by a Chinese judge through a video appearance.[215]

Litigants who are foreign nationals must provide copies of passports as evidence of their identification.[216] Verification of foreign litigants' identity may be conducted online as well.[217]

Chinese language is the official language in Chinese courts. The court may provide interpretation upon the parties' request but at the parties' expense.[218] Litigants could also bring their own interpreters. Documents submitted to the

---

210. Civil Procedure Law art. 259 and Civil Procedure Law Interpretations art. 520.

211. Civil Procedure Law art. 263.

212. Civil Procedure Law Interpretations art. 526.

213. *Id.* arts. 523, 524.

214. *Id.* art. 521.

215. Zuigao Renmin Fayuan Guanyu Wei Kuajing Susong Dangshiren Tigong Wangshang Lian Fuwu De Ruogan Guiding (最高人民法院关于为跨境诉讼当事人提供网上立案服务的若干规定) [The Supreme People's Court's Several Rules Concerning Online Case Acceptance Services for Parties in Cross-Border Litigations] (effective Feb. 3, 2021) [hereinafter the "SPC's Several Rules Concerning Online Case Acceptance Services for Parties in Cross-Border Litigations"] art. 6.

216. Civil Procedure Law Interpretations art. 521.

217. The SPC's Several Rules Concerning Online Case Acceptance Services for Parties in Cross-Border Litigations, art. 4.

218. Civil Procedure Law art. 262.

Chinese court must be in Chinese language or be accompanied with Chinese translations. [219]

12.5.2 Service of Process: Hague Service Convention

China is a signatory country of the Hague Service Convention. Chinese law on the service of judicial documents is consistent with the Convention. A Chinese court may serve a party whose domicile is outside China in the following manners: (1) in the manners prescribed in the international treaty between the country where the person to be served resides and China; (2) through diplomatic channels; (3) through the embassy or consulate of the People's Republic of China stationed in the country where the person to be served resides if the person to be served is a Chinese citizen; (4) through a litigation representative authorized by the person to be served to receive service of process; (5) through a representative office or a branch office or business agent authorized to receive service of process established in China by the person to be served; (6) by mail if service by mail is permitted under the law of the country where the person to be served resides, and if three months have elapsed after the date of postmark, the service acknowledgement is not returned, but based on all circumstances, it may be determined that process has been served, process shall be deemed served on the expiration date of the aforesaid period; (7) by fax, email, or any other means through which the receipt by the person to be served can be confirmed; or (8) if service of process by the aforesaid means is not possible, process shall be served by publication, and process shall be deemed served in three months after the date of publication.[220]

If a default judgment is entered against a party who does not domicile in China and the party was served by publication, the court must serve the default judgment by publication, and the default judgment will take effect after three months from the date of service of the default judgment by publication if the party fails to appeal within 30 days after the service of the default judgment by publication.[221] If a party was served by publication by the court of first instance, such party may be served by publication in the appeal, except when the party can be served by means other than publication.[222]

Where a person is served by mail outside of China, an acknowledgment of service (*songda huizheng*) must be included in the package. If the recipient fails to sign and return the acknowledgment of service, but has signed and returned a mailing receipt, the service should be deemed to have been

219. Civil Procedure Law Interpretations art. 525.
220. Civil Procedure Law art. 267.
221. Civil Procedure Law Interpretations art. 532.
222. *Id.* art. 535.

effectuated, and the date of delivery should be deemed as the date of service. After three months from the date of mailing, if the acknowledgment of service has not been returned to the court, and there is no sufficient evidence of the receipt of the mail, then the service by mail should be deemed as ineffective.[223]

12.5.3 Time to Respond

Where a defendant's domicile is not in China, the defendant has 30 days to file a written statement of defense after receiving the copy of the written complaint, and the defendant's time to answer may be extended at the court's discretion.[224]

A party who has no domicile in China has 30 days from the date of service of the written judgment or ruling to file an appeal against a judgment or ruling of a court of first instance; and 30 days to file a written response after receiving a copy of the written appeal. Extension of time to appeal or to respond to an appeal may be granted at the court's discretion.[225] If no appeal is taken within the time period for filing an appeal, the judgment and ruling of the court of first instance becomes legally effective.[226]

12.5.4 Judicial Assistance

A foreign court may request, and a Chinese court may provide, judicial assistance in service of process, investigation, and collection of evidence and other litigation activities either pursuant to international treaties to which China is a party or pursuant to reciprocity, provided such request does not violate China's sovereignty, national security, or public interest.[227] Requests for judicial assistance must be made through the channels prescribed in the relevant treaty or through diplomatic channels.[228] A foreign court's written request for judicial assistance must be accompanied with Chinese translations or translations in the languages specified in the relevant international treaty.[229] Chinese courts must provide requested judicial assistance in the manner prescribed Chinese law. If a foreign court requests that judicial assistance be provided in a specific manner, the Chinese court may assist in the manner requested, provided that the foreign court's request does not violate Chinese law.[230]

---

223. *Id.* art. 536.
224. Civil Procedure Law art. 268.
225. *Id.* art. 269.
226. Civil Procedure Law Interpretations art. 536.
227. Civil Procedure Law art. 276.
228. *Id.* art. 277 para. 1.
229. *Id.* art. 278.
230. *Id.* art. 279.

12.5.5 Taking Evidence in China

No foreign authority or individual may, without Chinese authority's permission, serve process, take testimony, conduct investigation, or collect evidence in China, except that a foreign embassy or consulate in China may serve process, investigate, and collect evidence from its own citizens, provided such activities do not violate Chinese law and are not compulsory.[231] China is a signatory country of the Hague Evidence Convention. Thus, a foreign court may request judicial assistance in evidence collection through the manners prescribed by the Convention. Strict compliance with Chinese law in taking evidence in China is critical, as unauthorized collection of evidence, including taking oral or written testimony from a witness present in China, is a violation of Chinese judicial sovereignty and could lead to serious legal consequences.

231. *Id*. art. 277.

Concluding Comments

The Civil Code marked the completion of a coherent, uniform legislative framework in Chinese family law. The new Civil Code requires a specialized family law judiciary capable of applying and implementing the code correctly and efficiently.[1] In June 2016, the SPC initiated a two-year family law pilot program in over 100 intermediate and first-instance courts throughout China.[2] Based on the experience acquired through the pilot program, the SPC started a nationwide family matter adjudication reform throughout the Chinese court

1. Chen Aiwu (陈爱武), jiashi anjian shenpan chengxu gaige de guancha yu sikao—jianyi minfa dian shidai woguo jiashi susong lifa de biyaoxing (家事案件审判程序改革的观察与思考 - 兼议民法典时代我国家事诉讼立法的必要性) [Observations and Thoughts on the Family Matter Adjudication Procedure Reform – Also on the Need for Our Country's Family Matter Litigation Legislation], Fazhi Xiandaihua Yanjiu (法治现代化研究) [Law and Modernization], 2020 Issue 4, 55–74.

2. Zuigao Renmin Fayuan Guanyu Kaizhan Jiashi Shenpan Fangshi He Gongzuo Jizhi Gaige Shidian Gongzuo De Yijian (最高人民法院关于开展家事审判方式和工作机制改革试点工作的意见) [The Supreme People's Court Opinions on Family Matter Adjudication Procedures and Mechanism Reform Pilot Program] (Apr. 23, 2016), http://www.court.gov.cn/zixun-xiangqing-37372.html; *see* Du Wanhua (杜万华), Lun Shenghua Jiashi Shenpan Fangshi He Gongzuo Jizhi Gaige (论深化家事审判方式和工作机制改革) [On Further Reforms of Family Matter Adjudication Procedures and Mechanisms], Zhongguo Yinyong Faxue (中国应用法学) [China Applied Jurisprudence] Vol. 2, 1–9 (2018) (the SPC's review of the family matter adjudication pilot program and pronouncement of comprehensive reform in family matter adjudication process in Chinese courts); *see also* Mu Wang (王 牧), Jiashi Shenpan Zhuanyehua De Shishi Beijing He Juti Jiangou (家事审判专业化的实施背景和具体建构) [The Context and Framework of the Specialization of Family Matter Adjudication] (a county court judge describing challenges faced by a county court in family matter adjudication and proposing some solutions), https://www.chinacourt.org/article/detail/2018/01/id/3145885.shtml.

system in 2018.[3] The goal of the reform is to institutionalize a highly specialized and problem-solving oriented family matter system.[4]

The reform requires Chinese courts to build a specialized family matter system within each court. Intermediate courts and basic-level courts are required to establish a specialized family matter division, or, at the minimum, designate a panel of judges to handle family matters.[5] Family matter division judges must receive training in sociology, education, and psychology in addition to law. The SPC requires that every collegiate bench in family matters include at least one woman, whether a female judge or a female juror.[6] Courts at all levels are required to establish a family matter mediation program,[7] family matter investigator program,[8] and psychological assistance programs.[9] These programs are staffed with community members, including community leaders, community service providers, mental health professionals, attorneys, and basic-level legal workers.[10]

Some new procedural rules in family matters are being implemented. Refined rules on mediation are incorporated in the new family matter adjudication procedure.[11] Chinese courts' investigative power has been expanded through court-appointed family matter investigators (*jiashi diaochayuan*).[12] Now, full financial disclosure is mandatory in all divorce cases,[13] personal safety orders may be issued during the pendency of divorce actions,[14] and custody and property issues may be bifurcated.[15] The procedural reform

3. Zuigao Renmin Fayuan Guanyu Jinyibu Shenhua Jiashi Shenpan Fangshi He Gongzuo Jizhi Gaige De Yijian (Shixing) (最高人民法院关于进一步深化家事审判方式和工作机制改革的意见(试行)) [The Supreme People's Court Opinions on Further Reforms of Family Matter Adjudication Procedures and Mechanisms (Trial Implementation)] (July 18, 2018) art. 46, (hereinafter the "Family Matter Adjudication Procedures").

4. Family Matter Adjudication Procedures art. 2. *See also* Chen Aiwu (陈爱武), *supra* note 1, at 56.

5. Family Matter Adjudication Procedures arts. 15–27.

6. *Id*. art. 47.

7. *Id*. arts. 6, 7.

8. *Id*. arts. 15, 16.

9. *Id*. arts. 28, 29.

10. *Id*. arts. 8, 17, 29.

11. *Id*. arts. 6–14.

12. *Id*. art. 15. China's new "family matter investigator" system is a legal transplant originated from Japan, Taiwan, and South Korea. *See* Feng Yuan & Yao Yiqi (冯源 姚毅奇), Jiashi Sifa Gaige Zhong Diaochaguan De Juese Ganyu (家事司法改革中调查官的角色干预) [Family Matter Judicial Reform Investigating Officers' Role and Intervention] Zhongguo Faxue (中国法学) [China Legal Science] Vol. 6 (2017) (discussing the origins of the family matter investigator program and the need for it in Chinese courts).

13. Family Matter Adjudication Procedures art. 44.

14. *Id*. arts. 35, 45.

15. *Id*. art. 39.

has installed in family matter proceedings therapeutic counseling and reconciliatory mechanisms, including "a psychological counseling procedure" (*xinli shudao chengxu*), mandatory divorce "cooling" period, psychological intervention, home visits, domestic violence prevention network, and post-action follow-up inquiries.[16] These new procedural mechanisms allow Chinese courts to recommend psychological therapy or counseling in family matters, particularly in cases involving domestic violence or children, and to "diagnose, restore and heal" marriages and families.[17]

The problem-solving, therapeutic family court model has been successful in enhancing separating families' ability to reconstruct positive relationships and has improved access to civil justice in the U.S. and other countries.[18] Its reconciliatory features certainly have natural appeal to Chinese people and family law reformers. However, the problem-solving family court model has some major failings. For example, using family courts as service providers to address individual problems or societal predicaments has rarely been effective, but has always been expensive.[19] The expansion of juridical power in micromanaging litigants' personal and family life risks due process violations, loss of privacy, and infringement of individual rights, particularly the rights of poor and vulnerable populations.[20] At the same time, surrendering some judicial authority in fact-finding and decision-making to nonlegal groups, such as mental health professionals, social workers, and nonlawyer mediators puts families at risk of bias and irreparable harm.[21] "Therapeutic justice" turns into "therapeutic tyranny" in many cases. To implement the

16. *Id.* arts. 28–34.

17. *Id.* art. 2.

18. Rebecca Aviel, *Family Law and the New Access to Justice*, 86 Fordham L. Rev. 2279, 2296 (2018); *see also* Hon. Lynda B. Munro (Ret.) et al., *Administrative Divorce Trends and Implications*, 50 Fam. L.Q. 427, 440–41 (2016).

19. For discussions of family courts' institutional incompetency in delivering social services, see Jana B. Singer, *Dispute Resolution and the Post-divorce Family: Implications of a Paradigm Shift*, 47 Fam. Ct. Rev. 363, 367 (2009); Jane C. Murphy, *Revitalizing the Adversary System in Family Law*, 78 U. Cin. L. Rev. 891, 897–900 (2010). For discussions of the evolvement of problem-solving family courts and the challenges and problems faced by problem-solving family courts, see Jane M. Spinak, *Romancing the Court*, 46 Fam. Ct. Rev. 258 (2008); *Family Defense and the Disappearing Problem-Solving Court*, 20 CUNY L. Rev. 171, 175 (2016).

20. Singer, *supra* note 19, at 367; *see also* Spinak, *supra* note 19, at 178–85 (detailing inadequate legal representation of indigent parents in termination of parental rights proceedings); Leigh Goodmark, *Law Is the Answer? Do We Know That for Sure?: Questioning the Efficacy of Legal Interventions for Battered Women*, 23 St. Louis U. Pub. L. Rev. 7 (2004) (detailing the problems faced by battered women in the justice system).

21. Murphy, *supra* note 19, at 900–05; *see also* Timothy M. Tippins & Jeffrey P. Wittmann, *Empirical and Ethical Problems with Custody Recommendations: A Call for Clinical Humility and Judicial Vigilance*, 43 Fam. Ct. Rev. 193 (2005) (outlining the jurisprudential and evidentiary problems regarding psychological opinions and recommendations in custody matters).

family matter adjudication reform, an astronomical amount of funding will be needed to train, recruit, and manage additional judicial, nonjudicial, and quasi-judicial staff. This includes mediators, financial evaluators, custody evaluators, parenting coordinators, and mental health service providers. For these reasons, the U.S. and some other jurisdictions have gradually turned away from the conventional adversarial procedure to a judicial system that promotes collaborative family dispute resolution.[22]

China's family law reform aims to inject Western concepts of therapeutic justice, holistic intervention, and expansive judicial discretion into China's conciliatory, relationship-preservation-oriented, mediation-centered family law tradition.[23] Chinese people have long cherished conciliation and revered judicial discretion. At the same time, Chinese people have a long tradition of protecting personal privacy and have resolutely resisted the state's invasions of family life. Therefore, the future of an interdisciplinary, therapeutic, problem-solving family law system is unclear in China.

---

22. For an overview of the paradigm shift in family dispute resolution in the United States, its underlying jurisprudence, and the problems arising from the family court restructuration, see Singer, *supra* note 19; Murphy, *supra* note 19, at 905; *see also* Patrick Parkinson, *The Idea of Family Relationship Centres in Australia*, 51 FAM. CT. REV. 195, 196 (2013) (describing the development of alternative family dispute resolution from a court-centric approach to a community-centric approach in Australia).

23. Du Wanhua (杜万华), Lun Shenghua Jiashi Shenpan Fangshi He Gongzuo Jizhi Gaige (论深化家事审判方式和工作机制改革) [On Further Reforms of Family Matter Adjudication Procedures and Mechanisms], Zhongguo Yinyong Faxue (中国应用法学) [China Applied Jurisprudence] Vol. 2, 1–9 (2018), 6–8.

Index

D

N

R

S

T

U

V

W

X

Y

Z